Taking SIDES

Clashing Views on Controversial Environmental Issues

Sixth Edition

Clashing Views on
Controversial
Environmental Issues

Sixth Edition

Edited, Selected, and with Introductions by

Theodore D. Goldfarb
State University of New York at Stony Brook

The Dushkin Publishing Group, Inc.

This book is dedicated to my children and all other children for whom the successful resolution of these issues is of great urgency.

Photo Acknowledgments

Part 1 Colorado Tourism Board
Part 2 Digital Stock
Part 3 Alcoa
Part 4 Saranac Lake/New York State Department of Commerce

Cover Art Acknowledgment

Charles Vitelli

Library of Congress Cataloging-in-Publication Data

Main entry under title:
    Taking sides: clashing views on controversial environmental issues/edited, selected, and with introductions by Theodore D. Goldfarb.—6th ed.
    Includes bibliographical references and index.
    1. Environmental policy. I. Goldfarb, Theodore D., *comp.*
        HC68   363.7
        1-56134-331-5

 Printed on Recycled Paper

The Dushkin Publishing Group, Inc.

PREFACE

For the past 18 years I have been teaching an environmental chemistry course, and my experience has been that the critical and complex relationship we have with our environment is of vital and growing concern to students, regardless of their majors. Consequently, for this sixth edition, I again sought to shape issues and to select articles that do not require a technical background or prerequisite courses in order to be understood. In addition to the sciences, this volume would be appropriate for such disciplines as philosophy, law, sociology, political science, economics, and allied health—any course where environmental topics are addressed.

Faculty are divided about whether it is appropriate to use a classroom to advocate a particular position on a controversial issue. Some believe that the proper role of a teacher is to maintain neutrality in order to present the material in as objective a manner as possible. Others, like myself, find that students rarely fail to recognize their instructors' points of view. Rather than reveal which side I am on through subtle hints, I prefer to be forthright about it, while doing my best to encourage students to develop their own positions, and I do not penalize them if they disagree with my views. No matter whether the goal is to attempt an objective presentation or to encourage advocacy, it is necessary to present both sides of any argument. To be a successful proponent of any position, it is essential to understand your opponents' arguments. The format of this text, with 36 essays arranged in pro and con pairs on 18 environmental controversies, is designed with these objectives in mind.

In the *introduction* to each issue, I present the historical context of the controversy and some of the key questions that divide the disputants. The *postscript* that follows each pair of essays includes comments offered to provoke thought about aspects of the issue that are suitable for classroom discussion. A careful reading of my remarks may reveal the positions I favor, but the essays themselves and the *suggestions for further reading* in each postscript should provide the student with the information needed to construct and support an independent perspective.

Changes to this edition   This sixth edition has been extensively revised and updated. There are seven completely new issues: *Will NAFTA Be Good For the Environment?* (Issue 1); *Does the Analysis of Existing Data Support Demands for Environmental Justice?* (Issue 4); *Should Property Owners Be Compensated When Environmental Restrictions Limit Development?* (Issue 6); *Should the Industrial Use of Chlorine Be Phased Out?* (Issue 7); *Should the New Clean Water Act Aim at "Zero Discharge"?* (Issue 9); *Is Protecting the Spotted Owl a Clever Strategy for Preserving Old-Growth Forests?* (Issue 11); and *Are Major Changes Needed to Avert a Global Environmental Crisis?* (Issue 18). For five of the issues retained from

i

the previous edition, the issue question has been significantly modified and both selections have been replaced in order to focus the debate more sharply and bring it up to date: Issue 8 on air quality; Issue 10 on the use of chemicals in agriculture; Issue 12 on hazardous waste; Issue 14 on nuclear waste; and Issue 16 on ozone layer depletion. The following additional selections have also been replaced: the YES selection for Issue 2 on wilderness preservation; both selections for Issue 5 on limiting population; and the YES selection for Issue 13 on municipal waste. The result is that 28 of the 36 selections in this sixth edition are new.

A word to the instructor   An *Instructor's Manual With Test Questions* (multiple-choice and essay) is available through the publisher for the instructor using *Taking Sides* in the classroom. Also available is a general guidebook, called *Using Taking Sides in the Classroom*, which has general suggestions for adapting the pro-con approach in any classroom setting.

Acknowledgments   I received many helpful comments and suggestions from friends and readers across the United States and Canada. Their suggestions have markedly enhanced the quality of this edition and are reflected in the new issues and the updated selections.

Special thanks go to those who responded to the questionnaire with specific suggestions for the sixth edition:

Ralph L. Amey
Occidental College

Alan P. Austin
University of Victoria

Ruth Bamberger
Drury College

Walter Block
College of the Holy Cross

Beverly A. Cigler
Pennsylvania State
  University–Harrisburg

Robin Collins
University of New
  Hampshire

Peter Crooks
University of
  Connecticut–Southeastern
  Branch

R. Laurence Davis
University of New Haven

David A. Firmage
Colby College

Rosann Fortner
Ohio State University

William Hallahan
Nazareth College of
  Rochester

Sara Keith
State University of New York
  at Syracuse

Joseph Mahoney
Kean College of New Jersey

Charles R. Maier
Wayne State College

Gail Marshall
West Georgia College

Priscilla Mattson
Middlesex Community
  College

George T. Matzko
Bob Jones University

Michael T. Mengak
Ferrum College

James A. Montgomery
De Paul University

Timothy G. O'Keefe
California Polytechnic
  University–San Luis
  Obispo

Harry W. Power
Rutgers University

Wendy S. Scattergood
Purdue University

Douglas Smith
Vanderbilt University

Sherilyn Smith
Siena College

Dennis L. Soden
University of Nevada

Peter Soule
Appalachian State University

Charles Taliaferro
Saint Olaf College

Donald Tarter
Marshall University

Howard Warshawsky
Roanoke College

Ralph J. Yulo, Jr.
Eastern Connecticut State
  University

Finally, I am grateful to Mimi Egan, publisher of the Taking Sides program, for her assistance.

Theodore D. Goldfarb
State University of New York at Stony Brook

CONTENTS IN BRIEF

PART 1 GENERAL PHILOSOPHICAL AND POLITICAL ISSUES 1

Issue 1.   Will NAFTA Be Good for the Environment?   **2**

Issue 2.   Does Wilderness Have Intrinsic Value?   **22**

Issue 3.   Should the Endangered Species Act Be Reauthorized?   **46**

Issue 4.   Does the Analysis of Existing Data Support Demands for Environmental Justice?   **68**

Issue 5.   Is Limiting Population Growth a Key Factor in Protecting the Global Environment?   **84**

Issue 6.   Should Property Owners Be Compensated When Environmental Restrictions Limit Development?   **102**

PART 2 THE ENVIRONMENT AND TECHNOLOGY 117

Issue 7.   Should the Industrial Use of Chlorine Be Phased Out?   **118**

Issue 8.   Is Stringent Enforcement of Existing Laws Needed to Improve Air Quality?   **144**

Issue 9.   Should the New Clean Water Act Aim at "Zero Discharge"?   **160**

Issue 10. Does Feeding People and Preserving Wildlands Require Chemical-Based Agriculture?   **178**

Issue 11. Is Protecting the Spotted Owl a Clever Strategy for Preserving Old-Growth Forests?   **194**

PART 3 DISPOSING OF WASTES 209

Issue 12. Hazardous Waste: Should the "Polluter Pays" Provision of Superfund Be Weakened?   **210**

Issue 13. Municipal Waste: Can Management Plans Based on Mandated Recycling Succeed?   **228**

Issue 14. Nuclear Waste: Should Plans for Underground Storage Be Put on Hold?   **248**

PART 4 THE ENVIRONMENT AND THE FUTURE 269

Issue 15. Can Incentives Devised by Industrial Nations Combat Tropical Deforestation?   **270**

Issue 16. Do the Projected Consequences of Ozone Depletion Justify Phasing Out Chlorofluorocarbons?   **288**

Issue 17. Are Aggressive International Efforts Needed to Slow Global Warming?   **308**

Issue 18. Are Major Changes Needed to Avert a Global Environmental Crisis?   **328**

CONTENTS

Preface   i

Introduction: The Environmental Movement   xii

PART 1   GENERAL PHILOSOPHICAL AND POLITICAL ISSUES   1

ISSUE 1.   Will NAFTA Be Good for the Environment?   2
YES: Robert A. Pastor, from "NAFTA's Green Opportunity," *Issues
in Science and Technology*   4
NO: Steven E. Sanderson, from "Mexico's Environmental Future,"
Current History   13

Political science professor Robert A. Pastor argues that the North American Free Trade Agreement (NAFTA) will likely reduce pollution problems
along the U.S.–Mexican border. Tropical conservation and development expert Steven E. Sanderson argues that the NAFTA negotiators are not taking
environmental concerns into consideration in promoting industrial and agricultural development.

ISSUE 2.   Does Wilderness Have Intrinsic Value?   22
YES: John Daniel, from "Toward Wild Heartlands," *Audubon*   24
NO: William Tucker, from "Is Nature Too Good for Us?" *Harper's
Magazine*   32

Wilderness magazine poetry editor John Daniel asserts that wilderness is a
valuable resource that must be protected. William Tucker, a writer and social
critic, asserts that wilderness areas are elitist preserves designed to keep
people out.

ISSUE 3.   Should the Endangered Species Act Be Reauthorized?   46
YES: Endangered Species Coalition, from *The Endangered Species
Act: A Commitment Worth Keeping*   48
NO: Suzanne Winckler, from "Stopgap Measures," *The Atlantic
Monthly*   60

A coalition of 50 environmental, conservation, and wildlife organizations
argues that the Endangered Species Act has successfully saved many species
from extinction. Natural history author Suzanne Winckler contends that it is
more important to protect critical ecosystems than near-extinct species.

ISSUE 4. Does the Analysis of Existing Data Support Demands for Environmental Justice? 68

YES: Robert D. Bullard, from "Grassroots Flowering: The Environmental Justice Movement Comes of Age," *The Amicus Journal* 70

NO: Michael Greenberg, from "Proving Environmental Inequity in Siting Locally Unwanted Land Uses," *Risk: Issues in Health and Safety* 76

Sociology professor and environmental justice movement theorist Robert D. Bullard argues that charges of environmental injustice made by grassroots activists are supported by solid evidence. Urban studies and community health professor Michael Greenberg proposes that charges of environmental racism are not supported by well-defined criteria or adequate analysis.

ISSUE 5. Is Limiting Population Growth a Key Factor in Protecting the Global Environment? 84

YES: Paul Harrison, from "Sex and the Single Planet: Need, Greed, and Earthly Limits," *The Amicus Journal* 86

NO: Betsy Hartmann, from "Population Fictions: The Malthusians Are Back in Town," *Dollars and Sense* 93

Author and Population Institute medal winner Paul Harrison argues that family planning programs should be implemented to prevent world population from exceeding carrying capacity. Betsy Hartmann, director of the Hampshire College Population and Development Program, argues that the real problem is not how many people there are but that controls over resource consumption are inadequate.

ISSUE 6. Should Property Owners Be Compensated When Environmental Restrictions Limit Development? 102

YES: Rick Henderson, from "Preservation Acts," *Reason* 104

NO: Doug Harbrecht, from "A Question of Property Rights and Wrongs," *National Wildlife* 110

Reason magazine's Washington editor Rick Henderson maintains that environmental restrictions cannot be placed on property owners without compensation. *Business Week's* Washington correspondent Doug Harbrecht claims that it is absurd to have to pay owners of private property for obeying environmental regulations.

PART 2   *THE ENVIRONMENT AND TECHNOLOGY*   **117**

ISSUE 7.   **Should the Industrial Use of Chlorine Be Phased Out?**   **118**

YES: Joe Thornton, from "Chlorine: Can't Live With It, Can Live Without It," Speech Prepared for the Chlorine-Free Debate Held in Conjunction With the International Joint Commission Seventh Biennial Meeting, Windsor, Ontario, Canada   **120**

NO: Ivan Amato, from "The Crusade to Ban Chlorine," *Garbage: The Independent Environmental Quarterly*   **132**

Greenpeace research coordinator Joe Thornton asserts that chlorinated organic compounds should be phased out to protect humans and animals from the toxic effects of these chemicals. Science writer Ivan Amato states that only a few chlorinated compounds are proven health threats and that no adequate substitutes for chlorine exist.

ISSUE 8.   **Is Stringent Enforcement of Existing Laws Needed to Improve Air Quality?**   **144**

YES: Will Nixon, from "The Air Down Here," *The Amicus Journal*   **146**

NO: Lester P. Lamm, from "Clean or Green: Political Correctness vs. Common Sense in Transportation," *Vital Speeches of the Day*   **151**

E Magazine associate editor Will Nixon supports the Clean Air Act but blames its failures on lax enforcement. Highway Users Federation president Lester P. Lamm sees new federal air and transportation laws as a threat to the economy.

ISSUE 9.   **Should the New Clean Water Act Aim at "Zero Discharge"?**   **160**

YES: Jeffery A. Foran and Robert W. Adler, from "Cleaner Water, But Not Clean Enough," *Issues in Science and Technology*   **162**

NO: Robert W. Hahn, from "Clean Water Policy," *The American Enterprise*   **170**

Environmental health and policy professor Jeffrey A. Foran and Clean Water Project director Robert W. Adler argue that revisions to the Clean Water Act should aim for the goal of zero discharge of toxic pollutants. American Enterprise Institute scholar Robert W. Hahn advocates a market-based approach to water regulation based on cost-benefit analyses.

**ISSUE 10. Does Feeding People and Preserving Wildlands
Require Chemical-Based Agriculture?**   178

YES: **Ronald Bailey,** from "Once and Future Farming," *Garbage: The
Independent Environmental Quarterly*   180

NO: **Paul Faeth,** from "We've Been Down That Road Before,"
Garbage: The Independent Environmental Quarterly   188

Environmental journalist Ronald Bailey claims that intensive farming, relying on pesticides and fertilizers, is needed to feed the world's people. A senior research associate in the economics and population program of the World Resources Institute, Paul Faeth counters that chemically intensive farming is less economically effective at increasing agricultural yields than organic farming.

**ISSUE 11. Is Protecting the Spotted Owl a Clever Strategy for
Preserving Old-Growth Forests?**   194

YES: **Jon Jefferson,** from "Timmmberr! How Two Lawyers and a
Spotted Owl Took a Cut Out of the Logging Industry," *ABA Journal*   196

NO: **Gene W. Wood,** from "Owl Conservation Strategy Flawed,"
The Journal of Forestry   202

Freelance writer Jon Jefferson lauds the successful legal strategy of environmental activists who organized their campaign to protect old-growth forests around a plan to save the northern spotted owl from extinction. Forest wildlife ecology professor Gene W. Wood concludes that choosing the owl as a surrogate for the forest is not the best plan for achieving the worthy goal of preserving both of them.

PART 3   *DISPOSING OF WASTES*   209

**ISSUE 12. Hazardous Waste: Should the "Polluter Pays"
Provision of Superfund Be Weakened?**   210

YES: **Bernard J. Reilly,** from "Stop Superfund Waste," *Issues in
Science and Technology*   212

NO: **Ted Williams,** from "The Sabotage of Superfund," *Audubon*   220

DuPont corporate counsel Bernard J. Reilly argues that the Superfund legislation has led to unfair standards and waste cleanup cost delegation. *Audubon* contributing editor Ted Williams warns against turning Superfund into a public welfare program for polluters.

**ISSUE 13. Municipal Waste: Can Management Plans Based on
Mandated Recycling Succeed?**   228

YES: John S. Van Volkenburgh and Randall L. Hartmann, from
"Recycling Incentives: An Example of the Public Process for Policy
Development," *MSW Management*   230

NO: Virginia I. Postrel and Lynn Scarlett, from "Talking Trash,"
Reason   237

Engineering analyst John S. Van Volkenburgh and county waste manager
Randall L. Hartmann support a municipal waste management program based
on a residential recycling incentive strategy. *Reason* editor Virginia I. Postrel
and solid waste researcher Lynn Scarlett argue that mandatory recycling
programs are ill-conceived and not cost effective.

**ISSUE 14. Nuclear Waste: Should Plans for Underground Storage
Be Put on Hold?**   248

YES: Nicholas Lenssen, from "Facing Up to Nuclear Waste," *World
Watch*   250

NO: Luther J. Carter, from "Ending the Gridlock on Nuclear Waste
Storage," *Issues in Science and Technology*   259

Nuclear waste researcher Nicholas Lenssen asserts that the search for a permanent nuclear waste repository should be delayed until the future of nuclear
power is decided. Science writer Luther J. Carter argues that now is the time to
begin using the proposed Yucca Mountain site for surface and underground
storage of nuclear waste.

PART 4   THE ENVIRONMENT AND THE FUTURE   269

**ISSUE 15. Can Incentives Devised by Industrial Nations Combat
Tropical Deforestation?**   270

YES: Martin T. Katzman and William G. Cale, Jr., from "Tropical
Forest Preservation Using Economic Incentives," *BioScience*   272

NO: Hannah Finan Roditi and James B. Goodno, from "Rainforest
Crunch: Combating Tropical Deforestation," *Dollars and Sense*   282

Economist Martin T. Katzman and science and mathematics dean William G.
Cale, Jr., propose a scheme whereby a consortium of industrialized nations
would implement an economic incentive program they claim could preserve
tropical forests. *Dollars and Sense* editorial associate Hannah Finan Roditi and
staff editor James B. Goodno emphasize the importance of grassroots tactics
in creating equitable plans to combat tropical deforestation.

ISSUE 16. **Do the Projected Consequences of Ozone Depletion Justify Phasing Out Chlorofluorocarbons?** 288

YES: Mary H. Cooper, from "Ozone Depletion," *CQ Researcher* 290

NO: Patricia Poore and Bill O'Donnell, from "Ozone," *Garbage: The Independent Environmental Quarterly* 299

CQ Researcher staff writer Mary H. Cooper argues that the evidence showing that chlorofluorocarbons (CFCs) are depleting the ozone layer justifies extraordinary international efforts to ward off the predicted health and environmental consequences. *Garbage* magazine's editor and publisher Patricia Poore and associate publisher Bill O'Donnell conclude that ozone depletion is not a crisis requiring an outright ban on CFCs.

ISSUE 17. **Are Aggressive International Efforts Needed to Slow Global Warming?** 308

YES: Richard Elliot Benedick, from "Equity and Ethics in a Global Climate Convention," *America* 310

NO: S. Fred Singer, from "Warming Theories Need Warning Label," *The Bulletin of the Atomic Scientists* 319

U.S. environmental diplomat Richard Elliot Benedick warns that waiting for scientific certainty about global warming before taking definitive action to prevent it could be disastrous. Environmental science professor S. Fred Singer claims that the world should not invest huge sums of money in response to the "phantom threat" of global warming.

ISSUE 18. **Are Major Changes Needed to Avert a Global Environmental Crisis?** 328

YES: Russell E. Train, from "A Call for Sustainability," *EPA Journal* 330

NO: Julian L. Simon, from "More People, Greater Wealth, More Resources, Healthier Environment," *Economic Affairs* 336

World Wildlife Fund chairman Russell E. Train argues that changing the course of the world's economic and industrial policies toward the goal of sustainable development will prevent serious global environmental deterioration. Professor of economics and business administration Julian L. Simon predicts that the market forces of a free economy will lead to improved standards of living and a healthier environment

Contributors 348

Index 354

INTRODUCTION

The Environmental Movement

Theodore D. Goldfarb

ENVIRONMENTAL CONSCIOUSNESS

In June 1992 Rio de Janeiro was the site of The United Nations Conference on Environment and Development (UNCED), popularly billed as the Earth Summit. UNCED, which was the follow-up to a much more modest United Nations conference held 20 years earlier, consisted of two massive, global conferences—one of official government delegations and the other of a diverse array of nongovernmental organizations (NGOs)—as well as a separate "Earth Parliament" comprised of 800 delegates of indigenous peoples. The most far-reaching outcome of UNCED was a 600-page agreement called Agenda 21, which sets guidelines for how, under UN leadership, the governments and businesses of the world should attempt to achieve economic growth, while maintaining environmental quality. Two years prior to the Earth Summit, on April 22, 1990, 200 million people in 140 countries around the world participated in a variety of activities to celebrate Earth Day. It was also a follow-up to an event that took place two decades earlier, the first Earth Day (celebrated only in the United States), which many social historians credit with spawning the ongoing global environmental movement.

Comparing the enormous increase in size, complexity, range of issues, and diversity of participation in either UNCED or Earth Day 1990 with its predecessor event reveals the explosive growth in political, scientific and technical, regulatory, financial, industrial, and educational activity related to an expanding list of environmental problems that has developed in the intervening years. Industrial development has reached a level at which pollutants threaten not only local environments but also the global ecosystems that control the Earth's climate and the ozone shield that filters out potentially lethal solar radiation. The elevation of environmental concern to a prominent position on the international political agenda persuaded commentators on Earth Day 1990 events to speculate that the world was entering "the decade —or even era—of the environment." The attention given to UNCED and the ambitious ongoing activities it has spawned appear to confirm this prediction.

THE HISTORY OF ENVIRONMENTALISM

The current interest in environmental issues in the United States has its historical roots in the conservation movement of the late nineteenth and early twentieth centuries. This earlier, more limited, recognition of the need for environmental preservation was a response to the destruction wrought by uncontrolled industrial exploitation of natural resources in the post–Civil War period. Clear-cutting forests, in addition to producing large devastated areas, resulted in secondary disasters. Bark and branches left in the cutover areas caused several major midwestern forest fires. Severe floods were caused by the loss of trees that previously had helped to reduce surface water runoff. The Sierra Club and the Audubon Society, the two oldest environmental organizations still active today, were founded around the turn of the century and helped to organize public opposition to the destructive practice of exploiting resources. Mining, grazing, and lumbering were brought under government control by such landmark legislation as the Forest Reserve Act of 1891 and the Forest Management Act of 1897. Schools of forestry were established at several of the land grant colleges to help develop the scientific expertise needed for the wise management of forest resources.

The present environmental movement can be traced back to 1962, when Rachel Carson's book *Silent Spring* appeared. The book's emotional warning about the inherent dangers in the excessive use of pesticides ignited the imagination of an enormous and disparate audience who had become uneasy about the proliferation of new synthetic chemicals in agriculture and industry. The atmospheric testing of nuclear weapons began to cause widespread public concern about the effects of nuclear radiation. City dwellers began to recognize the connection between the increasing prevalence of smoky, irritating air and the daily ritual of urban commuter traffic jams. The responses to Carson's book included not only a multitude of scientific and popular debates about the issues she had raised, but also a ground swell of public support for increased controls over all forms of pollution.

The rapid rise in the United States of public concern about environmental issues is apparent from the results of opinion polls. Similar surveys taken in 1965 and 1970 showed an increase from 17 to 53 percent in the number of respondents who rated "reducing pollution of air and water" as one of the three problems they would like the government to pay more attention to. By 1984, pollster Louis Harris was reporting to Congress that 69 percent of the public favored making the Clean Air Act more stringent. A CBS News/*New York Times* survey revealed that 74 percent of respondents in 1990 (up from 45 percent in 1981) supported protecting the environment *regardless of the cost.*

The growth of environmental consciousness in the United States swelled the ranks of the older voluntary organizations, such as the national Wildlife Federation, the Sierra Club, the Isaac Walton League, and the Audubon Society, and has led to the establishment of more than 200 new national and regional associations and 3,000 local ones. Such national and international groups as the Environmental Defense Fund, Friends of the Earth, the National Resources Defense Council, Environmental Action, the League of Conservation Voters, and Zero Population Growth have become proficient at lobbying for legislation, influencing elections, and litigating in the courts.

Critics of the environmental movement have frequently pointed out that the membership of these organizations comes from the upper socioeconomic classes. Recently, however, grassroots organizers have had considerable success in recruiting people of lower socioeconomic ranking and varied ethnic backgrounds to join in active campaigns to seek changes in policies that have resulted in their communities bearing much of the burden of environmental pollution and degradation.

Environmental literature has also grown exponentially since the appearance of *Silent Spring*. Many popular magazines, technical journals, and organizational newsletters devoted to environmental issues have been introduced, as well as hundreds of books, some of which, like Paul Ehrlich's *The Population Bomb* (1968) and Barry Commoner's *The Closing Circle* (1972), have become best-sellers.

CLASHING VIEWS FROM CONFLICTING VALUES

As with all social issues, those on opposite sides of environmental disputes have conflicting personal values. On some level, almost everyone would admit to being concerned about threats to the environment. However, enormous differences exist in individual perceptions about the seriousness of some environmental threats, their origins, their relative importance, and what to do about them. In most instances, very different conclusions, based on the same basic scientific evidence, can be expressed on these issues.

What are these different value systems that produce such heated debate? Some are obvious: An executive of a chemical company has a vested interest in placing greater value on the financial security of the company's stockholders than on the possible environmental effects of the company's operation. He or she is likely to interpret the potential health effects of what comes out of the plant's smokestacks or sewer pipes differently than would a resident of the surrounding community. These different interpretations need not involve any conscious dishonesty on anyone's part. There is likely to be sufficient scientific uncertainty about the pathological and ecological consequences of the company's effluents to enable both sides to reach very different conclusions from the available "facts."

Less obvious are the value differences among scientists that can divide them in an environmental dispute. Unfortunately, when questions are raised about the effects of personal value systems on scientific judgments, the twin myths of scientific objectivity and scientific neutrality get in the way. Neither the scientific community nor the general population appear to understand that scientists are very much influenced by subjective, value-laden considerations and will frequently evaluate data in a manner that supports their own interests. For example, a scientist employed by a pesticide manufacturer may be less likely than a similarly trained scientist working for an environmental organization to take data that show that one of the company's products is a low-level carcinogen in mice and interpret those data to mean that the product therefore poses a threat to human health.

Even self-proclaimed environmentalists frequently argue over environmental issues. Hunters, while supporting the prohibition of lumbering and mining on their favorite hunting grounds, strongly oppose the designation of these regions as wilderness areas because that would result in the prohibition of the vehicles they use to bring home their bounty. Also opposed to wilderness designation are foresters, who believe that forest lands should be scientifically managed rather than left alone to evolve naturally.

Political ideology can also have a profound effect on environmental attitudes. Those critical of the prevailing socioeconomic system are likely to attribute environmental problems to the industrial development supported by that system. Others are likelier to blame environmental degradation on more universal factors, such as population growth.

Changes in prevailing social attitudes influence public response to environmental issues. The American pioneers were likely to perceive their natural surroundings as being dominated by hostile forces that needed to be conquered or overcome. The notion that humans should conquer nature has only slowly been replaced by the alternative view of living in harmony with the natural environment, but the growing popularity of the environmental movement evidences the public's acceptance of this goal.

PROTECTING THE ENVIRONMENT

There has always been strong resistance to regulatory restraints on industrial and economic activity in the United States. The most ardent supporters of America's capitalist economy argue that pollution and other environmental effects have certain costs and that regulation will take place automatically through the marketplace. Despite mounting evidence that the social costs of polluted air and water are usually external to the economic mechanisms affecting prices and profits, prior to the 1960s, Congress imposed very few restrictions on the types of technology and products industry could use or produce.

As noted above, the turn-of-the-century conservation movement did result in legislation restricting the exploitation of lumber and minerals on federal lands. Similarly, in response to public outrage over numerous incidents of death and illness from adulterated foods, Congress established the Food and Drug Administration (FDA) in 1906.

Regulatory Legislation
The environmental movement of the 1960s and 1970s produced a profound and controversial change in the political climate concerning regulatory legislation. Concerns such as the proliferation of new synthetic chemicals in industry and agriculture, the increased use of hundreds of inadequately tested additives in foods, and the effects of automotive emissions were pressed on

Congress by increasingly influential environmental organizations. Beginning with the Food Additives Amendment of 1958, which required FDA approval of all new chemicals used in the processing and marketing of foods, a series of federal and state legislative and administrative actions resulted in the creation of numerous regulations and standards aimed at reducing and reversing environmental degradation.

Congress responded to the environmental movement with the National Environmental Policy Act of 1969. This act pronounced a national policy requiring an ecological impact assessment for any major federal action. The legislation called for the establishment of a three-member Council on Environmental Quality to initiate studies, make recommendations, and prepare an annual Environmental Quality Report. It also requires all agencies of the federal government to prepare a detailed environmental impact statement (EIS) for any major project or proposed legislation in which they are involved. Despite some initial attempts to evade this requirement, court suits by environmental groups have forced compliance, and now, new facilities like electrical power plants, interstate highways, dams, harbors, and interstate pipelines can proceed only after preparation and review of an EIS.

Another major step in increasing federal antipollution efforts was the establishment in 1970 of the Environmental Protection Agency (EPA). Many programs previously administered by a variety of agencies, such as the departments of the Interior, Agriculture, and Health, Education and Welfare, were transferred to this new, central, independent agency. The EPA was granted authority to do research, propose new legislation, and implement and enforce laws concerning air and water pollution, pesticide use, radiation exposure, toxic substances, solid waste, and noise abatement. The year 1970 also marked the establishment of the Occupational Safety and Health Administration (OSHA), the result of a long struggle by organized labor and independent occupational health organizations to focus attention on the special problems of the workplace.

The first major legislation to propose the establishment of national standards for pollution control was the Air Quality Act of 1967. The Clean Air Act of 1970 specified that ambient air quality standards were to be achieved by July 1, 1975 (a goal that was not met and remains elusive), and that automotive hydrocarbon, carbon monoxide, and nitrogen oxide emissions were to be reduced by 90 percent within five years—a deadline that has been repeatedly extended. Specific standards to limit the pollution content of effluent wastewater were prescribed in the Water Pollution Control Act of 1970. The Safe Drinking Water Act of 1974 authorized the EPA to establish federal drinking water standards, applicable to all public water supplies. The Occupational Safety and Health Act of 1970 allowed OSHA to establish strict standards for exposure to harmful substances in the workplace. The Environmental Pesticide Control Act of 1972 gave the EPA authority to regulate pesticide use and to control the sale of pesticides in interstate commerce. In 1976 the EPA was authorized to establish specific standards for the disposal of hazardous industrial wastes under the Resource Conservation and Recovery Act—but it wasn't until 1980 that the procedures for implementing this legislative mandate were announced. Finally, in 1976, the Toxic Substance Control Act became law, providing the basis for the regulation of public exposure to toxic materials not covered by any other legislation.

All of this environmental legislation in such a short time span produced a predictable reaction from industrial spokespeople and free-market economists. By the late 1970s attacks on what critics referred to as overregulation appeared with increasing frequency in the media. Antipollution legislation was criticized as a principal contributor to inflation and a serious impediment to continued industrial development.

One of the principal themes of Ronald Reagan's first presidential campaign was a pledge to get regulators off the backs of entrepreneurs. He interpreted his landslide victory in 1980 to mean that the public supported a sharp reversal of the federal government's role as regulator in all areas, including the environment. Two of Reagan's key appointees were Interior Secretary James Watt and EPA Administrator Ann Gorsuch Burford, both of whom set about to reverse the momentum of their agencies with respect to the regulation of pollution and environmental degradation. It soon became apparent that Reagan and his advisors had misread public attitudes. Sharp staffing and budget cuts at the EPA and OSHA produced a counterattack by environmental organizations whose membership rolls had continued to swell. Mounting public criticism of the neglect of environmental concerns by the Reagan administration was compounded by allegations of misconduct and criminal activity against environmental officials, including Ms. Burford, who was forced to resign. President Reagan attempted to mend fences with environmentalists by recalling William Ruckelshaus, the popular first EPA administrator, to again head the agency. But throughout Reagan's presidency, few new environmental initiatives were carried out.

Despite campaign promises to return to vigorous efforts to curb pollution, President George Bush received poor grades for the overall environmental policies of his administration. However, he can be credited with providing the support that resulted in the enactment of the long-stalled 1990 Clean Air Act amendments. Despite some criticisms concerning compromises with the automobile and fossil fuel industries, most environmentalists were pleased with many aspects of the new law, particularly its provisions designed to decrease the threat of acid rain. This early optimism was soon negated by what many perceived to be weak efforts to implement and enforce this legislation. Bush has also been faulted for his failure to implement an environmentally sound energy policy and his refusal to support other industrial nations' proposed initiatives to slow global warming and deforestation.

Once again a new president, Bill Clinton, was elected in 1992 on a platform that pledged to reverse the environmental neglect of his predecessors. This pledge was reinforced by the fact that his choice for vice president, Al Gore, had gained a reputation as an environmental activist. The administration has made some early progress in protecting the old-growth forests of the northwestern United States and in making a commitment to the international biodiversity agreement reached at the Earth Summit in Rio de Janeiro. However, after two years in office, Clinton has failed to promote action on such key legislation as the Endangered Species Act, the Clean Water Act, or the Resource Conservation and Recovery Act, all of which are stalled in Congress, awaiting needed revision and reauthorization. Having been encouraged by the appointment of environmental advocate Bruce Babbitt as secretary of the interior, environmentalists became disheartened by his failure to successfully press for restrictions on the ecological damage that results from the commercial exploitation of public lands.

The prospect that the Clinton administration will be more successful in satisfying its environmental critics during the next two years seems dim in view of the results of the mid-term congressional elections that have strengthened the position of those who oppose legislative prescriptions for environmental ailments.

RECENT DEVELOPMENTS

The 1990 Earth Day celebration prompted the publication of two articles critical of the mainstream environmental movement in the April 1990 issue of *The Nation*. In the first, "Ending the War Against the Earth," Barry Commoner summarizes the principal theme of his book *Making Peace With the Planet* (Pantheon Books, 1990). He argues that attempts to merely limit pollution due to existing inappropriate technology are doomed to failure. He calls for a program that would redesign industrial, agricultural, and transportation systems so that they will be environmentally benign and harmonious with the ecosphere. The other article, "The Trouble With Earth Day," by author and social critic Kirkpatrick Sale, presents four fundamental criticisms of the program organized by the planners of Earth Day. Sale contends that the focus on individual action is misguided because most environmental problems are a result of inappropriate systems of production or policies of governments or institutions that cannot be altered or reversed by each of us acting individually to adopt a more ecological lifestyle. Second, he complains about the decision to use most of the $3 million and unlimited publicity to put on a "week-long media bash" rather than to organize a long-range campaign with a continuing political thrust. Third, he accuses the organizers of having added support by accepting as partners many of the corporations, politicians, and lobbyists who have helped create existing problems. Finally, Sale points to the narrow anthropocentric focus on human peril and argues that it would be more appropriate to adopt an ecocentric perspective that would identify the solutions as those that would begin to restore the balance of the Earth's natural systems.

Sale's third complaint has been amplified by a dispute that has recently developed about the plans for the 25th anniversary of Earth Day, which will take place in April 1995. Many prominent individuals and organizations in the environmental organization fear that self-proclaimed "green" (or environmentally friendly) corporations are planning to use their wealth to serve a developmental agenda that does not meet the criteria of sustainability.

A very different form of criticism of environmentalism has emerged in the form of what has been popularly labeled the environmental backlash movement. With considerable funding and support from regulated industries, organizations such as Wise Use/Property Rights, the Council on Energy Awareness, and the Information Council on the Environment have been organizing around their opposition to environmental regulations. Some of these groups go so far as to claim that environmental problems such as ozone depletion and acid rain are nonexistent. A strategy employed by some of these groups to fight restrictions on land development has been to challenge the constitutionality of the government's right to "take" private property by designating it environmentally protected.

GLOBAL DEVELOPMENTS

Although initially lagging behind the United States in environmental regulation, other developed industrial countries have been moving rapidly over the past decade to catch up. In a few European countries where "green parties" have become influential participants in the political process, certain pollutant emission standards are now more stringent than their U.S. counterparts. A uniform system of environmental regulations and controls is prominent among the controversial issues being planned and implemented by the nations of the European Economic Community.

Although the feeding and clothing of their growing populations continue to be the dominant concerns of developing countries, they too are paying increasing attention to environmental protection. Suggestions that they forgo the use of industrial technologies that have resulted in environmental degradation in developed countries are often viewed as an additional obstacle to the goal of raising their standard of living.

During the past decade, attention has shifted from a focus on local pollution to concern about global environmental degradation. Studies of the potential effects of several gaseous atmospheric pollutants on the Earth's climate and its protective ozone layer have made it apparent that human activity has reached a level that can result in major impacts on the planetary ecosystems. A series of major international conferences of political as well as scientific leaders have been held with the goal of seeking solutions to threatening worldwide environmental problems. The "North-South" disputes that limited the agreements reached at the Rio Earth Summit were about how to promote future industrial development so as to avert or minimize the threats to the world's ecosystems, while satisfying the frequently conflicting socioeconomic needs of the developed and developing nations.

New Approaches

An evaluation of the apparent failure to control environmental decay in the past two decades has given rise to demands for new approaches. Environmental policy analysts have proposed that regulatory agencies adopt a more holistic approach to environmental protection, rather than continuing their attempts to impose separate controls on what are actually interconnected problems. The use of economic strategies, such as pollution taxes or the sale of licenses to those who wish to produce limited quantities of pollutants, has received increasing support as potentially more effective than regulatory emission standards. Indeed, the 1990 Clean Air Act amendments specifically include provisions for the trading of "pollution rights" among regulated industries. Such schemes continue to enrage many environmentalists who consider the sale of pollution rights to be unethical. Environmental activists point out that both population growth and increasing worldwide industrial development will result in increasing total quantities of pollutants released despite attempts to reduce the impact of pollution from current, specific sources. Such concerns have resulted in intensive discussion about the concept of "sustainable development," whose advocates propose replacing our entire system of energy production, transportation, and industrial technology with systems that are designed from the start to produce minimal cumulative environmental degradation. An excellent introduction to this concept is included in the 1987 World Commission on the Environment report *Our Common Future* (often referred to as the *Bruntland Report* after its principal author, commission chairperson Gro Harlem Bruntland).

A new militant wing, spearheaded by Greenpeace, has sprung up within the environmental movement. As a result of highly successful membership recruiting and fund-raising efforts, it has become the most powerful international grassroots environmental organization. More radical still are the politics and tactics of other "green" organizations such as Earth First! During a 1990 campaign that they called Redwood Summer, members chained themselves to trees to prevent the cutting of redwood trees in the ancient forests of northern California. The eco-radicals who constitute the small, but growing, extreme fringe of the environmental movement advocate such policies as a drastic reduction in the world's population and a return to much simpler, less materialistic lifestyles.

ECOLOGY AND ENVIRONMENTAL STUDIES

Efforts to protect the environment from the far-reaching effects of human activity require a detailed understanding of the intricate web of interconnected cycles that constitute our natural surroundings. The recent blossoming of ecology and environmental studies into respectable fields of scientific study has provided the basis for such an understanding. Traditional fields of scientific endeavor such as geology, chemistry, or physics are too narrowly focused to successfully describe a complex ecosystem. Thus, it is not surprising that chemists who helped promote the use of DDT and other pesticides failed to predict the harmful effects that accumulation of these substances in biological food chains had on birds and marine life.

Ecology and environmental studies involve a holistic study of the relationships among living organisms and their environment. It is clearly an ambitious undertaking, and ecologists are only beginning to advance our ability to predict the effects of human intrusions into natural ecosystems.

It has been suggested that our failure to recognize the potentially harmful effects of our activities is related to the way we lead our lives. Industrial development has produced lifestyles that separate most of us from direct contact with the natural systems upon which we depend for sustenance. We buy our food in supermarkets and get our water from a kitchen faucet. We tend to take the availability of these essentials for granted until something threatens the supply. It has been claimed that native peoples who lived off the land were more "in touch with nature" and were thus not likely to pollute their environment. This supposition has been discredited by studies showing that the practices of many Native American tribes, despite their generally greater respect for nature, seriously damaged the ecological systems on which they depended. What clearly distinguishes our society from that of our forebears is the increased capability to employ technology in ways that ultimately result in environmental degradation.

SOME THOUGHTS ON ARMED CONFLICT AND INTERNATIONAL COOPERATION

It has long been recognized that a major nuclear war would produce devastating environmental consequences. In *The Fate of the Earth* (Alfred A. Knopf, 1982), Jonathan Schell provides a chilling analysis of the likely effects of radioactive fallout, including destruction of the ozone layer and radioactive contamination of the food chain. In 1983 a group of eminent scientists initiated a controversial debate by predicting that a "nuclear winter" that could threaten the continued existence of human civilization might result from even a limited nuclear conflict.

Perhaps, as some political analysts suggest, the realignment of power following the demise of the Soviet Union has reduced the threat of nuclear war. Unfortunately, we have recently learned from the Persian Gulf War that modern, *conventional*, nonnuclear war can also produce catastrophic ecological damage. The intentional release of huge quantities of petroleum into the Persian Gulf and the ignition of the vast Kuwaiti oil fields produced severe water and air pollution problems whose long-term effects are still being assessed. Several analysts have suggested that environmental factors will figure prominently as both causes and effects of future armed conflicts. Whether or not this proves to be the case, it is beyond doubt that solutions to the growing list of threats to global and regional ecosystems will require unprecedented efforts toward international cooperation.

PART 1

General Philosophical and Political Issues

People who regard themselves as environmentalists can be found on both sides of all the issues in this section. But the participants in these debates nonetheless strongly disagree —due to differences in personal values, political beliefs, and what they perceive as their own self-interests—on how best to prevent environmental degeneration.

Understanding the general issues raised in this initial section is useful preparation for examining the more specific controversies that follow in later sections.

■ Will NAFTA Be Good for the Environment?

■ Does Wilderness Have Intrinsic Value?

■ Should the Endangered Species Act Be Reauthorized?

■ Does the Analysis of Existing Data Support Demands for Environmental Justice?

■ Is Limiting Population Growth a Key Factor in Protecting the Global Environment?

■ Should Property Owners Be Compensated When Environmental Restrictions Limit Development?

1

ISSUE 1

Will NAFTA Be Good for the Environment?

YES: Robert A. Pastor, from "NAFTA's Green Opportunity," *Issues in Science and Technology* (Summer 1993)

NO: Steven E. Sanderson, from "Mexico's Environmental Future," *Current History* (February 1993)

ISSUE SUMMARY

YES: Political science professor Robert A. Pastor sees the North American Free Trade Agreement (NAFTA) as reducing the incentives that have produced pollution problems on the U.S.–Mexican border.

NO: Tropical conservation and development expert Steven E. Sanderson argues that the NAFTA negotiations suggest that environmental concerns are being neglected in the interest of promoting industrial and agricultural development.

Most economists believe that the removal of trade restrictions is generally beneficial to all nations involved. They cite the concept of comparative advantage, which emphasizes the opportunity that free trade presumably gives to each country to exploit whatever particular advantage it may have in exportable commodities. In the past, however, the environmental effects of trade agreements have been ignored. The recently adopted North American Free Trade Agreement (NAFTA) resulted in a break with this tradition. Heated debate about the environmental implications of this treaty occurred at many levels during the latter stages of the negotiation and approval process. The concerns of the environmental community became intense enough to result in an ultimately unsuccessful lawsuit by the Sierra Club, Friends of the Earth, and Public Citizen arguing that the agreement could not be considered by Congress before a complete environmental impact statement had been prepared. This concern about the effects of the promotion of trade on the protection of the environment has continued during the current phase of international negotiations in Uruguay of the General Agreement on Tariffs and Trade (GATT), for which the Clinton administration is presently seeking congressional approval.

In order to satisfy complaints that environmental provisions of NAFTA are inadequate, the United States initiated negotiations with Mexico and Canada in April of 1993 that produced a set of "side agreements" to the treaty entitled the North American Agreement on Environmental Cooperation (NAATEC). NAATEC established a trilateral Commission for Environmental Cooperation charged with the task of scrutinizing the environmental repercussions of the trade pact and attempting to resolve disputes. This addition to the treaty resulted in a significant split in the environmental community with major organizations arguing both for and against ratification of NAFTA.

Opposition to NAFTA focuses on several potential negative impacts. One such impact is the effect of what are referred to as *trade disciplines*, which are intended to prevent parties to a trade agreement from unduly restricting trade. This concern was heightened when trade disciplines contained in GATT were successfully used by Mexico to prevent the United States from prohibiting the importing of tuna caught in a manner that killed dolphins. Another concern is based on the past tendency of parties to trade agreements to "harmonize" their environmental regulations downward to the least stringent level. Trade agreements can also enhance the movement of polluting industries over borders to the nation with the lowest environmental standards or the weakest enforcement procedures. This latter threat has particular significance in the case of NAFTA because of the *maquiladora* program that permits duty-free import of components into Mexico where they are processed and exported duty-free back to United States. The result of this program is the existence of many highly polluting factories along the southern side of the U.S.–Mexican border.

Robert A. Pastor is a political science professor at Emory University, where he directs the Latin American and Caribbean program at that university's Carter Center. While admitting that environmental concerns are not central to NAFTA, and that the trade agreement will not directly lead to the improvement of Mexico's environment, he argues that it will have the effect of bolstering the economy and thus making it easier for Mexico to respond to environmental problems. Steven E. Sanderson is a political science professor at the University of Florida where he directs the Tropical Conservation and Development Program. He projects growth in agriculture and energy production resulting from NAFTA, which, given Mexico's development model, is likely to lead to increased pollution.

YES

Robert A. Pastor

NAFTA'S GREEN OPPORTUNITY

For most of its history, Mexico has tried to keep its powerful northern neighbor, the United States, at a distance. It built tariff walls to limit trade; it devised investment rules to impede U.S. corporations; and it used a range of political techniques to block U.S. influence in its internal affairs. While U.S. leaders tried to expand ties, Mexico's leaders defined the limits to friendship.

In the spring of 1990, Mexican president Carlos Salinas de Gortari broke with this tradition of defensive nationalism and proposed a free trade agreement with the United States. President George Bush and, subsequently, Canadian Prime Minister Brian Mulroney accepted Salinas' challenge, and 2 1/2 years later the three signed the North American Free Trade Agreement (NAFTA). For the first time, a more trusting relationship among the North American countries seemed possible.

Besides raising new hopes, however, NAFTA has generated new risks and fears. NAFTA is the first reciprocal trade arrangement involving countries at such divergent levels of economic and political development. For different reasons, some groups in each country fear that integration will mean a loss of political control or a reduction of living standards. Environmental groups in the United States have been particularly concerned that economic growth resulting from such an agreement would exacerbate the already serious pollution problems on the border with Mexico. In addition, they have warned that the agreement could encourage U.S. industries to move to Mexico, where, they fear, environmental regulations will not be enforced, thereby putting pressure on the United States to lower its standards to match Mexico's.

Environmental concerns are not central to NAFTA or, in fact, to the overall relationship between Mexico and the United States. The principal environmental problem in U.S.–Mexican relations is pollution on the border; any solution to that problem will require international cooperation, whether or not NAFTA is approved. But environmental issues are of growing importance to both nations. In the United States, the environmental movement has become a powerful political force; in Mexico, there is an emerging popular awareness of the magnitude of the country's environmental problems.

From Robert A. Pastor, "NAFTA's Green Opportunity," *Issues in Science and Technology* (Summer 1993), pp. 47–54. Copyright © 1993 by The University of Texas at Dallas, Richardson, TX. Reprinted by permission.

Environmental activists in both countries view NAFTA as an instrument for influencing environmental policy.

U.S. trade negotiators initially rejected environmentalists' demands for maintaining and enforcing strong environmental standards. They insisted that their goal was to lower, not raise, barriers to competition. However, political pressure compelled the Bush administration eventually to seek a separate "flank agreement" on the environment. U.S. environmental groups judged this concession inadequate. The Clinton administration promised to negotiate a supplementary agreement explicitly linked to the treaty that includes stronger environmental provisions.

All three countries will benefit economically from NAFTA, and they are likely to benefit environmentally as well. Environmentalists' concerns will be addressed more effectively if the United States, Mexico, and Canada are wedded to a new economic relationship than if they are not. Their worries about the negative environmental effects of increased trade and competition can be assuaged. Indeed, environmentalists should favor NAFTA: The agreement represents an important opportunity to translate transnational environmental concerns into international agreements and to encourage Mexico to make its environmental program more effective.

BORDER POLLUTION

Mexico's gamble on free trade with the United States occurred at the very moment when the environmental movement first began to focus its attention on trade issues. No previous important trade agreement had included environmental issues. Few environmental-

ists knew much about trade policy, and few trade negotiators were prepared to address environmental demands. Communication was made still more difficult because the two groups speak different languages. Environmentalists want to restrict and regulate development; advocates of freer trade try to eliminate regulations and barriers that impede the flow of goods and services. Experience has shown, however, that growth and environmental protection are not necessarily incompatible.

The most pressing environmental issue raised in the NAFTA negotiations is whether the agreement would exacerbate pollution along the border. The chronic, severe environmental problems on the border are primarily the result of an explosion of economic and population growth in the past decade, largely due to U.S. and other foreign investment in factories on the Mexican side of the border. These factories, known as *maquiladoras*, take advantage of cheaper labor and a special tariff program that allows them to assemble parts imported from the United States and then re-export the assembled products.

Rapid industrialization has overburdened the region's thin infrastructure, and air pollution, water contamination and inadequate waste treatment have created serious health hazards. The National Wildlife Federation identifies the border pollution issue as its highest priority in U.S.–Mexican environmental relations, and the data support that conclusion. At Laredo, Texas, 25 million gallons of raw sewage flow into the Rio Grande every day. Contamination levels are 1,650 times greater than those considered safe for recreational use. In San Elizario, Texas, where a shared aquifer has been contaminated, 35 percent of the children contract hepatitis A by age 8, and 90 percent of adults have had it by age 35....

No one, least of all the people living along the border, disputes the seriousness of these environmental problems. Although environmentalists have expressed concerns that NAFTA would make these problems worse, two studies suggest that economic growth along the border is likely to be faster and dirtier if NAFTA is rejected than if it is approved. The main reason for this apparent paradox is that the *maquiladoras*, which rely on a partial exemption from tariffs, will theoretically become obsolete if NAFTA is approved and tariffs are eliminated. The only reason for future investment to occur near the border is proximity. However, there are more important factors that would encourage investors to locate their operations farther south.

First, absenteesim and high turnover of workers are chronic problems for companies on the border because workers soon learn that they can earn five to 10 times as much merely by crossing the border. Second, and partly because of the first, average wages in the *maquiladoras* are considerably higher than in the interior of the country. Third, the region's severe environmental and infrastructure problems will become an obstacle to investment on the border. The Mexican government already discourages investment in Mexico City and other congested urban areas. As the environmental costs of new investment in the border area increase and as better roads from the border to the interior reduce transportation costs, firms will look to invest in the interior. The government already provides incentives to invest in "priority zones"—not the border—that need development. Thus, by eliminating all tariffs, NAFTA is likely to reduce the environmental problems on

the border by eliminating the main incentive to invest there.

REGULATORY FEARS

The second key question is whether NAFTA would weaken environmental regulation in both countries. If the discrepancy in environmental standards served as a magnet attracting U.S. companies to Mexico, as some environmentalists fear, it could encourage U.S. communities to lower their standards.

Opponents of NAFTA have cited the decision of some Los Angeles furniture companies to move to Mexico to escape tough pollution laws as an example of what would happen if NAFTA were approved. The General Accounting Office conducted a study of this problem and found that from 1988 to 1990, between 11 and 28 furniture manufacturers in the Los Angeles area relocated to Mexico, affecting approximately 960 to 2,547 jobs. About 83 percent of the companies mentioned the differences in wages and workers' compensation as the major motives for relocating; 78 percent also cited stringent environmental controls. However, the number of companies involved represented only 1 percent to 3 percent of the total number of furniture manufacturers in the Los Angeles area, and only 2 percent to 10 percent of local furniture workers' jobs were affected. These percentages shrink to insignificance if one includes all furniture manufacturers in the United States. Clearly, this anecdote does not tell the whole story.

Studies of the decisionmaking processes of U.S. corporations that invest abroad indicate that environmental considerations have been negligible or nonexistent. Other studies have found little evidence that the cost of pollution abatement equipment influences decisions on where industries move. Princeton University analysts Gene Grossman and Alan Krueger found that the costs involved in complying with environmental laws "are small in relation to the other components of total cost that determine whether it is profitable to operate in the United States or Mexico." A second, more general study found that the weighted average cost of pollution abatement and control equipment was less than 1 percent of the cost of doing business, and the highest costs were just over 3 percent. These numbers are simply too low to be considered an incentive for relocation. Mexico's comparative advantage lies in low wages, not lax environmental regulations.

Moreover, there is substantial evidence that NAFTA would strengthen, rather than weaken, Mexico's environmental standards. In 1988, the Mexican government passed the General Law for Ecological Equilibrium and Environmental Protection, its first environmental law. Modeled on the U.S. Environmental Protection Act of 1970, the law prohibits air, water, and soil pollution and contamination by hazardous waste, pesticides, and toxic substances. In some ways, Mexico's law goes beyond U.S. laws—for example, by requiring an environmental impact statement (EIS) on any investment involving hazardous wastes. The United States requires an EIS only when a developer needs government credits or approval.

Salinas became president in December 1988, and he made the environment a high priority. After NAFTA negotiations began, Mexico's environmental efforts accelerated, particularly in Mexico City and on the border. The environmental budget increased by a factor of nine

in two years, and the number of environmental inspectors increased from 19 in 1989 to 100 in 1991, with half of those assigned to the border.

In 1992, Salinas created the Secretariat of Social Development (SEDESOL) to relate environmental concerns more directly to a wider range of governmental activities. He provided additional resources for environmental protection by more than quadrupling the environmental budget for the border area and increasing the number of inspectors there to 200. These new inspectors have closed 980 industrial sites, 82 of them permanently.

The most spectacular example of Mexico's new commitment to environmental protection was the decision by Salinas to close the oil refinery on the outskirts of Mexico City—at a cost of $500 million and 5,000 jobs. The government also replaced the capital's old gas-spewing buses, prohibited private cars from driving in the city one day a week, and required the use of cleaner-burning gasoline.

The pollution problems on the border are not as bad as in the capital, but they have a greater impact on the United States. U.S. and Mexican environmental agencies have been working together on the border since 1983, but the agreement that was signed then was too general to be effective. Here, too, NAFTA has injected life into environmental concerns.

In February 1992, after conducting hearings among groups in both countries and circulating a draft, the two governments formulated a three-year integrated plan for cleaning the border. President Bush pledged nearly $250 million in fiscal year 1993, a sum that included funding for three waste treatment projects. Mexico promised to spend $640 million over three years, to work closely with the

U.S. Environmental Protection Agency to train border environmental inspectors, and to develop data bases that could be used by both sides.

The integrated plan dealt with many of the problems that had been overlooked by the agreement of 1983. However, it promised more than its budget and personnel could possibly deliver, and many of the projects lacked specific implementation plans. Moreover, although the Mexican government has provided the funding it promised, the United States has thus far failed to come through with its pledged level of funding.

In a comprehensive analysis of the plan, Jan Gilbreath Rich of the University of Texas commended it as "the first large-scale attempt to integrate the planning and environmental strategies used by the two federal governments and a first attempt to recognize the direct link between natural resources and trade." Rich also notes that although the plan was compiled because of NAFTA, it deals with today's problems, rather than with those that will be faced if NAFTA is implemented. It is unclear whether or how the plan will be incorporated into NAFTA's supplementary agreement on the environment.

Mexico has a long way to go, but when one compares the progress that Mexico has made in the five years since enactment of its environmental law with what the United States accomplished in the two decades since passage of EPA, it is hard to avoid the conclusion that NAFTA has already had a profound and positive effect on the environment in Mexico. Some analysts believe that cooperation on environmental matters will improve even more after NAFTA is enacted. They point to the fact that the acid rain agreement between the United

States and Canada was reached after the trade agreement. In addition, NAFTA could eventually serve as a vehicle for transnational cooperation on global environmental issues such as rainforest destruction. Already, in yet another nod to NAFTA, Mexico has postponed the building of a large dam because of its implications for the rainforest.

INCLUSIONS AND OMISSIONS

Although the Bush administration officials insisted that they would address environmental issues only outside of NAFTA, political pressure compelled them to include language in the text of the agreement itself. The preamble to NAFTA includes 15 specific objectives, of which three relate to the environment: to "strengthen the development and enforcement of environmental laws and regulations, promote sustainable development," and implement the agreement "in a manner consistent with environmental protection and conservation."

Environmental issues are also addressed in four separate chapters of NAFTA. The most important are those on Standards and Sanitary and Phytosanitary Measures. These allow states and cities to enact strict standards and encourage governments to harmonize their standards upward. In addition, NAFTA adopts a more flexible test for evaluating the impact of environmental standards than currently exists in the General Agreement on Tariffs and Trade (GATT). Moreover, it deals explicitly with the "pollution haven" issue in the chapter on investment, which discourages countries from "derogating from" existing standards in order to "attract or maintain" investment and calls for the two governments to consult with each other in the event of a complaint on this issue.

Overall, NAFTA's environmental provisions are stronger than comparable provisions in the U.S.–Canadian Free Trade Agreement as well as those contemplated in the current text of the Uruguay Round of GATT negotiations. Despite this progress, the agreement falls short of its potential. Many of its provisions—for example, on pollution havens—are not tied to the dispute settlement mechanism, and there is no mechanism for monitoring or encouraging compliance with the new pollution control laws. In a Congressional hearing on NAFTA, Rep. Robert Matsui (D-Calif.) said: "Essentially, what the agreement now provides is a chance for Mexico to wink and not enforce its own laws and attract our business."

Another important issue that was omitted from NAFTA is whether to base standards on the process by which goods and services are produced. Countries may set product standards to exclude goods that are not safe, such as some pesticides. The tough question is whether a country should be able to set standards on the process by which goods are produced even if the product is not affected. For example, environmental groups have tried to prevent tuna from being imported because dolphins were not protected in the harvest. U.S. farmers might want to prevent tomatoes grown with a banned pesticide from being imported, even if there are no traces of pesticides on the food.

There are many complicated issues involved in setting process-based standards. Experts do not always agree on whether a particular process is immoral or environmentally unhealthy. Making those decisions across communities is difficult; doing it across sovereign borders will take patience and long negotiations.

In addition, some Americans argue that Mexican industry will receive a hidden subsidy if it does not have to maintain the same environmental standards on processes as well as products. Every policy difference between trading partners that gives a competitive edge to a company can be considered a kind of subsidy. These could include zoning regulations, uneven tax burdens, and small-business interest rates. The implicit logic of NAFTA, like the European Community, is that integration will move nations to harmonize standards and rules; otherwise, one side will have an improper advantage. The question of whether process standards are necessary to maintain a level playing field needs to be carefully investigated. Ideally, a mechanism should be established to evaluate each case on its own merits.

Finally, one of the hardest issues involved in NAFTA is who will pay for the environmental projects. So far, the U.S. Congress has not allocated sufficient funds even to pay for existing environmental programs on the border. Richard Gephardt (D-Mo.), the Majority Leader of the House of Representatives, has suggested a border tax. With total trade between the United States and Mexico amounting to $75 billion in 1992, a 1 percent tax would yield a fund of $750 million. This would meet most of the border environmental needs and allow for some infrastructural investments in Mexico and perhaps adjustment assistance in the United States. The main objection to the cross-border tax is that it is contrary to the purpose of NAFTA, which is to reduce barriers to trade. But under NAFTA, tariffs that greatly exceed 1 percent of trade will remain on many products for 5 years, and some will be kept in place for 15. We should place revenues representing 1 percent of trade from these existing tariffs in a special fund so that the short-term gains of trade will be reinvested in the long-term environmental and economic development of both countries.

ENFORCEMENT MEASURES

In response to concerns about the interpretation and enforcement of NAFTA's environmental provisions, top environmental officials of the United States, Mexico, and Canada met in September 1992. They agreed in principle to create a North American Commission on Environmental Cooperation to oversee the environmental aspects of the agreement. But the commission's mandate was vague, and it seemed more like a framework for periodic, high-level meetings than an institution aimed at making sure environmental goals would be pursued.

In October 1992, when presidential candidate Bill Clinton endorsed NAFTA, he pledged to negotiate a supplementary agreement on the environment and to establish a new commission to deal with the issue. The commission that he envisioned would have "substantial powers and resources," but its function would not be to enforce the agreement or the laws of the countries. Rather, it would use a variety of instruments—especially publicity and moral pressure—to encourage each government to enforce collective norms and its own laws. This commission would be more powerful than that proposed by the Bush administration but would not collectively enforce treaties, as the European Community Commission does.

In testimony before Congress in March, Mickey Kantor, Clinton's Special Trade Representative, described his view of the environmental commission as "a forum for reviewing and analyzing environmental issues on this continent." It would use independent experts, review complaints from citizens and governments, request information from environmental agencies in the three countries, and pursue "effective follow-up actions to ensure compliance." Kantor also said that the Clinton administration would seek additional measures to clean up the border and strengthen enforcement of national laws.

In a letter sent to Kantor in May 1993, the leaders of seven environmental groups pledged their support for NAFTA provided that the supplementary agreement included key provisions strengthening the commission's enforcement capabilities. They proposed a commission with a permanent secretariat and independent power to prepare reports, conduct investigations, and monitor compliance with environmental laws. If one government found another systematically failing to enforce its laws, then it could initiate a dispute settlement proceeding that could, under limited circumstances, permit the withdrawal of a trade concession. Presumably, the only issues that could trigger such actions would be cross-border or trade-related pollution, not problems such as persistent smog in Mexico City or Los Angeles.

The seven environmental groups also requested sufficient and sustainable funding for border projects, conservation programs, and the commission; negotiations on process standards; and the application of the dispute settlement system to environmental issues. Most of these suggestions are good ones. Mexico and Canada object to trade sanctions as the instrument to enforce environmental laws, and they would prefer a less independent and litigious commission, but both governments were willing to use NAFTA to strengthen environmental conditions and cooperation within North America.

Clinton's efforts to assuage the concerns of environmental groups and labor provoked an equal and opposite reaction from Republicans, who preferred Bush's original agreement. A majority of Republican senators warned Clinton in a letter on April 29 that if he created "whole new levels of regulation and bureaucracy relating to environmental protection and labor laws, he will lose most of the Republicans."

The conflicting pressures generated by environmentalists, Republicans, Mexico, and Canada may yield a compromise commission that will have substantial powers, but whose powers will not include enforcement or the imposition of sanctions. Such an independent commission could play an effective role in monitoring environmental problems, training Mexican inspectors, and raising North American consciousness. On the border, for instance, the commission could be given the authority to set emission standards, inspect businesses, and impose fines, using the funds to finance its operation and to clean up toxic wastes.

Although it would be desirable in the future to give the commission the power of collective enforcement, Mexico, Canada, and a significant number of members of Congress are not ready for such a proposal at this time. An editorial in the *New York Times* posed the problem: "Such sanctions raise tricky issues of sovereignty. Is the United States prepared to have sanctions applied to companies because an international tribunal finds them guilty of polluting the air over Los Angeles or hiring illegal aliens?"

NAFTA also calls for numerous committees, and President Clinton has proposed additional commissions on the environment and on work standards. An important question not addressed in NAFTA is how these committees and commissions ought to relate to one another. Over the long term, the best solution would be to have an umbrella North American Commission, with offices to deal with each of the fundamental issues relating to integration, instead of a multitude of independent commissions. Under the auspices of the larger commission, there could be offices for trade disputes, environmental issues, workers' rights, border development, human rights and migration, and the collection and harmonization of statistics. This North American Commission should be structured in a way that would foster constructive dialogue among the three governments on a future agenda including, perhaps, immigration.

Regrettably, none of the three governments has proposed a wider North American Commission. Mexico is reluctant to consider an institution for fear that the United States could control it. This stance ought to be reconsidered by Mexico because Washington is stronger in dealing with problems on a case-by-case basis than it would be if it had to submit to a genuinely trinational forum that employed agreed-upon principles and resolved disputes on the basis of a neutral set of rules. Indeed, such forums will be essential to sustain confidence that disputes will be settled fairly.

THE BROADER CONTEXT

... Rejection of NAFTA would sap Mexico's economic confidence, undermining the economy and perhaps its new economic policies; it would strengthen those who have long insisted that Americans should not be trusted. But the United States should not accept NAFTA just because the Mexican government wants it. A better rationale is that it is in our interest, that our future requires adaptation, and that the two countries can help each other acquire a global competitive edge.

Technological innovations and the communications revolution have increased the importance of trade in the United States, Mexico, and Canada. But trade, which benefits all three nations in the long term and in the aggregate, can also make a society more unequal, as occurred in the United States and Mexico in the 1980s. The people and businesses that are most mobile and competitive win; those that cannot move or adapt lose. Moreover, trade makes each country more dependent on the others. Such dependence is uncomfortable, and when jobs are lost as a result of import competition or industrial relocation, people resent their neighbors. Redistributive policies such as President Clinton's tax package and new training and adjustment-assistance programs are es-

sential to prevent the social fabric from tearing. The benefits of trade must be shared with those who will suffer the costs of increased competition and dislocation.

There is no magic in the marketplace to compensate for the economic inequalities generated by freer trade. Similarly, the market cannot correct the environmental repercussions resulting from the lowering of trade barriers. Only collective action by the governments of North America can respond to the old problems of border pollution and the new issues of ecological interdependence.

Incorporating social and environmental concerns into NAFTA will yield political and policy dividends. At a time when the domestic consensus behind trade policy has broken down, a broader NAFTA could attract new constituent groups. Instead of ignoring the adverse effects of freer trade on social and environmental problems, NAFTA can serve as an instrument to ameliorate these problems. NAFTA can not only reshape the relationship between the United States and Mexico, it can spur both governments to improve the environment.

NO

Steven E. Sanderson

MEXICO'S ENVIRONMENTAL FUTURE

After conducting the region's most profound economic reform and abandoning its historical antipathy to its northern neighbor, Mexico has become the darling of the United States these days. It is apparently now ready to face together with the United States what many call "the inevitable future" of North American integration. The government of President Carlos Salinas de Gortari has made headlines by committing itself to free trade, by abandoning land reforms instituted after the revolution, and by subscribing to international environmental agreements that break with the country's sorry record of past abuse. For many, especially conservative internationalists, Mexico has become a model citizen, a regional leader in international affairs.

But behind the headlines, environmental concerns were treated at separate tables from general economic concerns at the North American Free Trade Agreement (NAFTA) negotiations, even though there is no doubt that the economy and the environment are inextricably linked. Although the course of economic growth will determine Mexico's environmental future, virtually no one in a position to make policy is discussing the impact North American free trade will have on Mexico's environment, let alone Mexican economic reforms or land tenure changes. The architects of Mexico's impending wholesale integration into the world economy rarely speak about environmental protection. The ideology of the day has led free traders and fiscal reformers to condemn such concerns as belonging to an unaffordable nationalism of the past, and shrug off possible future costs.

Politicians have repeatedly stated that changes in economic policy actually strengthen environmental protection. From the United States trade representative to World Bank officials, talk of "sustainable," or ecologically sound, development is the order of the day. William Reilly, director of the Environmental Protection Agency under the Bush administration, hailed the agreement on free trade between the United States, Mexico, and Canada as "a watershed in the history of environmental protection, because it integrates economic and environmental concerns to an unprecedented degree." But the evidence strongly suggests that environmental concerns are being ignored.

FREE TRADE, REGARDLESS

One of the most important indicators of Mexico's environmental trajectory is NAFTA, which would establish a trilateral free trade zone. Surprisingly, there is no substantive treatment of the environment in the most recent draft text of the agreement. For example, the chapter on agriculture contains only a blanket expression of concern for "relevant ecological and other environmental conditions." The annex on the automotive industry refers neither to the environment nor to fuel efficiency, despite the alleged importance of environmental standards for automobile emissions and global concern over the release of greenhouse gases, which are believed to raise the temperature of the atmosphere. Perhaps most devastating, the word "environment" does not appear at all in the chapter on energy, nor any language professing concern for or recommending environmentally friendly energy policies for the free trade area.

Why the omission? First, the United States trade representative and other actors on the American side have always argued that crafting a treaty that addressed the environmental implications of free trade would create a "legislative Christmas tree" weighed down by ornaments inappropriate to the occasion. Such a document would not pass muster on Capitol Hill, or be welcomed in Mexico either.

Second, champions of economic integration—and of development in general—in both the United States and Mexico have neither the time, the intellectual disposition, nor the institutional mandate to deal with the environment. The environment is viewed as a "cost" billed against economic growth, while the opportunity to avoid unwanted future effects on the environment is missed. An otherwise valuable new assessment of NAFTA's impact published by the Brookings Institution barely touches on the environment, except in references to border pollution and in a more general essay by Robert Pastor, a member of President Jimmy Carter's administration. The leading policy volume on NAFTA, published by the Institute for International Economics, says the big environmental issue in NAFTA is who will put up money to spend on the environment—a question the trade negotiators largely shirked, according to the authors.

The third explanation for the omissions from NAFTA is even more troubling: that many policymakers worldwide believe good environmental outcomes naturally flow from sound economic practices. The global community has agreed since the 1987 report of the Brundtland Commission on the need to consider economic growth and development in light of environmental concerns, especially as the integration of the international economic system proceeds. And in the United Nations Conference on Environment and Development (UNCED) documents emerging from the "Earth Summit" in Rio de Janeiro last June, the world signed on to a concept of sustainable development that would link economics and environment from the outset, and that identified free trade and economic policy reforms as the most important vehicles for ensuring sustainable development. (This allows environmentalists advocating sustainable development to paint a positive portrait of the trade-development-environment connection without examining more disturbing possibilities.)

But the dissonant tones of international integration are much more difficult than the fair music of rhetorical agreement. Today nations around the world face an environmental dilemma. The global community has recognized that the environmental condition of one country is a complex product of the environmental policies and economic dynamics of the global system at large. But the selfsame community also treats each nation as a separate, closed environment, in which uses and abuses of natural resources stem from domestic "policy choices." For Mexico, international economic integration means that its environmental future is no longer its exclusive purview—if indeed it ever was. Mexican policymakers must include the United States (and to a much lesser extent, Canada) in their calculations, and it is hard to imagine that the relatively tiny Mexican economy could exert any control over the domestic policy of its giant neighbors. But though outcomes are mainly determined at the trilateral and at the global level, still it is Mexico that is held responsible.

For Mexico, the global economic system is, in large measure, the United States. And the United States, by ignoring environmental problems or separating them from general trade and growth issues, permits itself the luxury of displacing a great deal of its own environmental policy failure to Mexico—perhaps to be later re-exported back over the border in other forms. Arid lands agriculture is moving to Mexico from the western United States as land, water, and labor become harder to find and more expensive, and questions about the use of agricultural chemicals become more pressing. Mexico in turn responds to the exigencies of United States–Mexican relations and internal political pressures and creates economic institutions and processes without regard for their likely environ-

mental impact. For all the protests to the contrary, the environmental agenda is still marginal to the driving forces behind Mexican development and the United States–Mexican relations that frame it.

During the two years of negotiations over NAFTA, Mexico has often pushed its two northern neighbors toward agreement, so that NAFTA is very much a product of Mexican policy rather than a simple imposition of United States hegemony. Even so, given the widespread suspicion raised by the NAFTA talks and the general unhappiness of the developing countries with the Rio summit and the political jockeying surrounding it, some blame the United States for the environmental weakness of NAFTA. Others look to Mexico for new ways of tying economic recovery to environmental protection. It is impossible to leave NAFTA out when considering the Mexican environment (even though that is exactly what has been done up to now), for that reason alone, thinking about Mexico's environment requires an international focus. A look at agriculture and energy, only two out of a wide range of possible choices, will show how deeply Mexico's environmental futures are tied to international integration.

FOOD FACTS

Many of the reasons for Mexico's newfound internationalism are structural. Mexico cannot produce enough food for its burgeoning population or import the balance efficiently without recourse to free trade. Although Mexican agricultural production has increased substantially over the past two decades (the oft-repeated claim that Mexico's agriculture is stagnating is wrong), per capita agricultural production has not grown for a decade, hovering around levels that typified the early 1970s. In the past Mexico relied on heavy state intervention and costly public subsidies, as well as a restrictive import policy, to correct the food production problem. But none of these is politically or fiscally possible in the wake of the debt crisis and the subsequent economic reforms. The virtue of free trade and privatization of agriculture is that they allow the public sector to retire from the subsidy business and allow cheap border prices of foodstuffs to lower the cost for consumers of grain products, cooking oil, and other basic consumer items.

The environmental future of trade-based food policy is unclear. Everyone seems to agree that the reorganization of food production on the basis of free trade will inevitably mean marginal agricultural land will no longer be competitive; some, but not all, argue that it will go out of cultivation. In this scenario, the environmental cost of rain-fed agricultural production in Mexico will be displaced to the grain belt in the United States, which is much better suited ecologically to the purpose. Marginal land in Mexico—arid lands and steep hillsides—will return to a more natural state, reducing soil erosion and exhaustion.

Some argue that agricultural adjustment will be devastating for poor farmers. Most estimates suggest that the impact will be broad and deep, and that it will be especially serious for maize and bean producers. Under most models, a substantial portion of the estimated 12 million to 15 million poor farmers in Mexico are expected to move to urban areas. The net environmental impact of such a demographic shift is unknown. It would depend on how, when, and why the farmers moved to the city, and on the ability of the cities to absorb them productively. Certainly, hundreds of thousands of rural poor moving to squalid shantytowns on the fringes of Mexican cities is not a positive social or environmental outcome, even if their land were to lie fallow. Others suggest that the deteriorating living conditions of poor farmers under free trade will lead to more, not less, poverty-induced soil degradation and deforestation. And to the extent —often underestimated—that poor farmers generate employment for poor landless people, who also would be displaced, the risk of the poor "mining" marginal lands and remnants of forest is heightened. In a country that has lost 11 million hectares of forest in the past two decades, this last prospect is a grim one.

The United States is a probable hedge against such possibilities. Some large percentage of the displaced rural poor would likely find their way to the border, reflecting the "pull" of chronic labor shortages in agriculture and services in the United States and the hard "push" of agricultural adjustment. Thus a more relaxed immigration policy on the part of the United States would be a most welcome environmental outcome for Mexico, while a restrictive policy would have the opposite effect. In neither case is Mexico in control of this element of its environmental future.

Mexico appears to recognize the inevitability of its integration into the international agricultural system, dominated by its relationship with the United States. So that it faces that future as much as possible on its own terms, it is taking a leadership role in defining those terms. Mexico's export agriculture has thus been cited as one of the most important winners under free trade. Most analysts predict that a significant portion of fruit and winter vegetable production will shift southward (as has been occurring over the last two decades) from the United States to northern Mexican irrigation districts as California, Texas, and Florida become less hospitable sites. Beyond that shift, free trade will create additional demand in the United States, and Mexico will even replace other regional competitors to some extent (for example, Brazil, for frozen orange juice concentrate).

Despite the positive effect on the volume and balance of Mexico's trade, this has a number of disturbing environmental implications. The debate over water supply and distribution in the western United States may very well be displaced in some measure to Mexico. And as the urbanization of northern Mexico continues, the competition between urban centers and agriculturalists for scarce water is likely to escalate. This is not a new debate in Mexico. Since World War II, the north has fought over groundwater use, and in the process conservation has lost out. The prospect of intensifying agriculture in northern Mexico does not bode well for problems of aquifer depletion and salinization, fertilizer runoff and contamination, and the like.

Moreover, much of the cost advantage of Mexican export agriculture revolves around heavily subsidized agricultural inputs, especially water and energy. Agricultural exports are overwhelmingly energy-intensive, because of mechanized cultivation practices and heavy fertilizer use. Yet Mexico intends to reduce many subsidies to agriculture. Will water prices actually seek market levels, or will some subsidization continue? And will Mexican fuel prices rise to reflect market realities? If so, the economic outcome for agricultural exports will be much less

rosy; if not, Mexico will continue to subsidize energy and water consumption in the United States through a wasteful resource policy, with potentially disastrous environmental consequences. The essential question, though, is whether concern about the environment will take precedence over what are among the most promising exports in Mexico's agricultural sector. It certainly never has before.

THE OIL QUESTION

Mexico has a long history of oil production. Even before the revolution began in 1910 it was the world's largest oil exporter. After the Organization of Petroleum Exporting Countries (OPEC) enacted large price increases in 1973 and 1974, Mexico discovered huge new reserves and accelerated exploration and production to meet the needs of the 1970s oil boom. (Although Mexico was not a member of OPEC, it benefited from the high prevailing prices.) Now, after a decade of oil bust, the energy sector has reemerged as a determinant of domestic economic performance and environmental health.

Despite a decade of slow growth or no growth, energy consumption in Mexico grew 25 percent from 1980 to 1989, and average demand grew 3.4 percent annually. During that same period, the collapse of the oil boom and subsequent scandals within the state oil monopoly, Petróleos Mexicanos (PEMEX), caused investments in the sector to shrink drastically: from 1983 to 1991 PEMEX capital investments fell over 40 billion real pesos. Since then, Mexico has struggled to keep domestic production high enough to satisfy export and domestic demand.

The industrial growth projected as a result of economic recovery and integration through NAFTA will put tremendous new strains on domestic oil and gas production. If Mexico were to return to consumption rates of the good economic growth years of the 1970s, energy demand would grow at twice the rate it did during the 1980s. Problems with natural gas self-sufficiency cropped up some years ago, and the United States and Canada are both currently exporting natural gas to Mexico.

Demand for natural gas is expected to rise significantly over the next decade, as Mexico tries to change over its electrical energy production to natural gas-fired plants. The country is sure to take better advantage of its domestic gas, but much of its reserves are associated with southern oil fields, too remote for them to be competitive near the northern border. As a result, imports are likely to rise, with some expecting them to reach 1 billion cubic feet per day by the end of the century (current levels are about 350 million cubic feet per day). This would result in the production of cleaner technologies for energy production in Mexico.

The import solution does not follow for oil. As PEMEX is recapitalized and re-organized along more efficient lines, the main problem is to satisfy projected demand. Searching for more oil offshore and extracting more from known on-shore reserves are the two main methods being employed. But numerous know environmental risks are associated with increased onshore drilling near the Lacandon Forest, the largest patch of tropical moist forest in Mexico and PEMEX's prime site for new exploration. Similar risks accompany offshore drilling in the Bay of Campeche, with potential conse-quences for tourism, coastal aquaculture, and offshore fisheries from the states of Tabasco to Texas. Here let us isolate two additional problems accompanying this strategy: the implications of industrial growth for domestic fossil fuel use, and increased energy use for the global environment.

The growth of Mexican society has of course resulted in more fossil fuel use, and the rate has accelerated in recent years. Automobiles alone now account for about 80 percent of the severe air pollution in Mexico City; the number of cars has grown six times faster than the population between 1940 and 1982. The economic reforms since 1985 have already meant new industrialization and exports. With NAFTA, industrialization is projected to increase, and the border industries (maquiladoras)—which have operated under special tax regulations and always been prohibited from sell-ing in Mexico—will likely be folded into the general development plan. Certainly Mexico's hope is that industrial growth will speed up under NAFTA and pro-vide more jobs. (The Mexican economy requires about a million new jobs annu-ally just to cover new entrants into the labor market.)

What is disquieting is the virtual cer-tainty that recent growth rates in fos-sil fuel consumption and carbon dioxide emissions are bound to increase with free trade and economic reform. Mexico is al-ready the largest commercial consumer of energy in Latin America, far surpassing Brazil, which has nearly twice the popu-lation and economic output. Mexico's in-dustrial carbon dioxide emissions exceed Brazil's by more than 50 percent, mak-ing Mexico the leading source in Latin America; even so, per capita emissions in Mexico are a small fraction of the United

States figures, and would have to roughly triple for Mexico to break into the top 10 countries in the category.

But unless major changes take place in the way Mexico produces goods and services—reforms nowhere apparent in the country's current economic model —the steady upward trajectory of agricultural mechanization, industrial and commercial fuel-intensity, and carbon dioxide emissions is a part of the national environmental future. Critics in the United States have argued that Mexico should emulate American environmental standards, but as many have pointed out, Mexico's laws are as rigorous as any when it comes to industrial pollution. The real trouble lies in the fact that Mexico stands at the threshold of full integration into the community of developed nations —which has a miserable environmental record of its own, but has somehow been transformed into the standard for Mexico. The most positive possibilities for more open trade and freer competition lie in the more rapid transfer of clean technologies for new industrial production. And some customs receipts might be used for environmental cleanup and the implementation of safer standards.

REASSESSING THE FUTURE

The many economic reforms the Mexican government has undertaken are welcome to the extent that they eliminate gross distortions that allowed and even encouraged past environmental and economic abuses. But Mexico faces enormous environmental challenges for the future. If it displaces poor farmers from marginal lands, it must ensure that they have an alternative that is better socially and less harmful environmentally. It must also see to it that they do not make way for more intensive agriculture, with its energy waste and overuse of chemicals. If Mexico grows industrially, it must either devise new pathways to energy efficiency and lower levels of waste or risk becoming part of a Dickensian landscape of factories serving consumers in cleaner environments elsewhere. And if Mexico is to "mine" itself for oil, natural gas, water, and topsoil and export the products north, it should be confident that in the long run the proceeds will redound to the benefit of Mexicans.

Unfortunately, Mexico does not control the terms of its international integration. And its largest economic partner, the United States, is adopting a disingenuous position; it insists that Mexico emulate American environmental policies and trust that the benefits of free trade will be worth the environmental trouble. Free traders in the United States advocate doubling Mexican oil production in order to lower export prices, a policy that is environmentally unworthy on its face, and would contribute to more hydrocarbon consumption, not less. The United States has categorically refused to treat immigration in the free trade negotiations, and popular sentiment is certainly not pro-immigration. But "surplus population" is one of the consequences of economic efficiency in a country with a rapidly expanding population and a 3 percent growth rate in the labor force each year; it is well-nigh impossible for Mexico's teeming cities and worn-out, rain-fed lands to accept a million new hands a year without further environmental degradation. Just as the United States will benefit from relocating some difficult environmental problems to its south, so Mexico should be able to count on a willing partner to the north.

Whatever the bilateral, trilateral, or global framework, as Mexico looks into its environmental future, it must rely on something beyond the benevolence of the United States and Canada—or the global system, for that matter. To really make environmental progress, Mexico must reassess the use of energy in its economy, the cost of water and inorganic fertilizer in arid lands agriculture, and the virtues of industrializing on an American model. Otherwise, Mexico will not escape from the industrial and agricultural abuses that have beset societies of the developed world. Employing a model from the developed world's past is hardly a forward-looking strategy for a country with Mexico's potential.

POSTSCRIPT

Will NAFTA Be Good for the Environment?

Although Sanderson's article was written prior to the negotiations that produced the NAATEC environmental side agreements, it seems doubtful that his concerns about the potential negative environmental impacts of NAFTA would be significantly reduced by the creation of a commission that Pastor admits is unlikely to be given powers to enforce the safeguards proposed in the language of the side agreements nor to impose sanctions if there is blatant disregard for the spirit of these agreements. Optimism about environmental progress resulting from the economic benefits that may derive from freer trade requires a rejection of the type of analysis that projects the future behavior of an economically hard-pressed country such as Mexico on the basis of past developmental practices. The key question is whether or not increased global concern about environmental problems coupled with internal and external pressures from environmental activists may shift the political climate such that decisions will be made to devote a significant portion of increased financial resources to sound ecological management.

A somewhat more detailed analysis of NAFTA's likely environmental consequences by someone who shares much of Pastor's optimism is presented by Daniel Magraw in his article in the March 1994 issue of *Environment*. Also on the optimistic side is the brief piece by the Mexican researcher Roberto Sanchez in the April 1993 issue of *Technology Review*, in which he argues that Mexico's problems will require it to move slowly in implementing more environmentally sound technologies. On the pessimistic side is Michelle Swenarchuk, who argues that NAFTA will have a negative impact on Canadian environmental regulation (see the January 1993 issue of *Canadian Forum*). Ralph Nader, who opposed NAFTA partly on the basis of his analysis of its likely environmental impact, warns in the May/June 1994 issue of *Public Citizen* that GATT is a serious threat to U.S. environment and consumer protection laws. A symposium of differing views on free trade and the environment is included in the Fall 1993 issue of *The Amicus Journal*.

Two moving depictions of the squalid conditions that have resulted from the *maquiladoras* south of the U.S.–Mexico border are presented in the articles by Bruce Selcraig in the May/June 1994 issue of *Sierra* and Jeannie Ralston in the November/December 1994 issue of *Audubon*.

ISSUE 2

Does Wilderness Have Intrinsic Value?

YES: **John Daniel,** from "Toward Wild Heartlands," *Audubon* (September/ October 1994)

NO: **William Tucker,** from "Is Nature Too Good for Us?" *Harper's Magazine* (March 1982)

ISSUE SUMMARY

YES: *Wilderness* magazine poetry editor John Daniel philosophizes that wilderness may help us discern "the rightful limits of our place on this continent."

NO: William Tucker, a writer and social critic, asserts that wilderness areas are elitist preserves designed to keep people out.

The environmental destruction that resulted from the exploitation of natural resources for private profit during the founding of the United States and its early decades gave birth after the Civil War to the progressive conservation movement. Naturalists such as John Muir (1839–1914) and forester and politician Gifford Pinchot (1865–1946) worked to gain the support of powerful people who recognized the need for resource management. Political leaders such as Theodore Roosevelt (1858–1912) promoted legislation during the last quarter of the nineteenth century that led to the establishment of Yellowstone, Yosemite, and Mount Rainier national parks, and the Adirondack Forest Preserve. This period also witnessed the founding of the Sierra Club and the Audubon Society, whose influential upper-class members worked to promote the conservationist ethic.

Two conflicting positions on resource management emerged. Preservationists, like Muir, argued for the establishment of wilderness areas that would be off-limits to industrial or commercial development. Conservationists, like Roosevelt, supported the concept of "multiple use" of public lands, which permitted limited development and resource consumption to continue. The latter position prevailed and, under the Forest Management Act of 1897, mining, grazing, and lumbering were permitted on U.S. forest lands and were regulated through permits issued by the U.S. Forestry Division.

The first "primitive areas," where all development was prohibited, were designated in the 1920s. Aldo Leopold and Robert Marshall, two officers in the Forest Service, helped establish 70 such areas by administrative fiat. Leopold and Marshall did this in response to their own concerns about the failure of some of the National Forest Service's management practices. Many preservationists were heartened by this development, and the Wilderness Society was organized in 1935 to press for the preservation of additional undeveloped land.

It became increasingly apparent during the 1940s and 1950s that the administrative mechanism whereby land was designated as either available for development or off-limits was vulnerable. Because of pressure from commercial interests (lumber, mining, etc.), an increasing number of what were then called wilderness areas were lost through reclassification. This set the stage for an eight-year-long campaign that ended in 1964 with the passage of the Federal Wilderness Act. But this was by no means the end of the struggle. The process of implementing this legislation and determining which areas to set aside has been long and tortuous and will probably continue into the next century.

There are more clear-cut differences between values espoused by the opposing factions in the battle over wilderness preservation than in many other environmental conflicts. On one side are the naturalists who see undeveloped "wild" land as a precious resource, where people can go to seek solace and solitude—provided they do not leave their mark. On the opposite extreme are the entrepreneurs whose principal concern is the profit that can be made from utilizing the resources on these lands.

One consequence of the environmental movement has been the proliferation of studies that explore the impact of human developmental activities on remote, isolated regions of the globe. It has become apparent that industrial pollutants move through the air and water and find their way into every nook and cranny of the ecosphere. The notion of totally protecting any area of the Earth from contamination is an ideal that cannot be fully realized. This knowledge has increased the zeal of wilderness advocates who wish to minimize the impact of pollution on the few remaining relatively pristine ecosystems.

Advocates of wilderness preservation have also gained support from the growing recognition that protecting areas that are the habitats of many threatened species from destructive development may be the most effective means of achieving the vital goal of preserving biodiversity.

John Daniel is an award-winning essayist and the poetry editor of *Wilderness* magazine. His essay, written to celebrate the thirtieth anniversary of the enactment of the U.S. Wilderness Act, warns that the preservation of wild places will ultimately depend on how we choose to live our lives. He questions the wisdom of defining as progress any technology that threatens to replace a real experience of nature with an artificial image. William Tucker, a writer who is critical of environmentalism, views the wilderness movement as elitist and the idea of excluding most human activity from wilderness areas as a consequence of a misguided, romantic ecological ethic.

YES

John Daniel

TOWARD WILD HEARTLANDS

It has been 30 years since President Lyndon B. Johnson signed into law the most generous gesture we Americans have made toward the wild nature of this continent. The Wilderness Act of 1964 gave Congress the authority to declare certain unspoiled lands permanently off-limits to human occupation and development. Thus was born the National Wilderness Preservation System, which did the national park system one better. Wilderness allows no roads or vehicles—you enter on your own two feet, as explorers and settlers once entered the greater wilderness that was North America.

The wilderness system stands as a landmark of collective self-restraint on the part of the American people and the human species. Yet three decades after its inception, the most notable feature of the system—aside from the remarkable fact of its existence—is the meagerness of its size. Our subduing of the continent has been so extensive and thorough that all lands designated as wilderness constitute less than 4 percent of the United States; more than half of those are in Alaska. In the 48 contiguous states, the National Wilderness Preservation System amounts to 1.8 percent of our territory. It will grow in years to come, but not by much. Little undeveloped land remains, and efforts to designate new wilderness areas are met, unfailingly, by fierce and often overpowering resistance from those who have different ideas about the value of land.

Their ideas go back to the very beginnings of our history and culture. Europeans came to the New World not as hikers or nature lovers but as homemakers, community builders, land developers. They took freely of the continent's plenty and turned it to their uses. "In Europe," wrote Alexis de Tocqueville in the 1830s, "people talk a great deal of the wilds of America, but the Americans themselves never think about them; they are insensible to the wonders of inanimate nature and they may be said not to perceive the mighty forests that surround them till they fall beneath the hatchet."

There were those along the way who warned against excess. William Penn ordered an acre of woods left standing for every four cut. William Bartram catalogued the natural history of the Southeast and railed against early plantation agribusiness. Henry David Thoreau envisioned a 500- to 1,000-acre wilderness in every township. John Wesley Powell tried to show that the arid West couldn't support large populations or midwestern land-use practices. John Muir declaimed against commercial vandals in the temples of the wild. But those voices, to the extent they were heard at all, ran mostly against the American grain, ran counter to the spirit and even the common sense of a westering people who saw boundlessness before them.

And so we are left with a few hundred remnants of untamed land, most in the mountain West and most very small, which we call the National Wilderness Preservation System. Those remnants aren't nearly as secure as the ringing language of the Wilderness Act would seem to suggest. The act had holes in it to begin with, and its insufficiencies are becoming more evident as pressure builds against the last wild places. The pressure comes most obviously from extractive industries that value the land for what it can be made to produce, but they are only surrogates for a far more powerful force that will not be stopped by a line on a map or a sign at a trailhead. Ultimately, the fate of wilderness will be determined not by Congress or the President or any government agency, but by the way we live.

* * *

Climb Mount Hood, Mount Jefferson, or Mount Washington in the Oregon Cascades, and you will see the situation of American wilderness in microcosm. To the east, on the semiarid steppe that begins the Great Basin, you'll look out on irrigated pasture and alfalfa fields, a few pine-covered hills and volcanic outcrops, thin highways slanting off into distance. Looking west, through a haze of auto smog and smoke from field burning, you'll see the Willamette Valley, the paradise at the end of the Oregon Trail, bright green with pasture and orchards and fields of hay. You'll see towns and small cities, Interstate 5 with its continual glint of traffic, a network of highways and roads.

North and south along the wavy green Cascades going blue in the distance, you'll enjoy the sight of an occasional solitary volcano like the one you're standing on and a smattering of small lakes. But you'll find yourself staring at something else: an irregular patchwork of sheared ground along both flanks of the range, at some points reaching the crest, with white road-squiggles threading through it. The overall effect may suggest to you what it once suggested to me—mange on the sides and back of a dog. But mange is scraggly, uneven. These clearcut barrens are geometric, made with fine precision. Mange doesn't know what it's doing to the dog. What's working on these mountains knows exactly what it's doing.

Standing on that peak, you should be aware that almost every acre in your view, stripped or still wooded, is land you own. It's national forest land, part of a system of federal reserves we set aside a century ago, or thought we did, for wise future use. You should also know that up to one-fifth of the standing forest you see has been marked with flags and spray paint for timber sales or is planned for marking. The Northwest timber pipeline has been frozen for the past three years by conservationist lawsuits. It may reopen soon, at some reduced rate.

And what of wilderness in the scene before you? Is the mostly intact crest of the range protected as wilderness? Not much. The U.S. Forest Service currently manages the higher country for recreation and wildlife; but if its fir and lodgepole pine become valuable to the nation, it can be managed differently. The only congressionally protected wilderness within your view is a spare archipelago of little islands around the range's solitary volcanoes—Hood, Jefferson, Three-Fingered Jack, Washington, the Three Sisters, Diamond Peak. Those islands, the Wilderness Act has decreed, shall remain untrammeled by man.

We have protected those mountain islands in part because we love alpine scenery. But we love other terrains and biomes too. We love big trees, for instance —groves of centuries-old Douglas firs, their pocked and furrowed trunks as much as 15 feet around and 200 feet tall, their great broken crowns filtering sunlight to a muted clarity. Very few such groves stand within wilderness areas. Very few such groves stand at all. They yield the best and most timber, and so they are gone to clearcuts now, and we in the Pacific Northwest are fighting bitterly over the scraps of old-growth forest that remain. We wouldn't be having that fight, or not so bitterly, if a fair representation of old growth had been included in the wilderness system, but it was too commercially valuable for that.

The wilderness mountain on which you're standing, on the other hand, like most parcels in the system, is mostly rock and ice and straggly trees. It has scant commodity value at present. But the logic of the scraped and battered ground that surrounds you isn't hard to read, and if you love your mountain, it should make you nervous.

You can read the same logic, if not always so boldly written, in most any American landscape. You can read it in California's great Central Valley, for example, where 95 percent of the original wetlands have been lost to agribusiness and development. In the Southwest and the intermountain West, where little more than a century of stock grazing has set loose more soil erosion than occurred in the previous 10,000 years. In the Mississippi-Missouri river drainage, where half the original topsoil, the best in the world, has gone to sea, and the other half is going at a faster rate. In the ravaged hills and poisoned waters of West Virginia and eastern Kentucky, where coal has been ripped from the ground to give us power. You can read it, too, in skeletal forests and sterile lakes in the Smokies and Alleghenies and Adirondacks, where the coal has returned in precipitation as much as 400 times more acidic than ordinary rain.

This is the logic of the American chapter of the world economy, a living organism composed of us and all that we do. It is a beast more fearsome than any the Pilgrims could have imagined when they gazed on the wild shore of North America four centuries ago. What other creature could have silenced forever the raucous hordes of passenger pigeons that once streamed through the sky for days at a time? Or stripped the continent of 60 million buffalo and routed wolf and grizzly into a few remote strongholds? Or driven the great thunderbird of the California hills into zoos and the merest glimmer of its ancient life in the wild?

All humans exert control on wild nature to feed, clothe, and shelter themselves, but we are especially ambitious and gifted controllers. We take more and more from the land, and not only what we need—we take what our increasingly powerful technologies allow us to take, and what we take we learn to need, and our numbers grow, and we need more, and we take more.

We have begun to see how dangerous we are to the natural world, and so we have enacted a few restraints such as the Wilderness Act. But compromises were required to get the act through Congress. Stock grazing was grandfathered into many western wilderness areas, resulting in cropped grasslands and mucked-up springs and streams. Mining also was grandfathered in, and existing and potential areas were open to new claims until 1984. Claims have been filed in most wilderness areas in the West. And it's perfectly plausible that the Oregon mountain you're standing on may harbor a mineral that will become valuable in the 21st century. Will the stirring phrases of the Wilderness Act save it from harm? Maybe. But it would not be too surprising if the same regard for nature that surgically mutilated those forested slopes someday pushes up the mountain and starts blasting the rock beneath you.

In fact, the invasion is already under way, by proxy. The acid precipitation that is ruining lakes and forests in the East is now occurring in the West too, at lower but rising levels. Auto smog from the urban centers of the Pacific Coast has been drifting into the Cascades and the Sierra Nevada for years, passing freely across wilderness boundaries, disrupting photosynthesis in trees and weakening their resistance to disease. Unless our habits of energy consumption change, these effects will only increase. If we don't consume our wilderness for its raw materials, we may yet poison it to death.

* * *

No wild place will be safe from us until we reconsider our devout belief that economic growth is always and limitlessly good and examine our equally devout belief in the unlimited use of technology. Taken together, these two articles of faith compose a modern secular orthodoxy that pervades our culture. The object of its worship is the future—a future, we are told, in which our lives will be made safer, longer, healthier, better informed, and far more pleasurable. A new and improved future. And a future—this isn't in the advertising —that threatens not only the wild places of our continent but the very quality of wildness itself.

In the chorus of boosterism for a new technology, little is ever heard of its potential dangers, in part because the most significant dangers associated with any profound tampering with nature can't be foreseen. The nuclear enthusiasts of the 1950s promised that energy would be too cheap to meter, that radiation was containable and virtually harmless anyway. Forty years later, as the downwinders in Utah and Washington State have learned in the cruelest way, the costs and benefits of splitting the atom figure differently.

At this point in our technological history, it can only be naive to expect a different result from genetic engineering, which is currently the most prominent of our manipulative interventions into the life of the wild universe. The paradox of our obsessive urge to control is that we invariably release forces that will not *be* controlled, or that can be controlled only with great difficulty and at great expense.

But to judge genetic engineering by its possible effects is to judge it by an insufficient standard. It is necessary to ask not only whether it is wise, but also whether it is right. To revise in a laboratory what evolution has spent 4 billion years making must be an exhilarating experience. But for all our prodigious technical abilities, we cannot manufacture so much as one gene, one paramecium, one nerve fiber in the brain of a blue whale. We do not know how it happened that this rock-and-water planet stirred in its sleep and woke into sentient life, or how one fertile cell becomes an elephant, or how the uncountable lives we live among twine together in the wild mysteries we call ecosystems. Jack Ward Thomas, the new chief of the Forest Service, put it this way at last year's Northwest forest conference: "Ecosystems are more complex than we think. They're more complex than we *can* think."

We tend to revere technological inventors and interveners as heroes, as modern woodsmen penetrating the frontiers of human knowledge. I think we need a new kind of hero, one whose mission is not to breach limits but to understand them and to show us how to abide by those that are necessary and just—a hero capable of restraining what he *can* do in favor of what he *ought* to do for the good of the entire community. Some scientists, most corporate executives, and all members in good standing of the economic-technological orthodoxy will characterize this idea as a travesty, a capitulation of the questing human spirit. I call it growing up. As a child matures, he learns he is but one rightful member of a human community that sets limits on the satisfaction of his wishes. He then learns, I hope, what Aldo Leopold sketched as the "land ethic"— that his community extends beyond the human and includes other forms of life. And he also needs to learn that his known community opens around him into mysteries both beautiful and sacred, mysteries to which he belongs, mysteries which do not belong to him.

There is something in us deeply intolerant of mystery, something that drives us to prod and probe the natural world and crack open more and more of its secrets and tinker with its deepest workings. We open darknesses to the light of rationality as relentlessly as the early settlers once opened the eastern forests. We do this in the name of knowledge, but our knowledge is too often a knife—it cuts the world into pieces, wonders where its life and spirit have gone, and cuts again.

I don't mean to indict science in general. Many of the foremost champions of wild nature are scientists, and their work has done much to warn us of the environmental limits we are transgressing. I am arguing only against interventionist science that wants to splice genes, split atoms, or otherwise manipulate the wild—science aimed more at control than understanding, science that assumes ownership of the natural mysteries. When technological specialists come to believe that nature is answerable to their own prerogatives, they are not serving but endangering the greater community.

The same reasoning is evident in our seemingly boundless interest in a kind of pseudoknowledge its devotees call information. The "Information Superhighway" is being readied to convey us into our future, and to travel it, evidently, we need only buy the right machines and connections to machines. I hear little news about where the Superhighway is expected to lead us, and why. Apparently it will take us by means of information into a condition of more information for the reason that information is good for us.

We will have 500 channels of interactive television, it seems. A few of those channels will feed us "information" about weather and animals and natural landscapes, for which some of us will be hungry. Old proclivities die hard. But if we travel the highway far enough, we are bound to arrive at the condition for which television has been preparing us for decades—the electronic image of a redwood will replace the natural experience of a redwood, and so the real tree with roots in the ground will logically become expendable. In the evermore-real-seeming ghosts that haunt our screens, in the video-game sensory immersion of virtual reality, the new technology promises to complete the procedure of controlling nature, finally, by becoming it.

* * *

The psychologist and writer James Hillman has said that our inability to experience the beautiful is what separates us from the world. We are sick and therefore the land is sick because we no longer know its beauty, and our love for it has withered. His diagnosis may seem unlikely, given that we in America flock by the millions to the scenic splendors of our national parks and other natural areas. But there is something rote and decidedly passionless in our experience of natural beauty. I feel it whenever I stop at a scenic overlook, and I see it in other watchers. I rarely see enthusiasm or even animation, but mostly bored children and impassive parents showing the scenery to their cameras and video recorders. Though drawn to nature, we are still somehow insensible to it. Our lives are so removed from the land that it's become just a scene for us, an image to be captured and taken home. As tourists we don't damage the land as a mining or timber corporation would, but essentially we do what they do—we value the land for one of its extractable qualities. We have reduced nat-

ural beauty to postcard prettiness, another commodity for our consumption.

It's a different beauty of the land, a deeper and far more lively beauty, that we have largely forfeited. To know this beauty requires more than eyes and can't be done at a distance. It takes legs and sweat, hard breathing, and sometimes pain. It requires that we approach the land on its own terms, that we enter it respectfully and yield ourselves to its presence. The beauty I'm speaking of is simply the beauty of the given world— the land as it is, with its particular lives, its various weathers, its dynamic and singular wholeness. All of us feel some stirring for this beauty, some twitch or flood of yearning. Any scrap of nature provides a portion of it; but only our wild places can give us its full measure, and renew our love for it, and show us how it lives within ourselves.

Wilderness, the word, shares roots with *willfulness*, the condition of being ungovernable, beyond authority and control. When I ask myself what wilderness most truly is, what its beauty is most made of, willfulness is what I find—a vast, unconscious willfulness that bodies forth mountains from seas of magma, dreams the dark chaos of soil into forests of spiring trees, fashions meadowlarks and black bears from the long weaving strands of evolutionary time. In this willfulness I am something small—rightfully, refreshingly small. In the wild I experience myself and my kind in something like actual scale. And except perhaps for one willful mosquito or one paramount pebble beneath my sleeping bag, I am happy.

In our restless sight-seeing of nature, skimming down the road from one view to another, we see much more than we can absorb. In wilderness, we absorb much more than we see. We walk to rhythms longer than the conscious mind can know—the rhythm of sequoias rising, the Escalante carving its canyon, the slow titanic stirring of this crust of earth that bears us. The rhythm of the wild carries through shimmering aspen leaves and the blast of Mount St. Helens, through the boom of surf at Cape Perpetua and the hoarse whistle of a red-tailed hawk adrift in the summer sky. Life and death both dance to it—the browsing deer, the cougar that snaps the deer's neck and rips its belly, and the good carrion eaters that ultimately transform the cougar.

First and finally, wilderness is what we are. "Talk of mysteries!" wrote Thoreau. "Think of our life in nature,—daily to be shown matter, to come in contact with it,—rocks, trees, wind on our cheeks! the *solid* earth! the *actual* world!" If you follow the physicists, the actual world is made of willful little particles with names like *quark* and *gluon* that dodge in and out of existence, enlivening a universe born some 15 billion years ago, a form-seeking universe that has organized itself into nebulas, stars, planets, and Thoreau with wind on his cheeks. If you follow others, you find other accounts. There are many good books, but even the book you most believe in can tell no more than a glancing passage of the actual story of being. We want to understand, we want to know how it begins and ends and why, but the story, not our knowing, is what matters most. To be part of this—to rest in a mesa still warm with sun and watch the stars brighten to their fierce glitter, the little wind smelling of sage, while far away a coyote loosens his wail.... In this beauty, this mystery, I am glad to be alive. This beautiful mystery makes me whole.

If the sickness of the land is our sickness, its health can be our health. True empowerment comes from membership in the wild matrix that gave birth to us and sustains us even in our distance and contempt. We have much to learn from other members, if we can stop ourselves from destroying them. Much to learn from wild salmon, who leap the rapids with a faithfulness to home we have scarcely begun to imagine for ourselves. Much to learn from old-growth forest, how its diverse and vigorous commonwealth sustains itself through time. We might learn patience from the bristlecones, fortitude from monarch butterflies, the dignity of space and breathing room from junipers and saguaros.

When I spend too many hours reading newspapers or watching television, too many weeks breathing city air and hardening my ears to city noises, I don't believe we as a people are capable of learning anything more than how to operate the next machine. But wilderness, as Wallace Stegner wrote, is the geography of hope. When I'm able to pry myself out of town and let the land inform me, an unreasonable optimism comes over me. The land lets me feel no other way. It's been getting by for a long time, after all, and I expect it will outlive us and the worst we can do.

At our best, there is sanity among us, and it may prosper. There is a passionate caring for the wild in many of our younger people. If, with the help of the Wilderness Act and the system it created, we can nurse our wild remnants a few decades into the next century, we may see the emergence of the new heroism we need, a heroism capable of discerning the rightful and necessary limits of our place on this continent.

The Wilderness Act was a beginning, a momentous first step, but it accepts the premise of our unhealthy culture, fencing off only a few scraps of unspoiled land. The next step is to redefine wilderness according to the premise of nature's health—as entire, vigorous ecosystems and landscapes in the full array of their diversity. To define wilderness, in other words, as wilderness defines itself, and in that way restore and perpetuate the biotic well-being of our homeland.

That step will take centuries to complete. It means withdrawing ourselves a respectful distance, voluntarily closing roads and removing habitations, so that nature can expand and join some of the remnants into greater wilderness heartlands, large enough for grizzlies and wolves and wolverines to thrive, and those members of our own species who require a lot of room to get lost in. Wild heartlands not only of the western mountains, but heartlands of deserts and plains and prairies, heartlands of the southern and eastern forests. Regions outside those wildlands will be farmed and managed for multiple use—not as we have mismanaged our public and private lands, but with regard for the wildness that is the land's long-term health and fertility. And outside the buffer zones of multiple use will be the places where most of us live, in such numbers and economies as the vitality of the entire community will permit.

Maybe we are not capable of such a change. But if we can make that step, if we can find the generosity to give back a fair portion of all we have taken, then we will have a National Wilderness Preservation System worthy of this generous, beautiful, and hard-used continent. Then we may find ourselves members at last of the American land.

NO
William Tucker

IS NATURE TOO GOOD FOR US?

Probably nothing has been more central to the environmental movement than the concept of wilderness. "In wildness is the preservation of the world," wrote Thoreau, and environmental writers and speakers have intoned his message repeatedly. Wilderness, in the environmental pantheon, represents a particular kind of sanctuary in which all true values—that is, all nonhuman values—are reposited. Wildernesses are often described as "temples," "churches," and "sacred ground"—refuges for the proposed "new religion" based on environmental consciousness. Carrying the religious metaphor to the extreme, one of the most famous essays of the environmental era holds the Judeo-Christian religion responsible for "ecological crisis."

The wilderness issue also has a political edge. Since 1964, long-standing preservation groups like the Wilderness Society and the Sierra Club have been pressuring conservation agencies like the National Forest Service and the Bureau of Land Management to put large tracts of their holdings into permanent "wilderness designations," countering the "multiple use" concept that was one of the cornerstones of the Conservation Era of the early 1900s.

Preservation and conservation groups have been at odds since the end of the last century, and the rift between them has been a major controversy of environmentalism. The leaders of the Conservation Movement—most notably Theodore Roosevelt, Gifford Pinchot, and John Wesley Powell—called for rational, efficient development of land and other natural resources: multiple use, or reconciling competing uses of land, and also "highest use," or forfeiting more immediate profits from land development for more lasting gains. Preservationists, on the other hand, the followers of California woodsman John Muir, have advocated protecting land in its natural state, setting aside tracts and keeping them inviolate. "Wilderness area" battles have become one of the hottest political issues of the day, especially in western states—the current "Sagebrush Revolt" comes to mind—where large quantities of potentially commercially usable land are at stake.

The term "wilderness" generally connotes mountains, trees, clear streams, rushing waterfalls, grasslands, or parched deserts, but the concept has been institutionalized and has a careful legal definition as well. The one given

From William Tucker, "Is Nature Too Good for Us?" *Harper's Magazine* (March 1982). Adapted from William Tucker, *Progress and Privilege: America in the Age of Environmentalism* (Doubleday, 1982). Copyright © 1982 by William Tucker. Reprinted by permission.

by the 1964 Wilderness Act, and that most environmentalists favor, is that wilderness is an area "where man is a visitor but does not remain." People do not "leave footprints there," wilderness exponents often say. Wildernesses are, most importantly, areas in which *evidence of human activity is excluded;* they need not have any particular scenic, aesthetic, or recreational value. The values, as environmentalists usually say, are "ecological"—which means, roughly translated, that natural systems are allowed to operate as free from human interference as possible.

The concept of excluding human activity is not to be taken lightly. One of the major issues in wilderness areas has been whether or not federal agencies should fight forest fires. The general decision has been that they should not, except in cases where other lands are threatened. The federal agencies also do not fight the fires with motorized vehicles, which are prohibited in wilderness areas except in extreme emergencies. Thus in recent years both the National Forest Service and the National Park Service have taken to letting forest fires burn unchecked, to the frequent alarm of tourists. The defense is that many forests require periodic leveling by fire in order to make room for new growth. There are some pine trees, for instance, whose cones will break open and scatter their seeds only when burned. This theoretical justification has won some converts, but very few in the timber companies, which bridle at watching millions of board-feet go up in smoke when their own "harvesting" of mature forests has the same effect in clearing the way for new growth and does less damage to forest soils.

The effort to set aside permanent wilderness areas on federal lands began with the National Forest Service in the 1920s. The first permanent reservation was in the Gila National Forest in New Mexico. It was set aside by a young Forest Service officer named Aldo Leopold, who was later to write *A Sand County Almanac,* which has become one of the bibles of the wilderness movement. Robert Marshall, another Forest Service officer, continued the program, and by the 1950s nearly 14 million of the National Forest System's 186 million acres had been administratively designated wilderness preserves.

Leopold and Marshall had been disillusioned by one of the first great efforts at "game management" under the National Forest Service, carried out in the Kaibab Plateau, just north of the Grand Canyon. As early as 1906 federal officials began a program of "predator control" to increase the deer population in the area. Mountain lions, wolves, coyotes, and bobcats were systematically hunted and trapped by game officials. By 1920, the program appeared to be spectacularly successful. The deer population, formerly numbering 4,000, had grown to almost 100,000. But it was realized too late that it was the range's limited food resources that would threaten the deer's existence. During two severe winters, in 1924-26, 60 percent of the herd died, and by 1939 the population had shrunk to only 10,000. Deer populations (unlike human populations) were found to have no way of putting limits on their own reproduction. The case is still cited as the classic example of the "boom and bust" disequilibrium that comes from thoughtless intervention in an ecological system.

The idea of setting aside as wilderness areas larger and larger segments of federally controlled lands began to gain more support from the old preservationists' growing realizations, during the 1950s, that they had not won the battle during the Conservation Era, and that the national forests were not parks that would be protected forever from commercial activity.

Pinchot's plan for practicing "conservation" in the western forests was to encourage a partnership between the government and large industry. In order to discourage overcutting and destructive competition, he formulated a plan that would promote conservation activities among the larger timber companies while placing large segments of the western forests under federal control. It was a classic case of "market restriction," carried out by the joint efforts of larger businesses and government. Only the larger companies, Pinchot reasoned, could generate the profits that would allow them to cut their forest holdings *slowly* so that the trees would have time to grow back. In order to ensure these profit margins, the National Forest Service would hold most of its timber lands out of the market for some time. This would hold up the price of timber and prevent a rampage through the forests by smaller companies trying to beat small profit margins by cutting everything in sight. Then, in later years, the federal lands would gradually be worked into the "sustained yield" cycles, and timber rights put up for sale. It was when the national forests finally came up for cutting in the 1950s that the old preservation groups began to react.

The battle was fought in Congress. The 1960 Multiple Use and Sustained Yield Act tried to reaffirm the principles of the Conservation Movement. But the wilderness groups had their day in 1964 with the passing of the Wilderness Act. The law required all the federal land-management agencies—the National Forest Service,

the National Park Service, and the Fish and Wildlife Service—to review all their holdings, keeping in mind that "wilderness" now constituted a valid alternative in the "multiple use" concept—even though the concept of wilderness is essentially a rejection of the idea of multiple use. The Forest Service, with 190 million acres, and the Park Service and Fish and Wildlife Service, each with about 35 million acres, were all given twenty years to start designating wilderness areas. At the time, only 14.5 million acres of National Forest System land were in wilderness designations.

The results have been mixed. The wilderness concept appears valid if it is recognized for what it is—an attempt to create what are essentially "ecological museums" in scenic and biologically significant areas of these lands. But "wilderness," in the hands of environmentalists, has become an all-purpose tool for stopping economic activity as well. This is particularly crucial now because of the many mineral and energy resources available on western lands that environmentalists are trying to push through as wilderness designations. The original legislation specified that lands were to be surveyed for valuable mineral resources before they were put into wilderness preservation. Yet with so much land being reviewed at once, these inventories have been sketchy at best. And once land is locked up as wilderness, it becomes illegal even to explore it for mineral or energy resources.

Thus the situation in western states—where the federal government still owns 68 percent of the land, counting Alaska—has in recent years become a race between mining companies trying to prospect under severely restricted conditions, and environmental groups trying to lock the doors to resource development for good. This kind of permanent preservation —the antithesis of conservation—will probably have enormous effects on our future international trade in energy and mineral resources.

At stake in both the national forests and the Bureau of Land Management holdings are what are called the "roadless areas." Environmentalists call these lands "de facto wilderness," and say that because they have not yet been explored or developed for resources they should not be explored and developed in the future. The Forest Service began its Roadless Area Resources Evaluation (RARE) in 1972, while the Bureau of Land Management began four years later in 1976, after Congress brought its 174 million acres under jurisdiction of the 1964 act. The Forest Service is studying 62 million roadless acres, while the BLM is reviewing 24 million.

In 1974 the Forest Service recommended that 15 million of the 50 million acres then under study be designated as permanent wilderness. Environmental groups, which wanted much more set aside, immediately challenged the decision in court. Naturally, they had no trouble finding flaws in a study intended to cover such a huge amount of land, and in 1977 the Carter administration decided to start over with a "RARE II" study, completed in 1979. This has also been challenged by a consortium of environmental groups that includes the Sierra Club, the Wilderness Society, the National Wildlife Federation, and the Natural Resources Defense Council. The RARE II report also recommended putting about 15 million acres in permanent wilderness, with 36 million released for development and 11 million held for further study. The Bureau of Land Management is not scheduled to complete the study of its 24 million acres until 1991.

The effects of this campaign against resource development have been powerful. From 1972 to 1980, the price of a Douglas fir in Oregon increased 500 percent, largely due to the delays in timber sales from the national forests because of the battles over wilderness areas. Over the decade, timber production from the national forests declined slightly, putting far more pressure on the timber industry's own lands. The nation has now become an importer of logs, despite the vast resources on federal lands. In 1979, environmentalists succeeded in pressuring Congress into setting aside 750,000 acres in Idaho as the Sawtooth Wilderness and National Recreational Area. A resource survey, which was not completed until *after* the congressional action, showed that the area contained an estimated billion dollars' worth of molybdenum, zinc, silver, and gold. The same tract also contained a potential source of cobalt, an important mineral for which we are now dependent on foreign sources for 97 percent of what we use.

Perhaps most fiercely contested are the energy supplies believed to be lying under the geological strata running through Colorado, Wyoming, and Montana just east of the Rockies, called the Overthrust Belt. Much of this land is still administered by the Bureau of Land Management for multiple usage. But with the prospect of energy development, environmental groups have been rushing to try to have these high-plains areas designated as wilderness areas as well (cattle grazing is still allowed in wilderness tracts). On those lands permanently withdrawn from commercial use, mineral exploration will be allowed to continue until 1983. Any mines begun by then can continue on a very restricted basis. But the exploration in "roadless areas" is severely limited, in that in most cases there can be no roads constructed (and no use of off-road vehicles) while exploration is going on. Environmentalists have argued that wells can still be drilled and test mines explored using helicopters. But any such exploration is likely to be extraordinarily expensive and ineffective. Wilderness restrictions are now being drawn so tightly that people on the site are not allowed to leave their excrement in the area.

IMPOSSIBLE PARADISES

What is the purpose of all this? The standard environmental argument is that we have to "preserve these last few wild places before they all disappear." Yet it is obvious that something more is at stake. What is being purveyed is a view of the world in which human activity is defined as "bad" and natural conditions are defined as "good." What is being preserved is evidently much more than "ecosystems." What is being preserved is an *image* of wilderness as a semisacred place beyond humanity's intrusion.

It is instructive to consider how environmentalists themselves define the wilderness. David Brower, former director of the Sierra Club, wrote in his introduction to Paul Ehrlich's *The Population Bomb* (1968):

Whatever resources the wilderness still held would not sustain (man) in his old habits of growing and reaching without limits. Wilderness could, however, provide answers for questions he had not yet learned how to ask. He could predict that the day of creation was not over, that there would be wiser men, and they would thank him for leaving the source

of those answers. Wilderness would remain part of his geography of hope, as Wallace Stegner put it, and could, merely because wilderness endured on the planet, prevent man's world from becoming a cage.

The wilderness, he suggested, is a source of peace and freedom. Yet setting wilderness aside for the purposes of solitude doesn't always work very well. Environmentalists have discovered this over and over again, much to their chagrin. Every time a new "untouched paradise" is discovered, the first thing everyone wants to do is visit it. By their united enthusiasm to find these "sanctuaries," people bring the "cage" of society with them. Very quickly it becomes necessary to erect bars to keep people *out*—which is exactly what most of the "wilderness" legislation has been all about.

In 1964, for example, the Sierra Club published a book on the relatively "undiscovered" paradise of Kauai, the second most westerly island in the Hawaiian chain. It wasn't long before the island had been overrun with tourists. When *Time* magazine ran a feature on Kauai in 1979, one unhappy island resident wrote in to convey this telling sentiment: "We're hoping the shortages of jet fuel will stay around and keep people away from here." The age of environmentalism has also been marked by the near overrunning of popular national parks like Yosemite (which now has a full-time jail), intense pressure on woodland recreational areas, full bookings two and three years in advance for raft trips through the Grand Canyon, and dozens of other spectacles of people crowding into isolated areas to get away from it all. Environmentalists are often critical of these inundations, but they must recognize that they have at least contributed to them.

I am not arguing against wild things, scenic beauty, pristine landscapes, and scenic preservation. What I am questioning is the argument that wilderness is a value against which every other human activity must be judged, and that human beings are somehow unworthy of the landscape. The wilderness has been equated with freedom, but there are many different ideas about what constitutes freedom. In the Middle Ages, the saying was that "city air makes a man free," meaning that the harsh social burdens of medieval feudalism vanished once a person escaped into the heady anonymity of a metropolitan community. When city planner Jane Jacobs, author of *The Death and Life of Great American Cities*, was asked by an interviewer if "overpopulation" and "crowding into large cities" weren't making social prisoners of us all, her simple reply was: "Have you ever lived in a small town?"

It may seem unfair to itemize the personal idiosyncrasies of people who feel comfortable only in wilderness, but it must be remembered that the environmental movement has been shaped by many people who literally spent years of their lives living in isolation. John Muir, the founder of the National Parks movement and the Sierra Club, spent almost ten years living alone in the Sierra Mountains while learning to be a trail guide. David Brower, who headed the Sierra Club for over a decade and later broke with it to found the Friends of the Earth, also spent years as a mountaineer. Gary Snyder, the poet laureate of the environmental movement, has lived much of his life in wilderness isolation and has also spent several years in a Zen monastery.

All these people far outdid Thoreau in their desire to get a little perspective on the world. There is nothing reprehensible in this, and the literature and philosophy that merge from such experiences are often admirable. But it seems questionable to me that the ethic that comes out of this wilderness isolation—and the sense of ownership of natural landscapes that inevitably follows—can serve as the basis for a useful national philosophy.

THAT FRONTIER SPIRIT

The American frontier is generally agreed to have closed down physically in 1890, the year the last Indian Territory of Oklahoma was opened for the settlement. After that, the Conservation Movement arose quickly to protect the remaining resources and wilderness from heedless stripping and development. Along with this came a significant psychological change in the national character, as the "frontier spirit" diminished and social issues attracted greater attention. The Progressive Movement, the Social Gospel among religious groups, Populism, and Conservation all arose in quick succession immediately after the "closing of the frontier." It seems fair to say that it was only after the frontier had been settled and the sense of endless possibilities that came with open spaces had been constricted in the national consciousness that the country started "growing up."

Does this mean the new environmental consciousness has arisen because we are once again "running out of space"? I doubt it. Anyone taking an airplane across almost any part of the country is inevitably struck by how much greenery and open territory remain, and how little room our towns and cities really occupy. The amount of standing forest in the country, for example, has not diminished appreciably over the last fifty years, and is 75 percent of what it was in 1620. In addition, as environmentalists constantly remind us, trees are "renewable resources." If they continue to be handled intelligently, the forests will always grow back. As farming has moved out to the Great Plains of the Middle West, many eastern areas that were once farmed have reverted back to trees. Though mining operations can permanently scar hillsides and plains, they are usually very limited in scope (and as often as not, it is the roads leading to these mines that environmentalists find most objectionable).

It seems to be that the wilderness ethic has actually represented an attempt psychologically to reopen the American frontier. We have been desperate to maintain belief in unlimited, uncharted vistas within our borders, a preoccupation that has eclipsed the permanent shrinking of the rest of the world outside. Why else would it be so necessary to preserve such huge tracts of "roadless territory" simply because they are now roadless, regardless of their scenic, recreational, or aesthetic values? The environmental movement, among other things, has been a rather backward-looking effort to recapture America's lost innocence.

The central figure in this effort has been the backpacker. The backpacker is a young, unprepossessing person (inevitably white and upper middle class) who journeys into the wilderness as a passive observer. He or she brings his or her own food, treads softly, leaves no litter, and has no need to make use of any of the resources at hand. Backpackers bring all the necessary accouterments of civilization with them. All their needs have been met by the society from which they seek temporary release. The backpacker is freed from the need to support itself in order to enjoy the aesthetic and spiritual values that are made available by this temporary *removal* from the demands of nature. Many dangers—raging rivers or precipitous cliffs, for instance—become sought-out adventures.

Yet once the backpacker runs out of supplies and starts using resources around him—cutting trees for firewood, putting up a shelter against the rain—he is violating some aspect of the federal Wilderness Act. For example, one of the issues fought in the national forests revolves around tying one's horse to a tree. Purists claim the practice should be forbidden, since it may leave a trodden ring around the tree. They say horses should be hobbled and allowed to graze instead. In recent years, the National Forest Service has come under pressure from environmental groups to enforce this restriction.

Wildernesses, then, are essentially parks for the upper middle class. They are vacation reserves for people who want to rough it—with the assurance that few other people will have the time, energy, or means to follow them into the solitude. This is dramatically highlighted in one Sierra Club book that shows a picture of a professorial sort of individual backpacking off into the woods. The ironic caption is a quote from Julius Viancour, an official of the Western Council of Lumber and Sawmill Workers: "The inaccessible wilderness and primitive areas are off limits to most laboring people. We must have access...." The implication for Sierra Club readers is: "What do these beer-drinking, gun-toting, working people want to do in *our* woods?"

This class-oriented vision of wilderness as an upper-middle-class preserve is further illustrated by the fact that most of the opposition to wilderness designations comes not from industry but from owners of off-road vehicles. In most northern rural areas, snowmobiles are now regarded as the greatest invention since the automobile, and people are ready to fight rather than stay cooped up all winter in their houses. It seems ludicrous to them that snowmobiles (which can't be said even to endanger the ground) should be restricted from vast tracts of land so that the occasional city visitor can have solitude while hiking past on snowshoes.

The recent Boundary Waters Canoe Area controversy in northern Minnesota is an excellent example of the conflict. When the tract was first designated as wilderness in 1964, Congress included a special provision that allowed motorboats into the entire area. By the mid-1970s, outboards and inboards were roaming all over the wilderness, and environmental groups began asking that certain portions of the million-acre preserve be set aside exclusively for canoes. Local residents protested vigorously, arguing that fishing expeditions, via motorboats, contributed to their own recreation. Nevertheless, Congress eventually excluded motorboats from 670,000 acres to the north.

A more even split would seem fairer. It should certainly be possible to accommodate both forms of recreation in the area, and there is as much to be said for canoeing in solitude as there is for making rapid expeditions by powerboat. The natural landscape is not likely to suffer very much from either form of recreation. It is not absolute "ecological" values that are really at stake, but simply different tastes in recreation.

NOT ENTIRELY NATURE

At bottom, then, the mystique of the wilderness has been little more than a revival of Rousseau's Romanticism about the "state of nature." The notion that "only in wilderness are human beings truly free," a credo of environmentalists, is merely a variation on Rousseau's dictum that "man is born free, and everywhere he is in chains." According to Rousseau, only society could enslave people, and only in the "state of nature" was the "noble savage"—the preoccupation of so many early explorers—a fulfilled human being.

The "noble savage" and other indigenous peoples, however, have been carefully excised from the environmentalists' vision. Where environmental efforts have encountered primitive peoples, these indigenous residents have often proved one of the biggest problems. One of the most bitter issues in Alaska is the efforts by environmentalist groups to restrict Indians in their hunting practices.

At the same time, few modern wilderness enthusiasts could imagine, for example, the experience of the nineteenth-century artist J. Ross Browne, who wrote in *Harper's New Monthly Magazine* after visiting the Arizona territories in 1864:

Sketching in Arizona is... rather a ticklish pursuit.... I never before traveled through a country in which I was compelled to pursue the fine arts with a revolver strapped around my body, a double-barreled shot-gun lying across my knees, and half a dozen soldiers armed with Sharpe's carbines keeping guard in the distance. Even with all the safeguards... I am free to admit that on occasions of this kind I frequently looked behind to see how the country appeared in its rear aspect. An artist with an arrow in his back may be a very picturesque object... but I would rather draw him on paper than sit for the portrait myself.

Wilderness today means the land *after* the Indians have been cleared away but *before* the settlers have arrived. It represents an attempt to hold that particular moment forever frozen in time, that moment when the visionary American settler looked out on the land and imagined it as an empty paradise, waiting to be molded to our vision.

In the absence of the noble savage, the environmentalist substitutes himself. The wilderness, while free of human dangers, becomes a kind of basic-training ground for upper-middle-class values. Hence the rise of "survival" groups, where college kids are taken out into the woods for a week or two and let loose to prove their survival instincts. No risks are spared on these expeditions. Several people have died on them, and a string of lawsuits has already been launched by parents and survivors who didn't realize how seriously these survival courses were being taken.

The ultimate aim of these efforts is to test upper-middle-class values against the natural environment. "Survival" candidates cannot hunt, kill, or use much of the natural resources available. The true test is whether their zero-degree sleeping bags and dried-food kits prove equal to the hazards of the tasks. What happens is not necessarily related to nature. One could as easily test survival skills by turning a person loose without money or means in New York City for three days.

I do not mean to imply that these efforts do not require enormous amounts of courage and daring—"survival skills." I am only suggesting that what the backpacker or survival hiker encounters is

not entirely "nature," and that the effort to go "back to nature" is one that is carefully circumscribed by the most intensely civilized artifacts. Irving Babbitt, the early twentieth-century critic of Rousseau's Romanticism, is particularly vigorous in his dissent from the idea of civilized people going "back to nature." This type, he says, is actually "the least primitive of all beings":

> We have seen that the special form of unreality encouraged by the aesthetic romanticism of Rousseau is the dream of the simple life, the return to a nature that never existed, and that this dream made its special appeal to an age that was suffering from an excess of artificiality and conventionalism.

Babbitt notes shrewdly that our concept of the "state of nature" is actually one of the most sophisticated productions of civilization. Most primitive peoples, who live much closer to the soil than we do, are repelled by wilderness. The American colonists, when they first encountered the unspoiled landscape, saw nothing but a horrible desert, filled with savages.

What we really encounter when we talk about "wilderness," then, is one of the highest products of civilization. It is a reserve set up to keep people *out*, rather than a "state of nature" in which the inhabitants are "truly free." The only thing that makes people "free" in such a reservation is that they can leave so much behind when they enter. Those who try to stay too long find out how spurious this "freedom" is. After spending a year in a cabin in the north Canadian woods, Elizabeth Arthur wrote in *Island Sojourn:* "I never felt so completely tied to *objects,* resources, and the tools to shape them with."

What we are witnessing in the environmental movement's obsession with purified wilderness is what has often been called the "pastoral impulse." The image of nature as unspoiled, unspotted wilderness where we can go to learn the lessons of ecology is both a product of a complex, technological society and an escape from it. It is this undeniable paradox that forms the real problem of setting up "wildernesses." Only when we have created a society that gives us the leisure to appreciate it can we go out and experience what we imagine to be untrammeled nature. Yet if we lock up too much of our land in these reserves, we are cutting into our resources and endangering the very leisure that allows us to enjoy nature.

The answer is, of course, that we cannot simply let nature "take over" and assume that because we have kept roads and people out of huge tracts of land, then we have absolved ourselves of a national guilt. The concept of stewardship means taking responsibility, not simply letting nature take its course. Where tracts can be set aside from commercialism at no great cost, they should be. Where primitive hiking and recreation areas are appealing, they should be maintained. But if we think we are somehow appeasing the gods by *not* developing resources where they exist, then we are being very shortsighted. Conservation, not preservation, is once again the best guiding principle.

The cult of wilderness leads inevitably in the direction of religion. Once again, Irving Babbitt anticipated this fully.

> When pushed to a certain point the nature cult always tends toward sham spirituality.... Those to whom I may seem to be treating the nature cult with undue severity should remember that I am treating it only in its pseudo-religious aspect.... My quarrel is only with the asthete who assumes an apocalyptic pose and gives forth as a profound philosophy what is at best only a holiday or weekend view of existence....

It is often said that environmentalism could or should serve as the basis of a new religious consciousness, or a religious "reawakening." This religious trend is usually given an Oriental aura. E. F. Schumacher has a chapter on Buddhist economics in his classic *Small Is Beautiful*. Primitive animisms are also frequently cited as attitudes toward nature that are more "environmentally sound." One book on the environment states baldly that "the American Indian lived in almost perfect harmony with nature." Anthropologist Marvin Harris has even put forth the novel view that primitive man is an environmentalist, and that many cultural habits are unconscious efforts to reduce the population and conserve the environment. He says that the Hindu prohibition against eating cows and the Jewish tradition of not eating pork were both efforts to avoid the ecological destruction that would come with raising these grazing animals intensively. The implication in these arguments is usually that science and modern technology have somehow dulled our instinctive "environmental" impulses, and that Western "non-spiritual" technology puts us out of harmony with the "balance of nature."

Perhaps the most daring challenge to the environmental soundness of current religious tradition came early in the environmental movement, in a much quoted paper by Lynn White, professor of the history of science at UCLA. Writing in *Science* magazine in 1967, White traced "the historical roots of our ecological crisis" directly to the Western Judeo-

Christian tradition in which "man and nature are two things, and man is master." "By destroying pagan animism," he wrote, "Christianity made it possible to exploit nature in a mood of indifference to the feelings of natural objects." He continued:

Especially in its Western form, Christianity is the most anthropocentric religion the world has seen.... Christianity, in absolute contrast to ancient paganism and Asia's religions (except, perhaps, Zoroastrianism), not only established a dualism of man and nature but also insisted that it is God's will that man exploit nature for his proper ends.... In antiquity every tree, every spring, every stream, every hill had its own *genius loci*, its guardian spirit.... Before one cut a tree, mined a mountain, or dammed a brook, it was important to placate the spirit in charge of that particular situation, and keep it placated.

But the question here is not whether the Judeo-Christian tradition is worth saving in and of itself. It would be more than disappointing if we canceled the accomplishments of Judeo-Christian thought only to find that our treatment of nature had not changed a bit.

There can be no question that White is onto a favorite environmental theme here. What he calls the "Judeo-Christian tradition" is what other writers often term "Western civilization." It is easy to go through environmental books and find long outbursts about the evils that "civilization and progress" have brought us. The long list of Western achievements and advances, the scientific men of genius, are brought to task for creating our "environmental crisis." Sometimes the condemnation is of our brains, pure and simple. Here, for example, is the opening statement from a book about pesticides, written by the late Robert van den Bosch, an outstanding environmental advocate:

Our problem is that we are too smart for our own good, and for that matter, the good of the biosphere. The basic problem is that our brain enables us to evaluate, plan, and execute. Thus, while all other creatures are programmed by nature and subject to her whims, we have our own gray computer to motivate, for good or evil, our chemical engine.... Among living species, we are the only one possessed of arrogance, deliberate stupidity, greed, hate, jealousy, treachery, and the impulse to revenge, all of which may erupt spontaneously or be turned on at will.

At this rate, it can be seen that we don't even need religion to lead us astray. We are doomed from the start because we are not creatures of *instinct*, programmed from the start "by nature."

This type of primitivism has been a very strong, stable undercurrent in the environmental movement. It runs from the kind of fatalistic gibberish quoted above to the Romanticism that names primitive tribes "instinctive environmentalists," from the pessimistic predictions that human beings cannot learn to control their own numbers to the notion that only by remaining innocent children of nature, untouched by progress, can the rural populations of the world hope to feed themselves. At bottom, as many commentators have pointed out, environmentalism is reminiscent of the German Romanticism of the nineteenth century, which sought to shed Christian (and Roman) traditions and revive the Teutonic gods because they were "more in touch with nature."

But are progress, reason, Western civilization, science, and the cerebral cortex really at the root of the "environmental crisis"? Perhaps the best answer comes from an environmentalist himself, Dr. Rene Dubos, a world-renowned microbiologist, author of several prize-winning books on conservation and a founding member of the Natural Resources Defense Council. Dr. Dubos takes exception to the notion that Western Christianity has produced a uniquely exploitative attitude toward nature:

> Erosion of the land, destruction of animal and plant species, excessive exploitation of natural resources, and ecological disasters are not peculiar to the Judeo-Christian tradition and to scientific technology. At all times, and all over the world, man's thoughtless interventions into nature have had a variety of disastrous consequences or at least have changed profoundly the complexity of nature.

Dr. Dubos has catalogued the non-Western or non-Christian cultures that have done environmental damage. Plato observed, for instance, that the hills in Greece had been heedlessly stripped of wood, and erosion had been the result; the ancient Egyptians and Assyrians exterminated large numbers of wild animal species; Indian hunters presumably caused the extinction of many large paleolithic species in North America; Buddhist monks building temples in Asia contributed largely to deforestation. Dubos notes:

> All over the globe and at all times... men have pillaged nature and disturbed the ecological equilibrium... nor did they have a real choice of alternatives. If men are more destructive now... it is because they have at their command more powerful means of destruction, not because they have been influenced by the Bible. In fact, the Judeo-Christian peoples were probably the first to develop on a large scale a pervasive concern for land management and an ethic of nature.

The concern that Dr. Dubos cites is the same one we have rescued out of the perception of environmentalism as a movement based on aristocratic conservatism. That is the legitimate doctrine of *stewardship* of the land. In order to take this responsibility, however, we must recognize the part we play in nature—that "the land is ours." It will not do simply to worship nature, to create a cult of wilderness in which humanity is an eternal intruder and where human activity can only destroy.

"True conservation," writes Dubos, "means not only protecting nature against human misbehavior but also developing human activities which favor a creative, harmonious relationship between man and nature." This is a legitimate goal for the environmental movement.

POSTSCRIPT

Does Wilderness Have Intrinsic Value?

Daniel's rhapsodic descriptions of the beauty and wonder of wild areas would surely qualify him as a member of what Tucker refers to as the "cult of wilderness," but his preservationist motives include such practical ecological goals as preserving biodiversity, which Tucker does not discuss.

Despite the increasing popularity of backpacking, Tucker is correct in maintaining that it is still primarily a diversion of the economically privileged. Indeed, a lack of financial resources and leisure time prevents the majority of U.S. citizens from taking advantage of the tax-supported parks that multiple-use conservationists such as Tucker support, as well as enjoying a small fraction of the acreage that has been set aside as protected wilderness.

The controversy over oil development on Alaska's coastal plain is the most bitterly contested present struggle concerning proposals for exploitation of mineral resources in wilderness regions. The only positive result for environmentalists of the huge oil spill in Prince William Sound by the supertanker *Exxon Valdez* is that it has dealt a political setback to advocates of further oil exploration projects. The battle to preserve Alaskan wilderness is reviewed in articles by Duncan Frazier in *National Parks* (November/December 1987) and by George Laycock in *Audubon* (May 1988).

Another moving and thought-provoking commemoration of the thirtieth anniversary of the Wilderness Act is the essay "An Enduring Wilderness," by Bruce Hamilton, in the September/October 1994 issue of *Sierra*. For a comprehensive collection of essays on the subject, see *Voices for the Wilderness* (Balantine Books, 1969), edited by William Schwartz.

Those who are sympathetic to the concerns raised by Olson would probably find Bill McKibben's controversial book *The End of Nature* (Random House, 1990) both moving and deeply disturbing. More upbeat is the essay "The Heart and Soul of Culture," by Wilbur LaPage and Sally Ranney, *Parks and Recreation* (July 1988), which illustrates the profound influence of America's wild country on its writers, artists, and musicians. For a description of the transformation of wilderness preservation from an esoteric concern into a pragmatic international priority, see "Wilderness International," by Robert K. Olsen, *Wilderness* (Fall 1990).

ISSUE 3

Should the Endangered Species Act Be Reauthorized?

YES: Endangered Species Coalition, from *The Endangered Species Act: A Commitment Worth Keeping* (Wilderness Society, 1992)

NO: Suzanne Winckler, from "Stopgap Measures," *The Atlantic Monthly* (January 1992)

ISSUE SUMMARY

YES: A coalition of 50 environmental, conservation, and wildlife organizations argues that despite limited funding, the Endangered Species Act has succeeded in saving many species from extinction with minimal disruption of commerce.

NO: Natural history author Suzanne Winckler contends that we should protect critical ecosystems rather than near-extinct species.

Extinction of biological species is not necessarily a phenomenon initiated by human activity. Although the specific role of extinction in the process of evolution is still being researched and debated, it is generally accepted that the demise of any biological species is inevitable. Opponents of special efforts to protect endangered species invariably point this out. They also suggest that the role of *Homo sapiens* in causing extinction should not be distinguished from that of any other species.

This position is contrary to some well-established facts. Unlike other creatures that have inhabited the Earth, human beings are the first to possess the technological ability to cause wholesale extermination of species, genera, or even entire families of living creatures. This process is accelerating. Between 1600 and 1900, humans hunted about 75 known species of mammals and birds to extinction. Wildlife management efforts initiated during the twentieth century have been unsuccessful in stemming the tide, as indicated by the fact that the rate of extinction of species of mammals and birds has jumped to approximately one per year.

In 1973 the Endangered Species Act was adopted, and an international treaty was negotiated, in an effort to combat this worldwide problem. This act united a variety of industrial and business interests with the commercial hunters and trappers who traditionally objected to efforts to restrict their activities. However, opposition developed because the act prohibited construction projects that threatened to cause the extinction of any species. The most celebrated example of a confrontation brought about under this act was an effort by environmentalists to halt construction of the Tellico Dam in Loudon County, Tennessee, on the Little Tennessee River, because it threatened a small fish called the snail darter. Much publicity has also been given to the opposition of the lumber industry in efforts to protect the spotted owl whose habitat is in valued timber areas in the U.S. Northwest. Opponents of the act cite such controversies as evidence that the nation's economic well-being is undermined by such species preservation efforts. The act's supporters counter by claiming that the number of serious conflicts between development and species protection have been very few and that despite the uncompromising language of the law, no major project has been prevented because of its enforcement.

The battle over the act's reauthorization is one of the key environmental questions currently before the U.S. Congress. Scientists fear that the vitality of our ecology may be seriously threatened by the reduction of biological diversity resulting from the lost genetic resources contained in the extinct species. They note that the ability of species to evolve and adapt to environmental change depends on the existence of a vast pool of genetic material. This problem joins the issue of endangered species with that of wilderness preservation. Unfortunately, the need to set aside vast undeveloped areas to prevent wholesale extinction is more acute in the poorer, more crowded regions of the world where people are pressured by both their own basic needs and the demand of the industrialized world for their resources.

Concern about reduction in biodiversity due to species extinctions links the issues of wilderness preservation and endangered species. The ability of species to evolve and adapt to changing conditions requires the continued existence of a diverse pool of genetic material, which dwindles as species disappear. Tropical forest preservation is a key factor because of the enormous number of species confined to these ecosystems.

The Endangered Species Coalition consists of 50 diverse organizations concerned with wildlife preservation, conservation, and environmental protection that have joined together to publicize the successes achieved under the act, despite limited funding, and to urge Congress to reauthorize and strengthen the legislation. Suzanne Winckler, the author of two volumes of the *Smithsonian Guide to Historic America*, argues that the goal should be to preserve as many kinds of plants and animals as possible and that a better strategy would be to protect critical ecosystems rather than focusing on near-extinct species.

YES

Endangered Species Coalition

THE ENDANGERED SPECIES ACT: A COMMITMENT WORTH KEEPING

OVERVIEW: LIVING WITH ENDANGERED SPECIES

The Endangered Species Act is a problem-solving statute. The problem is the accelerating extinction of species caused mainly by destruction of their habitat. The solution is to list, watch out for, and help imperiled species.

Since Columbus reached the New World, some 500 plant and animal species have become extinct in the United States, among them the great auk, California grizzly, Roosevelt elk, and passenger pigeon. The President's Council on Environmental Quality estimates that human activity has caused a tenfold increase in the historical rate of extinctions, and between 1980 and 1990 dozens of species, subspecies, and populations came closer to extinction while awaiting federal protection. No responsible citizen or corporation can fail to be alarmed by this trend; no one wants to send an animal or plant species to its doom—or even stand idly by while this occurs.

On the contrary, we are becoming increasingly aware that each extinction means knowledge forfeited and opportunities lost—food sources never to be tapped, medicines never to be extracted. At the same time, however, endangered species serve as environmental indicators. As we discover the cause of a species' decline and take steps to reverse it, often we are identifying and removing threats to human quality of life as well—eliminating poisons from the air we breathe or the water we swim in, for example. The notion that the Endangered Species Act elevates the plant and animal kingdoms above humankind is a mistake, a product of myopia. The gains from maintaining as many species as humanly possible accrue to humanity itself.

Enacted in 1973 at the request of President Richard Nixon, the Act provides a flexible framework for resolving conflicts between development proposals and the survival of species. Sensational cases may grab headlines, but the overwhelming majority of conflicts are dealt with routinely and resolved. The history of administering the Act consistently bears this out: year after year, fewer than one percent of projects scrutinized by U.S. Fish and Wildlife

Service (principal administrator of the Act) have been blocked. The percentage for projects considered by the National Marine Fisheries Services is even smaller.

The Act has spawned dozens of offspring—the endangered species laws enacted by nearly every state. It also enjoys solid backing from the American public: a recent, bipartisan poll shows that two-thirds of voters in every region of the country support the Endangered Species Act, 40 percent support it strongly, and 73 percent say that a candidate's support for the Act is a reason to vote for him or her.

Finally, the Act does what it sets out to do: conserve endangered species. It has helped save from extinction the bald eagle, the peregrine falcon, the brown pelican, the California sea otter, the black-footed ferret, and others. Despite the chronic underfunding that has handicapped the endangered species program, its managers have done as good a job as possible of preserving the biological endowment of the nation and the world.

A WALK THROUGH THE ACT

The Endangered Species Act protects both *endangered* species, defined as those "in danger of extinction throughout all or a significant portion of [their] range," and *threatened* species, those likely to fall into the endangered category "within the foreseeable future." The term *species* also includes subspecies of fish, wildlife, and plants and geographically distinct populations of fish and vertebrate wildlife. In addition, the Act serves to fulfill the U.S. commitment to various treaties on wildlife conservation.

Two federal agencies are primarily responsible for administering the endangered species program: the U.S. Fish and Wildlife Service in the Interior Department for animals and plants found on land or in fresh water, the National Marine Fisheries Service for marine animals and plants.

The linchpin of the Act is the list of endangered and threatened species. Adding a species to the list invokes legal safeguards designed to help it recover. Section 9 prohibits importing, exporting, or trafficking across state lines in listed fish and wildlife species, as well as "taking" them—not just killing but harming them in any way, including the destruction of habitat. (The protection given to listed plants is more limited.)

The decision to list a species is purely biological, a factual call as to how close the creature is to extinction. Economic considerations can be factored in after the species is listed—in the drawing of boundaries for *critical habitat*, in the deliberations of a special *committee* authorized to grant exemptions from the Act (for more on both of these topics, see below), and elsewhere. Despite pleas to let economics influence listing, Congress has insisted on maintaining the list's scientific integrity.

Section 7 directs federal agencies to ensure that their actions do not "jeopardize the continued existence of [listed] species or result in the destruction or adverse modification" of critical habitat. In discharging this duty, federal agencies must consult with the appropriate service, and this is the stage where the vast majority of potential conflicts between activities and listed species are resolved, often informally.

On rare occasions, however, the differences cannot be ironed out and Section 7 will require an agency to forego a proposed activity. To alleviate possible hardships, Congress amended the law to allow appeal to a special committee composed of federal officials and a representative from any affected state. (In May, 1992, such a committee reviewed the conflict between protection of the threatened northern spotted owl and the logging of old-growth forests in the Pacific Northwest.) In certain circumstances, the committee may permit a proposed federal activity to go forward despite the harm it would cause to a listed species.

After listing a species and defining its critical habitat, the appropriate secretary prepares a recovery plan designed to restore the species to the point where it can be removed from the list.

COMEBACK STORIES: SPECIES THAT HAVE BEEN SAVED

In the mountains of southern California, a thunderbird spreads its great wings and soars through the sky. It peers down on a landscape it has never seen before, though its ancestors have flown here for thousands of years. The California condor, North America's largest bird, once hovered at the very brink of extinction. Since 1987, none of the birds had known freedom; all were in captivity, part of a last-ditch effort to rescue this majestic species from extinction. In the fall of 1991, that rescue effort reached a turning point with the release of condors back into the wild. Two young condors, offspring of the last captured birds, now glide over the mountainous Los Padres National Forest northwest of Los Angeles. Several dozen more "thunderbirds," as early Indians called them, remain behind at the Los Angeles Zoo and the San Diego Wild Animal Park to produce more chicks for future releases. Against almost insuperable odds, the Endangered Species Act is reversing the condor's slide toward extinction.

The condor's success story does not stand alone. Beginning in September, 1991, 50 young black-footed ferrets were released on a high windswept plain in south central Wyoming. Just over a decade ago the species was thought to be extinct. Then, in 1981, a ranch dog captured a ferret in a prairie dog town near Meeteetsee, Wyoming, east of Yellowstone National Park. State and federal wildlife biologists trapped six healthy animals to produce offspring for the reintroduction program. The remaining wild ferrets of Meeteetsee either died of canine distemper or were killed by predators.

Today, thanks to the collaboration of five zoos across the country, nearly 350 of these masked weasels are living in captivity. In 1992, biologists hoped to double the number of released ferrets, making use of other potential new sites in the Rocky Mountain states.

While these efforts do not guarantee that either the condor or the ferret will survive in the long run, without them it is virtually certain that both species would now be extinct. The California sea otter nearly met the same fate. The animal was once thought hunted to extinction, but a population of 40 animals came to light in 1938. Today, sea otter numbers [have] been increased to nearly 2,000, and its chances of survival are much improved.

No less dramatic is the story of the whooping crane—like the condor and ferret a charter member of the endangered species.

Its population had dropped to fewer than 20 birds when biologists launched a comprehensive conservation program to save it. Habitat preservation and a captive breeding program have increased the population of this tall, long-necked bird to more than 200. . . .

Loss of habitat is the most common reason for the endangerment of species; if this problem is addressed creatively, species loss can be averted. Near San Francisco, for instance, housing and commercial development threatened the last remaining habitat of the mission blue butterfly. This small, iridescent creature was known to exist only in a small mountain range that cuts across the San Francisco Peninsula. When the butterfly was listed as endangered in 1976, its fate appeared sealed by plans to build 8,500 houses and 2 million square feet of commercial space on San Bruno Mountain, its principal home. However, landowners, local, state, and federal officials, and environmentalists negotiated a land-use plan that eventually qualified for the first "incidental taking permit" under Section 10(a) of the Endangered Species Act. The plan scaled back the proposed development and protected much of the mountain permanently as open space. San Bruno Mountain is still home to its unique butterflies —and to people as well. . . .

The threat of extinction affects terrestrial and marine life, vertebrates and invertebrates, animals and plants, and the Endangered Species Act extends its protection to all of these. Eight species of whales are listed as endangered primarily because of overhunting by commercial whalers during the past two centuries. Because of the protection afforded by the Act and international treaties, several species are recovering, notably the gray whale.

These remarkable success stories have occurred despite the fact that the agencies with jurisdiction over the endangered species program, the Fish and Wildlife Service and National Marine Fisheries Service, are woefully understaffed and underfunded. As a result, for most of the hundreds of species on the endangered species list, progress toward recovery has barely begun. Yet comebacks by the condor, black-footed ferret, bald eagle, California sea otter, and others show that with sufficient funds and effort, the Endangered Species Act helps preserve and restore our vanishing natural heritage.

WHY CONSERVE SPECIES: THE STOREHOUSE OF BIODIVERSITY

In setting national priorities, some consider saving endangered species an expensive luxury, easily expendable in tough economic times. Such a view is extremely shortsighted. In fact, our own future welfare depends on preserving the natural diversity of the planet.

The variety of living species, called biological diversity or "biodiversity," is disappearing at a frightening rate. In recent years, species extinction has reached epidemic proportions, with most scientists believing we have entered a period of extinctions greater than any other since the disappearance of the dinosaurs 65 million years ago. Today's extinctions, however, are due almost entirely to one species: the human.

The loss of species should trigger alarm bells in the minds of responsible citizens. Like the asphyxiation of canaries lowered into mines used to detect life-threatening gases, the dramatic dying off of animal and plant species is telling us something: ecological systems have been so contaminated, degraded, or disrupted that they no longer support their native wildlife and may not long support us, either. The faster humans extinguish other life forms, the more we imperil ourselves.

Yet the destruction of animals and plants continues, primarily because most people fail to recognize the close connection between the well-being of humans and the health of the environment. Nature resembles an intricate tapestry, a marvelously complex construct of which humans are an integral part. By driving so many species to extinction, we have in effect grasped loose threads in that tapestry and begun to pull. . . .

Consider the direct benefits that humans derive from natural diversity. More than half of all medicines today can be traced to wild organisms, and chemicals from higher plants are the sole or major ingredient in one-quarter of all prescriptions written in the United States each year. They are responsible for saving thousands of lives.

For instance, the bark of the Pacific yew tree, found primarily in the fast-disappearing old-growth forests of the Pacific Northwest, is an important source of the drug taxol. The National Cancer Institute calls taxol the most promising new drug in 15 years because of its dramatic success in treating ovarian and breast cancer. The rosy periwinkle, a tropical plant, is a critical component in the treatment of childhood leukemia and Hodgkin's disease. . . .

The potential for further discoveries is enormous. In the words of Robert E. Jenkins, vice-president for science of The Nature Conservancy, "Humans have consciously been fighting parasites and diseases for only a few millennia, while other species have been evolutionarily fighting each other nearly since time began, leading to countless instances of metabolic substances produced by one organism that inhibit, deter, or outright kill another organism." Yet scientists have investigated a mere five percent of known plant species for their pharmaceutical applications. Each loss of a species snuffs out untold chances for possible treatments and cures.

Species diversity also contributes to the economy. A native wild corn species from Mexico has imbued crop hybrids here with the ability to resist blight. In 1970, a leaf blight fungus that wiped out 15 percent of the U.S. corn crop was stopped only by the introduction of genetic material from the Mexican plant. Wheat farmers must sow new varieties of wheat every 5 to 15 years to adapt to changing conditions, such as new pests and diseases. The genetic reservoir from which we draw new strains, however, consists of only a few plant varieties. Others may already have become extinct.

Finally, we have a strong moral interest in saving rare and endangered species. If, as Gandhi wrote, "the greatness of a nation and its moral progress can be judged by the way its animals are treated," then surely there can be few greater measures of our moral progress than the strength of our commitment to prevent the extinction of fellow creatures. It's easy to see the aesthetic virtues of the whooping crane and the California sea otter, but less glamorous species— plants, insects, and other invertebrates— are equally deserving of protection. They share the world with us, and we with them. When we exterminate them, we diminish ourselves. . . .

MAINTAINING A CREDIBLE LIST

The Endangered Species Act protects species listed as threatened or endangered by the Secretary of the Interior or the Secretary of Commerce, and it requires that listing decisions be based solely upon the best available scientific data. The list is intended to reflect an honest and objective assessment of the status of imperiled species. It neither includes species that do not require protection nor excludes species because their protection may be expensive or difficult.

Some have argued that listing decisions should not be strictly scientific, that economics should also play a role. In fact, for a brief period in the early 1980s, economic factors were part of listing decisions. Interior Secretary James Watt claimed this authority as a means of halting the addition of species to the list, but Congress wisely insisted that deciding whether a species is in danger should be [a] matter of scientific fact, uninfluenced by economics or politics. If the list has a shortcoming, it is not lack of credibility but incompleteness.

Within the past two centuries, more than 480 species of native plants and animals have vanished in the United States. Hawaii alone has lost half of its endemic birds and hundreds of plants and invertebrate species. Both the absolute number and the rate of extinctions are rising, largely because of the destruction of natural habitats. Moreover, extinction is only the most extreme manifestation of the loss of biological diversity: for every species that vanishes, countless populations and unique gene pools also die out.

Several types of ecosystem now occupy mere fragments of their former extents. Wetlands have been reduced by more than half since our nation was founded. All but 10 percent of the ancient forests of the Pacific Northwest have been logged. The tallgrass prairie, which once covered 400,000 square miles in the Midwest, has been reduced to less than one percent of that size. In the East, almost none of the virgin forest remains. Perhaps one-half of one percent of the longleaf pine community that once dominated 60 to 70 million acres of the southeastern upland coastal plain still exists. Less than 10 percent of the pitcher plant bogs of the Gulf Coast are left. As these habitat types disappear, the species they once supported are pushed to the brink of extinction, and sometimes over.

Given these pressures, it should be no surprise that more than 4,000 species or subspecies have been identified as candidates for listing. The number actually needing such protection may be even larger. As reported in the Council on Environmental Quality's 1991 annual report, data collected by state Natural Heritage Programs across the United States, shows that some 9,000 U.S. plant and animal species may be currently at risk....

The hitch is that listing is a complex and time-consuming process: much is at stake, and biologists have to "get it right." The Act contains an emergency provision for listing desperate cases in a hurry, but listing a species typically takes a year from start to finish. Because the appearance of a species on the list brings powerful legal tools into play, decisions must be accurate and based on the best available information—the list must have integrity. No decision to add a species to the list has ever been overturned in court, a tribute to the care with which the list has been compiled....

What ails the Endangered Species Act is clear. Limited resources have kept the federal government from listing five-sixths of the species thought likely to need protection.

THE IMPORTANCE OF PROTECTING SUBSPECIES AND POPULATIONS

The term "Endangered Species Act" is something of a misnomer, for the Act protects more than species. It permits the listing of any subspecies of plant or animal or "any distinct population segment" of any vertebrate species (i.e., mammals, birds, reptiles, amphibians, and fishes). The inclusion of subspecies and populations is sometimes attacked as unnecessary and excessive; in fact it represents both sound science and good public policy. To understand why this is so, we must first review the definitions of species, subspecies, and populations, and then consider how they function in the Act.

Most people have an intuitive grasp of what constitutes a species. We recognize an American robin as being different from an eastern bluebird, a red fox as distinct from a dog, a polar bear as different than a black or brown bear. The biological definition of a *species*, however, is based not on appearances but on reproductive behavior. A species consists of those individuals actually or potentially capable of reproducing among themselves and incapable of reproducing with other organisms. Robins do not breed with bluebirds.

A *population* refers to the interbreeding individuals of a species living in a given area. Individuals from different populations of the same species are biologically capable of breeding with each other; whether or not they do so depends upon how far apart the populations are. Populations can also be separated temporally, as in the case of salmon, where different groups of the same species spawn in the same rivers but at different times of the year. Since the Act refers to "distinct population segment[s]," it intends that listed populations show some degree of spatial or temporal isolation from other populations of the same species. Examples of populations protected under the Act include bald eagles, grizzly bears, and grey wolves found in the lower 48 states, gopher tortoises west of the Mobile and Tombigbee rivers, and the winter run of chinook salmon up the Sacramento River.

Populations of a given species from different regions may show characteristic differences in appearance and behavior. Such populations are classified as different *subspecies* or races, but they still belong to the same species. Subspecies protected by the Act include the Florida panther and Lahontan cutthroat trout. There are other subspecies of panther and cutthroat trout that are not considered endangered or threatened.

Reasons for protecting subspecies and populations fall into three categories: ecological, evolutionary, and aesthetic.

Ecological. Plants and animals do not live their lives in isolation. They interact with one another and with their physical environments. In doing so, they contribute to the health and resilience of ecosystems. With the extinction of a population or subspecies, an ecological niche is left empty. Populations and subspecies are also indicators of ecological health. The decline of bald eagles and peregrine falcons in many parts of the United States made people realize that DDT and other persistent pesticides were reaching dangerous levels in organisms at the top of the food chain. There were still thriving populations of bald eagles in Alaska and peregrine falcons in other countries, so neither species was in immediate danger of extinction. But the listing of bald eagle populations in the lower 48 states and of two North American subspecies of peregrine falcon called attention to the wider problem. Today, with the banning of DDT, numbers of both birds have increased, and potential threats to human health have receded.

Evolutionary. Natural environments are constantly changing, and over time species must adapt to these changes or perish. The key to adaptation is genetic diversity—the differences in genetic composition among individuals or between populations of a species. Populations and subspecies are the storehouses of genetic diversity. Today humans are transforming the world—depositing new chemicals in the air, land and water; altering the climate, spreading exotic species and diseases to new places; and replacing natural habitats with croplands and settlements. Under these circumstances, the long-term survival of many species will depend upon the genetic diversity stored in their subspecies and populations.

Aesthetic. By permitting subspecies and vertebrate populations to be listed, the Endangered Species Act ensures that more Americans will be able to enjoy some of our most awe-inspiring and unusual plants and animals. The alternative would be to restrict these species to increasingly remote and inaccessible areas. To see a bald eagle would require a trip to Alaska. Peregrine falcons would not dive off the skyscrapers of Baltimore or Manhattan in pursuit of pigeons. And visitors to Yellowstone National Park would have no hope of glimpsing a mother grizzly bear and her cubs ambling across a meadow. We could get by without these experiences, but would we want to? ...

It has been argued that eliminating protection of subspecies and populations would make the Act more workable....

One response to this suggestion is to point out that dropping protection for subspecies and populations would end years of effort to recover some of the best-known and most popular animals that the Act now protects. Among them are the bald eagle, peregrine falcon, California sea otter, grizzly bear, Florida panther, gray wolf, Sonoran pronghorn antelope, Aleutian Canada goose, Key deer, Everglade snail kite, Columbian white-tailed deer, masked bobwhite quail, and brown pelican.

But the argument as a whole has a fundamental flaw. The inclusion of subspecies and populations makes the Act *more* flexible, not less. Having the ability to list a subspecies or a population allows program managers to leave other subspecies and populations off the list. If an all-or-nothing choice were required between protecting a species everywhere or nowhere, the choice might have to be everywhere. Sacrificed would be the ability to apply the Act's protections selectively, where they are most needed, and to withhold them where they are not.

DOES THE ACT STAND IN THE WAY OF PROGRESS? A REAPPRAISAL

To listen to critics of the Endangered Species Act, one might conclude that it is annually derailing hundreds of meritorious and badly needed projects throughout the country, all because of the requirements imposed by Section 7. There is only one small problem with the claim: it doesn't square with the facts.

Section 7 is the most effective and, hence, most controversial, provision in the Act. It reflects a deliberate congressional policy that federal agencies should not contribute to the further decline and extinction of species. In particular, it directs federal agencies to ensure that actions they authorize, fund, or carry out are not likely to jeopardize the continued existence of any endangered or threatened species, or result in adverse modification or destruction of any such species' critical habitat. In compliance with Section 7, federal agencies consult with the Secretary of the Interior or the Secretary of Commerce before undertaking or authorizing projects that might adversely affect listed species or their critical habitats....

Studies of Fish and Wildlife Service files demonstrate that Section 7 has not been a major impediment to economic activities. Indeed, in the 13-year period from 1979 through 1991, formal consultation with the Service led to the cancellation of only a minute fraction of proposed federal activities. The most recent study shows that between 1987 and 1991 the Service engaged in 71,560 informal consultations and 2,000 formal ones. Only 18 proposals, fewer than 1 percent of those going as far as a formal consultation, were positively identified as blocked by Section 7.

The fraction is even smaller for projects examined by the National Marine Fisheries Service. Between 1987 and 1991 the Service formally reviewed 248 projects; only one was canceled because of Section 7.

How important were the few projects halted during those years? Probably not very, since in no case but that of the spotted owl did a disappointed party utilize the Act's provisions, authorizing exemption from Section 7.

The above numbers stand in stark contrast to the sweeping and unsubstanti-ated claims made by critics of the Act. The numbers also demonstrate that the consultation process is not unduly burdensome or unreasonable, and that the vast majority of biological opinions allow proposed projects to proceed with only minor modification....

JOBS, DOLLARS, AND SPECIES: A BALANCING ACT

Of all the myths bandied about by opponents of the Endangered Species Act, perhaps the most misleading is this: it rigidly excludes consideration of economics, such as the effect of blocking a project on jobs in the community, and exalts protection of plants and wildlife over human needs. One response is that conservation is good business, in that protecting plants and wildlife helps meet our need for a stable food supply, offers the hope and reality of promising cures for cancer and other diseases, and provides myriad other societal benefits. Even aside from those vital considerations, however, the Act contains ample opportunity for balancing the costs and benefits of saving species.

Indeed, in only one area does the Act exclude consideration of economic or other non-biological factors. When the Secretary of the Interior or Commerce decides whether to list a species as threatened or endangered, he or she must do so based solely on biological factors. In adopting this limitation, Congress wisely recognized that the question of whether a species is in peril is a scientific one and does not depend on how much it will cost to save the species. On the other hand, once a species is listed, the questions of what steps to take to save it and what degree of habitat destruction to allow are fraught with economic, political, ethical, and other social considerations. Congress recognized this as well and, in crafting the Act, struck an effective balance between those concerns and the needs of vanishing species.

For example, while the Act requires the designation of critical habitat for listed species, it specifies that likely economic and other impacts be considered before any land is designated. In addition, the Act permits the exclusion of land from critical habitat if it can be shown that the costs of including a particular area outweigh the benefits to the species. Applying this rule in the case of the threatened northern spotted owl, the Fish and Wildlife Service dropped 3 million acres of state, private, and and other non-federal land from proposed critical habitat....

Economic considerations also come heavily into play in evaluating the impact of federal permits and projects on threatened and endangered species. When the Fish and Wildlife Service or the National Marine Fisheries Service concludes that a proposed federal action is likely to jeopardize a threatened or endangered species, it suggests "reasonable and prudent alternatives" that will not result in jeopardy. Reasonable and prudent alternatives must be economically and technologically feasible and fulfill the purposes of the proposed agency action. For example, the National Marine Fisheries Service has concluded that one type of harbor dredging carried out by the Corps of Engineers along the southeastern United States coast jeopardizes threatened and endangered sea turtles. Rather than ban dredging, however, the Service has offered the Corps the reasonable and prudent alternatives of either employing a different type of dredge or dredging during cold-water months,

when turtles are least likely to be present. Within the existing provisions of the Act, then, both the conservation needs of sea turtles and the economic needs of port cities for ease of navigation can be met.

Even in the rarest of instances, when no reasonable and prudent alternative is available, the Act provides for an ultimate balancing of a species' continued existence against the demands of society. In the wake of the famous snail darter controversy, Congress created the Endangered Species Committee. This ad-hoc Cabinet-level body is empowered to exempt projects from the Act's restrictions when it determines that the benefits of the project clearly outweigh the benefits of conserving a species and no alternative action is available. Since its creation in 1978, such a committee has been called upon only three times to make this difficult decision—testimony to the Act's flexibility in balancing societal needs for economic development with protection of species....

As it now stands, the Act is far from the rigid, anti-human monolith that its opponents portray it to be. Rather, through the careful balancing allowed by its provisions, the Act represents a recognition by Congress and the American people that we can meet our needs for economic development without sacrificing the right of future generations to a world as rich in plants and wildlife as our own.

CREATIVITY IN THE FIELD: HABITAT CONSERVATION PLANS

On a brushy mountaintop just south of San Francisco, bright blue butterflies dart through meadows of native wildflowers. Nearby stands a newly built community of houses and offices. The butterflies are an endangered species—the mission blue butterfly—and the construction of the new houses and offices has provided sorely needed funds to ensure their continued survival.

Farther south, near Palm Springs, a speckled lizard scurries across the hot sand, then quickly buries itself beneath the surface. Here too, new houses and thriving new businesses stand nearby. And here too, the structures are part of a plan to save a threatened species—the Coachella Valley fringe-toed lizard.

In growing numbers all across the country, habitat conservation plans are reconciling the needs of endangered species with the continued growth and prosperity of surrounding communities. Clark Country, Nevada, has recently done such a plan for the desert tortoise. Travis County, Texas, and the City of Austin are doing one for a half dozen rare species native to the area. And Riverside County, California, has done one for a desert-dwelling curiosity, the Stephens' kangaroo rat.

These examples and others like them exemplify a new strategy to preserve endangered species, one that emphasizes the carrot more than the stick. This is an important development, since the limits of exclusive reliance on the stick approach are becoming apparent. The stick works best when there is a single, obvious, and overriding threat to a species—like DDT to the bald eagle or a dam planned on the only river in which a rare fish occurs. In these situations, there may be no choice: ban DDT, stop the dam, or lose a species.

For most imperiled species, however, the situation is not so simple. Instead of one large and obvious villain threatening to gobble up the habitat of a rare species in a single bite, there are many

smaller threats, each nibbling away at the same habitat. There are not enough sticks with which to pursue each of these problems and the sticks that exist are not well suited for that purpose anyway. On the other hand, in such situations there may be many different potential strategies for saving a species. The challenge is to find the strategy that combines a high probability of success with a low likelihood of painful economic sacrifice....

Habitat conservation planning was an idea added to the Endangered Species Act in 1982, at the behest of land development interests. Slow to take hold at first, it is now growing geometrically. With all the attention given to a few prominent controversies, we should not lose sight of this new tool and its success in reconciling protection of endangered species with development.

THE CHALLENGE AHEAD

We have all been heartened by recent good-news items on endangered species, especially the reintroduction to the wild of the California condor, black-footed ferret, red wolf, and other scarce animals that had survived only in captivity.

Yet a few triumphs are not enough to reverse the overall trend. The Congressional Research Service, and the Interior Department's Inspector General have each issued recent reports concluding that the goal of bringing species back from near extinction may be unreachable at current funding levels. The threat of extinction menaces more species than at any time since the Act was passed. Efforts to meet the mandate of the Act will require a greater commitment of resources than has been available to date.

Conservation groups working for recovery of endangered species have documented the amount of money needed to make the federal endangered species program capable of achieving the Act's goals: a recommended funding level that eventually reaches $100 million annually. Such a commitment would unquestionably accelerate federal and state efforts to meet the Act's goals and increase the program's successes. We believe it must be made....

Recovery is the ultimate goal of the Act and the heart of the endangered species program. Species awaiting listing are often subject to years of delay. Some species have slipped over the edge while waiting to be listed. Once listed, they can languish until a recovery plan is prepared, and even then, the plan may not be implemented for lack of funds. Such problems cannot be overcome simply by a new priority system; more dollars and more manpower must be made available.

Above all, the Act must be kept strong. Cutting back on the Act's protections would send the worst possible signal about this country's commitment to the environment, especially to those developing nations that are being urged to save their rainforests and other habitats rich in unique species. Much more than symbolism is at stake, however. A weakened Endangered Species Act would mean a return to extinctions as usual.

Dr. Lewis Thomas, former dean of the Yale Medical School and former president of the Memorial Sloan Kettering Cancer Center, has entitled his new book of essays *The Fragile Species*. The reference is to ourselves, whose existence is predicated on a biosphere that seems to be unraveling in every direction. "The animal species chiefly at risk for the near term," Thomas writes, "is humankind. If there is to be a mass extinction just ahead, we will be the most conspicuous victims. Despite our vast numbers, we should now be classifying ourselves as an immediately endangered species, on grounds of our total dependence on other vulnerable species for our food, and our simultaneous dependence, as a social species, on each other."

At an exceedingly modest cost and with minimal disruption of commerce, the endangered species program has made striking progress toward reversing the trend of pell mell extinctions and improving the outlook for human well-being. Keeping the Act's structure intact and increasing its funding levels are the best safeguards we have for the biological trust fund we will be passing on to our descendants.

NO

Suzanne Winckler

STOPGAP MEASURES

> If our goal is to preserve as many kinds of plants and animals as possible, it makes little sense to spend limited funds on heroic steps to rescue a handful of near-extinct species. A more effective strategy would focus on protecting ecosystems that support maximum biological diversity

To say that the Endangered Species Act is not working is to sound ungrateful for what it has accomplished. Inasmuch as tens, if not hundreds, of organisms that would undoubtedly be extinct by now—including the Attwater's prairie chicken, the Florida panther, the black-footed ferret, the Kirtland's warbler, and the Puerto Rican parrot—are instead hanging on by a thread, the act has been a success.

The continued existence, however precarious, of these species is deeply satisfying to many people. The creatures are beautiful (the whooping crane); they stand for ideals that are important to us culturally (the bald eagle); they exhibit incredible behavior (the Attwater's prairie chicken); they are stunning emblems of the closest we can come to pristine wilderness (the grizzly bear). Our knowledge of their presence in the wild helps assuage our guilt about what we've done to them in particular and to the natural world in general, which might imply that the Endangered Species Act is ultimately designed to treat our own brand of sickness and not theirs. Regardless of what these animals do to make us feel better, they are the walking wounded of the world, and it costs millions of dollars to keep them out of there.

That it saves organisms from extinction is faint praise for a law with the far loftier aspiration of "better safeguarding, for the benefit of all citizens, the Nation's heritage in fish, wildlife, and plants." It is the stated purpose of the law not just to keep species from going extinct but to return them to viability. In this regard it is failing.

The Endangered Species Act takes under its wing an array of taxa—from full species (whooping crane) to subspecies (Attwater's prairie chicken) to discrete populations of species (the Mojave population of the desert tortoise). "Taxon" (plural "taxa") refers to any of the groupings into which taxonomists classify organisms. As of last November the federal government listed 1,196

NO Suzanne Winckler / 61

taxa around the world—more than half of them occurring in the United States and its territories—as either endangered or threatened, one of which dubious distinctions is necessary for care under the act. Another 3,500 or so are waiting for review. Among this second group—known as candidate species or Category 1 and Category 2 species—are many plants and animals acknowledged by scientists to be in far worse danger than species that have already qualified. They languish in bureaucratic limbo because of a perennial problem of the act: it never has enough funding. A number of candidate species have gone extinct before they could be considered for listing.

The process for listing threatened and endangered species is complicated, but if there is an overriding criterion for listing, it is that the species is demonstrably imperiled. John Fay, a botanist with the Division of Endangered Species of the U.S. Fish and Wildlife Service, explains the implicit ranking process: "We try to set our priorities so that those species that face the greatest threat are the ones we address first. The alternative—intervening with things that are in better shape—would mean losing a substantial number of species in immediate danger. And within the terms of the Endangered Species Act that's unacceptable."

This is what critics point to as a major failing of the act. It intervenes in a way that no intelligent nurse, paramedic, or doctor would under analogous circumstances. It has thrown out the window any concept of triage. It does not sort and care for species in such a way as to maximize the number of surviving species. On the contrary, it attempts to save the hardest cases, the equivalent of the terminally ill and the brain-dead. It pays less attention to species that would be easier and cheaper to save—species that require treatment akin to minor surgery, a splint, or a Band-Aid. The act has no concept of preventive medicine, of keeping healthy species from peril. Consequently, many animals and plants that were common twenty years ago—were even considered in some realms to be pests—are now entitled to care under the Endangered Species Act.

One reason the act eschews triage is that its enforcers, not to mention many endangered-species watchdogs, do not want—and do not want to allow anyone else—to "play God." There is no doubt that such a role confers awesome responsibilities. The triage of species and the triage of individuals of one species (as it is practiced in emergency rooms and on battlefields) differ by several orders of magnitude. Few people would want the ethical burden of deciding the fate of a whole species—of saying, for instance, that the blunt-nosed leopard lizard can go but the humpback whale stays. John Fay says, "All we can do is try to preserve our options. My absolutely favorite quote is from Aldo Leopold: 'To save every cog in the wheel is the first precaution of intelligent tinkering.' That's what we're trying to do. We don't know which ones are important. We don't know which ones are going to disappear."

Moral neutrality is noble, but it creates problems in the categories of money (there has never been enough allocated to save every cog; there is no promise of more in the future) and biology (the cogs we are saving are so crippled, so compromised, that they can barely perform their assigned functions in their respective niches). To refuse to play God is to play the devil by default. . . .

UNCERTAIN RETURN
ON INVESTMENT

In 1988 Congress began to require that the Fish and Wildlife Service submit annual reports on federal expenditures for the U.S. roster of endangered and threatened species. (The federal government spends little money on foreign species.) This is not an easy task—at least thirteen federal agencies make regular outlays of money for endangered species. Nor are the reports ever likely to be more than a best guess of expenditures, since endangered-species activities often merge with other operations. For example, prescribed burning—setting fires to remove the brushy vegetation once held at bay by natural fires—is a management tool at Francis Marion National Forest, in coastal South Carolina, which aids not only endangered red-cockaded woodpeckers but also game species like turkey and quail.

While there is much to be said for making the protectors of endangered species accountable for how they spend our money, the expense reports (two have been prepared so far, for 1989 and 1990) are sadly divisive documents that reinforce the individual-species thrust of the Endangered Species Act. They provide ammunition not only for those who are alarmed by how much we're spending on, say, the Higgins' eye pearly mussel ($437,700 in 1989; $367,000 in 1990) but also for those who are upset at what we're *not* spending on, say, the desert tortoise, a species that because of a strange upper-respiratory disease is dropping dead at an alarming pace in the Mojave Desert. The tortoise got almost $500,000 in 1989. Its advocates saw that boosted to more than $4 million in 1990.

By focusing on individual species, the expenditure reports perpetuate a chronic lack of attention to the big picture. Environmentalists are defending expenditures for the plants and animals to which they have, for whatever reason, chosen allegiance when instead they should be addressing a whole different set of questions and concerns. Why does the list of endangered and threatened species keep getting longer? Why have only a few species ever been taken off the list? Where on earth will the money come from to care for every new addition to the lengthening list?

The biggest question the expenditure reports should provoke is this: Why is half of all the money earmarked for endangered and threatened species being spent on only twelve of them? In 1990, of $102 million apportioned among 591 taxa, a total of $55 million went to twelve. They are, in descending order of expenditures, the northern spotted owl, the least Bell's vireo, the grizzly bear, the red-cockaded woodpecker, the Florida panther, the desert tortoise, the bald eagle, the ocelot, the jaguarundi, the peregrine falcon, the California least tern, and the Chinook salmon. The apportionment does not become much more equal after this first dozen. The next dozen species—which include the gray wolf, the southern sea otter, and the Puerto Rican parrot —received the next $19 million. In other words, the remaining quarter of funding —$28 million—was shared among about 570 other organisms.

The fortunate two dozen or so creatures that command three quarters of the money are among the most beautiful on earth. They have captured the hearts of a wide assortment of people. These people would better serve the objects of their affections if they cared for whole ecosystems—the degradation of which is largely responsible for our degraded wildlife—with the same fervor.

Intensive care for animals and plants is costly. It is not cheap to hire airplanes and helicopters for the surveillance of populations (as was done before the last California condors were taken from the wild), set up captive-breeding facilities (for the bald eagle, the peregrine falcon, the whooping crane, and the black-footed ferret), translocate animals, either in order to invigorate isolated gene pools (the grizzly bear, the red-cockaded woodpecker), release individuals back into the wild (successfully accomplished with the peregine falcon), attempt to establish breeding populations (tried and failed with the whooping crane), or keep parasitic cowbirds out of the nests of endangered birds (being done year in and year out for the Kirtland's warbler, the golden-cheeked warbler, and the black-capped vireo). When we focus treatment on the most afflicted, we can expect to pay.

It is true that the Endangered Species Act inherited some desperate cases when it went into effect. The whooping crane, the California condor, and the Kirtland's warbler are examples of species that were rare to begin with and suffered from the presence of people within their ranges. Thirty years before the Endangered Species Act, biologists had begun the arduous and expensive endeavor of bringing the whooping crane back, from a single flock of fourteen individuals in the wild. After fifty years of intensive management, the wild flock of whooping cranes numbers about 140 birds. This population—like small populations—is intensely vulnerable: last winter nine birds, representing six percent of the flock, were lost.

It is also true that many endangered and threatened species need only moderate sums of money to survive. For instance, certain narrowly endemic plants —plants that have evolved in rare micro-habitats, such as the bunched cory cactus and the McKittrick pennyroyal—require little more than the purchase of the land on which they grow, and small outlays for monitoring and law enforcement (cacti, for example, are particularly susceptible to rapacious collectors).

But for every one of these bargain species there is a very expensive one waiting for a constituency to care enough, waiting to get a little more endangered, or waiting for its recovery plan to be approved. To name just a few, they include the black-capped vireo, the golden-cheeked warbler, several of the Columbia River salmon stocks, the humpback whale, the San Marcos gambusia, Texas wild rice, and the thirty-odd species of freshwater mussels now menaced by the accidental introduction of the alien zebra mussel.

LAST-DITCH SPENDING

... In order to save the most-endangered species, the act diverts attention and money from the much more crucial goal of preserving overall biological diversity —that is, preserving the maximum number of healthy species in ecosystems that require a minimum of maintenance. The way to save species is to save the places where they live. By extension, the way to save the greatest number of species is to save the places that house the richest biological inventory. One example is the 17,800-acre Sacramento National Wildlife Refuge, where, according to J. Michael Scott, a research biologist with the U.S. Fish and Wildlife Service, and his colleagues, there are 257 vertebrate species, 170 of which have resident populations. "The populations of many of these species number in the tens of thousands," Scott et al. write. "The annual cost of managing this system, estimated at one million dollars, is less than the annual expenditures on the recovery effort for the critically endangered California condor." The comparatively low cost of maintenance leads Scott and his colleagues to conclude, "Prevention is cheaper than treatment."

The Endangered Species Act has institutionalized the bizarre notion that the primary legal justification for the preservation of an ecosystem is a species teetering on the brink of extinction. That it is one of the most magnificent landscapes in North America is somehow no longer reason enough to preserve the last remnants of the Pacific old-growth forest. Instead, the only legal mechanism available is to require the preservation of some minimum configuration of that forest in hopes of keeping the northern spotted owl—one species among thousands that dwell there—from going extinct. At the same time, the boreal forests of Minnesota, Wisconsin, and upper Michigan, the marshes and wetlands rimming our coasts, and the prairie potholes of the Midwest, the riparian woodlands along streams in the West, and other ecosystems will continue to shrink until they yield evidence of the endangered species that will warrant their preservation. . . .

[T]he Endangered Species Act is treating the symptom and not the disease. The increasing numbers of plants and animals that are becoming biological wards of the government are a manifestation of what can only be described as an ecosystems crisis. Yet the servants of the Endangered Species Act, charged explicitly with habi-

tat conservation, have never excelled at the real-estate business. They have come to rely on heroic measures for saving one species at a time in large part because they have failed at the alternative of saving habitat. The act has continually gone against the grain of the American desire to exploit the natural resources of this continent, its arterial system of fresh water, and its surrounding seas without considering the consequences.

Defenders of the act, many of whom know exactly what's wrong with it and willingly discuss its flaws in private, worry that public criticism will play into the hands of the pro-development groups who perennially try to weaken it. Many environmentalists are girding for just such an assault this spring, when the act comes up in Congress for reauthorization. They should not fear criticism from within their own ranks, however. When adversaries of the act assail its shortcomings—when, for example, they complain that we are spending too much money on endangered species—environmentalists have an obvious counteroffensive: The reason the act has engendered a costly and unwieldy bureaucracy for the perpetual care of compromised organisms is that pro-development groups have been so successful at evading the central principle of the act—the preservation of ecosystems. The very people who complain about the act are the ones who have made it malfunction.

GAP ANALYSIS

Over the past decade steadily increasing numbers of zoologists, botanists, geneticists, environmental-policy makers, land managers, geographers, and developers have been making the case that it is time to focus on the rational, systematic, continent-wide preservation of those ecosystems that suport maximum biological diversity. A leader in this cause has been J. Michael Scott, who was the project leader for the California-condor recovery program from 1984 to 1986, and before that spent ten years in Hawaii, which harbors the greatest concentration of endangered birds in the world. Hawaii also holds an appalling number of endangered plants, of which the Cooke's kokio, a tree, is considered the most endangered species in the world. Only half of one Cooke's kokio exists; it is grafted onto a related species in a botanical garden in Hawaii.

On behalf of the Fish and Wildlife Service, Scott and a team of twenty-six ornithologists, botanists, and statisticians were assigned the task of conducting an inventory of the forest birds of the Hawaiian Islands; they produced one of the classic documents in field ornithology, *Forest Bird Communities of the Hawaiian Islands*. During years of camping in the rain and slogging in the mud (Hawaii harbors the wettest places on earth) and worrying about the people on his team ("I count as our biggest achievement outside the scientific realm that we got through six years of that kind of survey in remote country and we didn't lose a single person"), Scott began to get his first inklings of what was wrong with the management of endangered species. He began to see the gaps.

For their study Scott and his team made Mylar maps of the vegetation of each island, of the range of each species of bird, and of the existing federal, state, and private land holdings that preserved the presumed habitats of these species. When the maps were laid on top of one another, the lack of overlap was glaringly apparent: the areas of greatest avian diversity were outside the protection of preserves.

In this simple fashion Scott performed one of the first exercises in what has come to be called "gap analysis" (F. William Burley, an Oregon biologist and rancher, is usually credited with coining the term). Gap analysis looks for unprotected landscapes that are rich in species. Far faster than a man stacking maps, and with the ability to manipulate much more information, computers store, manage, retrieve, and analyze vast amounts of information from satellite imagery and data bases that show for a particular landscape the different species on it, their distribution, and various habitat factors (vegetation, soil type, geologic elements) and cultural features (zoning, roadways, land ownership, dominant land use). Much of the species information being used comes from information gathered by the Nature Conservancy, a private land-preservation organization that has been a leader in the assessment of ecosystems in North America.

The development of gap analysis as a technique for locating areas of rich biological diversity has coincided with increased concern about rapidly dwindling tropical ecosystems. Biologists and policy-makers working in the tropics have been quick to use gap-analysis approaches to try to find and save the richest examples of those ecosystems. Scott came up against endangered-species bias when he began looking for funding to start doing some gap analysis of North American ecosystems. "I got no buyers for two years," he says. He kept hearing, " 'Come back in twenty-five years and we'll talk to you. Right now we're up to our eyeballs in endangered species.' But look, I said, this is the way to get around it." Scott and his colleagues, funded by the Idaho Department of Fish and Game, the U.S. Fish and Wildlife Service, and the National Fish and Wildlife Foundation, have completed a gap analysis for Idaho. "The same sorts of patterns we were finding in Hawaii hold true for Idaho," Scott says. "Even with a state that has more than fifty percent federal landownership, we're still finding large numbers of natural vegetation types that are completely outside natural preserve areas." Gap analysis is also in progress or about to begin in seventeen other states.

Analyzing the gaps in protected biological diversity across North America will be merely a stimulating computer game for a handful of biologists and geographers unless the new method is applied to rethinking and rearranging land use on the continent. "What I envision," Scott says, "is making this information available to people who are in a position to make management decisions—federal landowners, for instance, who can see their property plays a role in the protection of biological diversity, where a shift in land management could afford more protection to an area of high species richness or to a vegetation type that is unprotected in other areas. That requires no expenditures of dollars. That's simply a shift in management."

Scott believes that gap analysis can steer bureaucracies toward buying unprotected areas that are rich in species —and away from ecosystems that, however beautiful to behold, are already adequately protected. Gap analysis promotes the greatest biodiversity at the least cost to the taxpayer. By also identifying areas of potential conflict (areas where oil exploration is occurring, for example), gap analysis allows buyers to find the species-rich land least encumbered by controversy. Gap analysis locates lands owned by willing sellers, not by parties who are intractable and litigious—and this is its strongest virtue.

Perhaps Michael Scott has impossibly lofty goals for gap analysis; perhaps he is simply tired of the good fight; perhaps the evolved policies of the Endangered Species Act are the best we can hope for in an imperfect world. But when I think of biologists frantically building nest holes for red-cockaded woodpeckers, or keeping vigil under the last few Puerto Rican parrot nests in the wild, or watching black-footed ferrets die of canine distemper, or abandoning their efforts to establish another flock of whooping cranes at Gays Lake, Idaho, or pitching cowbirds out of the nests of Kirtland's warblers year in and year out, I no longer call to mind the words of Aldo Leopold or Henry David Thoreau or John Muir or any of the Native American chiefs who spoke so eloquently long ago about the sacredness of the earth and mankind's debt to the beasts. Instead, I think of Hampton Carson, a geneticist and an authority on endangered Hawaiian flora and fauna, who once wrote, "Nature is a better stockkeeper than we are."

POSTSCRIPT

Should the Endangered Species Act Be Reauthorized?

The Endangered Species Coalition points out that the act is flexible and that economic consequences are considered in deciding how to respond to the listing of a species as threatened or endangered. This is certainly not the impression conveyed to the public by the rhetoric of the reelection campaign of George Bush and Dan Quayle, who portrayed those who were concerned about saving the northern spotted owl as advocating measures that would devastate the timber industry. Winckler agrees with the goal of reducing the rate of species extinctions but she claims that the act is failing to do this. (The coalition disputes this claim.) Her preferred strategy would require the identification of those ecosystems that are the habitats for the maximum number and diversity of species. Even if her claim is true that the technique of gap analysis provides an objective means of accomplishing this complex task, it is not clear that the result will be the identification of a sufficient number of "species-rich land(s) least encumbered by controversy." The history of environmental regulation suggests that a more complex strategy, such as that proposed by Winckler, is less likely to be successfully implemented than the present, more straightforward focus on saving specific, identified, endangered species.

In a recent ruling, a Federal Appeals Court has narrowly interpreted the present Endangered Species Act as not preventing the destruction of the habitat that sustains a species. If this surprising decision is not overturned by the Supreme Court, the effectiveness of the law will be essentially nullified.

In the May 1994 issue of *Outdoor Life*, Michael Hanbach supports the renewal of the Endangered Species Act from the sportsman's perspective and presents an analysis of the present Congressional debate. For additional arguments favoring reauthorization see "A Tough Law to Solve Tough Problems," by Frances Hunt and William Robert Irvin, *Journal of Forestry* (August 1992); "How Much Is a Species Worth?" by Jerry Adler and Mary Hager, *National Wildlife* (April/May 1992); "Saving the Endangered Species Act," by Linda Rancourt, *National Parks* (March/April 1992); "The Endangered Species Act: Too Tough, Too Weak, or Too Late?" by Tom Horton, *Audubon* (March/April 1992); and "Making Room in the Ark," by John Volkman, *Environment* (May 1992). Arguing that the act is economically too costly are John Heissenbuttel and William Murray in "A Troubled Law in Need of Revision," *Journal of Forestry* (August 1992).

ISSUE 4

Does the Analysis of Existing Data Support Demands for Environmental Justice?

YES: Robert D. Bullard, from "Grassroots Flowering: The Environmental Justice Movement Comes of Age," *The Amicus Journal* (Spring 1994)

NO: Michael Greenberg, from "Proving Environmental Inequity in Siting Locally Unwanted Land Uses," *Risk: Issues in Health and Safety* (Summer 1993)

ISSUE SUMMARY

YES: Sociology professor and environmental justice movement theorist Robert D. Bullard argues that the principles formulated by the grassroots activists who support the growing movement are founded on conclusive evidence.

NO: Urban studies and community health professor Michael Greenberg proposes that charges of environmental racism need to be supported by better defined criteria and more thorough analyses.

The environmental movement has often been described as reflecting the idealist aspirations of white middle- and upper-income people. Indeed, poor people and minority groups were not well represented among those who gathered for the teach-ins and other events organized to celebrate the first Earth Day in April 1970. The planners and leaders of that event were all white and relatively affluent. The speeches they made and the goals they set took little note of the special needs of the poor or of the possible relationship between racial oppression and the burdens of pollution. Only later did some of the growing environmental organizations even begin to discuss the need to reach out in their organizing efforts to low-income communities and ethnic minority neighborhoods.

The dearth of African Americans, Native Americans, Hispanics and poor white people among the early environmental activists was passed off as a reflection of the pressing need such people felt to pay attention more "basic" social concerns such as hunger, homelessness, and safety.

Until very recently, little media attention has been given to publicizing the fact that, after a slow start, the involvement of poor and minority people in grassroots environmental organizing has been growing dramatically for more than a decade. Triggered in 1982 by demonstrations to protest the decision to locate a poorly planned PCB disposal site adjacent to impoverished African American and Native American communities in Warren County, North Carolina, the movement for environmental justice has grown to encompass local, regional, and national groups organized to protest what they claim is systematic discrimination in the setting of environmental goals and the siting of polluting industries and waste disposal facilities in their backyards.

Recognition of the demands of this movement by mainstream environmental organizations and government officials has been slow in coming. It was not until 1990 that the United States Environmental Protection Agency (USEPA) issued a report, "Environmental Equity: Reducing Risks for All Communities," which acknowledged the need to pay attention to many of the concerns being raised by environmental justice activists. In that same year leaders of the Southwest Organizing Project sent a letter demanding a dialogue with U.S. environmental organizations in which they charged that, "Your organizations continue to support and promote policies that emphasize the cleanup and preservation of the environment on the backs of working people in general and people of color in particular." At the 1992 United Nations Earth Summit in Rio de Janeiro, a set of "Principles of Environmental Justice" was widely circulated and discussed. In 1993 the USEPA opened an Office of Environmental Equity with plans for cleaning up sites in several poor communities. On February 11, 1994, President Clinton made the cause of environmental equity a national priority by issuing a sweeping Executive Order on Environmental Justice.

As might be expected the environmental justice movement has given rise to several controversies. Critics of the charges of environmental racism claim that inequities in the siting of sources of pollution are simply the result of market forces that make the poor neighborhoods where minorities live the economically logical choice for the location of such facilities. Others claim that apparent inequities result because once these facilities are built, they depress real estate values, turning the neighborhoods into poor and minority communities. A more fundamental concern is whether simplistic efforts to combat environmental racism will simply shift pollution to poor white neighborhoods.

Sociology professor Robert D. Bullard has emerged as one of the most influential leaders of the movement. He believes that existing studies adequately justify the charges of environmental injustice and racism that motivate the increasingly powerful grassroots organization he describes in his essay. While not denying the likely existence of environmental inequity, Professor Michael Greenberg, an environmental policy researcher, argues that more carefully designed studies are needed to justify the economic impacts that will result if specific charges of environmental racism due to the siting of locally unwanted land uses (LULUs) are taken on face value.

YES

Robert D. Bullard

GRASSROOTS FLOWERING: THE ENVIRONMENTAL JUSTICE MOVEMENT COMES OF AGE

The year is 1967. The place is Houston. And the issue, though it does not yet go by this name, is environmental justice. Two student groups join forces to demonstrate against the treatment of the city's African American citizens; one is protesting discriminatory discipline at a junior high school, the other the siting of a city-owned garbage dump in a mostly African American community—a dump where an eight-year-old girl has fallen and drowned. The days of demonstrations that follow, culminating in a violent confrontation with Houston police and the arrest of several hundred students, are the first protests on record against environmental racism.

The environmental theme was to sound repeatedly in civil rights struggles long before environmental justice emerged as a movement unto itself. Indeed, it was a garbage strike that brought Martin Luther King, Jr., to Memphis in 1968, where he was assassinated. King's mission was to assist garbage workers protesting their unequal pay and unsafe working conditions.

Another landmark garbage dispute took place in 1979, when a middle-income Houston neighborhood brought the first lawsuit challenging discriminatory waste facility siting under the 1964 civil rights laws. The neighborhood had been selected for a municipal solid waste landfill, and the young African American attorney who filed the lawsuit (my wife, Linda McKeever Bullard) argued that "the placement of the landfill in the black community is a classic case of institutional racism ... and the last time I checked, racial discrimination is illegal." Though her clients did not succeed in stopping the landfill, they did convince the city council to adopt an ordinance restricting the location of waste facilities—no small feat in a city that still boasts of its status as "the only major U.S. city without zoning."

* * *

But it was in 1982, in the rural, mostly African American Warren County of North Carolina, that environmental justice took root, earned a name, and was transformed from a local issue into a nationwide movement. The spark was the selection of Warren County as the disposal site for PCB-tainted soil from fourteen other North Carolina counties. Over 500 demonstrators were arrested, including such national figures as District of Columbia Delegate Walter Fauntroy, chairman of the Congressional Black Caucus at the time; Reverend Benjamin F. Chavis, Jr., then of the United Church of Christ (UCC) Commission for Racial Justice (and currently director of the NAACP); and Reverend Joseph Lowery, head of the Southern Christian Leadership Conference.

The demonstrators were the first Americans jailed for protesting the siting of a waste facility. They did not succeed in blocking the landfill, but they drew national attention to inequities in siting and galvanized African American church leaders, civil rights organizers, and grassroots activists around environmental issues. And in the process, they put the term "environmental racism" on the map. Reverend Chavis defined environmental racism as "racial discrimination in environmental policymaking, enforcement of regulations and laws, and targeting of communities of color for toxic waste disposal and siting of polluting industries."

Moreover, the episode gave rise to two of the foundation documents of the environmental justice movement. The Warren County protesters prompted Delegate Fauntroy to request an investigation by the U.S. General Accounting Office of hazardous waste facility siting in eight southern states. The report, released in 1983, revealed that although African Americans made up only a fifth of the population in the region, three-fourths of the hazardous waste landfills were sited in predominantly African American communities. The other report was *Toxic Wastes and Race*, probably the single most influential document of the early environmental justice movement. This statistical study, released in 1987 by the Commission for Racial Justice, demonstrated that race is a stronger factor than class in predicting the location of toxic waste sites.

By the end of the decade, environmental justice struggles were going on all over the South. In the book *Dumping in Dixie* (1990), I examined five local disputes, in states from Texas to West Virginia, as case studies of the tactics and thinking of communities of color addressing environmental causes. The grass-roots leaders in these communities conclusively dispelled the myth that African Americans are not concerned about or involved in environmental issues.

* * *

In the few years since, the environmental justice movement has made a difference in the lives of people from West Harlem to East Los Angeles. The 1990s have seen grass roots organizing win a community buy-out of the contaminated Carver Terrace neighborhood in Texarkana, Texas, and the shutdown of a hazardous waste incinerator in Chicago's Southside. Sioux activists defeated a 6,000-acre landfill slated for the Rosebud reservation in South Dakota (a proposal dubbed "Dances with Garbage"). Activists have defeated a Formosa Plastics plant proposed for Wallace, Louisiana, hazardous waste incinerators in East Los Angeles and Kettleman City, California, and a hazardous waste landfill in Noxubee County, Mississippi.

Often, work at the grassroots level has had impacts beyond the local community. For example, in a precedent-setting lawsuit, NRDC, the NAACP Legal Defense and Educational Fund, the American Civil Liberties Union, and Alameda County Legal Aid sued California for not living up to federally mandated rules on testing children receiving Medicaid for lead. The 1991 out-of-court settlement resulted in a $10–15 million lead screening program for over 557,000 California children.

* * *

After dozens of such success stories, the environmental justice movement is no longer "just" a grassroots movement, but a grassroots movement that is a powerful national force. Its national role was cemented in October 1991 with the convening of the First National People of Color Environmental Leadership Summit—probably the single most important environmental justice event of the early 1990s. The Summit was attended by over 650 grassroots and national leaders, including delegates from all fifty states, Puerto Rico, Chile, Mexico, and the Marshall Islands. It broadened the focus of the movement beyond anti-toxics campaigns, and demonstrated that it is possible to build a multi-issue, multi-racial, and multi-regional grassroots movement around environmental justice.

In the wake of the summit, grassroots environmental justice groups have become the fastest growing segment of the environmental movement. Frontline leaders have taken the initiative in building regional networks, following the example of the Southwest Network for Environmental and Economic Justice (SNEEJ). SNEEJ has been meeting since 1990, and its goal, according to co-chair Richard Moore, is to build not just a network but "a net that works." SNEEJ's

multi-issue, multi-ethnic, and multi-state association embraces six western states and several Native American nations. More recently, its reach has become international, with the integration of U.S.–Mexico border issues into its organizing and education strategy; this past August, SNEEJ convened its annual gathering in San Diego, California, and Tijuana, Mexico.

In the spirit of the "net that works," the Southern Organizing Committee for Economic and Social Justice in December 1992 held a regional labor and environment conference at Xavier University in New Orleans—the first follow-up gathering to the summit. It attracted over 2,500 participants, including over 500 youth. Other networks are in various stages of formation. The Indigenous Environmental Network was formed in 1992 and the Asian Pacific Environmental Network in 1993. The Northeast, Northwest, and Midwest regions have convened organizational meetings and are exploring region-wide gatherings in 1994.

* * *

As the movement mushrooms, its influence on others is growing. Charles Lee, director of research at the UCC Commission for Racial Justice, has commented that the 1991 Summit "put to rest forever any notion that people of color were not already providing significant leadership on environmental issues." Indeed, the U.S. environmental justice movement had a significant impact at the United Nation's international conference on the environment at Rio de Janeiro in 1992, where the "Principles of Environmental Justice" adopted at the 1991 People of Color Summit were circulated and used by nongovernmental organizations.

At home, the environmental justice movement has broadened the very definition of environmentalism. Partly as a result of the movement's work, the public's concept of "the environment" now includes endangered urban habitats, childhood lead poisoning, energy and transportation, facility siting, equal protection, and a host of other issues related to where people live, work, and play.

Correspondingly, grassroots environmental struggles have gained the support of a broad cross-section of groups that have not always worked on environmental issues, including civil rights, labor, and public health organizations. And environmental justice has now entered the vocabulary of some industry officials. During the November hearing of the congressional Transportation and Hazardous Materials Subcommittee, representatives from Waste Management, Inc. and the National Association of Manufacturers joined the chorus of grass-roots community groups and African American leaders espousing the importance of environmental justice.

As for the national environmental and conservation groups, the environmental justice message now reverberates through many of them. Some national groups have begun to diversify their staffs and boards and incorporate environmental justice into their missions. Dana Alston, a longtime environmental justice activist currently with the Public Welfare Foundation, maintains that environmental justice leaders have provided the vision for the larger movement. For Alston, the "vision of the environment is woven into an overall framework of social, racial, and economic justice."

*   *   *

Environmental justice has also "trickled up" from the grassroots to influence the national political leadership—so much so that it is becoming a significant political force in state and federal government. Arkansas and Louisiana have already passed environmental justice laws. Five other states have legislation pending to address environmental disparities. And a half-dozen bills have been introduced in Congress. Among the measures proposed are a national program to identify the top hundred "environmental high-impact areas" needing remediation, a prohibition on siting new waste facilities in environmentally disadvantaged communities, and a ban on exporting wastes to developing countries. One bill, introduced by Senator Paul Wellstone (D-Minnesota), uses the language in Title VI of the Civil Rights Act of 1964 to require that any federally financed program involving toxic chemicals and the public health be conducted in a non-discriminatory fashion.

The trickle-up effect can also be seen in the executive branch. It started in 1991, under Environmental Protection Agency (EPA) administrator William Reilly. Reilly met with an ad hoc group of environmental justice leaders on a quarterly basis, created an Office of Environmental Equity, and took the lead in working with other federal public health agencies to identify key research needs. With the coming of the Clinton administration, environmental justice activists mobilized their forces to build on this long-overdue progress. Activists assisted in preparing a briefing book for newly designated EPA administrator Carol Browner, and Benjamin Chavis and I served on the administration's transition team. Deeohn Ferris of the Lawyers' Committee for Civil Rights took the lead in drafting an Environmental Justice Transition Paper for the administration, shaped in part through the direct input of hundreds of grassroots groups.

There were immediate results in the rhetoric of the new administration. In April, Carol Browner named environmental justice as one of the four top priorities of her agency, and Vice President Al Gore has stressed the "crisis" of environmental inequity in a number of speeches. And, while the first year of the administration was not a bumper year for environmental justice initiatives, there were some tangible products. For the first time in EPA's history, its Office of Civil Rights began investigating charges of environmental discrimination under Title VI of the Civil Rights Act of 1964. Several studies of hazardous waste and demographics were initiated. The Department of Justice began formulating a plan for increased enforcement of environmental laws in minority communities.

Moreover, in 1993 the U.S. Civil Rights Commission at last added an environmental side to its long history of addressing discrimination in education and employment. It weighed in on the debate over "Cancer Alley," the petrochemical corridor in Louisiana, with a report confirming what most residents of the area already knew: that African American communities in Cancer Alley "are disproportionately impacted by the present State and local government systems for permitting and expansion of hazardous waste and chemical facilities."

* * *

Perhaps most significantly, on February 11 President Clinton signed an Executive Order on Environmental Justice—a sug-

gestion put forward in the Environmental Justice Transition Paper. The Order offers guidance to all federal agencies in addressing environmental justice through Title VI (which prohibits use of federal funds in ways that have racially discriminatory effect) and through the National Environmental Policy Act.

Environmental justice activists hardly expect the Executive Order to be a silver bullet that will fix the problems of environmental racism and unequal protection overnight. Nevertheless, the Order is important because it is a concrete sign that the administration has heard what many activists have been saying all along: environmental justice must become a priority at the highest levels of government. Moreover, the Order could serve as an opening for activists to work directly with federal agencies in shaping their policies. The agencies have one year to develop implementation plans for the Order. To be effective, these plans must be developed in consultation with the environmental justice groups that served as the catalysts for getting this issue on the agenda. The environmental justice community needs to become a partner— not a junior or silent partner, but a full partner—in the process.

Some of the groundwork for such a partnership was laid at a February symposium on environmental justice and health research needs, which was co-sponsored by half-a-dozen federal agencies; grassroots, civil rights, and environmental justice leaders; and health professionals, research scientists, and academics. As a joint effort between federal agencies and activists, the symposium is something of a landmark. Charles Lee believes that it represented a turning point in the quest for "an open process that allows the victims of toxic contamination to function with integrity in planning and decision-making."

If Lee is right, then the symposium and the Executive Order point to a future in which environmental justice activists and environmentally burdened communities will be increasingly potent forces influencing federal policy. But endangered communities are not waiting for the government or the polluting industries to get their acts together. Hazel Johnson, of Chicago's Southside, observes, "It seems like our own government, which is supposed to represent the people's interests, represents the polluters—who usually do not comply with laws that regulate them." Johnson and many others are already on the front lines, working for vigorous enforcement of existing environmental, public health, housing, and civil rights laws where they live. Their grassroots activism gave birth to the environmental justice movement, and it will be the movement's core and its strength in the future.

NO

Michael Greenberg

PROVING ENVIRONMENTAL INEQUITY IN SITING LOCALLY UNWANTED LAND USES

INTRODUCTION

Hazardous waste management facilities, airports, prisons, and other locally unwanted land uses (LULUs) cause tension and political conflict. For example, hazardous waste management facilities, argue recent reports, have been deliberately sited in poor and minority neighborhoods already suffering from political, economic and social inequities. Government, industry, and even national environmental groups have been charged with "toxic racism" and "environmental racism" for causing or ignoring the problem.

Hazardous waste management facilities appear to be disproportionately located in poor and in African- and Hispanic-American communities. But are municipal landfills, electricity generating facilities, solid waste transfer stations, airports, sewage plants, highways, maximum security prisons, drug halfway houses, housing projects, hospices for people with AIDS, garbage incinerators, and other LULUs also disproportionately located in minority and poor communities? It is tempting to answer "yes," a temptation prevalent at conferences and sometimes in print. Yet, the stigma of being branded a racist organization is so odious that the accusation demands proof.

Proof begins with a definition of inequity and a formal process to test for it. This paper proposes a definition of inequity; offers a five-step process to measure it; compares the choices made in two of the best known inequity studies to those made in the five-step process; and illustrates the application of the process with national and state case studies of a particular LULU —waste-to-energy facilities. The discussion addresses some of the difficult issues that should be resolved by a representative panel.

DEFINITION AND PROCESS TO EVALUATE INEQUITY

Equity means different things to different people. To some, equity focuses on outcome. The guiding principle is that the spatial-temporal distribution of

From Michael Greenberg, "Proving Environmental Inequity in Siting Locally Unwanted Land Uses," *Risk: Issues in Health and Safety*, vol. 235 (Summer 1993). Copyright © 1993 by The Franklin Pierce Law Center. Reprinted by permission. Notes omitted.

benefits and burdens should be balanced; i.e., those who generate the need for the LULU should suffer the burden, not future generations or existing populations that gain relatively little from it. Consequently, if a disproportionate number of LULUs are found in disadvantaged communities, then inequity exists, i.e., correlation of LULUs and disadvantaged populations is sufficient to declare outcome inequity; deliberate intent (cause-and-effect) to site in areas populated by disadvantaged persons need not be proven.

A second definition focuses on process. If appropriate environmental, health, physical, legal, economic, and political criteria are applied to every area, then the results are fair even if they disproportionately burden some groups and benefit others. In other words, process inequity means that normal facility-siting criteria were deliberately ignored to locate LULUs in disadvantaged communities.

It is not the purpose of this study to choose between process and outcome inequity. Both are important. I focus on outcome because much has been written about it and little done to define criteria for analyzing it. I describe a five-step process to test for outcome inequity.

(1) Who Are the Populations to Be Studied?
A consensual list of disadvantaged populations, e.g., African-, Hispanic- and Native-American; poor; young and old; infirm and future generations, is needed. Without it, interest groups have focused on racial, ethnic and income inequities. But there is good reason to be concerned about the very young and old, more vulnerable to environmental hazards because of immunological deficiencies, and those who are pregnant or have pre-existing health problems.

(2) What Are the LULUs to Be Assessed? What Subset of Each LULU Is Most Indicative of Outcome Inequity?
No definitive list of LULUs (e.g., nuclear generating stations, high and low-level nuclear waste sites, hazardous waste sites, landfills, etc.) exists, nor an index that compares them. Within any single type of land use category, a distinction can be made between larger, newer facilities located adjacent to areas with more population and smaller, older ones in areas with few inhabitants. This distinction is that old facilities may have been built before the existence of evidence that they may affect public health, environment, and community. Or they may have been built as pilot plants. The same rationalization cannot be made for large LULUs constructed or planned for population centers during the last fifteen years. Someone in the siting process should have been thinking about local concerns. Thus, greater inequity in newer and larger LULUs is implicit evidence of conscious recent efforts to target areas occupied by powerless people.

(3) What Are the Burdens to Be Studied?
Science measures burden by doing risk assessments and environmental and socioeconomic impact statements. But these exist *only for some LULUs* at some locations. Thus, researchers have assumed that when outcome inequity exists, the community is disproportionately or potentially burdened by health effects, environmental contamination, property devaluation, and social and political stresses.

(4) What Are the Geographical Areas to Be Compared?
Typically, researchers use census blocks, census tracts, zip code areas, special

districts, cities, boroughs, towns, and counties as burdened areas and states or the U.S. as a whole as benefit areas. The choices can make an enormous difference. The area that most benefits should be compared to the area that bears the brunt of the fiscal, social, economic and environmental costs associated with the LULU.

(5) What Are the Statistical Methods to Be Used in Evaluation?

Ideally the location history of each LULU should be studied and a mathematical model constructed to capture that history. Lacking detailed histories and data, researchers have tended to compare the arithmetic means of benefit and burden areas.

Different statistics can lead to different conclusions about equity. In order to avoid unsubstantiated accusations, inequity should be demonstrated with at least two different types of statistics, at least one of which should be parametric (e.g., arithmetic mean) and one nonparametric (e.g., comparison of proportions).

TWO EXAMPLES FROM THE LITERATURE

The typical inequity report is about a disadvantaged minority neighborhood or city, or is a historical analysis of zoning, land use, and legal cases. The reports are hypothesis-generators and provide insights about process inequity. However, few studies are useful to examine outcome inequity.

PLAYING WITH FIRE and TOXIC WASTE AND RACE IN THE U.S. are exceptions. The first compared average proportion of white residents, home owners, and the average income, home value, and rent of zip codes hosting 16 ex-

isting commercial hazardous waste incinerators and 24 proposed incinerators with the U.S. average values. The authors found average percent of minority population in zip code areas with facilities was 89% higher than the U.S.; and average income was 15% lower.

The analysts distinguished between existing and proposed commercial hazardous waste facilities. In other words, they explicitly made choices about which LULUs to compare (choice 2 of five). However, no other choice was explicit. There was no discussion of the elderly, young or other populations at risk (choice 1); no discussion of why the U.S. was the area of benefit (choice 4); and no discussion of alternative statistical methods (choice 5).

Using their raw data, I calculated 95% confidence limits for the nonwhite and income variables. These exceeded national averages, i.e., we cannot reject the null hypothesis at $p < 0.05$ that their values for zip code areas with commercial hazardous waste facilities are the same as those for the U.S. average as a whole.

Benjamin Goldman, the analyst for TOXIC WASTE AND RACE IN THE U.S., has been the most explicit about the five choices. With respect to types of LULUs (choice 2), he compared four sets of zip code areas: (1) without an operating commercial hazardous waste treatment, storage, and disposal facility; (2) with one facility, but no landfill; (3) with one landfill that is not among the five largest in the U.S.; and (4) with one of the five largest landfills or with one more treatment, storage, and disposal facility. In addition to comparing the four groups, tests were made with only the largest capacity facilities.

With respect to geographical areas to compare (choice 4), Goldman used zip codes hosting hazardous waste facilities as the burdened areas. Recognizing the limitation of using a single area of benefit, he compared the zip code areas to the U.S. as a whole, the zip code areas within each of the ten U.S. Environmental Protection Agency (EPA) regions; and zip code areas within each of 43 states with sufficient data.

Five statistical methods were tried (choice 5). Difference-of-mean tests, matched-pair t-tests, and non-parametric versions of these tests were used to explore differences between each of the four groups of zip code areas described above. The matched-pair tests were particularly important. Each zip code with commercial hazardous waste management facilities was compared to the parts of the surrounding county without commercial facilities to control for local variations in market conditions and socioeconomic status. Discriminant analysis was used to identify variables best able to explain differences between the four mutually exclusive sets of zip code areas.

The only obvious limitation of this study was the choice of test populations. Goldman used percent minority, mean household income, mean housing value and indicators of hazardous waste production as the test populations (choice 1). The data base included elderly and young populations. But they were not tested for inequity.

The choice 1 decision had a marked impact on the perception of this most widely sited study. The national and regional discriminant analysis test results showed percent nonwhite to be frequently a significant discriminator with p ranging from <.01 to .20.

Mean family income was a much less powerful indicator. Yet, mean family income was a more powerful variable in the matched-pair tests. For example, percent minority was statistically significant in 5 in the 10 EPA regions and 5 of the 43 state comparisons. But the comparable results for mean income were 8 of 10 EPA regions and 10 of 43 states.

In short, Goldman's study made a series of carefully reasoned choices about types of LULUs, geographical areas and statistical methods. Yet, the limited choice of test populations when combined with the lack of emphasis on the matched-pair analyses in the final report has resulted in this report being cited as the strongest evidence of outcome inequity to African- and Hispanic-Americans. There clearly is outcome inequity for nonwhites, but there may even be greater outcome inequity for other populations that were not tested....

DISCUSSION

Because "environmental racism" and similar slogans can lead to serious political and economic impacts for owners and operators, I urge the U.S. government to ask an organization with high credibility and objectivity to conduct a policy analysis of environmental inequity based upon an agreed upon protocol devised by representatives of government, industry, advocate groups and university scientists.

EPA has unilaterally begun an effort. In response to sports and charges of environmental racism, Administrator William Reilly stated that "talk of environmental racism at EPA and charges that the agency's efforts pay less regard to the environments of poor people infuriate me. I am determined to get to the bottom of these charges to refute or respond to them." He appointed an Environmental Equity Working Group of 40 EPA professionals to consider the evidence and recommend a response. Among the recommendations of the group were to increase the priority given to environmental equity issues, establish and maintain a data base by income and race, and develop a research plan.

While I applaud EPA's initiatives, I do not believe that an internal working group of one agency can do a comprehensive analysis that will be recognized by all the stakeholders. At a minimum, I recommend that representatives of Housing and Urban Development, the Department of Justice, state and local governments, labor unions, as well as EPA be included. Furthermore, the interests of racial/ethnic minorities, labor unions, the impaired, the elderly, children and global environment groups must all be represented in a consensus on a set of principles for assessing process and outcome inequity. A government-wide commission is probably necessary.

To fairly assess process equity requires a protocol that can evaluate the inequity of commonly used siting processes. It also requires principles that can suggest the rights and responsibilities of different government, corporate, and private organizations, as well as individuals in siting and managing LULUs. A good deal of interesting academic and practical work has already been done on process equity. In comparison, little empirical work has been done on a protocol for outcome inequity. Each of the steps defined above raises issues that should be considered. For example, with respect to Step 1 (choice of populations to study), a list of disadvantaged populations is needed. African- Hispanic-, Native- and poor Americans seem to be the focus of attention. The young and elderly should also be included.

But should recent immigrant groups also be included? Or must they also be poor? In addition, consideration should be given to future generations. But how should future generations be represented? One way is by including aquifers and forest areas, salt-water swamps, and endangered species, all of which may be extremely important to future generations, as well as those already living.

With respect to Step 2, a panel needs to provide a prioritized list of LULUs to evaluate. Steps 2 and 3 (list of burdens) need to be considered simultaneously. Health risk is the most obvious way to rank them. But environmental risk should be considered. Also, economic impact, social and political implications cannot be neglected because they affect public perceptions. Selection of burdens to evaluate influences choice of LULUs to evaluate.

At a minimum, the closest approximation to neighborhood (zip code, census blocks or tracts) and municipality should be used as areas of potential burden (Step 4). Careful consideration needs to be given to a method of defining primary and secondary areas of benefit for each type of LULU and a way of weighting these areas in an overall aggregate analysis.

It is inevitable that landfills, power plants and other types of LULU will burden someone. The burden becomes inequitable when a specific type of LULU consistently burdens many powerless populations. Having chosen populations to be tested, LULUs to be examined, burdens to be studied, and areas of burden and benefit it remains to select methods for testing the hypothesis that outcome inequity exists (Step 5). This paper has demonstrated that one parametric and one nonparametric method should be used at a minimum. But more are doubtlessly needed, including perhaps a multivariate statistical model that can control for the reality that variables, such as poverty, race, and age are frequently related.

Finally, we need a protocol that covers adequate reporting of results. Does adequate reporting include formally stated hypotheses and null hypotheses, and require pre-selected levels of statistical significance? What should be the requirements for reporting data quality and limitations? Should researchers be required to state the power of the statistical tests to detect false results, especially false negatives? Most important, what should be the responsibilities to report both findings of equity and inequity for each type of LULU?

It is not my goal to state how existing inequities should be addressed, nor which should be given priority. Rather, my goal is to suggest that we can only avoid unfair branding of owners and operators of LULUs by arriving at consensual principles of outcome and process inequity and protocols for fairly testing for them. I hope the five steps presented and illustrated here engage others who will join in searching for a scientifically sound and fair process of resolving conflicting interests in the location of LULUs.

POSTSCRIPT

Does the Analysis of Existing Data Support Demands for Environmental Justice?

Greenberg proposes that a carefully constructed set of definitions and statistical criteria, agreed upon by representatives of many different interest groups, be employed by an objective organization to test the validity of serious charges of environmental inequity and racism. This may seem like a reasonable course of action to an academic social scientist, but it seems highly unlikely that grassroots activists would accept the proposition that they should put their demands on hold until this idealistic proposal is realized. Greenberg appears to acknowledge inequity in the siting of at least one LULU—hazardous waste management facilities. (In August 1994 the Commission for Racial Justice of the United Church of Christ published an update of the 1987 study cited by Greenberg that presents evidence that the percentage of minority group members living near hazardous waste facilities continues to grow.) It may be that inappropriate generalizations to other LULUs and other types of inequity are being made. But in the real sociopolitical world such generalizations are to be expected, and the standards of proof that Greenberg proposes are rarely, if ever, realized. It seems likely that the Environmental Protection Agency (EPA) and other federal agencies will choose to move ahead with actions designed to respond to both perceived as well as proven problems raised by environmental justice activists who have now been empowered by a presidential order. Perhaps more important than demanding validation of all of the charges are efforts designed to ensure that actions taken in the name of environmental equity do not result in shifting the burdens of pollution, resulting from the use of inappropriate technology, from one population group to another.

A student of the environmental justice movement would do well to begin by reading some of the many other articles and books written or edited by Robert D. Bullard. His most recent book is *Unequal Protection: Environmental Justice and Communities of Color* (Sierra Club Books, 1994). A set of principles for overcoming racism in environmental decision making is the focus of a detailed analysis of the problem in an article by Bullard in the May 1994 issue of *Environment*.

Several books and scores of articles by other authors have been written about this issue during the past decade. One such recent book that examines the growth and political influence of the grassroots movement is *Ecopopulism: Toxic Waste and the Movement for Environmental Justice* by Andrew Szasz (Uni-

82

versity of Minnesota Press, 1994). The entire March/April 1992 issue of the *EPA Journal* was devoted to the environmental equity issue, and it contains articles by agency officials, movement activists, politicians, and environmental journalists on many aspects of the controversy. The EPA's 1992 report, *Environmental Equity*, is reviewed by Julie A. Roque in the June 1993 issue of *Environment*. A roundtable debate on environmental racism was featured in the May/June 1993 issue of *Sierra*. For an examination of the link between ecology and social justice from a class analysis perspective see Michael Heiman's lead article in the Summer 1988 issue of *The Egg*. In her article in the Spring 1994 issue of *Dissent*, Ruth Rosen presents a history of the environmental justice movement that stresses how it has woven together strands of the civil rights and environmental struggles. *Race, Poverty, and the Environment*, published by the San Francisco–based Earth Island Institute, is a journal that covers this issue on a regular basis.

The suggestion that environmental inequity is the result of normal market dynamics rather than racism or discrimination is explored by Robert Braile in the Summer 1994 issue of *Garbage*. Braile cites recent articles by several authors who, like Greenberg, question the data analyses used to support charges of environmental racism.

ISSUE 5

Is Limiting Population Growth a Key Factor in Protecting the Global Environment?

YES: Paul Harrison, from "Sex and the Single Planet: Need, Greed, and Earthly Limits," *The Amicus Journal* (Winter 1994)

NO: Betsy Hartmann, from "Population Fictions: The Malthusians Are Back in Town," *Dollars and Sense* (September/October 1994)

ISSUE SUMMARY

YES: Author and Population Institute medal winner Paul Harrison argues for family planning programs that take into account women's rights and socioeconomic concerns in order to prevent world population from exceeding carrying capacity.

NO: Betsy Hartmann, director of the Hampshire College Population and Development Program, argues that the "real problem is not human *numbers* but undemocratic human *systems* of labor and resource exploitation, often backed by military repression."

The debate about whether human population growth is a fundamental cause of ecological problems and whether population control should be a central strategy in protecting the environment has long historical roots.

Those seriously concerned about uncontrolled human population growth are often referred to as "Malthusians" after the English parson Thomas Malthus, whose "Essay on the Principle of Population" was first published in 1798. Malthus warned that the human race was doomed because geometric population increases would inexorably outstrip productive capacity, leading to famine and poverty. His predictions were undermined by technological improvements in agriculture and the widespread use of birth control (rejected by Malthus on moral grounds), which brought the rate of population growth in industrialized countries under control during the twentieth century.

The theory of the demographic transition was developed to explain why Malthus's dire predictions had not come true. This theory proposes that the first effect of economic development is to lower death rates. This causes a population boom, but stability is again achieved as economic and social changes lead to lower birth rates. This pattern has indeed been followed in Europe, the United States, Canada, and Japan. The less-developed countries of the Third World have more recently experienced rapidly falling death rates. Thus far, the economic and social changes needed to bring down birth rates have not occurred, and many countries in Asia and Latin America suffer from exponential population growth. This fact has given rise to a group of neo-Malthusian theorists who contend that it is unlikely that Third World countries will undergo the transition to lower birth rates required to avoid catastrophe due to overpopulation.

Biologist Paul Ehrlich's best seller *The Population Bomb* (Balantine Books, 1968) popularized his view that population growth in both the developed and developing world must be halted to avert worldwide ecological disaster. Ecologist Garrett Hardin extended the neo-Malthusian argument by proposing that some Third World nations have gone so far down the road of population-induced resource scarcity that they are beyond salvation and should be allowed to perish rather than risk sinking the remaining world economies.

Barry Commoner, an early prominent critic of the neo-Malthusian perspective, argues in *The Closing Circle* (Alfred A. Knopf, 1971) and his subsequent popular books and articles that inappropriate technology is the principal cause of local and global environmental degradation. While not denying that population growth is a contributing factor, he favors promoting ecologically sound development rather than population-control strategies that ignore socioeconomic realities.

Enthusiasts for population control as a sociopolitical and environmental strategy have always been opposed by religious leaders whose creeds reject any overt means of birth control. Recently the traditional population control policy planners have also been confronted with charges of sexism and paternalism by women's groups, minority groups, and representatives of developing nations who argue that the needs and interests of their constituencies have been ignored by the primarily white, male policy planners of the developed world. At the September 1994 World Population Conference in Cairo, organizers and spokespeople for these interests succeeded in promoting policy statements that reflected sensitivity to many of their concerns.

Paul Harrison, who won a Population Institute Global Media award for his book *The Third Revolution* (Penguin Books, 1993), argues that "population growth combined with... consumption and technology damages the environment." He proposes "quality family planning and reproductive health services, mother and child health care, women's rights and women's education" as a four-point program to rapidly decrease population growth. Betsy Hartmann, who directs the Hampshire College Population and Development Program, claims that "the threat to livelihoods, democracy and the environment posed by the fertility of poor women hardly compares to that posed by the consumption patterns of the rich or the ravages of militaries." She proposes greater democratic control over resources rather than narrow population control as an environmental strategy.

YES

Paul Harrison

SEX AND THE SINGLE PLANET:
NEED, GREED, AND EARTHLY LIMITS

Population touches on sex, gender, parenthood, religion, politics—all the deepest aspects of our humanity. Start a debate on the topic, and the temperature quickly warms up. In the preparations for next year's World Population Conference in Cairo, the link between population growth and environmental damage is one of the hottest topics.

The sheer numbers involved today make it hard to ignore the link. The last forty years saw the fastest rise in human numbers in all previous history, from only 2.5 billion people in 1950 to 5.6 billion today. This same period saw natural habitats shrinking and species dying at an accelerating rate. The ozone hole appeared, and the threat of global warming emerged.

Worse is in store. Each year in the 1980s saw an extra 85 million people on earth. The second half of the 1990s will add an additional 94 million people per year. That is equivalent to a new United States every thirty-three months, another Britain every seven months, a Washington every six days. A whole earth of 1800 was added in just one decade, according to United Nations Population Division statistics. After 2000, annual additions will slow, but by 2050 the United Nations expects the human race to total just over 10 billion —an extra earth of 1980 on top of today's, according to U.N. projections.

If population growth does not cause or aggravate environmental problems, as many feminists, socialists, and economists claim, then we do not need to worry about these numbers. If it does, then the problems of the last decade may be only a foretaste of what is to come.

At the local level, links between growing population densities and land degradation are becoming clearer in some cases. Take the case of Madagascar. Madagascar's forests have been reduced to a narrowing strip along the eastern escarpment. Of the original forest cover of 27.6 million acres, only 18.8 million acres remained in 1950. Today this has been halved to 9.4 million acres—which means that habitat for the island's unique wildlife has been halved in just forty years. Every year some 3 percent of the remaining forest is cleared, almost all of that to provide land for populations expanding at 3.2 percent a year.

The story of one village, Ambodiavi-avy, near Ranomafana, shows the process at work. Fifty years ago, the whole area was dense forest. Eight families, thirty-two people in all, came here in 1947, after French colonials burned down their old village. At first they farmed only the valley bottoms, which they easily irrigated from the stream running down from the hilltops. There was no shortage of land. Each family took as much as they were capable of working. During the course of the next forty-three years, the village population swelled ten times over, to 320, and the number of families grew to thirty-six. Natural growth was supplemented by immigration from the overcrowded plateaus, where all cultivable land is occupied. By the 1950s, the valley bottom lands had filled up completely. New couples started to clear forest on the sloping valley sides. They moved gradually up-hill; today, they are two-thirds of the way to the hilltops.

Villager Zafindraibe's small paddy field feeds his family of five for only four months of the year. In 1990 he felled and burned five acres of steep forest land to plant hill rice. The next year cassava would take over. After that the plot should be left fallow for at least six or seven years.

Now population growth is forcing farmers to cut back the fallow cycle. As land shortage increases, a growing number of families can no longer afford to leave the hillsides fallow long enough to restore their fertility. They return more and more often. Each year it is cultivated, the hillside plot loses more topsoil, organic matter, nutrients.

* * *

The debate over this link between population growth and the environment has raged back and forth since 1798. In that year Thomas Malthus, in his notorious *Essay on Population*, suggested that population tended to grow faster than the food supply. Human numbers would always be checked by famine and mortality.

Socialists from William Cobbett to Karl Marx attacked Malthus's arguments. U.S. land reformer Henry George, in *Progress and Poverty* (1879), argued that the huge U.S. population growth had surged side by side with huge increases in wealth. Poverty, said George, was caused not by overpopulation, but by warfare and unjust laws. Poverty caused population growth, not the other way around.

In modern times, U.S. ecologist Paul Ehrlich has played the Malthus role. "No geological event in a billion years has posed a threat to terrestrial life comparable to that of human overpopulation," he argued back in 1970, urging compulsion if voluntary methods failed. His early extremism (such as suggesting cutting off aid to certain Third World countries) has mellowed into a more balanced analysis (for example, he acknowledges the need for more than just contraceptives to attack the problem). But doomsday rhetoric remains in his 1990 book, *The Population Explosion*, which predicts "many hundreds of millions" of famine deaths if we do not halt human population growth.

Today's anti-Malthusians come in all shades, from far left to far right. For radical writers Susan George and Frances Moore Lappé, poverty and inequality are the root causes of environmental degradation, not population. For Barry Commoner the chief threat is misguided technology. Economist Julian Simon sees moderate population growth as no problem at all, but as a tonic for economic growth. More people mean more brains to think up more solutions. "There is no meaningful limit to our capacity to keep growing forever," he wrote in 1981 in *The Ultimate Resource.*

Other voices in the debate focus on ethics and human rights. Orthodox Catholics and fundamentalist Muslims oppose artificial contraception or abortion. A wide range of feminists stress women's rights to choose or refuse and downplay the impact of population growth. "Blaming global environmental degradation on population growth," argued the Global Committee on Women, Population and the Environment before Rio, "stimulates an atmosphere of crisis. It helps lay the groundwork for an intensification of top-down population control programs that are deeply disrespectful of women."

There is no debate quite like this one for sound and fury. As the forgoing examples show, positions are emotional and polarized. Factions pick on one or two elements as the basic problem, and ignore all the others. Thinking proceeds in black-and-white slogans.

Often debaters seem to be locked into the single question: Is population growth a crucial factor in environmental degradation—or not? However, if we frame our inquiry in this simplistic way, only two answers are possible—yes or no —and only two conclusions—obsession with family planning, or opposition to family planning. Both of these positions lead to abuse or neglect of women's rights.

There has to be a way out of this blind alley. Perhaps we can make a start by accepting that *all* the factors mentioned by the rival schools are important. All interact to create the damage. Sometimes one factor is dominant, sometimes another. Population is always there. In some fields it plays the lead role, in others no more than a bit part.

Most observers agree that it is not just population growth that damages the environment. The amount each person consumes matters too, and so does the technology used in production and waste disposal. These three factors work inseparably in every type of damage. Each of them is affected by many other factors, from the status of women to the ownership of land, from the level of democracy to the efficiency of the market. If we adopt this complex, nuanced view, much of the crazy controversy evaporates, and the hard work of measuring impact and designing policy begins.

A number of success stories have emerged. One hallmark of these successes is the recognition that population should be an integral part of long-range resource management.

* * *

Take a snapshot at one particular moment, and there is no way of saying which of the three factors carries the main blame for damage. It would be like asking whether brain, bone, or muscle plays the main role in walking. But if we compare changes over time, we can get an idea of their relative strengths. Results vary a lot, depending on which country or which type of damage we are looking at.

In Madagascar, population growth bears the main blame for deforestation and loss of biodiversity. As described before, the island's rain forests have shrunk to a narrow strip. Increased consumption—a rise in living standards —and technology tend to play less and less of a role in this devastation. Incomes and food intake today are lower than thirty years ago. Farming methods have not changed in centuries.

Population growth is running at 3 percent a year. When technology is stagnant, every extra human means less forest and wildlife.

By contrast, population growth played only a minor role in creating the ozone hole. The main blame lay with rising consumption and technology change. Between 1940 and 1980, world chlorofluorocarbon (CFC) emissions grew at more than 15 percent a year. Almost all of this was in developed countries, where population grew at less than 1 percent a year. So population growth accounted for less than 7 percent (one-fifteenth) of increased CFC emissions.

A central issue in the controversy is whether we are on course to pass the earth's carrying capacity—the maximum population that the environment can support indefinitely. Malthusians like Dennis and Donnella Meadows suggest in their book *Beyond the Limits* that we have already passed the limits in some areas such as alteration of the atmosphere. Anti-Malthusians like Julian Simon insist that we can go on raising the limits through technology.

Here, too, a compromise comes closer to reality. Humans *have* raised the ceiling on growth many times in the past. When hunter-gatherers ran short of wild foods, they turned to farming. When western Europeans started to run out of wood in the seventeenth century, they turned to coal. The process continues today. When one resource runs down, its price changes, and we increase productivity or exploration, bring in substitutes, or reduce use. In other words, we do not just stand by and watch helplessly while the world collapses. We respond and adapt. We change our technology, our consumption patterns, even the number of children we have. It is because we can

adapt so fast that we are the dominant species on earth.

So far adaptation has kept us well stocked with minerals despite rising use. It has proved Malthus wrong by raising food production roughly in line with the five-and-a-half-fold growth in population since his time. But it has not worked at all well in maintaining stocks of natural resources like forests, water, sea fish, or biodiversity, nor with preserving the health of sinks for liquid and gaseous wastes such as lakes, oceans, and atmosphere. These are common property resources—no one owns them—so what Garrett Hardin called the "tragedy of the commons" applies. Everyone overuses or abuses the source or sink, fearing that if they hold back others will reap the gains.

Problems like erosion, acid rain, or global warming are not easy to diagnose or cure. Sometimes we do not even know they are happening until they are far advanced, as in the case of the ozone hole. Like cancer, they build up slowly and often pass unseen till things come to a head. Farmers in Burkina Faso did not believe their land was eroding away until someone left a ruler stuck into the soil; then they saw that the level had gone down an inch in a year.

Environmental quality follows a U-shaped curve. Things get worse before they get better, on everything from biodiversity and soil erosion to air and water quality. But everything hinges on how long the downswing lasts—and how serious or irreversible are the problems it gives rise to. Given time we will develop institutions to control overfishing or ocean pollution, stop acid rain or halt global warming. But time is the crux of the matter. Adaptable though we are, we rarely act in time to prevent severe damage. In one area after another, from whales to ozone holes, we have let crises happen before taking action.

Over the next few decades we face the risk of irreversible damage on several fronts. If we lose 10 or 20 percent of species, we may never restore that diversity. If the global climate flips, then all our ability to adapt will not stave off disaster. Rather than wait for global crisis, prudence dictates that we should take action now.

However, the way we look at causes deeply affects the search for solutions. That is why the debate on population and environment matters. If we say that damage results only from technology, only from overconsumption, only from injustice, or only from population, we will act on only one element of the equation. But damage results from population, consumption, and technology multiplied together, so we must act on all three. And we cannot neglect the many factors from inequality to women's rights and free markets that influence all others.

* * *

Consumption will be the hardest nut to crack. Reducing overconsumption may be good for the soul, but the world's poorest billion must *increase* their consumption to escape poverty. The middle 3 billion will not willingly rein in their ambitions. The middle classes in India and China are already launched on the consumer road that Europe took in the 1950s. They are moving faster down that road, and their consumer class probably outnumbers North America's already. Even in the rich countries, consumption goes on growing at roughly 2 percent a year, with hiccups during recession. Consumption can be cut if consumers and producers have to pay

for the damage they do through higher prices or taxes—but, politically, it is not easy. Politicians who threaten to raise taxes risk electoral defeat.

So technological change must reduce the *impact* of consumption. But it will be a Herculean task for technology to do the job alone. The massive oil price rises of 1973 and 1979–80 stimulated big advances in energy efficiency. Between 1973 and 1988 gasoline consumption per mile in western countries fell by 29 percent. But this technology gain was wiped out by a rise in car numbers of 58 percent, due to the combined growth of population and consumption. The result was a rise in gasoline consumption of 17 percent.

Population and consumption will go on raising the hurdles that technology must leap. By 2050, world population will have grown by 80 percent, on the U.N. medium projection. Even at the low 1980s growth rate of 1.2 percent a year, consumption per person will have doubled. Technology would have to cut the damage done by each unit of consumption by 72 percent, just to keep total damage rising at today's destructive rate.

Yet the International Panel on Climate Change says we ought to *cut* carbon dioxide output by 60 percent from today's levels. If incomes and population grow as above, technology would have to cut the emissions for each unit of consumption by a massive 89 percent by 2050. This would require a 3.8 percent reduction every year for fifty-seven years.

Such a cut is not utterly impossible, but it would demand massive commitment on all sides. Introducing the 85 miles-per-gallon car could deliver a cut of almost exactly this size in the transport sector, if it took ten years to go into mass production, and another fifteen years to saturate the market. But the combined growth of population and car ownership could easily halve the gain.

Technology change will have a far easier job if it is backed by action on the population front. Population efforts are slow-acting at first: for the first fifteen years the difference is slight. The U.N.'s low population projection points to what might be achieved if all countries did their best in bringing birth rates down. Yet for 2010, the low projection for world population is only 1.2 percent less than the medium projection. Over the longer term, though, there are big benefits. By 2025 the low projection is 7.3 percent less than the medium—621 million fewer people, or a whole Europe plus Japan. By 2050 the low figure is 22 percent or 2.206 billion people less—equal to the whole world's population around 1930.

With a concerted effort in all countries (including the United States), world population could peak at 8.5 billion or less in 2050 and, after that, come down. And it is clear that this would reduce environmental impact and lower the hurdles that improved technology will have to leap.

What do we need to do to bring it about? Here, too, the debate rages. Diehard Malthusians talk of the need for crash programs of "population control." Horrified feminists answer that a woman's fertility is her own business, not a target for male policy measures. The objective should be reproductive health and choice, not simply bringing numbers down, they argue.

Yet this conflict, too, is an artificial one. The best way to bring numbers down fast is to pump resources not into crash or compulsory programs narrowly focused on family planning, but into broad women's development programs that most feminists would welcome. How do we get enough resources out of male governments to do this properly? Only by using the arguments about environment and economy that feminists do not allow.

Coercion and crash programs defeat their own aims. "Population control" is impossible without killing people: the term implies coercion and should be dropped forthwith. Coercion rouses protests that sooner or later bring it to an end. India's brief and brutal experiment with forced sterilization in 1975–76 led within a year to the fall of Indira Gandhi's government. The progress of family planning in India was set back a decade.

Mass saturation with just one or two family planning methods is equally doomed to failure. With female contraceptives, side-effects are common: women need good advice and medical backup to deal with them or avoid them. Left to handle them alone, they will stop using contraceptives and go on having five children each. Once mistrust has been aroused, it will make the job harder even when better programs are finally brought in.

If we want to bring population growth rates down rapidly, we must learn from the real success stories like Thailand. In the early 1960s, the average Thai woman was having 6.4 children. Today she is having only 2.2. This represents a drop of 3.5 percent per year—as speedy as the fastest change in technology.

Such success was achieved, without a whiff of coercion, by universal access to a wide and free choice of family planning methods, with good-quality advice and medical backup. Mother and child health was improved, women's rights were advanced, and female education leveled up with male.

All these measures are worthwhile in their own right. They improve the quality of life for women and men alike. And there are economic spin-offs. Thai incomes grew at 6 percent a year in the 1980s. A healthy and educated work force attracts foreign investment and can compete in the modern high-tech world.

Quality family planning and reproductive health services, mother and child health, women's rights, and women's education—this four-point program is the best way to achieve a rapid slowdown in population growth. It can improve the quality of life directly, through health and education benefits, and it improves the status of women. It creates a healthy and educated work force. It gives people the knowledge with which they can fight for their own rights. It might also help to raise incomes, and it will certainly help to slow environmental damage.

With its human, economic, and environmental benefits, there are few programs that will offer better value for money over the coming decades.

NO

Betsy Hartmann

POPULATION FICTIONS: THE MALTHUSIANS ARE BACK IN TOWN

In the corridors of power, the tailors are back at work, stitching yet another invisible robe to fool the emperor and the people. After 12 years in which the Reagan and Bush administrations downplayed population control as a major aim of U.S. foreign policy, the Clinton administration is playing catch-up. World attention will focus on the issue this month in Cairo, when leaders from the United States and abroad gather at the United Nations' third International Conference on Population and Development. Cloaked in the rhetoric of environmentalism and—ironically—women's rights, population control is back in vogue.

At the UN's second International Conference on Population in Mexico City in 1984, the Reagan administration asserted that rapid population growth is a "neutral phenomenon" that becomes a problem only when the free market is subverted by "too much governmental control of economies." Under the Republicans, the U.S. withdrew funding from any international family planning agencies that perform abortions or even counsel women about them. Aid was cut off to the International Planned Parenthood Foundation as well as the UN Fund for Population Activities (UNFPA).

The Clinton administration, by contrast, is requesting $585 million for population programs in fiscal year 1995, up from $502 million the year before. This aid is channelled through the U.S. Agency for International Development (USAID), which has made population control a central element of its new "Sustainable Development" mission for the post Cold War era. The USAID's draft strategy paper of October 1993 identifies rapid population growth as a key "strategic threat" which "consumes all other economic gains, drives environmental damage, exacerbates poverty, and impedes "democratic governance."

Clinton's more liberal stand on abortion is certainly welcome, but even that has yet to translate into effective Congressional action or foreign policy. Announced in April, USAID's new policy on abortion funding overseas is still very restrictive: It will finance abortion only in cases of rape, incest, and life endangerment, the same conditions the Hyde amendment puts on federal Medicaid funds. Along with the mainstream environmental movement, the administration pays lip service to women's rights but continues to back practices—such as promoting long-acting contraceptive methods like Norplant without follow-up medical care—that are actually harmful to women's health.

POPULATION MYTHS

It is true that population growth (which is actually slowing in most areas of the world) can put additional pressure on resources in specific regions. But the threat to livelihoods, democracy and the global environment posed by the fertility of poor women is hardly comparable to that posed by the consumption patterns of the rich or the ravages of militaries.

The industrialized nations, home to 22% of the world's population, consume 60% of the world's food, 70% of its energy, 75% of its metals, and 85% of its wood. They generate almost three-quarters of all carbon dioxide emissions, which in turn comprise nearly half of the manmade greenhouse gases in the atmosphere, and are responsible for most of the ozone depletion. Militaries are the other big offenders. The German Research Institute for Peace Policy estimates that one-fifth of all global environmental degradation is due to military activities. The U.S. military is the largest domestic oil consumer and generates more toxic waste than the five largest multinational chemical companies combined.

What about the environmental degradation that occurs within developing countries? The UNFPA's *State of World Population 1992* boldly claims that population growth "is responsible for around 79% of deforestation, 72% of arable land expansion, and 69% of growth in livestock numbers." Elsewhere it maintains that the "bottom billion," the very poorest people in developing countries, "often impose greater environmental injury than the other 3 billion of their citizens put together."

Blaming such a large proportion of environmental degradation on the world's poorest people is untenable, scientifically and ethically. It is no secret that in Latin America the extension of cattle ranching —mainly for export, not domestic consumption—has been the primary impetus behind deforestation. And it is rich people who own the ranches, not the poor, as most countries in Latin America have a highly inequitable distribution of land. In Southeast Asia the main culprit is commercial logging, again mainly for export.

In developing countries, according to USAID, rapid population growth also "renders inadequate or obsolete any investment in schools, housing, food production capacity and infrastructure." But are increasing numbers of poor people really the main drain on national budgets? The UN's 1993 *Human Development Report* estimates that developing countries spend only one-tenth of their national budgets on human development priorities. Their military expenditures meanwhile soared from 91% of combined health and education expenditures in 1977 to 169% in 1990. And in any case, the social spending that there is often flows to the rich. A disproportionate share of health budgets frequently goes to expensive hospital services in urban areas rather than to primary care for the poor, and educational resources are often devoted to schools for the sons and daughters of the wealthy.

The "structural adjustment" programs imposed by the World Bank have not helped matters, forcing Third World countries to slash social spending in order to service external debts. The burden of growing inequality has fallen disproportionately on women, children, and minorities who have borne the brunt of structural adjustment policies in reduced access to food, health care and education. But in USAID's view, population growth is at the root of their misery: "As expanding populations demand an even greater number of jobs, a climate is created where workers, especially women and minorities, are oppressed."

A COSTLY CONSENSUS

In the collective psyche of the national security establishment, population growth is now becoming a great scapegoat and enemy, a substitute for the Evil Empire. A 1992 study by the Carnegie Endowment for International Peace warned that population growth threatens "international stability" and called for "a multilateral effort to drastically expand family planning services." A widely cited February 1993 *Scientific American* article by Thomas Homer-Dixon, Jeffrey Boutwell and George Rathjens identifies rapidly expanding populations as a major factor in growing resource scarcities that are "contributing to violent conflicts in many parts of the developing world."

In the pages of respectable journals, racist metaphors are acceptable again, as the concept of noble savage gives way to post-modern barbarian. In an *Atlantic Monthly* article on the "coming anarchy" caused by population growth and resource depletion, Robert Kaplan likens poor West African children to ants.

Their older brothers and fathers (and poor, nonwhite males in general) are "re-primitivized" men who find liberation in violence, since their natural aggression has not been "tranquilized" by the civilizing influences of the Western Enlightenment and middle-class existence.

The scaremongering of security analysts is complemented by the population propaganda of mainstream environmental organizations. U.S. environmentalism has long had a strong neo-Malthusian wing which views Man as the inevitable enemy of Nature. The Sierra Club backed Stanford biologist Paul Ehrlich's 1968 tract *The Population Bomb*, which featured lurid predictions of impending famine and supported compulsory sterilization in India as "coercion in a good cause."

By the late 1980s, population growth had transformed from just one of several preoccupations of the mainstream environmental movement into an intense passion. Groups such as the National Wildlife Federation and the National Audubon Society beefed up their population programs, hoping to attract new membership. Meanwhile, population lobbyists such as the influential Population Crisis Committee (renamed Population Action International) seized on environmental concerns as a new rationale for their existence.

The marriage of convenience between the population and environment establishments led to many joint efforts in advance of the 1992 UN Conference on Environment and Development (UNCED) in Rio de Janeiro. In 1990, Audubon, National Wildlife, Sierra Club, Planned Parenthood Federation of America, and the Population Crisis Committee began a joint Campaign on Population and the Environment. Its major objective was "to expand public awareness of the link between population growth, environmental degradation and the resulting human suffering."

Despite their efforts, the U.S. population/environment lobby had a rude awakening at Rio. In the formal intergovernmental negotiations, many developing nations refused to put population on the UNCED agenda, claiming it would divert attention from the North's responsibility for the environmental crisis. At the same time the nongovernmental Women's Action Agenda 21, endorsed by 1500 women activists from around the world, condemned suggestions that women's fertility rates were to blame for environmental degradation.

In the aftermath of Rio, "the woman question" has forced the population/environment lobby to amend its strategy. Many organizations are emphasizing women's rights in their preparations for the Cairo conference. Women's empowerment—through literacy programs, job opportunities, and access to health care and family planning—is now seen as a prerequisite for the reduction of population growth.

While this is a step forward, the population/environment lobby largely treats the protection of women's rights as a means to population reduction, rather than as a worthy pursuit in itself. Its inclusion—and co-optation—of feminist concerns is part of a larger strategy to create a broad population control "consensus" among the American public. Behind this effort is a small group of powerful actors: the Pew Charitable Trusts Global Stewardship Initiative; the U.S. State Department through the office of Timothy Wirth, Undersecretary for Global Affairs; the UNFPA; and Ted Turner of the powerful Turner Broadcasting System, producer of CNN.

Although the Pew Initiative's "White Paper" lists "population growth and unsustainable patterns of consumption" as its two targets, population growth is by far its main concern. Among Pew's explicit goals are to "forge consensus and to increase public understanding of, and commitment to act on, population and consumption challenges." Its targeted constituencies in the United States are environmental organizations, religious communities, and international affairs and foreign policy specialists.

Pew and the Turner Foundation have sponsored "high visibility" town meetings on population around the country, featuring Ted Turner's wife Jane Fonda, who is also UNFPA's "Goodwill Ambassador." At the Atlanta meeting, covered on Turner's CNN, Fonda attributed the collapse of two ancient Native American communities to overpopulation.

To prepare for the Cairo conference, the Pew Initiative hired three opinion research firms to gauge public understanding of the connections between population, environment and consumption so as to "mobilize Americans" on these issues. The researchers found that the public generally did not feel strongly about population growth or see it as a "personal threat." Their conclusion: An "emotional component" is needed to kindle population fears. Those interviewed complained that they had already been overexposed to "images of stark misery, such as starving children." Although the study notes that these images may in fact "work," it recommends finding "more current, targeted visual devices." One strategy is to build on people's pessimism about the future: "For women, particularly, relating the problems of excess population growth to children's future offers possibilities."

SACRIFICED RIGHTS

Whatever nods the new "consensus" makes towards women's broader rights and needs, family planning is its highest priority. USAID views family planning as "the single most effective means" of reducing population growth; it intends to provide "birth control to every woman in the developing world who wants it by the end of the decade."

The promotion of female contraception as the technical fix for the "population problem" ignores male responsibility for birth-control and undermines the quality of health and family planning services. The overriding objective is to drive down the birth rate as quickly and cheaply as possible, rather than to address people's broader health needs.

In Bangladesh, for example, at least one-third of the health budget is devoted to population control. The principal means is poor-quality female sterilization with incentives for those who undergo the procedure, including cash payments for "wages lost" and transportation costs, as well as a piece of clothing (justified as "surgical apparel"). The World Bank and population specialists are now heralding Bangladesh as a great family planning success story. But at what human cost? Because of the health system's nearly exclusive emphasis on population control, most Bangladeshis have little or no access to primary health care, and infant and maternal death rates remain at tragically high levels.

Lowering the birth rate by itself has hardly solved the country's problems. Poverty in Bangladesh has much more to do with inequitable land ownership and the urban elite's stranglehold over external resources, including foreign aid, than it does with numbers of people. The great irony is that many people in Bangladesh wanted birth control well before the aggressive and often coercive sterilization campaign launched by the government with the help of the World Bank and AID. A truly voluntary family planning program, as part of more comprehensive health services, would have yielded similar demographic results, without deepening human suffering.

The prejudice against basic health care is also reflected in the UN's first draft of the "Program of Action" for the Cairo conference. It asks the international community to spend $10.2 billion on population and family planning by the year 2000, and only $1.2 billion on broader reproductive health services such as maternity care. After pressure from women's groups and more progressive governments, the UN raised this figure to $5 billion, but family planning still has a two-to-one advantage. Meanwhile, the Vatican is attacking women's rights by bracketing for further negotiation any language in the Cairo document which refers to abortion, contraception or sexuality. Women are caught between a rock and a hard place, bracketed by the Vatican, and targeted by the population establishment.

The current focus of population programs is on the introduction of long-acting, provider-dependent contraceptive technologies. The hormonal implant Norplant, for example, which is inserted in a woman's arm, is effective for five years and can only be removed by trained medical personnel. But often, these methods are administered in health systems that are ill-equipped to distribute them safely or ethically; In population programs in Indonesia, Bangladesh and Egypt, researchers have documented many instances of women being denied access to Norplant removal, as well as receiving inadequate counselling, screening, and follow-up care.

A number of new contraceptives in the pipeline pose even more serious problems, in terms of both health risks and the potential for abuse at the hands of zealous population control officials. The non-surgical quinacrine sterilization pellet, which drug specialists suspect may be linked to cancer, can be administered surreptitiously (it was given to Vietnamese women during IUD checks without their knowledge in 1993). Also potentially dangerous are vaccines which immunize women against reproductive hormones. Their long-term reversibility has not yet been tested, and the World Health Organization has expressed some concern about the drugs' interaction with the immune system, especially in people infected with the AIDS virus. Simpler barrier methods, such as condoms and diaphragms, which also protect against sexually transmitted diseases, continue to receive considerably less attention and resources in population programs since they are viewed as less effective in preventing births.

Recently, a network of women formed a caucus on gender issues in order to pressure USAID to live up to its rhetoric about meeting women's broader reproductive health needs. The caucus emerged in the wake of a controversial USAID decision to award a $9 million contract for studying the impact of family planning on women's lives to Family Health International, a North-Carolina-based population agency, rather than to women's organizations with more diverse and critical perspectives.

Progressive environmentalists also intend to monitor USAID's planned initiative to involve Third World environmental groups in building "grass roots awareness around the issue of population and family planning." They fear that USAID funds will be used to steer these groups away from addressing the politically sensitive root causes of environmental degradation—such as land concentration, and corporate logging and ranching—toward a narrow population control agenda.

TROUBLE AT HOME

Within the United States, the toughest battle will be challenging the multimillion dollar public opinion "consensus" manufactured by Pew, the State Department, and CNN. Not only does this consensus promote heightened U.S. involvement in population control overseas, but by targeting women's fertility, it helps lay the ground, intentionally or not, for similar domestic efforts.

The Clinton administration is considering whether to endorse state policies that deny additional cash benefits to women who have babies while on welfare. (This despite the fact that women on welfare have only two children on average.) A number of population and environment groups are also fomenting dangerous resentment against immigrant women. The Washington-based Carrying Capacity Network, for example, states that the United States has every right to impose stricter immigration controls "as increasing numbers of women from Mexico, China and other areas of the world come to the United States for the purpose of giving birth on U.S. soil." And in many circles, Norplant is touted as the wonder drug which will cure the epidemic of crime and poverty allegedly caused by illegitimacy.

Such simple solutions to complex social problems not only don't work, they often breed misogyny and racism, and they prevent positive public action on finding real solutions. Curbing industrial and military pollution, for example, will do far more to solve the environmental crisis than controlling the wombs of poor women who, after all, exert the least pressure on global resources.

The real problem is not human *numbers* but undemocratic human systems of labor and resource exploitation, often backed by military repression. We need to rethink the whole notion of "carrying capacity"—are we really pressing up against the earth's limits because there are too many of us? It would make more sense to talk about "political carrying capacity," defined as the limited capacity of the environment and economy to sustain inequality and injustice. Viewed this way, the solution to environmental degradation and economic decline lies in greater democratic control over resources, not in a narrow population control agenda.

POSTSCRIPT

Is Limiting Population Growth a Key Factor in Protecting the Global Environment?

Harrison extols the virtues of Thailand's population-control program, which he claims has achieved success in significantly reducing birthrates without coercion while promoting women's health care and female education. He implies that this policy contributed to a growth in average income and the ability to "compete in the modern high-tech world." He does not, however, respond to Hartmann's argument that such policies alone do not ensure a reduction in environmental degradation.

Recent U.S. policy does not support the positions espoused in either of the two preceding articles. Contributions to worldwide birth control efforts have been curtailed by both the Reagan and Bush administrations. They have also opposed direct governmental involvement in constraining industry to adopt ecologically sound development strategies.

Anyone with a serious interest in environmental issues should certainly read Paul Ehrlich's *The Population Bomb* (Ballantine Books, 1968) and Barry Commoner's *The Closing Circle* (Alfred A. Knopf, 1971). Ehrlich was so distressed by the arguments contained in Commoner's popular book that he co-authored a detailed critique with environmental scientist John P. Holden, which Commoner answered with a lengthy response. These two no-holds-barred pieces were published as a "Dialogue" in the May 1972 issue of the *Bulletin of the Atomic Scientists*. They are interesting reading, not only for their technical content but as a rare example of respected scientists airing their professional and personal antagonisms in public.

Another frequently cited controversial essay in support of the neo-Malthusian analysis is "The Tragedy of the Commons," by Garrett Hardin, which first appeared in the December 13, 1968 issue of *Science*. For a thorough attempt to justify his authoritarian response to the world population problem, see Hardin's book *Exploring New Ethics for Survival* (Viking Press, 1972).

An economic and political analyst who is concerned about the connections among population growth, resource depletion, and pollution—but who rejects Hardin's proposed solutions—is Lester Brown, director of the Worldwatch Institute. His world view is detailed in *The Twenty-Ninth Day* (W. W. Norton, 1978).

Anyone willing to entertain the propositions that pollution has not been increasing, natural resources are not becoming scarce, the world food situation is improving, and population growth is actually beneficial, might find economist Julian Simon's *The Ultimate Resource* (Princeton University Press, 1982) amusing, if not convincing.

For a recent assessment of the need to control population growth by several international authorities, including Commoner, see "A Forum: How Big is the Population Factor?" in the July/August 1990 issue of *EPA Journal*. Ehrlich presents his current views on the issue in an article he coauthored with Anne Ehrlich entitled "The Population Explosion," *The Amicus Journal* (Winter 1990). A series of articles on the connections among population, development, and environmental degradation appears in the February 1992 issue of *Ambio*.

Harrison's essay is part of a special section entitled "Population, Consumption & Environment" in the Winter 1994 issue of *The Amicus Journal*, which includes other articles focusing on the needs and concerns of Third World people, along with brief statements representing the views of people from all over the world about the issues that were to be debated at the 1994 Cairo population conference. The Spring 1994 issue of that journal includes an essay by Jodi L. Jacobson that addresses some of the same concerns raised by Hartmann. Distinguished environmentalist Michael Brower addresses the population debate in the Fall 1994 issue of *Nucleus*, the magazine of the Union of Concerned Scientists. A provocative response to the Cairo meeting is the article by Norway's prime minister and sustainable devlopment advocate Gro Harlem Brundtland in the December 1994 issue of *Environment*.

ISSUE 6

Should Property Owners Be Compensated When Environmental Restrictions Limit Development?

YES: Rick Henderson, from "Preservation Acts," *Reason* (October 1994)

NO: Doug Harbrecht, from "A Question of Property Rights and Wrongs," *National Wildlife* (October/November 1994)

ISSUE SUMMARY

YES: *Reason* magazine's Washington editor Rick Henderson applauds recent court decisions preventing the imposition of environmental restrictions on property owners without compensation.

NO: *Business Week's* Washington correspondent Doug Harbrecht claims that it is absurd to have to pay owners of private property for obeying environmental regulations.

The question of possible conflicts between the public interest and a private landowner's development plans for his or her property is not a new issue. It has, however, taken on new meaning over the past decade as a result of a growing U.S. property rights movement that has been attempting, with some success, to prevent local, federal, and state governments from imposing environmentally motivated restrictions on the use of private property without due compensation for any resulting loss of value to the landholder

Those who defend the absolute development rights of landowners frequently justify their position by quoting from the writings of seventeenth century political philosopher John Locke. They further cite as a legal basis for their position the eminent domain clause of the Fifth Amendment, which prohibits the government from "taking" private property for public use without just compensation.

Opponents of the property rights activists point out that Locke based his position on the abundant availability of land that prevailed in his day and that he considered undeveloped land to be of no value, a position that would find few supporters today. They argue further that the environmental problems that have resulted from population pressures coupled with inappropriate development could hardly have been foreseen by a seventeenth century philosopher. In their view the language of the Fifth Amendment was meant to preclude actual seizure of property by the government, not loss of value resulting from regulatory restrictions.

The courts have historically supported this latter interpretation. However, in a few recent cases, court rulings have interpreted the "taking" of property as possible, including those cases where the regulatory restriction was such as to render the property totally worthless or where the public benefits resulting from the restriction could not be shown to be at least commensurate with the loss of value suffered by the property owner.

Only the most extreme property rights advocates argue that all regulations require compensation to a landowner for the potential value of activities they preclude. Few would support the rights of a landowner to profit from a project that results in a serious pollution problem not confined to the owner's property. It is also generally recognized that investment in property is a speculative activity and that the purchaser should be aware that potential actions by governments or private parties can result in either the enhancement or the diminution of the worth or value of the property.

Rick Henderson is the Washington editor for *Reason*, a magazine that supports the libertarian political perspective. In his article he reports favorably on a series of legislative initiatives at the state and federal level, as well as recent court decisions that are advancing the agenda of the property rights movement. Doug Harbrecht is a Washington-based correspondent for *Business Week*. In his view environmental laws do more to protect rather than reduce property rights. He fears that legislative proposals that would require compensation to property owners for decreases in value resulting from such laws will make it economically impossible for the government to require an ecologically sound development policy.

YES

Rick Henderson

PRESERVATION ACTS

Brandt Child planned to build a campground and golf course on land he owns outside Moab, Utah. But after he started construction, the Fish and Wildlife Service claimed that the natural springs on Child's land provide habitat for the endangered Kanab Ambersnail. The government halted construction and forced Child to fence off the property, rendering it worthless. Child claims that the effective condemnation of his land has cost him $2.5 million.

In 1986, Maine residents Gaston and Monique Roberge wanted to provide money for their retirement by selling a lot they had purchased 22 years earlier. After the Roberges got an offer of $440,000 for the land, the U.S. Army Corps of Engineers claimed that the property was a wetland and that the Roberges had let the city illegally "fill" the property with dirt in 1976. When the Roberges removed the dirt, the property became less desirable as a home site; offers to buy the land disappeared. After spending thousands of dollars hiring consultants to comply with bureaucratic edicts, the Roberges have exhausted their retirement investments, still have no offers for their land, and live on Social Security.

Richard Ehrlich owns a piece of property in Culver City, California, on which he constructed a private tennis club. The tennis club went out of business. Ehrlich then tried to get permission to build 30 condominiums on the land. Culver City, a separately incorporated town surrounded by Los Angeles, approved Ehrlich's proposal on the condition that he pay the city $280,000 so that it could build public tennis courts to "replace" the courts at Ehrlich's club. The condo association would also have to maintain the public courts after they were built.

Stories like these have become all too common over the past decade or so, as state, city, and federal regulations have encroached ever further into the lives of even small property owners. But as such regulations, especially those ostensibly intended to protect wetlands and endangered species, affect average property owners and business operators, hundreds of grass-roots private property organizations and inholders groups are fighting back. And people like Child, the Roberges, and Ehrlich are increasingly winning. In

From Rick Henderson, "Preservation Acts," *Reason* (October 1994). Copyright © 1994 by The Reason Foundation, 3415 S. Sepulveda Blvd., Suite 400, Los Angeles, CA 90034. Reprinted by permission. For a sample issue, please call (310) 391-2245.

legislatures, the courts, and among the general public, the property-rights movement is chalking up victories.

On July 14, for instance, the House of Representatives passed an amendment to the California Desert Protection Act that could deter some regulatory "takings" of private property like those mentioned above. The amendment, sponsored by Rep. Billy Tauzin (D-La.), would prevent the government from reducing the appraised value of private property it acquires when the land harbors threatened or endangered species. If Tauzin's amendment applied to the entire Endangered Species Act, environmental regulators would have to pay Brandt Child the fair market value of his property before the snails were found.

Even though the Tauzin amendment, which passed by a 281–148 vote, applies only to the desert bill, it should help the owners of 700,000 acres of private property who would have otherwise lost most uses of their land. And the amendment caught environmentalist sponsors of the bill, led by Rep. George Miller (D-Calif.), off guard. After the amendment passed, Miller temporarily removed the bill from consideration; it passed two weeks later, 298 to 128, with the amendment attached. Sen. Bennett Johnston (D-La.) will head the conference committee that reconciles the Senate and House versions; he has assured Tauzin and the amendment's supporters that the amendment will be part of the final bill.

* * *

The Fifth Amendment to the U.S. Constitution requires the government to provide "just compensation" any time regulators or legislators "take" private property for public use. Until recently, individuals would receive payment only for those takings resulting from eminent domain—in other words, when land was condemned so that government could build a highway or some other public-works project.

But the 1985 publication of University of Chicago law professor Richard Epstein's *Takings: Private Property and the Power of Eminent Domain* provided intellectual ammunition for the argument that regulations can restrict a land owner's rights just as much as overtly condemning property. Epstein's reasoning swept through law schools and into the courts, where Reagan appointees used the new takings rationale to limit the reach of environmental regulators. Such public-interest law firms as the Pacific Legal Foundation, the Washington Legal Foundation, the Institute for Justice, and Defenders of Property Rights represented clients who were victims of regulatory takings and filed amicus briefs in federal and state court cases.

In three federal cases, *Nollan v. California Coastal Commission* (1987), *Lucas v. South Carolina Coastal Council* (1992), and *Dolan v. City of Tigard* (1994), the U.S. Supreme Court ruled that land-use planners could no longer expect a free lunch. Regulations meant to serve legitimate public purposes must not place a disproportionate burden on the property owners being regulated.

Meanwhile, hundreds of grass-roots property-rights groups were springing up nationwide. Often these "groups" consist of the members of one family whose land was made worthless by wetlands regulations, the Endangered Species Act, or other environmental statutes. Legislators are responding to these groups, and the property owners they represent, by enacting laws that pare back new regulations.

* * *

The property-rights agenda is advancing on three fronts:

1) State legislatures and state referenda. The high-profile court cases and environmental bills focus on federal court decisions and two national laws—the Endangered Species Act and the wetlands provision of the Clean Water Act. But most regulatory takings result from the actions of state environmental agencies and local planners. Not surprisingly, much property-rights ferment takes place outside Washington.

Since 1991, 36 states have considered property-protection laws. Six states enacted bills before 1994; five others passed them this year. Peggy Riegle, chairman of the Fairness to Landowners Committee, says 86 bills were introduced this year alone. These bills either require regulators to study the costs of proposed regulations or they establish procedures that allow land owners affected by regulations to receive compensation.

Voters in as many as three states will decide property-rights referenda this fall. Massachusetts voters will determine whether to repeal rent control. If it qualifies for the ballot, Floridians will vote on a property-rights amendment to the state constitution. And in Arizona, voters will resolve the fate of a property-rights bill that would require every state agency to determine the impact of new regulations on property owners and decide how to compensate land owners when any proposed regulation reduces property values.

The Arizona initiative passed the state legislature in 1992. But green groups exercised a provision in the state constitution that allows a bill signed by the governor to be brought before voters as a referendum; if the initiative fails at the ballot box, the law won't go into effect. The November vote on Proposition 300 could have national implications for the property-rights movement. Phoenix political consultant Bob Robb says the outcome "will be cited by the winning side as an indication of the popular support for property rights."

Local politics could hurt the initiative. Robb points out that the Grand Canyon State is an unusual mix of populist conservatives and conservationists, a state that simultaneously sent Barry Goldwater to the Senate, Mo Udall to the House, and Bruce Babbitt to the governor's mansion. "The legislature is strongly pro-business and hostile to environmentalists," says Robb. "On environmental issues," by contrast, "the people have a strong preservationist ethic." Property-rights protections, though they benefit many average citizens, aren't really populist measures but protections against tyrannical majorities or powerful activist groups.

And while initiatives and referenda often provide legislative vehicles for political outsiders, qualifying and passing an initiative can take years of education and promotion and cost hundreds of thousands of dollars. Peggy Riegle says backing initiatives isn't as important for the property-rights movement as lobbying legislators because many lawmakers are receptive to land owners and have passed property-rights bills. Arizona's vote may test the movement's broader appeal.

2) Federal courts. The *Dolan* decision marks a departure from earlier takings cases for two reasons: It prohibits the regulators' use of "unconstitutional conditions" in land-use restrictions, and it requires the government to prove—before enforcing regulations—that there is a "rough proportionality" between its regulations and the "legitimate state interests" it is trying to advance.

The Court has traditionally prohibited governments from forcing individuals to surrender civil liberties in exchange for other rights. For instance, it clearly would be unconstitutional for a city to permit a person to build a home only if the home owner gave up his right to vote in the next election. The *Dolan* decision extended the unconstitutional conditions doctrine to property rights. Here, it ruled that a business owner can't be forced to build a public bike path in exchange for a permit to expand an existing hardware store without giving the owner compensation.

* * *

The Court also challenged the long-standing notion that business regulations are less important than restrictions on free speech or other civil liberties. Since the 1930s, the courts have established a hierarchy of rights: Certain civil liberties, such as voting and free speech, have received greater protection than property rights. As a result, most business regulations, no matter how draconian, have withstood constitutional challenges.

In *Dolan,* the Court began to restore property rights to the level of other civil liberties. Governments must now prove that their regulations, including land-use restrictions, are proportional to the public purposes they are trying to achieve. Otherwise, courts can strike down those regulations. Chief Justice William Rehnquist wrote for the majority: "We see no reason why the Takings Clause of the Fifth Amendment, as much a part of the Bill of Rights as the First Amendment or Fourth Amendment, should be relegated to the status of a poor relation in these comparable circumstances."

While the *Dolan* case dealt with an "exaction" (a condition placed on land use) that involved an actual invasion of private property, the Court strongly suggested that certain development fees and other monetary exactions might be unconstitutional as well. Three days after *Dolan* was decided, the Court ordered the California Court of Appeals to reconsider its ruling against Richard Ehrlich, the California tennis-club owner.

Ehrlich challenged the impact fee Culver City assessed, arguing that the tennis courts he operated were private. The Court of Appeals agreed with the city: "We do not find the distinction between public and private recreational facilities to be compelling," ruled the court. "The City had a legitimate need for community recreational facilities, whether public or private, and both the land-use restriction and the mitigation fee served that same need."

Counters James Burling, senior property-rights attorney at the Pacific Legal Foundation [PFL], "The city may need additional lights, sewage treatment, and streets" as a consequence of building new condos. "But there's not a *need* for a new park or tennis courts." PLF will file an amicus brief in support of Ehrlich.

Since nearly 90 percent of local governments impose monetary exactions on new development (up from 10 percent in 1960), a favorable ruling in *Ehrlich* could foreclose many land-use restrictions. "Applied consistently," says attorney Scott Bullock of the Institute for Justice, "the *Dolan* precedent will strike down unjustified exactions and largely end what was a growth industry in government-condoned extortion."

3) Congress. Tauzin's amendment to the desert bill was the fourth major victory for the property-rights movement in this session. Earlier, property protections were added to the bills establishing the National Biological Survey and elevating the Environmental Protection Agency to cabinet status. After the amendments were added, greens removed both bills from consideration.

The Senate also added amendments to the Safe Drinking Water Act requiring a "takings-impact analysis" for any regulation that might cause a taking of property and mandating cost-benefit analyses for any regulations costing more than $100 million. In the House, property-rights advocates and representatives from small towns that might not be able to afford expensive new purification systems may add even tougher amendments. Greens may take the drinking water bill off the table for the rest of the year as well.

Until now, property-rights advocates in Congress have mostly played defense, attaching amendments to noxious bills with the hope that they could weaken them. Democratic congressional barons have bottled up stand-alone proposals by Tauzin, Rep. Jimmy Hayes (D-La.), and former Sen. Steve Symms (R-Idaho) in the environment committees, never letting them reach the floor of the House or Senate for a vote.

But property protectors are fighting back. Tauzin has proposed HR 3875, the Private Property Owners Bill of Rights. Tauzin's bill would define as a taking any regulation under the Endangered Species Act or the wetlands provision of the Clean Water Act that reduces a land owner's property value by 50 percent or more. To keep the bill from being gutted or bottled up in committee, he has filed a discharge petition—a procedure that requires the entire House to consider the bill without any modifications. Before the petition can take effect, Tauzin must collect the signatures of 217 other members. At press time, the discharge petition had 140 signers.

In the Senate, Phil Gramm (R-Tex.) will soon introduce a more radical bill, the Private Property Rights Restoration Act. Gramm's bill would assume that a taking occurs when any new regulation "restricts, limits, or otherwise infringes a right to real property that would otherwise exist." The bill would give a property owner standing to sue the government for compensation when a regulation temporarily or permanently reduces the owner's property value by at least 25 percent or $10,000, whichever is less. (The bill would exempt regulations that prevent pollution and other "public nuisances.")

The Institute for Justice's Bullock says lawmakers are proposing bills that more closely conform with court rulings. "Legislators are saying, 'If the Court takes the Constitution seriously, we should too,'" he says. "These decisions encourage [legislators] to be bolder."

Such boldness may be needed. Paul Kamenar, president of the Washington Legal Foundation, warns that bills that rely on "neat formulas" for determining compensation won't keep regulators entirely at bay. "The government will still try to get around the formula," he says. "A bigger help would be to clear the underbrush of procedural hurdles"—such impediments as obtaining permits, hiring consultants, and going through lengthy administrative appeals—"a property owner has to get through to make a claim against the government." Those hurdles, he says, "discourage 99.9 percent of property owners who do have a legitimate claim from pursuing it in court."

While constitutional law changes incrementally, property owners seem to have the momentum. Riegle says environmentalists, who have relied upon bluster and apocalyptic rhetoric to frighten legislators into action, have lost control of the legislative agenda. In the past, she says, property-rights advocates were on the defensive, "always holding a shield while environmentalists were carrying the sword. Now we have the sword. And they're not good at playing defense."

NO

Doug Harbrecht

A QUESTION OF PROPERTY RIGHTS AND WRONGS

Ralph Seidel's livelihood depends on the clean waters of Natrona Creek in rural Pratt County, Kansas, where he owns a golf course, a private fishing resort and a trailer park. But for more than two decades, starting in the late 1960s, neighboring cattle outfit Pratt Feeders dumped livestock wastes into the creek, causing repeated fish kills, according to state environmental officials. When the company's pollution-control permits came up for renewal a few years ago, Seidel organized a public uprising that led to state changes in Pratt Feeders' permits requiring more stringent treatment of its waste water.

Seidel's property rights, not Pratt's, were the issue. "That's what 'property rights' has always meant for conservationists: protections for average Americans and their property," says National Wildlife Federation [NWF] attorney Glenn Sugameli. But a new property-rights movement is afoot, one that could lead polluters like Pratt Feeders—to claim loss of *their* property rights through regulations. All over the country, ranchers, developers, mining companies and others are charging that property owners should be "compensated" if obeying the law lowers the value of private property or results in less-than-anticipated corporate profit.

The notion may seem absurd. "The whole idea that the government needs to pay people not to do bad things is ridiculous," says John Humbach, a property-rights expert at Pace University. "The reason the government exists in the first place is to define what is for the common good and what's not."

Absurd or not, the movement has become a political force to be reckoned with, linked as it is to the powerful notion that landowners should be allowed to do what they want with their property. "People better start taking this movement seriously," says Robert Meltz, a property-law expert at the Congressional Research Service. "This isn't just some fringe element anymore." The proof can be found in Congress, where proposed property-rights amendments are delaying nearly all major environmental legislation.

The new movement has the potential to disrupt a delicate balance between private greed and public need forged over two centuries of U.S. property law, legal experts say. The outcome will affect the survival of endangered wildlife, and it threatens not only environmental protections like pollution laws, but also zoning regulations and even obscenity laws. "Extremists are trying to take away the ability of Americans to act through their government to protect neighboring private-property owners and the public welfare," says NWF's Sugameli.

In Congress, property-rights debates have held up renewal of the Endangered Species Act, originally slated for 1993, and reauthorization of the Clean Water Act. Property-rights issues have also helped hold up bills to reform the Mining Law of 1872, elevate the Environmental Protection Agency to Cabinet status and reauthorize the Safe Drinking Water Act. The delays are due in large part to property-rights lobbying for amendments such as a ban on volunteers collecting data on private land for the National Biological Survey or a requirement that the government do "loss-of-value" assessments when regulations "could" cause a change in the worth of private property ranging from land to stocks and bonds.

At the state level, "takings" bills similar to those in Congress have been introduced in 37 state legislatures in the past two years; nearly all have been defeated. Many of the bills would require taxpayers to "compensate" landowners, including corporations, for property values diminished because of regulation. Such payments could be extremely costly, and the measures could erode state authority to protect public health and safety—as well as wreak havoc on long-established planning tools such as zoning.

For the most part, the new movement is not faring well in the courts either but it has scored some wins. In one case directly affecting wildlife, last March the U.S. Court of Appeals for the District of Columbia struck down a U.S. Fish and Wildlife Service regulation that prevented private landowners from destroying habitat of federally listed species.

The court declared the provision as "neither clearly authorized by Congress nor a 'reasonable interpretation'" of the Endangered Species Act. The Clinton Administration has asked the court to reconsider the decision. If it stands, the ruling would allow landowners to take actions such as chopping down a tree containing the nest of an endangered red-cockaded woodpecker or bulldozing a beach where threatened sea turtles lay their eggs—*as long as the animals are not around.* No matter that the animals later would return to their habitat; no protections would exist in their absence.

While that case raises the issue of how much conservation laws apply to private land, it is technically a question of the intent of Congress in passing the Endangered Species Act. In contrast, the heart of most of the property-rights debate lies in a Fifth Amendment clause in the Constitution's Bill of Rights: "... nor shall private property be taken for public use, without just compensation." Legal historians interpret the original intent as requiring that landowners be paid when the government seizes property for public conveniences like roads and dams.

No one disagrees that if the government takes all of a person's property for public use, then just compensation is required. But the new movement pushes the argument a big step further, contending that regulation of landowners' ability to do as they wish with their property is a "taking" as well. The movement was sparked by the 1987 book *Takings*, by University of Chicago professor Richard Epstein. Epstein argued that the broad definition of a taking "invalidates much of the 20th-century legislation."

Such arguments mask the myriad ways governments increase the value of public property. Partly for this reason, editorial boards at newspapers across the country have condemned property-rights legislation. In one April 1994 editorial, *The Atlanta Constitution* called the demands of property rights forces "pure hypocrisy." As an example, it cited Arizona, "one of the fastest-growing states in the country and a hotbed of property-rights legislation. But its cities and suburbs would still be worthless desert if not for water brought from hundreds of miles away, at huge expense to the federal government."

Other examples: Developers in coastal areas that depend on taxpayer-subsidized insurance and agri-businesses that thrive with federal price support and crop insurance. Property values often exist only because of sewers, roads and other government-paid amenities.

The takings argument has quickly reached the level of the absurd. "Compensation" has been asked for costs incurred in widening restroom doors to allow wheelchair access required by law, losses due to limits on the sale and import of assault rifles—and even losses due to restrictions on "dial-a-porn" services.

In Mississippi and Georgia, religious groups have joined environmentalists in opposing proposed property-rights legislation. The bills would require taxpayers to compensate pornography dealers prevented from locating next to schools and churches. "Where this leads is to the end of government's role as protector of the little guy and provider of amenities the market alone cannot provide," says Jessica Mathews, a se-

nior fellow at the Council on Foreign Relations. "Things like public health, worker safety, civil rights, environment, planning, historic preservation and anti-discrimination measures."

The rule of law in the United States has long been that landowners must not use their land in any way that creates a public or private nuisance (in other words, harms the public or neighbors). "(A)ll property in this country is held under the implied obligation that the owner's use of it shall not be injurious to the community," the Supreme Court ruled 100 years ago. In a string of cases since then, the high court has consistently reaffirmed that bedrock principle.

In 1992, the Supreme Court did rule conditionally in favor of South Carolina developer David Lucas, who had been denied permission to build on two ocean-front lots after the state adopted a coastal-zone management plan. Lucas owned two lots appraised at $1 million. The Court ruled he was entitled to compensation in part *if* the action deprived him of "all economically viable use" of his land. The case then went back to the state courts, where it was eventually settled. Justice Antonin Scalia, who wrote the Supreme Court's majority opinion, warned that anyone who purchases property always takes a risk that government regulation will diminish its value. He wrote that a lakebed owner "would not be entitled to compensation when he is denied the requisite permit to engage in a landfilling operation that would have the effect of flooding others' land." In other words, says NWF attorney Sugameli, "Property ownership does not include the right to flood your neighbors."

Even permits for livestock grazing on public land, claim "takings" advocates, are property. In Nevada, rancher Wayne

Hage is suing the U.S. government for $28 million in damages for diminishing the value of his property (his permit) in a number of ways. But the range that Hage's cattle roamed is not his. It's yours: 700,000 acres of the Toiyabe National Forest in Nevada he leased from the federal government. In 1990, the Forest Service warned Hage he was letting his cattle overgraze. The animals were devouring vegetation along clear-running streams among the mountain meadows and piñon pine, birch and aspen trees—and in the process destroying key habitat for fish, birds, elk and other wildlife.

After Hage didn't respond to repeated warnings, in July 1991 contract cowboys protected by armed Forest Service rangers rounded up 73 of Hage's scofflaw bovines. Later, 31 more were taken in. Hage sold off the remainder of his herd of 2,000 and has taken his grievances to court. Among them are his claims that the government ruined his business by introducing elk, which competed with his cattle for grass; allowing backpackers and elk to drink from springs used by his livestock; and restricting how heavily his cattle could graze streamside vegetation. Federal officials say that by ignoring grazing regulations, Hage has only himself to blame for his troubles. On behalf of several environmental groups and the state of Nevada, the National Wildlife Federation is actively participating in the case as a friend of the court.

So-called property-rights advocates like to portray themselves as average Janes and Joes fighting the daunting power of federal bureaucrats and tree-hugging elites. Says J. T. "Jake" Commins, executive vice president of the antiregulation Montana Farm Bureau, "Walt Whitman was speaking to the universal aspiration of humanity throughout history when he said, 'A man is not whole and complete unless he owns a house and the ground it stands on.'"

But loss of regulations often benefits big landowners most. Charles Geisler, a sociologist at Cornell University, has found that the nation's land is concentrated in the hands of the wealthy few. According to the Department of Agriculture, almost three quarters of all the privately owned land in the country is owned by less than 5 percent of the landowning population. "This is important to keep in mind when the property-rights people talk about fighting for the little guy," says Geisler.

Who are the nation's largest private landowners? Timber and mining companies, agri-businesses, developers and energy conglomerates, says Geisler. These owners appear to be prime movers behind the property-rights movement.

One example: When M & J Coal Company of Marion County, West Virginia, was ordered by federal officials not to mine portions of coal deposits because a gas line ruptured and huge cracks opened on the land of homeowners living over the underground mine, the company sued. Though it earned a 34.5 percent annual profit on the mine, the company claimed the restrictions were a "regulatory taking" for which it was entitled to $580,000 in lost profits. The court rejected the claim earlier this year; the company has appealed.

In Wyoming, the Clajon Corporation recently challenged in court state limits on the number of hunting licenses issued to large landowners. As owner of a large ranch, Clajon contended that it owned the right to hunt wildlife on its land and that the state's hunting-license limit was a taking of the company's property rights. The Wyoming Wildlife Federation and NWF's Rocky Mountain Natural Resource Center were leaders in fighting the claims, which were thrown out by Wyoming's federal district court in June.

Despite such cases, legal experts do not dismiss the takings movement in general. Even Humbach of Pace University maintains environmentalists have two decades of their own success partly to blame for the current backlash. "People concerned about the wise use of land should be equally concerned about misapplied and heavy-handed government rules that turn average Americans into poster children for the property-rights movement," he says.

Environmentalists might even agree with that notion—at least up to the mention of poster children. "I am convinced there is no actual case of an 'American poster child' for the property-rights movement," says NWF's Sugameli. NWF has examined hundreds of such purported cases. "And every single case either falls apart or doesn't exist at all," he says.

One example: the well-publicized 1988 jailing of Hungarian immigrant John Pozsgai for filling in a small wetland next to his Pennsylvania diesel mechanic shop. Property-rights advocates portray Pozsgai as a hapless victim who only meant to make his own land useful. But according to the Environmental Protection Agency, engineers told Pozsgai before he bought the property that there were wetlands on it; he even used that information to negotiate a $20,000 reduction in the land's purchase price. He then refused to obtain the required federal permit to fill his wetlands, filled them without the permit and ignored repeated official notification to stop doing so. Said the judge during Pozsgai's sentencing, "It is hard to visualize a more stubborn violator of the laws that were designed to protect the environment."

Such cases aside, environmentalists say they do recognize a need for collaboration. "The whole environmental community should be advancing the view that environmental laws are vital to protecting property rights, not taking them away, says Michael Bean, chairman of the Wildlife Program of the nonprofit Environmental Defense Fund. To that end, the group is exploring a plan to help save the endangered red-cockaded woodpecker in the pine forests of North Carolina, where private landowners own most of the prime habitat. The idea involves "land-use credits" for leaving large stands of trees untouched. The credits could take the form of lower taxes, regulatory relief from parts of the Endangered Species Act or some other tangible asset.

And in Kern County, California, conservationists have long supported a plan aimed at allowing developers to build near habitat of the endangered kit fox in return for undisturbed parcel setasides and a developer-funded conservation program, both of which would aid the fox.

That sort of thinking may be the best hope for habitat and wildlife in the future. "In recent years, proponents of various private property-rights amendments have come to view the protection of private-property rights and government regulation as mutually exclusive goals," says Senator John Chafee (R-Rhode Island). "That view is wrong." In the end, property rights are as much an issue for Ralph Seidel and the elk in Toiyabe National Forest as for Wayne Hage. The framers of the Constitution wouldn't have had it any other way.

POSTSCRIPT

Should Property Owners Be Compensated When Environmental Restrictions Limit Development?

Harbrecht takes comfort from the fact that, thus far, the legislative program of the property rights movement has not been very successful. However, with the election of a Republican Congress, the prospects of such legislation as Senator Phil Gramm's (R-Texas) Private Property Rights Restoration Act, described in Henderson's article, will be considerably improved. Even with a Democratic majority in both houses, property rights lobbyists were successful in preventing the enactment of revised endangered species and clean water legislation. It seems likely that the Clinton administration will be forced to accept at least some of the proposed property compensation amendments to win approval from the reconstituted legislature for either of these major environmental laws.

University of Chicago law professor Richard Epstein's book *Takings: Private Property and the Power of Eminent Domain* (Harvard University Press, 1985) is credited with providing the property rights movement with legal arguments, which have been used in courtroom challenges, to regulations that have invoked the Fifth Amendment. For a concise debate between Epstein and John Echeverria about the legal aspects of the issue, see the May/June 1992 issue of the *Cato Policy Report*, published by the Cato Institute, Washington, D.C.

For another slant by an environmentalist who opposes the property rights position, see Carl Pope's article in the March 1994 issue of *Sierra*. For the perspective of those who see environmental restrictions on property rights as part of a leftist-inspired government conspiracy to control all aspects of our lives, see William Norman Rigg's article in the August 9, 1993, issue of *New American*.

Chapter two of *Foundations of Environmental Ethics*, by Eugene C. Hargrove (Prentice Hall, 1989), is a review of philosophical attitudes toward land use and property rights.

PART 2

The Environment and Technology

Most of the environmental concerns that are the focus of current regulatory debates are directly related to modern industrial development—the pace of which has been accelerating dramatically since World War II. Thousands of new synthetic chemicals have been introduced into manufacturing processes and agricultural pursuits. New technology, its byproducts, and the exponential increases in the production and use of energy have all contributed to the release of environmental pollutants. How to continue to improve the standard of living for the world's people without increasing ecological stress and exposure to toxins is the key question that underlies the issues debated in this section.

- Should the Industrial Use of Chlorine
  Be Phased Out?

- Is Stringent Enforcement of Existing
  Laws Needed to Improve Air Quality?

- Should the New Clean Water Act
  Aim at "Zero Discharge"?

- Does Feeding People and Preserving
  Wildlands Require Chemical-Based
  Agriculture?

- Is Protecting the Spotted Owl a Clever
  Strategy for Preserving Old-Growth
  Forests?

ISSUE 7

Should the Industrial Use of Chlorine Be Phased Out?

YES: Joe Thornton, from "Chlorine: Can't Live With It, Can Live Without It," Speech Prepared for the Chlorine-Free Debate Held in Conjunction With the International Joint Commission Seventh Biennial Meeting, Windsor, Ontario, Canada (October 1993)

NO: Ivan Amato, from "The Crusade to Ban Chlorine," *Garbage: The Independent Environmental Quarterly* (Summer 1994)

ISSUE SUMMARY

YES: Greenpeace research coordinator Joe Thornton presents the case for a systematic phaseout of chlorinated organic compounds as the only effective means of protecting humans and animals from the toxic effects of these chemicals.

NO: Science writer Ivan Amato emphasizes the industry's argument that only a few chlorinated compounds are proven health threats, and he states that Greenpeace's claims that substitutes exist are misleading.

In 1991 Greenpeace, the largest international grassroots environmental organization, launched a campaign to phase out most industrial uses of chlorine and chlorinated organic compounds. The basis for this strategy is the growing evidence that a wide variety of chlorinated compounds—such as dioxins, PCBs, chlorinated pesticides, vinyl chloride, carbon tetrachloride, and chloroform—are highly toxic or carcinogenic and that chlorine-containing compounds are destroying the protective ozone layer.

Prior to the 1970s the legislative restriction on the production, sale, or use of industrial chemicals in both capitalist and socialist economies was limited to a very small number of substances that were either clear and obvious threats to public health, such as the use of mercury- or arsenic-containing agricultural chemicals or radioactive isotopes. The growing environmental consciousness about the potential human health and ecological impacts due to the enormous number of synthetic chemicals introduced into industrial use following World War II has resulted in the enactment of numerous laws. These laws have been designed to reduce environmental pollution or public exposure to a rapidly growing list of proven, or suspected, hazardous substances. These laws attempt to limit air emissions, water contamination, land contamination, food contamination, and industrial exposure.

Efforts to find a scientifically valid, economically and politically feasible strategy for protecting the public and the ecosphere from the deleterious effects of hazardous substances have proven to be problematic and controversial. Lack of adequate data for valid risk assessments, inability to do direct, controlled tests on human subjects, questions about the validity of deducing human health concerns from animal test data, the difficulty of interpreting the results of epidemiological studies, lack of access to industrial data that is considered prioritory, and the complications due to possible synergistic effects among different pollutants are among the factors that have plagued regulatory agencies.

Most of the early efforts to limit exposure to proven or suspected toxins focused on carcinogenesis. This was because of legitimate public concern about rising cancer rates and the belief that cancer could be a likely outcome of exposure to low levels of synthetic chemicals. More recently, evidence that exposure to chemicals could affect the immune system and sexual development has meant that these possible health consequences of exposure to toxins are now being included in risk assessments as well.

With few exceptions the practice has been to consider each suspected toxic chemical individually. This expensive and time-consuming approach has resulted in a growing backlog of untested, industrial chemicals being introduced into processes or products that result in exposure to workers and consumers. Citizen's groups concerned about hazardous chemicals have unsuccessfully lobbied for a change in the regulatory philosophy that generally considers a new industrial chemical innocent as a potential health hazard until proven guilty.

The chemical industry was caught off guard by the rapidity with which the proposal to phase out nonessential uses of chlorine compounds led to endorsements and action. Chlorine gas has been eliminated as a bleach for pulp and paper in Europe. Norway has commissioned research on the policy effects of a total chlorine ban, and the International Joint Commission on the Great Lakes has recommended a broad organochlorine phaseout. The American Public Health Association issued a resolution in 1993 supporting a reduction in industrial uses of chlorine, and in February 1994 EPA administrator Carol Browner joined the chorus by announcing that the agency may consider a reduction and prohibition of chlorine and chlorine-containing compounds in connection with the rewriting of the Clean Water Act.

A counterattack has recently been launched in the form of a well-financed lobbying effort by the chemical industry to convince government officials and the public that the benefits of chlorine compounds outweigh the risks. This campaign appears to be succeeding in slowing the anti-chlorine bandwagon.

Pros and cons of the issue are discussed in detail in the following articles by Greenpeace research coordinator Joe Thornton and science writer Ivan Amato.

YES   Joe Thornton

CHLORINE: CAN'T LIVE WITH IT, CAN LIVE WITHOUT IT

In medicine, an ounce of prevention is worth a pound of cure. When it comes to the global environment, however, an ounce of prevention is priceless, for serious damage to the biosphere cannot be repaired before the health of millions of humans and other species has been affected. Already, toxic chlorine-based organic chemicals—called organochlorines—have contaminated the global environment and caused widespread damage to human health and the ecosystem; these chemicals cannot be removed from the tissues of the human population, the food chain or the general environment. It is time for society to adopt a precautionary strategy to prevent further damage by organochlorines.

My purpose here is three-fold: first, to show that organochlorines are a major hazard to health and the global environment; second, to show that for the purpose of environmental policy these thousands of related chemicals should be treated as a class, and that a planned phase-out of the industrial production and use of chlorine and organochlorines is necessary to prevent further injury to health and the environment; and third, to show that a phase-out of chlorine is technologically and economically feasible.

Already, numerous international institutions have called for a chlorine phase-out. For instance, the International Joint Commission on the Great Lakes (IJC)—a binational advisory body to the governments of the U.S. and Canada—concluded in 1992 and reiterated in 1994 that chlorine-based organic chemicals are a primary hazard to human health and the environment. On the IJC's list of the eleven pollutants requiring the most urgent action, eight are organochlorines; of the 362 on the "secondary track," more than half are chlorinated. The IJC argued that these chemicals should be treated as a class and subject to a policy of Zero Discharge, and recommended that the governments of the U.S. and Canada should, "in consultation with industry and other affected interests, develop timetables to sunset the use of chlorine and chlorine-containing compounds as industrial feedstocks."

Such diverse organizations as the Paris Commission on the Northeast Atlantic—a ministerial convention of 15 European governments—the

International Whaling Commission, the Arctic Wildlife Congress, and the 21-nation Barcelona Convention on the Mediterranean have all concluded that discharges of persistent, bioaccumulative substances—particularly organochlorines—should be eliminated entirely.

In late 1993, the American Public Health Association, the nation's premier organization of public health scientists and professionals, resolved that "chlorinated organic chemicals are found to pose public health risks involving the workplace, consumer products, and the general environment," and recognized that "elimination of chlorine and/or chlorinated organic compounds from certain manufacturing processes, products, and uses may be the most cost-effective and health protective way to reduce health and environmental exposures to chlorinated organic compounds." The APHA concluded that organochlorines should be treated as a class, presumed harmful unless shown otherwise, and phased-out, with exceptions made only if a given use or substance can be proven safe or essential.

And in early 1994, the Clinton White House announced as part of its proposal for the Clean Water Act that the Environmental Protection Agency (EPA) be authorized to conduct a study and develop a strategy to "substitute, reduce, or prohibit the use of chlorine and chlorine-containing compounds." The White House specifically sited growing evidence that links contamination of the environment by these persistent toxic substances "not only to cancer but also to neurological, reproductive, developmental, and immunological adverse effects."

WHAT ARE ORGANOCHLORINES?

Organochlorines are the products and by-products of industrial chlorine chemistry. In nature, chlorine exists almost solely in its stable ionic form, called chloride. Chloride ions circulate constantly through our bodies and the ecosystem, primarily in the familiar form of sea salt (sodium chloride, NaCl); these ions do not react or combine with the carbon-based organic matter that is the basis of living things.

The chemical industry takes this sea salt and subjects it to a powerful electric current, transforming ionic chloride into elemental chlorine gas (Cl_2), along with the co-product sodium hydroxide. The energy input in this "chlor-alkali process" fundamentally changes the chemical character of the chlorine atom. Unlike natural chloride, chlorine gas is a toxic, greenish gas that is highly unstable, combining quickly and randomly with organic matter to produce a new class of chemicals called organochlorines.

Since World War II, the chlorine industry has grown very rapidly, reaching production of 40 million tons of chlorine each year. Of this, about 80 percent is used within the chemical industry to manufacture 11,000 different organochlorine products, including plastics, pesticides, and solvents. The remainder is sold to other industries—most of it to the pulp and paper industry—for uses such as bleaching and disinfection. In addition to the many organochlorines produced on purpose, thousands more—including dioxin—are formed as accidental by-products in all uses of chlorine, and whenever organochlorines are used or disposed in reactive environments, such as incinerators.

Chlorine is useful in industry for the same reasons it is a hazard to health and the environment. Its reactivity makes it a powerful bleach and disinfectant —and an effective reactant in chemical synthesis—but this quality results in the formation of unintended by-products. Organochlorines tend to be very stable, resisting natural breakdown processes, so they are useful as plastics, refrigerants, di-electric fluids, pesticides, and other chemicals, but this same quality makes them long-lived in the environment and in the bodies of living organisms. Further, organochlorines tend to be oil-soluble, so they work well as degreasing solvents, but this causes them to concentrate in the tissues of living things. And organochlorines tend to be toxic, so they are powerful pesticides and drugs; the negative impacts of this characteristic are obvious.

In contrast to the now large-scale industrial production of these chemicals, organochlorines are largely foreign to living systems. Only one organochlorine is produced naturally in significant amounts—chloromethane, the simplest organochlorine, which serves in the natural regulation of the stratospheric ozone layer. Several hundred organochlorines are produced in trace amounts, primarily by lower organisms such as algae and fungi; none are known to occur naturally in the tissues of mammals or terrestrial vertebrates, and none circulate freely and ubiquitously throughout the general environment. Moreover, the organisms that produce organochlorines do so precisely because of their toxicity or other biological activity: organochlorines serve in nature not in the mainstream of biochemistry but as chemical defenses against predators and parasites, as pesticides, and as signalling molecules (i.e., pheromones). The limited role of organochlorines in nature confirms the view that this class of compounds is hazardous to complex living organisms.

GLOBAL CHLORINE POLLUTION

After only about fifty years of large-scale industrial chlorine production, the entire planet is now blanketed with a cocktail of hundreds or thousands of toxic, long-lived organochlorines. This is because of the huge quantities of these chemicals produced by the chemical industry, and because organochlorines tend to persist in the environment and build up in the food chain. Even those organochlorines that do break down almost always degrade into other organochlorines— which are often more toxic and/or persistent than the original substance— compounding the problem further.

In the Great Lakes, for instance, 168 organochlorines have been unequivocally identified in the water, sediments or food chain—making up about half of all the pollutants that have been found in that ecosystem. The list includes the most infamous organochlorines—PCBs, dioxins, and pesticides like DDT and aldrin— but it also contains scores of lesser known organochlorines. Great Lakes contaminants span the entire spectrum of the class of these substances—including simple chlorinated solvents and refrigerants, a host of chlorinated benzenes, phenols and toluenes, a selection of exotic chlorinated by-products, alcohols, acids, and the newer chlorinated pesticides like atrazine and alachlor.

The problem, of course, is not just in North America but is truly global. Because organochlorines tend to be so persistent in the environment, they can travel thousands of miles on currents of wind and water, resulting in a distribution that affects everyone on the planet. In the Arctic circle, for instance, far from any known sources of these compounds, some of the world's highest concentrations of organochlorines can be found in the tissues of polar bears, people, and other species.

And because many organochlorines are more soluble in fat than in water, they bioaccumulate, concentrating in the fatty tissues of living things and multiplying in concentration as they move up the food chain. Concentrations of these chemicals in the bodies of predator species may be millions of times greater than the levels found in the ambient environment. Thus, the bulk of the general population's exposure to many of these compounds occur through the food supply—particularly foods high in fat such as fish, meats, and dairy products.

Since humans are inextricably connected with our environment—though we often forget it—we too are contaminated. Because we are at the top of the foodchain, we bear some of the highest exposures of all. 177 organochlorines have been identified in the fat, blood, mother's milk, semen, and breath of the general population of the U.S. and Canada. These chemicals are in absolutely everyone's body, not just people living near pulp mills and chemical plants.... Organochlorines accumulated in the body are also passed from one generation to the next through the placenta and through mothers' milk.

Worst of all, these 177 organochlorines that have been identified are just the tip of the iceberg: they represent only a fraction of the thousands of contaminants that are known present in our bodies but have not yet been specifically identified....

HEALTH AND ENVIRONMENTAL IMPACTS

The health damage that organochlorines can cause has been well-established, though the existing data may only hint at the full-scale of the problem. Organochlorines are known to disrupt the body's hormones, to cause genetic mutations and metabolic changes, to cause or promote cancer, to reduce fertility, impair childhood development, cause neurological damage, and suppress the function of the immune system. The International Agency for Research on Cancer has identified 117 organochlorines or groups of organochlorines that are known or suspected carcinogens.

Some organochlorines are among the most potent poisons ever studied, though the potency and specific effects vary from one chemical to another. A recent study for the U.S. and Canadian pulp and paper industry admitted that adding chlorine to an organic chemical almost always increases its toxicity, persistence, and tendency to bioaccumulate.

As the America Public Health Association concluded, "virtually all organochlorines that have been studied exhibit at least one of a wide range of serious toxic effects..., often at extremely low doses, and many chlorinated organic compounds... are recognized as significant workplace hazards." A large body of scientific literature shows that people exposed in the workplace to a wide variety of organochlorines—pesticides, PCBs, dioxins, solvents, vinyl chloride, chemical intermediates, and so on—have elevated rates of cancer, infertility, hormonal abnormalities, nervous system damage, and other effects.

By itself, this information is enough to justify a phase-out of these chemicals.

Common sense tells us that we should not be exposing ourselves and other species to chemicals that can cause such a wide range of severe health effects. If they persist or bioaccumulate—making the impacts long-lived and virtually irreversible—the folly of dumping these compounds into the environment becomes even more obvious....

Because these chemicals are persistent and ubiquitous, we confront a threat to our health unlike most hazards associated with toxic chemicals: a global hazard to the health of the entire population, not simply a local set of exposures and health risks.... Although it is so difficult for epidemiologists and environmental scientists to catalogue long-term, large-scale damage and trace it back to its causes, a large body of scientific information that has emerged over the last few years indicates that organochlorines are causing a global epidemic of serious health effects among people and wildlife.

Some of the best information comes from the Great Lakes—one of the best-studied large ecosystems in the world. Here, scientists have documented severe chemically-induced epidemics among 14 species—virtually every predator species in the ecosystem, from bald eagles to salmon, mink to snapping turtles, herring gulls to humans. In each case, the consumption of Great Lakes fish contaminated with organochlorine mixtures appears to be the cause. These epidemics primarily affect reproduction and development, with effects including population declines, inability to reproduce, physical and behavioral feminization of males, birth defects, embryonic mortality, wasting syndrome and other developmental effects, behavioral changes and learning impairment, and immune system suppression. Most alarming, the ef-

fects are most severe not in the exposed generation but in its offspring, and they are often not apparent until the offspring reach adulthood.

The problem is not getting any better. Some of the pesticides and PCBs that were restricted in the 1970s declined somewhat by the mid-1980s, but those chemicals have now stabilized at levels that are still unsafe. Others, such as the chlorinated dibenzofurans, are actually increasing. This summer, four newborn eaglets were discovered with life-threatening birth defects, including crossed bills and clubbed feet, that are consistent with organochlorine exposure. Finding one deformed eagle in a single year would be cause for concern; finding four, especially in a population that is bearing few young anyway, is truly alarming.

Similar effects are occurring worldwide. Epidemics of infertility, reproductive problems, hormonal disruptions and population declines have been documented among seals, fish and birds in the Baltic, the North Sea, the Wadden Sea, the Mediterranean, and the Pacific coast of North America. And organochlorines have been implicated in the mass die-offs of dolphins in recent years, as immune suppression caused by these chemicals appears to have made the animals more susceptible to infectious diseases.

What does this evidence mean for humans? Because they tend to have shorter generation times and more consistent feeding habits than people, wildlife are canaries in the coal mine for effects that can be expected in humans....

In fact, the evidence suggests that the impacts on human health are starting to occur already. In Michigan, a series of studies has found that children born to mothers who had eaten just two to three meals per month of organochlorine-contaminated Great Lakes fish were born sooner, weighed less, and had smaller heads. As they developed, these children suffered an impaired ability to learn, with measurable impacts on short-term memory. These impacts lasted for years, and the severity correlated with the concentrations of organochlorines in the mother's blood. The results from Michigan are consistent with other studies from Wisconsin, North Carolina, Taiwan, and New York state that have found similar behavioral and neurological effects among the offspring of women and animals exposed to PCB, dioxin, or contaminated Great Lakes fish. Based on the severity of the effects and the low doses at which they occur, scientists have concluded that a substantial number of children from the general population may be suffering from this "diminished potential" due to chemical exposures.

Since World War II, average sperm density among men worldwide has declined by about half, and the proportion of men who are infertile has increased accordingly. Dioxin, PCBs, pesticides and other organochlorines that disrupt the body's hormones are known to cause male reproductive impairment, including low sperm counts, feminization, smaller gonad size, and reduced sex drive—even when only a tiny dose is fed to the mother on a single critical day of pregnancy. Several studies have found a relationship between low sperm count and high concentrations of certain organochlorines in a man's semen or blood. Recent articles in the scientific literature have argued that organochlorine exposure of the male fetus before birth may be an important factor in the worldwide decline in male fertility. This body of evidence also suggests that organochlorines may also be factors in testicular cancer and other defects of the male reproductive tracts, both of which can be caused by hormone-disruptors and have increased by 2- to 4-fold in recent decades.

Organochlorines have also been linked in a number of excellent studies to the worldwide epidemic of breast cancer that now strikes about one in nine women in most industrialized nations. Chlorinated solvents and the by-products of chlorination in drinking water have been linked to leukemia, bladder cancer, and colorectal cancer. And a recent large study by the New Jersey Department of Health links these same chemicals in drinking water to increased risk of spontaneous abortion, low birth weight, and a number of types of birth defects, particularly those —such as malformations of the cardiovascular system—that have been rising at an alarming rate among the general population.

In 1994, U.S. EPA released its long-awaited reassessment of the toxicity of dioxin. This three-year effort concluded that dioxin has severe effects upon a wide range of organ systems in humans and animals, that the evidence from studies of people suggests that dioxin has caused cancer, hormonal changes, and an array of biochemical effects in groups of people exposed to dioxin in the workplace or in their community, and that the most severe effects of dioxin are impairment of reproduction, development, and immune system function. Particularly sobering is EPA's conclusion that the current "background" body burden of dioxin and related chemicals in the tissues of the general U.S. population is already in the range at which these effects are known to occur in laboratory animals. There is no margin of safety remaining.

Finally, a few words about the impacts of the destruction of the stratospheric ozone layer, which has been caused primarily by chlorine-containing refrigerants and solvents. The United Nations Environment Programme has estimated that current ozone depletion trends will result in an additional 300,000 cases of skin cancer every year, plus at least 1.6 million cases of cataracts and an unknown but probably very large number of cases of immune suppression. Also expected are worldwide decreases in the productivity of agriculture and the marine foodchain, possibly leading to serious consequences for both humans and the global ecosystem.

... I will stop with these examples, and make two points about all the effects that have been linked to organochlorines. First, none were predicted before the chemicals went into commerce, and all required a lag time of decades before they were discovered. Once the evidence was in, the damage was irreversible. Second, in no study have scientists been able to pinpoint individual chemicals that are responsible for these health and ecological impacts, because it is the mixture of hundreds of organochlorines—along with other factors—that is causing the injury.

POLICY APPROACHES TO ORGANOCHLORINE POLLUTION

... The chemical industry would have us regulate organochlorines one by one. Risk assessments can be used, the industry argues, to determine exposure levels that are safe and environmental concentrations that do not exceed the ecosystem's "assimilative capacity." From these assessments, "acceptable discharges" can be calculated, and the industry proposes using pollution control and disposal devices—filters, incinerators, and the like—to keep releases within those limits.

But this is precisely the current regulatory system, which is primarily reactive: it attempts to control chemicals after they have been produced, and these actions are taken only after the chemicals have been shown to cause harm. The industry's suggestion represents no change from the status quo, really.... This may explain part of why the industry advocates it.

... We need a fundamental shift to a precautionary, public health-based approach. Such a policy seeks to *prevent* damage to our health and the environment before it happens; it accepts the irreversibility of harm and the limits of our scientific knowledge and technological control over toxic chemicals. This new approach is based upon three central ideas: the precautionary principle, zero discharge, and clean production processes.

First, the precautionary principle. Our current system is reactive: it takes action only after harm has already occurred. DDT, PCBs, and CFCs were phased-out, but only after overwhelming evidence linked them to severe impacts on health and the environment. The precautionary principle, which has already been adopted by the UN and other international fora, says that chemicals that *may* cause harm should not be discharged into the environment. In the face of scientific uncertainty, we should err on the side of caution. This idea is analogous to the first laws of medicine and public health practice: first do no harm, with prevention the goal.

Second, zero discharge. Approving "acceptable" discharges of persistent toxic chemicals is a recipe for disaster, because these chemicals—even when released in small amounts—build up in the environment over time, eventually reaching levels that cause health effects. The assumption that the environment has an "assimilable capacity" for pollution may be appropriate for conventional pollutants like oil and grease, which break down in the environment. But for persistent toxic substances, as the IJC has said, the ecosystem's assimilative capacity is zero....

Finally, clean production. We know that "back-end" solutions—pollution control and disposal measures that deal with chemicals and wastes after they are produced—have failed utterly to prevent toxic discharges, because they merely move chemicals from one environmental medium to another. Only front-end solutions—eliminating the production and use of toxic substances and feedstocks—truly prevent environmental contamination. As Barry Commoner has shown, the history of environmental regulations for the last two decades supports the view that pollution control has been marginally effective at best, while bans and phase-outs—on leaded gasoline, PCBs, and certain pesticides, for example—are responsible for all of our major success stories.

... [W]e need to eliminate the use of chlorine and chlorinated compounds by installing chlorine free alternative production processes. As discussed below, chlorine-free technologies are available for all major uses of chlorine—including plastics, pesticides, paper bleaching, solvents, and other chemical uses.

TREATING ORGANOCHLORINES AS A CLASS

The current system, which regulates each compound one-by-one, considers chemicals "innocent until proven guilty."

There are 80,000 chemicals in commerce—11,000 of them organochlorines—plus thousands more formed as accidental by-products. Only a handful have been subject to thorough hazard assessments, and many have not even been identified. Although virtually all organochlorines that have been tested have turned out to cause one or more adverse effects, we continue to presume that the untested ones are safe.

Chemicals do not have constitutional or human rights. The current system mistakenly grants chemicals the right to be considered innocent until proven guilty, while treating people as if we were guinea pigs who should be experimentally exposed to untested chemicals.... It is people who are innocent until proven guilty, and it is people who have the right not be exposed to chemicals that may harm their health.

... The precautionary principle tells us that synthetic chemicals—and the industrial processes that generate them—should be presumed harmful until demonstrated safe and compatible with the basic processes of the ecosystem....

Reversing the burden of proof also allows us to leave behind the cumbersome focus on individual organochlorines numbering in the thousands, and in the impossible bureaucracy that approach creates. Instead, we can target the far smaller set of processes and feedstocks that produce these diverse mixtures. For instance, dioxin and related compounds appear to be formed in virtually all uses of elemental chlorine (including the manufacture of a full range of organochlorine products, including pesticides, solvents, PVC feedstocks, and chemical intermediates), in many uses of organochlorines (especially those that take place in reactive or high-temperature environments) and whenever organochlorines are burned in incinerators, recycling facilities, or in accidental fires. Dioxin is even produced when chlorine gas is produced from salt. Even if our goal is simply to eliminate pollution by dioxin—the single most hazardous organochlorine known—we would have to restrict the use of chlorine in dozens of processes, along with the myriad of individual organochlorine products that are associated with dioxin at some point in their lifecycle.

We do know that all these organochlorines share a common root: the chlorine feedstock. That fact presents the opportunity for a clear and focused chemical policy: we should seek to replace chlorine-based processes with clean alternatives. With a single program, we can eliminate the largest and most hazardous group of toxic pollutants on the planet—a goal that the regulatory bureaucracy now in place has not even been able to consider.

IMPLEMENTING A CHLORINE PHASE-OUT

A chlorine phase-out does not mean that all chlorine-based processes are banned overnight. The process of conversion should be well-planned in order to set priorities, minimize costs, maximize benefits, and insure that both are equitably distributed. The program should begin with a reversal of the burden of proof: organochlorines and the processes that produce them will be presumed to be phased-out unless industry can provide convincing evidence of their safety.

Second, priorities should be set so that the largest, most polluting processes for which alternatives are available now are addressed first. PVC, pulp and paper, solvents, pesticides, other major chem-ical manufacturing processes, incineration of chlorine-containing waste, and in-plant water disinfection are logical priorities. Of course, products that serve a compelling social need for which alternatives are not yet available—such as certain pharmaceuticals, which account for well under one percent of all chlorine use—could be exempted.

Finally, a transition fund should be established to insure that workers and communities do not bear the economic burden of the transformation to a non-toxic economy. This fund, financed with revenues from a tax on chlorine and related products, should be used for two purposes. First, the fund should be used [for] local new investment and to create new jobs in clean production processes in the same communities in which dislocation is most likely, thus placing priority on keeping people employed. Second, workers whose jobs are eliminated should be offered meaningful assistance, protection, and new opportunities: one proposal is the GI Bill for Workers, advocated by the Oil, Chemical and Atomic Workers International Union, would provide full income, up to four years of higher education, and health care coverage to all workers whose jobs are lost because of phase-outs of industries that are incompatible with environmental concerns. Governance of the transition planning fund should include full participation by all interested parties—particularly workers and communities.

CHLORINE ALTERNATIVES AND ECONOMICS

The chemical industry has responded to the calls for a chlorine phase-out by arguing that such a program will result in exorbitant costs (about $100 billion per year) and massive job losses in the U.S. and Canada. The industry's scenario, however, is based upon invalid assumptions that drastically overestimate the costs and underestimate the benefits of a well-planned transition from chlorine-based process to clean production.

In fact, society can realize significant economic gains in this transition, provided that the process is guided by careful planning to use the best alternatives, set sensible priorities, minimize costs, maximize benefits, and insure that both are equitably distributed. Safe, effective alternatives are available now for all major uses of chlorine, preserving or even increasing employment. Further, a prevention-based approach would eliminate the gargantuan social costs and economic drag caused by expenditures on pollution control ($90–$150 billion per year in the U.S.) and contaminated site remediation (up to $750 billion to remediate the current legacy of toxic sites). Further, the International Joint Commission's Virtual Elimination Task Force has estimated that health care costs associated with the effects of persistent toxic substances range from $100 to $200 billion per year. The net contribution of polluting industries to our economy does not appear to be positive.

By prioritizing major chlorine use-sectors, the cost of the phase-out can be substantially reduced. The industry's alarming figures assume that the chlorine phase-out will be implemented all at once, without thought or prioritization and without any attempt to use the most effective and least expensive alternatives. Even based on the industry's own inflated estimates, 97 percent of all chlorine use could be phased out for just $22 billion per year—one-fifth of the assumed cost of a total phase-out and only a fraction of the amount spent annually on toxics-related health care.

The industry has also drastically inflated its estimates of job loss by assuming that all jobs that involve chlorinated chemicals in some way will be lost when chlorine is restricted. But alternative processes will be used instead of chlorine, a chlorine phase-out does not mean that all productive economic activity once associated with chlorinated chemicals will stop.... In many cases, these alternatives create jobs because they are more labor-intensive than the current chemical-intensive processes.

For instance, traditional materials or chlorine-free plastics can substitute for all major uses of PVC plastic—the largest single chlorine use sector. There are dozens of communities, several hospitals and numerous manufacturers of autos, furniture, flooring, and packaged products—mostly in Europe—that have entirely or virtually eliminated the use of PVC. For instance, Tarkett AG—one of the world's largest flooring manufacturers—recently announced it will phase-out all PVC products from its line in favor of chlorine-free plastics and other materials. Tarkett workers will still be employed; they will simply use a different material to produce flooring.

Pulp and paper mills use chlorine to bleach wood pulp bright white, releasing huge quantities of organochlorine discharges in the process. But oxygen-based bleaching processes (using ozone, hydrogen peroxide, oxygen gas, enzymes, and improved control over production conditions) are capable of producing top-quality chlorine-free paper. Already, there are 55 mills around the world producing totally-chlorine-free (TCF) paper for the most demanding uses, including the large-circulation high-profile newsweeklies Der Spiegel and Stern in Germany. TCF production is rapidly coming to dominate paper production and consumption in Western Europe, and the North American industry risks being left behind in the global marketplace if it does not adopt these technologies. In fact, chlorine-free pulp production—following an initial investment—is less expensive than chlorine bleaching because of reduced costs for chemicals, pollution control and disposal, and energy consumption; by switching to chlorine-free bleaching, the North American industry could reduce its operating costs by over $500 million per year.

Chlorinated solvents—used primarily for cleaning and coating in manufacturing industries—are the next largest chlorine use sectors. But in the last 5 years, dozens of manufacturers of electronics, autos, and other types of equipment—including IBM and GE—have begun to eliminate chlorinated solvents in favor of process changes, such as aqueous or mechanical cleaning and coating. According to the U.S. Office of Technology Assessment, these changes result in net savings due to reduced costs for chemical procurement, waste disposal, and liability. For example, U.S. EPA concluded last year that clothing dry cleaners can replace chlorinated solvents with a water-based process that is just as effective but requires a 42 percent lower capital investment and provides a 78 percent better return on investment, a 5 percent increase in profits, a 21 percent increase in jobs and a 38 percent increase in total wages.

As for chlorinated pesticides, the U.S. National Academy of Sciences has found that farmers who eliminate their use of pesticides in favor of organic agriculture lower their costs and increase their yields. Farmers now spend close to $8 billion per year on synthetic pesticides, of which 99 percent are dispersed into the environment without ever reaching their target crop....

Wastewater treatment accounts for about 4 percent of chlorine use, while drinking water treatment uses less than 1 percent of the chlorine in the U.S. Alternatives are available in [this] sector, as well. Hundreds of wastewater treatment plants in the U.S. and Canada are already using ultraviolet light for disinfection prior to discharge, with operating costs lower than those associated with chlorine. Several hundred drinking water systems—mostly in Europe, including those in Berlin and Amsterdam—use UV, ozone, or modern filtration methods to provide safe, chlorine-free water to their communities.

There is no doubt that phasing out chlorine will require substantial technological conversion. Based on industry estimates, the investment in new technology would itself stimulate the creation of about 925,000 job-years of employment. But while we expect the net economic effect to be positive, there will be real disruption for some sectors—specifically those involved in the production of chlorine and chlorinated chemicals. Some chemical firms will have to establish a new production line or go out of business. There are already signs that the largest chemical manufacturers—including Dow, DuPont, Monsanto, and Bayer—are introducing chlorine-free products and seeking to eliminate chlorine from their own processes to anticipate the trend away from chlorine. But who is thinking about the chemical industry workers and communities whose jobs may be moved or lost in the transition? The transition planning fund described above can help preserve jobs, prevent dislocation, and provide meaningful protection for workers and communities, who should not bear the burden of the conversion to a non-toxic economy.

CONCLUSION

Chlorine pollution is not a fact of life. It is the result of decisions made by industry in the last five decades to produce and use toxic synthetic chemicals for convenience, efficiency, or profit. And it is our society that has decided to permit industry to make such choices. We as citizens have the right not to be contaminated by toxic chemicals. We have the right not to worry that our grandchildren will be denied the opportunity to live full and healthy lives because their world has been contaminated by long-lived poisons. We have the right to decide —based on current scientific evidence and our commitment to an ethical public policy on health and the environment— that chlorine chemistry should no longer play a role in our society's production processes.

NO

Ivan Amato

THE CRUSADE TO BAN CHLORINE

Only in the past year or two did the chemical industry realize a meteor was coming its way: a dead-serious proposal to eliminate or drastically curtail the industrial use of chlorine, skillfully brought to legislators and the public by Greenpeace and other environmentalists known for anti-technology positions. "This is the most significant threat to chemistry that has ever been posed," says Brad Lienhart, a longtime industry executive who heads the Chemical Manufacturers Association's new $5 million campaign to counter as much of that threat as possible, for as long as possible.

At issue is the industry's previously unquestioned right to use massive amounts of chlorine, number 17 on the Periodic Table of Elements. Since the end of World War II, chlorine, a pale green gas in its elemental form, has become central to the chemical industry, and thus to thousands of processes and consumer products. "It is the single most important ingredient in modern [industrial] chemistry," says W. Joseph Stearns, director of chlorine issues for Dow Chemical Company, one of the largest producers and users of chlorine.

"It is such a valuable and useful molecule because it does so many things and is involved in so many end products," remarks John Sesody, vice president and general manager of Elf Atochem North America's basic chemical business. Chemists and chemical engineers acknowledge that chlorine is dangerous to use and handle, but argue that industry can manage these dangers well enough for society to safely enjoy chlorine's many benefits.

In fact, many in the chemical industry are passionate about the overall good they say chlorine chemistry does for society (as passionate as the anti-chlorine forces are about its potential for damage). With uses ranging from making pesticides to commodity polymers to synthesizing pharmaceuticals and disinfecting 98% of the nation's water supply, say defenders, chlorine is a substance society cannot do without.

Detractors couldn't disagree more. Polarizing the issue perfectly, "There are no uses, of chlorine that we regard as safe," remarks Joe Thornton, a Greenpeace research analyst who in 1991 authored Greenpeace's case for a chlorine phaseout in a document titled "The Product is the Poison."

Among the documented "criminal actions" of some chlorine-containing chemicals: contaminating riverbeds and lush aquatic habitats such as the Great Lakes water basin; accumulating in the tissue of birds and other wildlife, where they contribute to reproductive disorders and increased incidence of disease; and causing a rare form of liver cancer in some plastics workers who were exposed to high amounts of vinyl chloride monomer (the building block of polyvinylchloride [PVC]) during the 1960s, before the Occupational Safety and Health Administration imposed stringent exposure regulations.

Chlorinated organic molecules have been found in human tissues, and anti-chlorine advocates assert they may be responsible for some of the increase in breast-cancer rates over the past few decades. *No one can claim a causal link* between chlorine-containing chemicals and breast cancer, but the mere suggestion alarms the anti-chlorine camp enough for them to call for its phaseout. As alternatives are available for at least some chlorine-containing products and processes, activists conclude it's better to play it safe and simply banish the element from industry. For example, activists have claimed in all sincerity, we could return to metal piping instead of PVC.

SCIENCE ISN'T THE NAME OF THE PLAYING FIELD

When asked what they think of the call to eliminate industrial use of chlorine, most chemists throw back a "yeah, right" look. Then they denounce it. "The idea of banning chlorine is patently ridiculous and scientifically indefensible," says Steven Safe, a Texas A&M toxicologist who for 20 years has studied such chlorinated compounds as dioxins and PCBs [polychlorinated biphenyls]. Mario Molina, the atmospheric chemist now at M.I.T. who, with Sherwood Rowland, first identified the link between CFCs [chlorofluorocarbons] and ozone depletion, agrees. He told *Science* magazine last summer that banning chlorine "isn't taken seriously from a scientific point of view."

Industry may have been counting on science to throw out this challenge. Yet many participants and observers of the debate doubt that standard scientific study will play a decisive role in determining the fate of chlorine chemistry. Each side of the chlorine debate has corralled vast amounts of data (quite often the same data) to support their diametrically opposed arguments. But public perception can change much more quickly than science can unambiguously determine the real impact of chlorine on the environment and on human health.

That point hit industry in the solar plexus this past February when EPA [Environmental Protection Agency] Administrator Carol Browner was quoted in the *New York Times*, the *Washington Post*, and other national media as saying that the agency's proposals for reauthorizing the Clean Water Act would include a "national strategy for substituting, reducing, or prohibiting the use of chlorine and chlorinated compounds." Ms. Browner's bombshell drew 2,000 angry letters from citizens and elected officials, and an additional 300 letters from industry, says an EPA source who asked not to be identified. "We quickly answered the ones from Congress, and now we are getting into the boxes [of letters.]"

The EPA's reply, which its public-affairs office has been busy delivering to reporters, is more in line with what most scientists would suggest. The Agency's prepared statement says it "will study chlorine and chlorinated compounds to determine whether actions may be necessary to protect aquatic resources from discharges of these compounds, and it is premature to draw any conclusions about EPA's final actions before the study is completed." Even if the study becomes part of a reauthorized Clean Water Act, it is extremely unlikely that any action would be in the form of a blanket ban on chlorine, say EPA insiders.

Despite that clarification, the potential fact of industrial life without elemental chlorine, which the coverage of Ms. Browner's statements displayed in neon, puts raw fear into the heart of chlorine's defenders.

The chemical industry has never been known as a master of public relations. Greenpeace, on the other hand, the most aggressive member of the anti-chlorine consortium, could have written the book. With their "Chlorine Free" campaign, Greenpeace and allies have used every outlet to make their case.

Realizing the court of public relations will likely adjudicate the chlorine debate, the Chemical Manufacturer's Association established and bankrolled the Chlorine Coordinating Council (since renamed the Chlorine Chemistry Council [CCC]), with Brad Lienhart as its managing director. The group hopes to counter what it views as anti-chlorine prejudice fueled more by environmentalist hysteria than hard science and sober risk assessment. Chlorine compounds, they say, ought to be regulated like other compounds—based on determinations of their individual risks and benefits, not on the mere presence of chlorine atoms in their molecular anatomies.

As its first order of business, the CCC commissioned reports on chlorine which included a massive analysis—totaling 10 volumes and 4,000 pages—of the toxicological literature on chlorinated organic compounds. The Chlorine Institute, an older industry group devoted "to the safe production, handling, and use of chlorine," has even prepared packaged school lessons and a video that takes students on a tour of chlorine's role in everyday products. Big chemical companies including Dow have created new full-time positions such as Director of Chlorine Issues. The aim of this emerging infrastructure, says Lienhart, is to offer the public a different view of chlorine chemistry than the one anti-chlorine forces have been purveying unchallenged for years.

Industry remains the underdog. Last October 15, the anti-chlorine lobby got the likes of Bella Abzug, the fiery former New York congresswoman and a cancer survivor, to publicly endorse a Greenpeace document linking the rise of chlorine chemistry over the past few decades to rising rates of breast cancer. The Associated Press reported the event and sent the story over the wires. That sort of lachrymose (and toxicologically meaningless) coverage just isn't available to the CCC.

ELEMENTAL CHLORINE IS A CORNERSTONE OF INDUSTRIAL CHEMISTRY

To the community of manufacturers, chlorine remains a cornerstone of chemistry, playing a role in virtually every nook and cranny of modern society. By volume, chlorine is one of the largest chemical feedstocks, rivaling even petroleum. Global chlorine production now hovers around 38 million tons a year.

NO Ivan Amato / 135

In the United States, the number is more like 11 million tons of chlorine.

The Chlorine Institute reports that about 28% of the chlorine supply goes into making plastics, mostly polyvinyl-chloride (PVC), from which thousands of products are derived, among them wall coverings, floor tiles, siding, pipes, shoe soles, electrical insulation, automobile components, and medical equipment. Saran Wrap is made from another major chlorine-containing polymer —polyvinylidene chloride. Just over one-third of the chlorine supply is used for synthesizing an estimated 11,000 commercial chemicals. Among the lengthy list of chlorine-dependent products are most herbicides and pesticides, dyes, chlorosilanes for making semiconductor materials, carbon tetrachloride for making nonstick cookware and refrigerants, dichlorophenyl sulfone for making computer components and power-tool housings, propylene chlorohydrin that is used first to make propylene oxide, which in turn is used to make a range of products including lubricants, coatings, brake fluids, cleaners, adhesives, pharmaceuticals, and soft-drink syrups.

Just under one-fifth of the chlorine supply is consumed by chlorinated solvents such as methylene chloride, a degreaser and paint stripper, although demand for such solvents is declining as manufacturers switch to water-based and otherwise less environmentally troublesome materials and methods. Approximately 14% of the chlorine supply is used for bleaching pulp and paper; the pulp and paper industry is likewise undergoing a transition toward bleaching processes that use less chlorine or no chlorine at all. The remaining few percent of the chlorine supply goes mostly into agents for purifying drinking and waste water, and for manufacturing pharmaceuticals.

Although undisputed estimates are hard to come by, in one way or another chlorine use amounts to at least tens of billions of dollars of commerce each year in the United States alone. It employs directly or indirectly at least hundreds of thousands of people. The highest estimates, from a widely cited and much disputed economic analysis conducted for the Chlorine Institute by the Charles River Associates consulting firm in Boston, contends that chlorine accounts for $91 billion of economic input in the U.S. and, directly and indirectly, over 1.3 million jobs.

THE SEEDS OF CONTROVERSY WERE PLANTED IN THE 1960s

The controversy began well before Greenpeace focused its worldwide campaign on chlorine chemistry in the mid-1980s, following the lead of Germany's Green Party. Never mind the once undisputed public-health successes of chlorine use in disinfecting water, controlling insect-borne diseases, and manufacturing pharmaceuticals. Such benefits to society can easily be forgotten once the anti-chlorine alliance unleashes its ordnance.

Consider DDT, an insecticide so effective against malaria that the World Health Organization once considered shortages as threats to public health. DDT, which stands for dichlorodiphenyl-trichloro-ethane and includes five chlorine atoms in its molecular structure, became the rallying point of the then-nascent environmental movement when Rachel Carson documented its unanticipated effects on the environment and wildlife in her 1962 book *Silent Spring*. (Although DDT has never been proved to be a significant human hazard, it was banned from use in the U.S. because it was known to bioaccumulate or be deposited in body fat at relatively low levels of exposure.)

Add the notoriety of chlorovillain PCBs, or polychlorinated biphenyls, a family of about 180 compounds that have anywhere from two to ten chlorine atoms in their molecular anatomies. PCBs' stability, low flammability; and insulating properties made them favorites for electrical and hydraulic equipment, but those same properties (along with their solubility in fat) likewise enabled them to accumulate to levels of concern in the cells and fat tissue of animals and people.

DDT and PCBs are not the only so-called organochlorine compounds that have a place among chemicals non grata. Even inorganic chlorine compounds that do not themselves persist in the environment, and presumably pose little long-term risk on their own, can break down into harmful molecules that do stick around. When the elemental chlorine used to bleach paper and the volatile chemicals used to make PVC plastic break down in the environment, they can spawn polychlorinated dibenzodioxins (PCDDs) and polychlorinated dibenzofurans (PCDFs). Both are suspected human carcinogens and both have documented adverse affects on wildlife in the Great Lakes region and elsewhere.

CFCs, or chlorofluorocarbons, whose nontoxicity, low cost, and physical and chemical properties had for decades made them just about perfect for large-scale cleaning and refrigeration uses, have become perhaps the best known and most vilified chlorinated compounds of all. CFCs' probable ozone-depleting properties, which never occurred to their originators in the 1930s, now overshadow all that's good about them. By the end of 1995, industry will halt the manufacture of CFCs in accordance with the international Montreal Protocol, a global response that anti-chlorine advocates view as an important precedent for their more ambitious goal of banning the industrial use of chlorine entirely.

The above-noted "chemical black list" represents a tiny fraction of the chlorinated compounds in use. Even so, activists in Germany's Green Party and then at Greenpeace began, as Brad Lienhart puts it, "connecting the dots" between those few notorious chlorovillains and all chlorine-containing compounds. Even though the majority of chlorinated compounds have never been studied for their toxicological effects, Greenpeace views them as a single class of chemicals that should be considered unfit for commercial use until proven safe—a virtual impossibility, both scientifically and economically.

If Greenpeace were alone in its fight against chlorine, the Dows, Monsantos, and Du Ponts of the world might not have much to worry about. But the chemical industry decided that the call for a ban was more than environmentalist bravado when a normally conservative United States/Canadian commission, the International Joint Commission [IJC], officially announced comprehensive anti-chlorine recommendations, to their respective governments in their biannual report of 1992.

The IJC's scientific panels and advisors convinced its six commissioners that chlorinated compounds are persistent enough in the Great Lakes region that a recommendation to phase them out is prudent. Although the Commission concedes that many of the synthetic chlorinated organic substances identified in the water, sediment, and biota of the region have not been identified as individually toxic, it concludes that many of these chemicals—because of their shared chemical characteristics—will be identified as persistent toxicants.

The IJC recommended in 1992 that the U.S. and Canada "develop timetables to sunset [phase out] the use of chlorine and chlorine-containing compounds as industrial feedstocks, and the means of reducing or eliminating other uses [such as water treatment and paper bleaching] be examined." Moreover, other treaty organizations that oversee the use of international waters have articulated similar antichlorine positions.

"The IJC lit up our lives," says Rick Hinds, legislative director of Greenpeace's toxics campaign.

Despite rigorous lobbying by the CCC to stop lumping the entire menagerie of chlorine-containing compounds into one huge regulatory class, the IJC is standing firm. Its 1994 biannual report, issued following its most recent gathering in Windsor, Ontario, redoubled calls for sunsetting chlorine. Brad Lienhart, who participated in the IJC meeting, thinks that some gains were made despite the anti-chlorine message. The IJC's Virtual Elimination Task Force, which develops strategies to eventually eliminate all toxic inputs to the Great Lakes, agreed there is a need for "a thorough and complete analysis of chlorine chemistry before any schedule for sunsetting chlorine is implemented," Mr. Lienhart says. He believes such an analysis will vindicate much of chlorine chemistry as a sensible, environmentally responsible choice for manufacturers.

Following that mild concession by the IJC, though, another voice joined the anti-chlorine chorus. In early November,

the American Public Health Association, which represents 50,000 public-health workers, registered some of the strongest anti-chlorine positions yet heard. A final draft of the APHA's position states "the only feasible and prudent approach to eliminating the release and discharge of chlorinated organic chemicals and consequent exposure is to avoid the use of chlorine and its compounds in manufacturing processes." The resolution concedes that not all uses of chlorine, especially such public-health uses as disinfecting drinking water and pharmaceutical production, have feasible alternatives—thereby implying that those uses of chlorine ought to be continued. But APHA calls for provisions to retrain workers displaced from a shrinking chlorine industry.

THE CASES FOR AND AGAINST MAY REST ON RISK OR BENEFIT TO SOCIETY

Like looking at clouds, both sides can see what they want in existing data, or commission hand-picked scientists to do studies that lend credence to their respective interpretations.

In lieu of objective scientific debate, methodological and philosophical issues are at the fore. One of the largest gulfs between the two camps centers on the unprecedented call to consider all chlorinated compounds in use as a single class subject to regulatory action. The case for banning all industrial uses of chlorine is easier to explain, which gives it a decided advantage over the more complicated argument of chlorine's defenders. The basic argument starts with reference to DDT, PCBS, dioxins, CFCs and a few other compounds that have documented effects. Next the argument points out that all of these compounds have one thing in common, namely, the presence of chlorine atoms in their molecular structures.

Finally, the argument takes an inferential step—and this is the precise point of contention. It concludes that, because of this commonality, all other chlorine compounds are suspected environmental and biological hazards. The concept of "reverse onus" would be applied to all chlorinated compounds: an assumption that they produce toxicity unless otherwise proved by the seller. Since chlorine detractors admit that most chlorine-dependent compounds have never been shown to have hazardous effects and have never even been studied, they refer to this conclusion as "the precautionary principle."

Another key component of the argument points to correlations between the presence of chlorinated organics in sediments, water basins, and tissues of animals and humans, on the one hand, and, on the other, incidences of wildlife population declines, reproductive and developmental anomalies in animals and people, and various diseases, including cancer. Theo Colborn, a Fellow at the World Wildlife Fund who chaired an often-cited gathering of toxicologists, ecologists, immunologists, and other scientists three years ago, said in an interview that "we have reached a point [of loading toxic synthetic chemicals in the environment and living tissue] that we ought to be concerned about releasing more."

The so-called "precautionary principle" is seductively simple. There are simply too many chlorinated compounds to study on a one-by-one basis to assess their safety. "There aren't enough rats in the world to assess individual compounds and what their combined effects might

be," says Tufts University biologist Ana Soto, who is studying how compounds including PCBs can mimic the hormonal effects of estrogen.

Nevertheless, the pro-chlorine advocates assert that the only scientifically defensible way to ascertain chlorine's health and environmental effects is to do toxicological, epidemiological, and other studies of specific organochlorine chemicals. They point out that the scientific data simply does not exist to implicate any but a very few organochlorine compounds, such as DDT and PCBs—which have been studied for many years. Brad Lienhart tirelessly points out that the many thousands of organochlorine compounds in use cannot legitimately be thought of as a single class because they are chemically, physically, and biologically heterogeneous. Adds W. Joseph Stearns, Dow's director of chlorine issues: "The substantive part of this issue is that *some* organochlorines are persistent toxics, not that all organochlorines contain chlorine."

Indeed, many organochlorine compounds have short lifespans in the natural world. Mr. Stearns argues that to condemn any compound because it contains chlorine in its molecular structure will lead to a whole host of environmental regulations that the actual risks do not call for. And depriving society of thousands of useful, chlorine-based products without ascertaining if the risks are unacceptable, says the pro-chlorine camp, is a misguided formula that will greatly damage the nation's economic strength and standard of living.

GREENPEACE'S INSISTENCE THAT "SUBSTITUTES EXIST" IS MISLEADING

Chlorine's defenders can point out the importance of its use in modern industrial chemistry, and try to explain the complex toxicological reasons why tens of thousands of compounds having nothing in common but chlorine should not be treated as a single class of chemicals. But their strongest argument may be that, while substitutes for chlorine and chlorinated compounds may exist in many cases, the costs to switch are prohibitive and the substitutes not necessarily any less risky.

Susan Sieber, a toxicologist and Deputy Director of the Division of Cancer Etiology at the National Cancer Institute, warns that hasty blanket bans can have the unwanted effect of pushing alternatives that are worse. "You need to assess the risks and benefits," she says.

Attempts at sober assessment that would fall between the two camps have begun in earnest. One example is a 180-page report that the M.I.T. Program in Technology, Business and Environment prepared for the Norwegian government and European industry groups. The report begins the daunting task of assessing the economic, social, and environmental costs and gains of non-chlorine substitutes, focusing on several areas including cleaning solvents in the electronics industry, polyvinylchloride (PVC) plastic, chlorinated pesticides, and chlorine-based bleaching agents.

The report notes that a trend toward chlorine-free bleaching technologies in the paper industry shows that major categories of chlorine use are not absolutely necessary for the industries that have been heavy chlorine users. "This suggests that concerns over the unavailability of such alternatives in other cases of chlorine use may be overblown," concludes the summary of the report's findings.

Availability of substitutes, however, is only part of the story. Among the big caveats:

• Substitutes carry their own environmental and health effects. For example, water-based substitutes for CFCs in the electronics industry add a new source of water pollution. The return of hydrocarbon coolants and insulating fluids for electrical transformers has brought back the fire hazards that PCBs had virtually eliminated.

• Chlorine-based technologies themselves may have been less hazardous replacements for nastier technologies. A chlorine-dependent route to titanium dioxide, a widely used pigment in white paint, replaced the dangerous lead-based pigments that contributed to a public-health calamity. The chlorine-dependent process produces one-sixth the hazardous waste of an alternative process that relies on sulfuric acid.

• Affordable alternatives that can perform as well as the chlorine-dependent product may not exist. In these cases, technological innovation and development can take a long time, at great cost. The report cites the absence of any drop-in replacements for CFCs that automakers could use for air conditioning systems of cars after the CFC ban goes into effect.

FEW SEE THE WHOLE PICTURE, BUT LEGISLATORS AND USER GROUPS HAVE BEGUN TO REACT

Greenpeace believes it has industry on the run. "The writing is on the wall," says Jay Palter, Toronto director of the group's Chlorine Free campaign. "A chlorine phaseout is inevitable and industry is just stalling for time."

Industry representatives don't see it that way. "Greenpeace is not fundamentally changing the way we do business," says Michael W. Berezo, director of environmental strategy for Monsanto. At the moment, neither EPA nor its Canadian counterpart, Environment Canada, has accepted the notion that all chlorine compounds ought to be regulated or phased out as a class. Berezo does concede that the ascent of the chlorine issue is pushing Monsanto and other companies to look more aggressively at alternatives to chlorine-containing chemicals. But industry's dilemmas lack easy answers.

Specific user groups have begun to wrestle with the chlorine issue as it affects them. The Jan/Feb '94 issue of the newsletter *Environment Building News* ran a 10-page article titled "Should We Phase Out PVC?" The report makes a Herculean effort to integrate the available information on PVC's benefits and the dangers stemming from its manufacture into a picture that might guide its readers. After concluding that its account left more questions than answers, the article counseled the 1,200 builders and architects who subscribe to the newsletter to "seek out better, safer, and more environmentally responsible alternatives" to polyvinylchloride—without actually suggesting that readers completely avoid vinyl materials. PVC accounts for more than a quarter of worldwide chlorine use,

so such recommendations can have far-reaching effects.

Perhaps the most newsworthy feature of the chlorine controversy is that it has progressed to the point where a ban is being taken seriously by governments and industry. And even if the meteor of a ban is deflected by pragmatic concerns, chlorine chemistry may be forever changed by an asteroid shower of legislation. In October, Rep. Bill Richardson (D-NM) delighted environmentalists by reintroducing a bill that would legislate chlorine out of the pulp and paper industry within five years. In October, the Clinton administration nearly issued an executive order that would have mandated government to buy paper made without chlorine. (The requirement didn't make it into the final order.)

Even a year ago, engineering professor David Marks, who is coordinating M.I.T.'s $1.8 million cross-disciplinary study of chlorine, thought the anti-chlorine movement couldn't box its way out of an unbleached paper bag. Now he wonders. "The chlorine industry could wake up one day and see many anti-chlorine bills on the table in Congress," he warns. "Things are moving so fast, it's hard to tell how it will end up."

Industry is well aware how quickly a few Bella Abzugs can alter public perception. Despite the difficulties in switching to chlorine-free production, progressive companies are eyeing such strategies as pollution prevention and substitution to preempt future, more costly adjustments. Truly farsighted companies aim to turn anti-chlorine sentiment into a market. Dow has created a new business entity called Advanced Cleaning Systems, which provides water-based cleaning technology and support services for green industrial niches. And Louisiana

Pacific, one of the country's largest paper manufacturers, is trumpeting its new chlorine-free bleaching process at a plant in Samoa, California.

Should there be a chlorine phaseout, it would probably occur in a piecemeal fashion, hopping from product category to product category. Both sides will continue to debate the data on what effects chlorinated compounds have on the environment and human health. But it seems quite possible that even without government-imposed limits, public perception and the market forces that follow from it will dictate the future of chlorine's role in industry and society.

POSTSCRIPT

Should the Industrial Use of Chlorine Be Phased Out?

Industry claims that the cost of eliminating those chlorinated organics that are either not essential or for which there are available substitutes would be prohibitive, as well as suspect without an independent assessment by an agency that does not have a vested interest in maintaining the status quo. Similar claims, which greeted the initial demands to phase out most uses of asbestos and chlorofluorocarbons, proved to be vastly overstated. Omitted from the chlorine industry's economic analysis of the issue is the savings that would accrue to the general public from a general restriction on chlorinated compounds, due to the fact that regulatory agencies would be relieved of the financial burden of assessing the hazards of individual compounds and enforcing regulations for each one that required restriction. On the other hand, Thornton's claim that "97% of all chlorine use could be phased out for just $22 billion per year" would most likely not stand up to the scrutiny of an unbiased analysis.

Transition Planning for the Chlorine Phaseout and *Chlorine, Human Health and the Environment: The Breast Cancer Report* are publications available from Greenpeace. The technical arguments used by the chlorine industry in their opposition to the phaseout are contained in the April 1993 *Assessment of the Economic Benefits of Chlor-Alkali Chemicals to the United States and Canadian Economies*, prepared by Charles River Associates, Inc., for the chlorine industry. A more even-handed analysis is "The Crusade Against Chlorine," by Ivan Amato, in the July 9, 1994, issue of *Science*. An article that strongly condemns the anti-chlorine initiative as a "campaign against modern industrial society" is "Chemical Warfare," by Michael Fumento, *Reason* (June 1994).

The evolving political strategies and arguments of the parties in the chlorine controversy can be followed by reading Bette Hileman's News Focus article in the April 19, 1993, issue of *Chemical and Engineering News*, as well as the News Focus article Hileman coauthored with Janice R. Long and Elisabeth M. Kirschner in the November 21, 1994, issue of the same journal.

ISSUE 8

Is Stringent Enforcement of Existing Laws Needed to Improve Air Quality?

YES: Will Nixon, from "The Air Down Here," *The Amicus Journal* (Summer 1994)

NO: Lester P. Lamm, from "Clean or Green: Political Correctness vs. Common Sense in Transportation," *Vital Speeches of the Day* (May 15, 1994)

ISSUE SUMMARY

YES: *E Magazine* associate editor Will Nixon claims that the Clean Air Act "may be the most ambitious pollution program on the books," and its failures are due to lax enforcement.

NO: Highway Users Federation president Lester P. Lamm sees new federal air and transportation laws as a threat to the economy. He supports proposed national highway system improvements as the route to cleaner air and less congested roads

The fouling of air due to the burning of fuels has long plagued the inhabitants of populated areas. After the industrial revolution, the emissions from factory smokestacks were added to the pollution resulting from cooking and household heating. The increased use of coal combined with local meteorological conditions in London produced the dense, smoky, foggy condition first referred to as "smog" by Dr. H. A. Des Vouex in the early 1900s.

Dr. Des Vouex organized British smoke abatement societies. Despite the efforts of these organizations, the problem grew worse and spread to other industrial centers during the first half of the twentieth century. In December 1930, a dense smog in Belgium's Meuse Valley resulted in 60 deaths and an estimated 6,000 illnesses due to the combined effect of the dust and sulfur oxides from coal combustion. This event, and a similar one in Donora, Pennsylvania, received public attention but little response. Serious smog control efforts did not begin until a disastrous "killer smog" in London in December 1952 resulted in approximately 4,000 deaths.

The first major air pollution control victory was the regulation of high-sulfur coal burning in populated areas. The last life-threatening London smog incidents were recorded in the mid-1960s. Unfortunately, a new smog problem, linked to the rush hour traffic in large cities such as Los Angeles, was fast developing. This highly irritating, smelly, smoky haze—now referred to as photochemical smog—is caused by sunlight acting on air laden with nitrogen oxides, unburned hydrocarbons from automotive exhausts, and other sources. The resulting chemical reactions produce ozone and a variety of more exotic chemicals that are very irritating to lungs and nasal passages—even at very low levels.

The Clean Air Act of 1963 was the first comprehensive U.S. legislation aimed at controlling air pollution from both stationary sources (factories and power plants) and mobile sources (cars and trucks). Under this law and its early amendments, regulations have been issued to establish maximum levels for both ambient air concentrations and emissions from tailpipes and smokestacks for common pollutants such as sulfur dioxide, suspended particulates (dust), carbon monoxide, nitrogen dioxide, ozone, and airborne lead. Although these standards, coupled with required state plans to reduce air pollution, have had a significant impact, the exponential growth in the number of motor vehicles has resulted in only a modest average reduction in pollutant levels. Many urban areas in the United States still exceed the limit for one or more pollutants. Satellite photographs reveal chronic pollution over vast areas, such as the entire U.S. northeastern coast. Even more severe air pollution plagues other industrialized urban centers around the globe, such as Mexico City.

After years of debate Congress finally passed the 1990 Clean Air Act amendments. This complex piece of legislation includes significantly more stringent standards and extends controls to many additional sources of air emissions. It is designed to produce a marked improvement in air quality by the end of the century, as well as to reduce the incidence of acid precipitation that occurs when nitrogen- and sulfur-oxide emissions return to earth hundreds of miles from their sources in the form of rain, snow, or fog laden with sulfuric and nitric acids. In addition, a new congressional initiative, the Intermodal Surface Transportation Efficiency Act (ISTEA), was signed in 1991 into law aimed at stimulating the changes in human and freight transport that would facilitate compliance with the Clean Air Act goals. Both of these acts were initially received favorably by most clean air advocates, but they have stimulated recent sharp criticism due to the slow pace with which they are being implemented.

Will Nixon, associate editor of *E Magazine*, describes the frustration experienced by grassroots air quality advocates in attempting to organize support for the enforcement of the complex Clean Air Act amendments. However, Nixon sees this legislation, coupled with ISTEA, as providing the strong legal mandate required for air pollution reduction. Lester P. Lamm, president of the Highway Users Federation, views both the Clean Air Act amendments and ISTEA as draconian "Big Brother" laws that will force Americans to change their lifestyles. He claims that clean air and personal mobility can both be achieved by strong support for legislation to improve the national highway system, which will reduce road congestion.

YES

Will Nixon

THE AIR DOWN HERE

In the United States, the ill winds blow in many directions. From her house near the Maine coast, Lee Buffinton can watch a brown bank of summer smog, which migrates up the Atlantic seaboard every summer, wash inland from the ocean to ruin her day. With her scarred lungs, a legacy of childhood illnesses, she is a human pollution monitor able to tell when the ozone levels rise above her state's safety standard, as they do more than thirty days every summer. She must quit her gardening or tennis and take to a hammock with a cup of herbal tea because any exercise would make her sick. "I can get a scratchy throat, congestion, a headache. That can work itself into coughing, wheezing, shortness of breath," she says. "Just hiking up the hill from my garden does it."

Gloria Inverso lives in "Rocky" country near the Italian market and the famed Pat's Cheese Steak stand in South Philadelphia. She is the third generation on her block of look-alike brick row houses (which tourists often peer into, expecting to see the nineteenth century). But in 1989 the city rezoned her neighborhood, opening the way for the fifty-four auto repair and auto body shops she now counts within six square blocks. Inverso also faces dry cleaners, sign painting shops—all in all, a major pollution source divided into dozens of parts. Her ordeal began at the Labor Day block party in 1990, when she arrived late and found that everyone had already taken their picnic food inside because the boys had come down with bloody noses from breathing air that smelled like bottles and bottles of nail polish remover. Since then, Inverso has had two dogs die. A neighbor's cat went crazy after three weeks of sitting in the windowsill. "Birds have dropped dead like a Raid commercial with their feet in the air," she says. "Everybody sounds like they have a cold 365 days a year." She loses her breath sometimes just walking up a few stairs, and she has shed thirty to forty pounds. "I have mucus in my chest and sinus drips. I can't eat. It's a great weight loss program for anyone who doesn't want to spend money."

To live in Altgeld Gardens on the south side of Chicago, a neighborhood ringed with chemical factories and fronted by a sewage treatment plant, Patricia Jackson of People for Community Recovery needs two basic pieces of asthma equipment: a steroid inhaler used twice a day and a medicated inhaler used five times a day. "If I didn't, I'd be gasping for breath every half hour," she says. Before she moved here, an inhaler would last her six months to a year; now she buys a new one every month. And she's not alone. "If someone sees you use an inhaler, they say, 'Oh you've got asthma too.' It's very common here," she adds. "Some people are confined to their homes with respiratory machines, and two died from asthma this winter. I was speaking on the phone with a woman in Denver, Colorado, who works at the National Jewish Center. As soon as she heard where I live, she said, 'You've got to get out of there.' I know, but it's not that easy."

* * *

In 1990, President Bush signed the Clean Air Act Amendments, a legal behemoth more than 700 pages long designed to solve countless problems like these. All told, this multifarious law aims to reduce toxic air emissions by over 70 percent; cut the sulfur dioxide emissions that cause acid rain by almost 50 percent; phase out chlorofluorocarbons and other ozone-depleting substances; and ensure that the vast majority of Americans live in areas with healthy air by the year 2000 —no small task, since the Environmental Protection Agency (EPA) estimates that at present, 140 million people live in counties prone to polluted air.

To accomplish all this, the Clean Air Act takes a decentralized approach to the mightily decentralized problem of air pollution. It deals with—just for starters —diesel buses, paint fumes, electric utilities, and highway planning; chemical plants, lawn mowers, carpooling, and dry cleaners; marine terminals, employee parking privileges, and the chemistry of gasoline. And, to fragment the process

still further, some of these issues are in the hands of the EPA, some in the hands of the states.

Activists working to enforce the 1990 Act have had some notable success stories. There was the decision last February by the Ozone Transport Commission (which coordinates clean air efforts along the smogbound Atlantic seaboard) to petition EPA to impose California's strict new auto emissions standards on states from Virginia to Maine. There was EPA's decision to hold public hearings in "Cancer Alley," the mostly African-American region between Louisiana and Texas, in order to give citizens a chance to testify on its weak organic chemical plant rules. After hearing hours of anguished testimony from people who live near the plants, EPA toughened up some of the regulations.

* * *

Yet some environmentalists fear that, all in all, the 1990 Act faces the same fate as earlier clean air laws: good plans on paper that are resisted in practice. The EPA has fallen behind in conducting studies and issuing regulations. States keep missing their annual deadlines to implement stages of the Act. States with serious ozone problems, for instance, must put together customized smog control plans by November of this year —but few seem ready to make this critical deadline, says Deborah Sheiman, an NRDC senior researcher. "What we are watching is the imminent collapse of one of the most important clean air programs on the books," she adds. And, in one of the 1990 Act's hottest political showdowns, California recently wriggled out of the EPA's specifications for an improved auto inspection program to catch the 20 percent of cars that are causing 60 percent of the pollution.

And, as if delays and compromises were not enough, there is mounting scientific evidence that the EPA has set its "healthy" levels for the two most widespread pollutants, ozone smog and fine particles (or particulate matter), too high. Its limit for ozone is a one-hour concentration of 0.12 parts per million, but current tests find that people can suffer fatigue, congestion, and other ill effects from breathing ozone at 0.08 parts per million over the course of a day. Epidemiological studies in a number of cities, including six tracked by a Harvard team since 1974, have found a strong link between fine particulates and mortality—even at levels better than EPA's standard—with estimates running from 50,000 to 70,000 premature deaths a year. The American Lung Association has sued under the Clean Air Act to have EPA improve its ozone and particulate standards, but it will take years before the agency reaches a decision.

* * *

There are several reasons why clean air will not come easy. Industry has been well equipped to aid the bureaucratic weakening of the original vision of the law, bringing on a phalanx of attorneys and lobbyists to influence each new regulation as it comes up. The EPA's new rules on toxic emissions from dry cleaning operations, for example, are laxer than California's.

Meanwhile, the breathing public, even those who suffer greatly from air pollution, plays little part in the debate. Air pollution is hard to see and harder to understand. Hospitals have no "particulate wards" for the heart and lung patients put at risk by breathing diesel exhaust, and, as Carlos Martinez of the Labor/Community Strategy Center in Southern California puts it, "If people don't know what's killing them, they won't react."

Ozone smog is almost as bad. On the one hand, it is easy to confuse ground-level ozone smog with the stratospheric ozone layer: "I have literally had two people tell me that they heard there was an ozone alert, so they put extra sunscreen on their children," says Lee Buffinton. On the other, people affected by breathing ozone often do not know what hit them. Buffinton comments, "I was at a meeting one muggy summer night, and half of the people in the audience had raspy voices and coughs. Someone said, 'What is this pollen?' I said, 'I think it's the air pollution.' They looked at me like, '*What?*'"

The Clean Air Act itself does not help. To the ordinary citizen, it is a Pandora's box of atmospheric pollution chemistry, abstruse policy concepts, and acronyms galore. Anyone wanting to join the fun must learn fluency with the terms SIP, NO_x, RACT, MACT, VOC, HOV, ECO, UAM, and VMT. (Pop quiz: Which is a complicated way of saying "Leave the car at home"?) Indeed, one activist in Washington, D.C., has found the campaign for state smog-reduction plans to be the most difficult he has ever worked on.

In defense of all the complexity, Bill Sessa, a spokesman for the California Air Resources Board, quotes a federal official who once said, "Even the simplest air quality issue is more complicated than the most complex water or solid waste issue." But the upshot is that Clean Air Act issues tend to remain the purview of full-time clean air professionals—advocates, public officials, and industry lawyers who understand its concepts and speak its language.

Gloria Inverso and Patricia Jackson focus their community work on siting issues and on coping with asthma, respectively, though stringent air quality regulations would also bring them relief. GHASP (Galveston Houston Alliance to Stop Pollution) has just a dozen members agitating for a tough state air plan, even though Houston has an ozone problem second only to that of Los Angeles. GHASP leader Brandt Mannchen comments that local conservation issues such as protecting Galveston Bay attract more public support. And when one checks in with asthma support groups in Los Angeles—surely the most likely hotbeds of grassroots clean air activism in the country—the story is the same: food labeling is more likely to be on the agenda than ozone.

* * *

With public involvement in clean air policy low, and only a limited number of beleaguered air quality advocates to defend it, the Clean Air Act has become an easy target of criticism. It is now fashionable, in many Washington circles, to regard the Act as a dinosaur typical of an outdated "command and control" approach. "Newer environmental thinking calls for upfront pollution prevention rather than end-of-the-tailpipe controls, and that's great," says Jayne Mardock of the Clean Air Network, a national umbrella organization of clean air advocates. "But you can't throw the baby out with the bathwater. I'll be the first to throw my hat in the air when all air pollution has been prevented, but until that day we still need to control the pollution because we're still breathing it."

Indeed, one of the best-kept secrets of the Clean Air Act is that, when it is enforced, it works. Without it, we might be living by now in the *"air noir"* atmosphere of the movie "Batman" or of metropolises like Mexico City, where you can read your fate in the black smoke signals rising from the tailpipes. Since it was first passed in 1970, the Clean Air Act had dramatically cleaned up our skies by filtering our industrial economy, adding everything from catalytic converters on cars to smokestack scrubbers on coal-burning utilities. Between 1983 and 1992, airborne lead fell 89 percent as leaded gasoline was phased out. Carbon monoxide fell 34 percent, even as Americans drove 37 percent more miles. Ozone, a tricky one to average because it varies so much with hot and cool summers, declined about 10 percent.

Even the effects of the 1990 Amendments have already registered at the air monitors. In twenty-eight metropolitan areas with winter carbon monoxide problems, for instance, the EPA made gas stations switch to oxygenated gasoline that costs up to five cents a gallon extra but burns cleaner. In 1992, these areas saw their peak levels of carbon monoxide drop by 13 percent—virtually eliminating violations of the carbon monoxide standard.

* * *

And the Clean Air Act is having benefits in other areas, as well. It amounts to an industrial development policy for new pollution control equipment. The EPA cites a recent study showing that environmental protection is already a $100 billion industry, and that the air pollution control industry alone will grow by $50 billion to $70 billion over today's revenues by the year 2000. That could translate into 300,000 new jobs. And it is an area of technology with strong export potential, as Bill

Sessa confirms: "Literally every piece of hardware that reduces pollution on cars anywhere in the world was developed for California."

In addition, Project California predicts that California's mandate to auto manufacturers, requiring them to start selling a certain quota of electric vehicles in the next few years, could produce 71,000 jobs by the year 2010. (Project California is a committee of industry, academics, labor, and state officials seeking to develop new clusters of high-tech environmental industries.) Indeed one of the biggest boosters of the electric-vehicles mandate is the state machinists union.

Similar results could follow as the EPA moves to regulate in other fields. After twenty years of focussing primarily on passenger cars, the agency is starting to pay much more attention to all of the other fossil-fuel engines operating in our society: diesel buses and trucks, farm and construction equipment, lawn and gardening machinery, motor boats and jet skis, perhaps even locomotives and jet planes. Many of these engines will undergo the same kinds of radical improvements that cars have made, cleaning up by 95 percent since 1970 (though it is worth noting that electric cars will still be 200 times cleaner over their lifetimes than gasoline-powered cars). Cleaning up the motors for lawn mowers and chain saws, for instance, which have long been designed with no thought for air quality, will take a far more efficient design or a catalytic converter the size of a fifty-cent piece.

* * *

But, in the end, the Clean Air Act does admit that reinventing technology is not enough. Engines can only be so clean, and when their number is growing by leaps and bounds, the aggregate pollution will increase in spite of every improvement at the tailpipe. "If car use had gone up in Chicago at the same rate as population instead of twelve times faster, we would have 20 to 25 percent less hydrocarbons and nitrogen oxides [the main ingredients of ozone smog]," says Ron Burke of the American Lung Association in Chicago. In Maine, the population grew 8 percent during the 1980s while the number of miles driven leaped by 60 percent.

And so the Clean Air Act, for all its reputation as the fuddy-duddy of environmental laws, contains what may be the most ambitious pollution prevention program on the books: a mandate for society to put the brakes on the sprawling exurban subdivisions, industrial parks, and highway extensions that turn us into such drive-oholics in the first place. Much as utilities have discovered "least-cost planning," which allows them to use energy efficiency as the cheaper alternative to building new power plants, so too will metropolitan planning councils, local zoning boards, and state transportation departments have to learn a new way of life. In tandem with the Surface Transportation Efficiency Act of 1991—which supplies the "carrot" of federal funds for transportation infrastructure—the Clean Air Act requires the states to ensure that the sum total of new road-building in a year adds no new pollution.

Will it work? How well? How soon? Stay tuned. And remember: the script is still being written. Anyone with an interest in the outcome needs to take part.

NO
Lester P. Lamm

CLEAN OR GREEN: POLITICAL CORRECTNESS VS. COMMON SENSE IN TRANSPORTATION

Delivered before the Detroit Economic Club, Detroit, Michigan, March 29, 1994

It is a pleasure to be here in Detroit, a place that is the very symbol of economic revival, the name badge of the century-old U.S. auto industry which itself has been a leader in America's response to the changing international challenges of our time.

Dismissed by short-sighted pundits only a few years ago, your auto industry has tightened its belt, whipped itself into shape and, let me put it like this, kicked a little tailgate.

It has been a magnificent renaissance, one that I know is a source of pride to the people of Detroit and to the nation. The auto industry has led a national trend. Maybe you've seen reports of last year's cross-national McKinsey & Company study on productivity. In both the service and manufacturing sectors, America is leaving the rest of the world in the dust. And that, of course, means a better, more hopeful, happier future for ourselves and our children.

One major reason for our productivity preeminence is, my topic today, our highway system—Our roads carry 82 percent of our intercity passenger traffic, 94 percent of our commuter miles traveled and almost 80 percent of U.S. freight by dollar value. They are truly the backbone of transportation in the United States.

Just-in-time delivery is now the key to productivity improvements in nearly every industry and thus America's highways are a major component of your continued success.

Also for those of you involved in transportation products or services, our uniquely American desire for individual mobility is your base market as well.

Transportation productivity is, in a sense, my theme for today—What we must do to ensure its continued growth, and two laws and the regulations that go with them that may well decimate it.

I am here to sound an alarm!

To tell you that every business in America—in both services and manufacturing—needs to wake up to a threat to the arteries that bring its employees to work and take its products to markets.

You—and every American needs to know—that transportation service, and, to a noticeable extent, your markets are being threatened by two laws which are creating an artificial conflict between basic values all Americans support—continued economic growth and a cleaner environment. The laws are the Clean Air Act Amendments of 1990 and the Intermodal Surface Transportation Efficiency Act of 1991.

Let me start with the Clean Air Act Amendments. And I will put the nature of the threat as simply and directly as possible. The final regulations that implement this law will soon apply nationwide—although in some areas they are already in force. This law is of course not new to you, you've had to respond as "stationary sources" for years.

What you may not know is that the second shoe is on its way. You, your plants, your suppliers, customers, and employees are also "mobile sources," and do we have a treat in store for you!

The mobile source mandates threaten to be a disaster for business growth and productivity.

For one example, new mobile source regulations will mandate that 10 urban areas in 11 states—New York City, Chicago, Los Angeles—areas where your companies are actively doing business—reduce dramatically, and artificially, the number of motor vehicles on their roads during peak travel periods.

Businesses with as few as 100 employees at a single site will be required to develop plans to increase the average occupancy of their workers' vehicles by 25 percent.

The penalty if they don't? Or if the bureaucrats in charge of enforcement don't like their plans? Fines of up to $50,000 a day.

California has been enforcing these rules since 1991, and already some outrageous stories are accumulating. For example Kaiser Permanente—the health maintenance organization—offered their employees cash incentives to carpool.

Auditors for the local air quality maintenance district thought that the incentives should be stronger—including more free lunches for workers to keep them from driving out to eat. So they slapped Kaiser with a $125,000 fine (proving, yet again, that there is no such thing as a free lunch). Kaiser could have appealed.

But—get this—the district board hears appeals and rules on its own decisions. So Kaiser negotiated a settlement, which was to apply the fine to car pool development costs.

According to one study, in 1992 California employers spent $160 million complying with these rules. To give credit, the result was fewer cars on the road—but, at a cost of $3,000 a car.

But even that amazing number may be dramatically below the true costs.

For example, according to the *Los Angeles Business Journal*, just companies alone—Douglas Aircraft and Southern California Edison—are spending a million dollars a year on compliance—each!

And according to a senior officer in the San Diego Economic Development Corporation, in her words, "This one regulation is at the top of the list as to why companies would like to leave California."

The best estimate is that employers are spending up to $1,000 per employee per year on this Clean Air Act rule alone.

As the head of the environmental department at one Bethlehem Steel facility has said, "I've got 6,000 people at my plant. I want the biggest bang for my buck. For $6 million, I could do a lot more for the environment." Those are his words, not mine.

Now think about what that cost means, not to a giant like Bethlehem Steel, but to a small, growing company, the kind that creates most of America's new jobs each year. If you have a company with 99 employees on site, you don't face these expenses. Hire the 100th man or woman and you do.

In other words, that employee could cost you as much as $100,000.

There has been talk in recent years of companies deciding to stop hiring, rather than cross such a regulatory threshold. These clean air regulations are a prime example of why that is so.

We are talking about a massive tax on American business and particularly on growing companies that are thinking of crossing the 100 employee threshold. The amazing thing here is that of the many ways to improve air quality, this one government mandate is about the most expensive and least effective way!

It's not hard to find alternatives.

Ten percent of the cars on the road produce 50 to 60 percent of the vehicle-caused pollution. I'm not talking about antique and collectible classic cars. I'm talking about the old, poorly maintained smoke-belching clunkers. Perhaps we should just buy these cars and take them off the road.

In fact, some private companies have —for about $750 per car on average.

And for every dollar spent to increase the number of employees riding in each car, those buy-back programs got the same air quality results for a cost of... one penny.

Buy for a dollar what you can get for a penny. Come to think of it, isn't that how many things are done in Washington?

And there are other more cost-effective ways to reduce pollution. We could:

• Link the 90 percent of the nation's traffic lights that aren't yet connected to computers;
• Increase the use of flexible work hours and telecommuting;
• Improve our highway capacity, to eliminate bottlenecks;
• Invest more to develop a market for smart cars and smart highways;
• Remotely monitor tail pipe emissions of passing cars and target polluting vehicles for repair; and
• Invest in the National Highway System. I'll outline the benefits of this new program later.

The common thread is that these solutions use better technology or common sense institutional changes, and steer clear of the behavioral changes that average Americans associate with Big Brother government mandates.

Taken together these six solutions will improve traffic management, increase traffic flow, reduce gridlock and congestion, cut wasteful idling emissions, and substantially lower pollution at lower cost.

And, at much greater public acceptance.

Why aren't these more effective solutions gaining more support in Southern

California? Because they rely on good traffic management and enhanced mobility. And the environmental extremists who brought us these laws are opposed to greater mobility.

This is no accident or an example of the government fumbling the ball—it is a shrewd and calculated strategy.

To show you what I mean, let me turn to the other law I mentioned, known by its acronym, ISTEA. This is the program for improving and upgrading our transit systems, highways and bridges. You depend on the transportation systems to remain competitive.

For example, most manufacturing today depends on just-in-time logistics. Chrysler alone receives 1,700 truck shipments a day—nine out of ten on just-in-time schedules. Meanwhile, at a single General Motors plant, 23 trucks a day arrive from one particular supplier more than 200 miles away, and each truck must get there within a fifteen minute window.

But it is not manufacturing productivity alone that depends on highways. Toys-R-Us, Safeway Foods and many other retailers hold costs and prices down by using trucks and highways well.

We highway users pay the full cost of this efficient system, through the Highway Trust Fund, each time we purchase fuel. And in fact highway taxes also pay for much of the federal public transit programs.

The ISTEA law also mandated that a portion of the highway dollars be devoted specifically to help meet air quality requirements. In the first few years we are seeing some strange proposals for using these funds, such as $4 million for bicycle paths in a northern industrial city.

Nothing wrong with bicycles, but are bicycle paths as useful in the midwest's winter of 1994 as a comparable investment in roadway surfacing? Are bicycle paths even a cost-effective way to improve air quality?

A recent report from Congress' General Accounting Office says they are not. However, it's clear that there is a small group of environmental extremists who steadfastly resist any discussion of cost effectiveness or scientific analysis of risks before they saddle American business with another serious inflexible federal regulation.

It's clear, also, that these same fringe groups have some strange plans in mind for how this country should establish highway investment policies as our economy continues to grow.

Congress is now considering the National Highway System—also proposed in the 1991 ISTEA. The NHS is a strategic investment program for nearly 160,000 miles of the nation's most important highways. Most of these roads exist already, but have not received the attention they need in recent years. You know the NHS as the Lodge, The Davison, Michigan Avenue, 9 Mile Road, M-59 and other major arteries.

These roadways will be the focus of federal funding for the rest of the decade.

The NHS is the highway system that will carry America into the 21st century. The system will make up only four percent of all roads, but it will carry 40 percent of all highway traffic, 75 percent of truck traffic and reduce national traffic congestion losses that currently waste $40 billion a year. It will be the foundation for increased transportation productivity for decades to come.

And yet we are facing a concerted effort in Washington to divert and dilute its funding, and to destroy its strategic purpose. The same groups of anti-mobility extremists see a National Highway System that:

- Can't be expanded to keep up with a growing economy;
- Could have gaps at county or state lines or national borders; and,
- Is seen as a "slush fund," whose funds could be diverted by politicians for any other use.

My point here is a serious one—that extremists in the environmental community seem to have declared war on the automobile, on the people who drive automobiles, and, on the roads on which they drive. Maybe if they were offering people real choices and letting them decide, that would be one thing. But increasingly we are seeing proposals for government to employ "behavioral strategies," to forcibly limit personal choice and individual freedom.

Translated that means—Do it my way —or it's the highway. Given that choice —I'll take the highway.

But on their agenda—choice is out. Mandates, commands, and state control are in.

They tell us that the environment is the basic issue. Well, let me remind you of what radio commentator Paul Harvey calls "the rest of the story."

The fact is that, whether you're talking about carbon monoxide, volatile organic compounds, or nitrogen oxides, cleaner fuels developed by the petroleum industry and the cleaner cars and trucks produced by Detroit have massively reduced the average vehicle's contribution to air pollution.

I'm talking 96 percent for vehicle emissions over the last 30 years—and over the last decade nearly 40 percent in the case of volatile organic compounds. And just this month the *Journal of Science* reported that global levels of atmospheric carbon monoxide have declined dramatically— nearly 20 percent since 1991.

In fact, without the new technology of today's cars, trucks, and fuels, these pollutants would have gone up dramatically over the past decade. Instead they have fallen dramatically. In other words, cars and trucks are no longer the bulk of the problem. But they remain the prime targets.

We hear calls for mandating so-called zero-emission vehicles. Well, we all want automobiles to be clean and fuel efficient. But the zero emission vehicles will cost $40,000 each, and come with much lower performance. These will not be vehicles of choice, or the normal family car. And, EPA says they may not even pollute less, when power plant emissions are considered!

Whatever it is, the cry from the green extremists always seems to call for the most expensive solution—the least practical—the least acceptable. They seem united against mobility, against choice for your customers, against efficient transportation and against transportation productivity growth.

In other words, the environmental pharmacy always prescribes the same treatment—*make* the people do this, or *forbid* them to do that. The environmentalist's prescription doesn't recognize commuters' complex needs:

- the need of working parents—especially working mothers—to drop off and pick up children at day-care centers on the way to and from work;
- the need to run errands and keep appointments during the day;
- the need to shop for groceries after work;

- the need to leave work in a hurry in case of a family emergency;
- and the need to have more choices, and the right and the freedom to choose.

Like some troop of avenging angels, these same environmental extremists seem bent on punishing us for our prosperity and shredding and re-weaving our social fabric to fit their personal preferences.

I am not the first to note that all too often the worthy goal of protecting the environment is warped into an excuse and a cover for Big Brother command and control.

Does this mean that it is time to abandon the work of cleaning up after ourselves and helping leave a clean world for our children and grandchildren? Absolutely not.

But it is time to turn our back on Big Brother environmental extremism— to say that choice and mobility and prosperity and freedom also benefit the environment.

Countries start to pay attention to environmental issues only when per capita income passes a certain threshold, when basic bread-and-butter needs are covered. They continue to pay attention primarily in periods of strong economic growth.

I am here today because I believe that on these issues of clean air and transportation, some of the most important battles between Big Brother environmentalism and free market environmentalism, will be fought, and I would like to enlist your support.

I believe that these elite environmental extremists are poised and committed to try to undo the spectacular accomplishments of the great industry that is uniquely known by the city in which it resides, Detroit.

They wanted to control the behavior of your customers by making your product more expensive, more highly regulated, less popular and less useful. They would love to see your customers park your product in the garage and use other means of transportation, and not by choice.

So, today we in America have before us two visions for our transportation and our environmental future.

The first is a vision that would clog the engine of the great American job machine with bureaucracy, paperwork and ill-considered regulations. It would divert our national energy and wealth from solutions that are proven successes to those that are proven failures. It is a vision that fears growth rather than cheers growth.

One that would trade prosperity for austerity.

The second vision of the future would increase the mobility and freedom of the American people and American business —to allow each of us to do most—what each does best. It is a future of growth and opportunity, of jobs and economic security. And, ironically, it is a future that would make possible the goals that both we and the environmentalists *do* share in common: less congested roads, cleaner air, and better quality of life for all Americans.

We have the blueprint for this future. It is centered on an effective National Highway System. Strategic federal funding priorities for NHS for the rest of the decade will lead to more good jobs, reduced congestion costs, more productive, less costly transportation, improved North American trade corridors, and U.S. goods which remain cost-competitive in domestic and world markets. This new program of strategic highway investment will allow us to keep alive the economic miracles you and your colleagues in American business create every day.

We at the Highway Users Federation are fighting hard for the National Highway System. We need you to fight too.

Congress must approve the National Highway System this year or in 1995, at the latest. The funding, the concept, the opportunity disappears if they fail to act in time. We need you to talk to your friends in Congress. We need you to join a growing coalition of businesses and individuals who recognize that the National Highway System is essential to a brighter transportation future for all Americans—but particularly for the industry we know as Detroit.

If we win—America wins a system that provides the continued convenience and freedom of mobility that Americans have come to cherish.

It is vital that *our* vision—yours and mine—win. Surely America can agree that this is the right vision—a better vision. A freer vision. A more American vision.

Free choice. Economic growth. Free mobility. And a better transportation future in balance with a cleaner environment.

That is what we must work for. That is what we must achieve.

Thank you.

POSTSCRIPT

Is Stringent Enforcement of Existing Laws Needed to Improve Air Quality?

Lamm cites the reduction in vehicle emissions of air pollutants achieved during the past 30 years, but he fails to acknowledge that this achievement resulted from the type of regulatory strategy he condemns. He also neglects to point out that the improvement in ambient air quality resulting from the large per-vehicle reduction has been largely negated in many urban areas due to the exponential increase in vehicles on the road. The grassroots, clean air activists, whose activities and frustrations are described in Nixon's article, are hardly agents of the "Big Brother" governmental bureaucracy that Lamm suggests is forcing unwilling citizens to give up their right to own and operate any type of vehicle they choose.

Dissatisfaction with present governmental efforts to control air emissions is certainly not confined to those committed to opposing restrictions on automobile use. In his article entitled "Hot Air" in the May/June 1994 issue of *Public Citizen*, Christopher Dyson castigates the policies of the Clinton administration with regard to vehicle emissions that may contribute to global warming. Another significant source of criticism comes from those who argue that we need to design new sustainable, nonpolluting technologies rather than continue to focus on so-called end-of-the-pipe controls. Hilary F. French advocates this approach in her article in the July/August 1990 issue of *Energy Policy*.

For technical details about the 1990 Clean Air Act amendments and the regulatory strategy they embody, see the January/February 1991 issue of *EPA Journal*. Contrary to the impression conveyed by Lamm's article, many strategies, including some that Lamm advocates, were evaluated by the EPA and its consultants during the decade of political struggle that preceded the enactment of the amendments. Disputes continue among technical experts about the best strategies for improving air quality. For one critical evaluation of the likely impact of several of the motor vehicle emission standards in the new law see "Achieving Acceptable Air Quality: Some Reflections on Controlling Vehicle Emissions," by J. G. Calvert, J. B. Heywood, R. F. Sawyer, and H. H. Seinfeld, *Science* (July 2, 1993).

For a very different analysis than that of Lamm about the future of personal transportation and how various scenarios concerning the automobile are likely to affect the environment, see the article by Stephen Wilkinson in the May/June 1993 issue of *Audubon*.

ISSUE 9

Should the New Clean Water Act Aim at "Zero Discharge"?

YES: Jeffery A. Foran and Robert W. Adler, from "Cleaner Water, But Not Clean Enough," *Issues in Science and Technology* (Winter 1993/1994)

NO: Robert W. Hahn, from "Clean Water Policy," *The American Enterprise* (November/December 1993)

ISSUE SUMMARY

YES: Environmental health and policy professor Jeffrey A. Foran and Clean Water Project director Robert W. Adler argue that the goal of zero discharge of toxic pollutants can be achieved if the revisions to the Clean Water Act are designed to promote pollution prevention rather than control.

NO: American Enterprise Institute scholar Robert W. Hahn advocates a market-based approach based on cost-benefit analysis as a replacement for the present "command and control" approach to water regulation.

In 1621 Robert Burton wrote in *The Anatomy of Melancholy*, "They that use filthy, standing, ill-coloured, thick, muddy water [will] have muddy, ill-coloured, impure and infirm bodies. And because the body works upon the mind, they shall have grosser understandings, dull, foggy, melancholy spirits, and be really subject to all manner of infirmities." Although modern science has long since discredited this particular kind of causal analysis, one can nevertheless say that water pollution had long been recognized as a health hazard. The most important factor in increasing life expectancy in developed countries has been the prevention of contamination of public water supplies by human and animal wastes.

Recent concerns about water purity relate to the increasing contamination of both surface and groundwater by all manner of toxic and hazardous chemicals that are the by-products of our modern industrial societies. In the United States, the first comprehensive attempt to respond to this problem was the 1972 Clean Water Act followed by the 1974 Safe Drinking Water Act. By limiting the permissible discharge of contaminants into bodies of water and establishing water quality standards, this legislation, along with strengthening amendments enacted in 1977 and 1987, has had a significant impact resulting in marked improvement in some of the most polluted lakes and rivers, such as Lake Erie and the Hudson River.

But industrial expansion and population increases have resulted in the need for new strategies to stem the spread of water pollution. The International Joint Commission on the Great Lakes has called for stringent measures to halt the accumulation of chemical toxins in the water and sediments of those commercially important bodies of water. Groundwater, previously considered a reliable source of pure water, is becoming increasingly polluted. Fish kills and algal blooms are becoming more frequent in the bays and estuaries that border areas of high population density. In the spring of 1993 more than 350,000 Milwaukee residents became ill due to the contamination of their water supply, which derives from Lake Michigan, by the *Cryptosporidium* protozoan. This event, along with other recent episodes of infestation of public water supplies by toxic organisms, has alerted the public to the continued vulnerability of drinking water.

The Clean Water Act was among the major environmental laws that were scheduled for reauthorization when President Clinton was elected in 1992. A major revision of the legislation was anticipated early in his term of office that would both strengthen existing regulatory mandates as well as extend federal water protection to include previously neglected problems. Several bills were introduced in Congress, but consideration of all them has been stalled by major disputes that have developed over how to respond to such economically sensitive problems as the protection of wetlands.

One of the goals stated in the original 1972 Clean Water Act was to ultimately achieve zero discharge of pollutants into navigable bodies of water. In practice, the so-called end-of-the-pipe strategies that have been employed in the implementation of the legislation have abandoned this goal. Jeffrey A. Foran, formerly a professor and director of the Environmental Health and Policy Program at George Washington University and presently director of the Risk Science Institute in Washington, D.C., and attorney Robert W. Adler, who directs the Natural Resources Defense Council's Clean Water Project, propose that by shifting its strategy to encourage "pollution-prevention activities such as chemical substitution and process changes that reduce pollution at the source," the original zero discharge goal may be achievable.

Robert W. Hahn, who is both a resident scholar at the American Enterprise Institute and an adjunct research fellow at Harvard University, also advocates a major change in clean water strategies away from "command and control" regulation, but not with the aim of achieving zero discharge. He calls for a risk-benefit assessment of Clean Water Act goals, followed by the use of marketplace incentives—such as subsidies, pollution charges, and marketable permits—to achieve those goals that are economically justified.

YES

Jeffery A. Foran and
Robert W. Adler

CLEANER WATER, BUT NOT CLEAN ENOUGH

The Clean Water Act has undeniably helped control and reduce pollution of the nation's surface waters. Many gross pollution problems that existed a generation ago have been eliminated. Thirty years ago, Lake Erie had deteriorated so much that an article in *Science News* declared the lake dead. In 1969, the Cuyahoga River, which was heavily contaminated with flammable oils and grease, actually caught fire. These particular problems, of course, no longer exist. In addition, more subtle but no less important pollution problems have also improved since the 1960s. For example, levels of polychlorinated biphenyls (PCBs) have declined dramatically in fish and other aquatic biota in systems such as the Great Lakes.

The Clean Water Act, which was passed in 1972, has been a critical factor behind improving water quality. Major amendments enacted in 1977 and 1987 included provisions aimed at further improving the regulation of toxic substances. But despite its many successes, the Clean Water Act (CWA) and its amendments have failed to adequately control many sources of toxic pollutants.

For example, the act required that by 1983 all surface waters should have attained a quality that "provides for the protection and propagation of fish, shellfish, and wildlife and provides for recreation in and on the water." Surface waters that achieve this level of quality are classified under the act as fishable and swimmable. Yet, according to the Environmental Protection Agency's (EPA) most recent National Water Quality Inventory, at least a third of assessed rivers, half of assessed estuaries, and more than half of assessed lakes are not yet clean enough to merit this classification.

Continuing pollution problems in surface waters have also led the U.S./Canadian International Joint Commission (IJC), a quasi-governmental body that oversees quality issues in waters shared by the two nations, to designate 42 regions in the Great Lakes basin as highly contaminated. Also, nearly all states now declare that at least some fish taken by sport anglers from contaminated lakes and streams should not be consumed. And the cost of losses in recreational fishing, swimming, and boating opportunities caused by the discharge of toxic pollutants is estimated by the U.S. General Accounting Office (GAO) to be as high as $800 million per year.

The types of pollutants that continue to cause water quality impairments are widely varied. A total of 362 contaminants, including metals such as lead and mercury, an array of pesticides, and organic industrial chemicals such as PCBs and dioxin, have been found in the Great Lakes ecosystem. Eleven of these substances have been classified by the IJC as pollutants of "critical concern."

Research conducted by the IJC and others in the Great Lakes basin has provided specific information on the loads of some highly toxic pollutants that are discharged to surface waters. For example, Lake Superior receives nearly 500 pounds of PCBs (mainly from nonpoint sources) annually, and Lakes Michigan, Huron, Erie, and Ontario receive up to 5,000 pounds annually (mainly from nonpoint sources, although over 1,000 pounds are discharged to Lakes Erie and Ontario from point sources annually). Between 1,000 and 5,000 pounds of mercury are discharged to each of the Great Lakes annually mainly from nonpoint sources, although point sources appear to contribute the major portion of mercury in Lake Erie. Large loads of lead are also contributed to the Great Lakes, mainly from point sources. Over 1,000 pounds of lead are discharged annually to Lakes Superior and Huron, over 8,000 pounds are discharged to Lake Ontario, over 30,000 pounds are discharged to Lake Erie, and over 50,000 pounds are discharged to Lake Michigan annually.

Pollutants in water are responsible for damage to wildlife that includes eggshell thinning, reduced hatching success and infertility, immune system suppression, behavioral changes, physical impairments such as crossed beaks and clubfeet as well as adverse effects on populations and communities of organisms. Similarly, the health of human populations has been affected by toxic substances in surface waters. For example, cognitive and other deficits have been documented in children born of mothers who were exposed to PCBs through consumption of large quantities of contaminated fish.

Congress is expected to reauthorize and possibly amend the CWA again early in 1994. This presents an opportunity to correct the law's flaws, which have allowed some water-pollution problems to remain. In particular, we see a need to strengthen the provisions aimed at preventing pollution rather than relying on mechanisms to treat pollution at the point of discharge.

SOURCES OF FAILURE

The objective of the CWA is to restore and maintain the chemical, physical, and biological integrity of the nation's waters. In pursuit of that objective, the act explicitly states as one goal that "the discharge of pollutants into the navigable waters be eliminated." Congress designated 1985 as the date to achieve the zero-discharge goal. A 1992 IJC report found that the United States had yet to completely eliminate the discharge of any persistent toxic substance. Failure to achieve this goal and the act's other objectives, as well as continuing water-quality problems, are attributable to inadequacies in the existing water quality regulatory process.

To understand the reasons for our failure to achieve the act's goals, it is necessary to examine the two approaches that are used concurrently under the act to control toxic substances discharged to surface waters. The first approach is the mandated use of specific treatment technology for discharges from point sources of pollution, such as industry and waste treatment plants. For each category of industry, EPA issues industrywide effluent limitations defined as the "best available technology economically achievable." However, the designated technology may not be adequate to protect all surface waters from harm.

The second approach was developed for situations where technology-based controls do not protect water quality. This "water-quality-based" approach requires EPA and the states to set maximum allowable concentrations of toxic pollutants in surface waters without regard to economic impacts or technological achievability. The concentrations are supposed to be low enough so that they pose no threat to individual organisms (including humans) or to populations, species, communities, and ecosystems. Safe concentrations of toxic pollutants are defined under the CWA by chemical-specific, numeric Water Quality Criteria (WQC). In principle, WQCs could be set at zero where necessary to protect human health and the environment. In practice, however, WQCs are set well above zero, based on often-contentious concepts of risk assessment or implicit assumptions about technological and economic attainability.

States are required under the CWA to adopt WQCs and to use them in determining how much to control the discharge of toxic pollutants from point sources as well as from nonpoint sources (such as agricultural runoff and pollutants from the atmosphere). What the states do, though it is not necessarily sanctioned by the law, is to require that pollutant concentrations meet WQC in lakes or streams only after a discharge has been diluted by mixing with water in the receiving system. Thus an industry or waste-water treatment plant is allowed to discharge toxic pollutants in its effluent at concentrations higher than WQC for those pollutants, so long as pollutant concentrations are then diluted enough in the receiving water to meet WQC.

There are two problems with this approach. First, it does not force dischargers to comply with the CWA mandate of zero-discharge of pollutants to surface waters. In fact, the entire WQC system is based on the assumption that there is an acceptable level of pollutant discharge. Second, WQC and dilution capacity are used even where the ability of the environment to assimilate pollutants has been exceeded, or where adverse impacts have occurred, particularly in receiving systems far downstream from the point of discharge. Even though a lake has unacceptable levels of a pollutant, the pollutant can be discharged into a stream that empties into the lake so long as it is diluted to acceptable levels in the stream.

Under the 1972 act, technology-based effluent guidelines were supposed to require pollution-reduction technologies that not only became increasingly more stringent until zero-discharge was achieved, but that, in theory, would progress from end-of-pipe treatment approaches to changes in manufacturing processes and other strategies that would actually prevent pollution at its sources. This progression was expected to continue to reduce pollutants while also reducing the economic burden associated with installing increasingly costly treatment technology at the point of discharge. Unfortunately, EPA has been locked into a largely end-of-pipe treatment approach to pollutant control. The result has been only partial progress toward zero-discharge under the technology-based approach, along with ever-rising costs associated with more stringent forms of waste treatment.

The water-quality-based approach to toxicant control could also force technology toward increasingly strict pollution control requirements—and, ultimately, zero-discharge. But that will not happen as long as the operating assumption is that there are acceptable levels of pollution in surface waters and that we can count on receiving systems to dilute toxic effluents.

A POLLUTION-PREVENTION STRATEGY

The most effective way to reduce the discharge of a toxic pollutant into water is to reduce the use of the chemical or its precursors. Pollution prevention can be attained by reducing the use of a chemical through changes in industrial processes (including more efficient use of chemicals), substitute chemicals, and recycling. Or reduction (and in some cases elimination) may be accomplished by the phaseout of chemicals, product changes or bans, and behavior changes that affect consumption, use, or disposal of products that create pollutants.

Each prevention strategy should result in less waste production and toxic pollutant release, not just to surface waters but to other parts of the environment as well. Thus, prevention will reduce discharges of toxic pollutants below the levels pos-

sible with waste treatment alone. Ultimately, where a toxic chemical is eliminated via substitution, process change, or other mechanisms, or where environmental releases are eliminated, the discharge of that chemical will also be eliminated. The zero-discharge goal of the CWA can thus be met without risk-based arguments about acceptable pollutant levels, without the use of dilution to determine discharge limits, and without increasingly expensive treatment technologies applied at the point of discharge.

The difficulty of choosing chemical-specific pollution-prevention mechanisms and developing a schedule for their implementation is a potential obstacle to achieving pollution prevention. We therefore propose a scientific priority-setting process to determine a chemical's toxicity and assess the potential for exposure to it.

Exposure is assessed by evaluating a chemical's propensity to accumulate in the tissues of fish and other organisms, its persistence in the environment, and the amount that is released to the environment. Toxicity to aquatic plants and animals, as well as to terrestrial species (including birds and humans), is assessed by criteria that include death, impairment of growth and reproduction, and other adverse impacts, including cancer, from short- and long-term exposures.

Each toxicity and exposure component includes a set of triggers to determine whether a chemical can be classified as of high, moderate, or low concern relative to other chemicals. Once chemicals have been screened and classified, appropriate pollution-prevention activities and schedules for those activities (including the time it will take to reach zero-discharge) can be chosen.

Other factors may also influence the choice of pollution-prevention activities and the time it will take to implement them. For example, where it is determined that a hazardous chemical should be phased out of an industrial process, the pace of the phaseout may be influenced by whether there are safer substitutes, by the availability of different technologies that may not use toxic chemicals, and by the cost of developing these new chemicals or technologies. It should be generally recognized, however, that although such considerations may determine the length of time it takes to phase out a hazardous chemical, they should not affect the basic decision to phase it out.

MAKING IT LAW

Two different approaches should be taken to incorporate pollution-prevention measures into the CWA. First, the provisions of the law designed to implement technology-based and water-quality-based controls should be fine-tuned to point EPA back in the direction of zero-discharge. Fairly modest statutory changes might achieve the desired results. Second, broader changes and new requirements should be added to promote planning for pollution prevention by government and private parties.

Several requirements of the CWA should be modified to maximize the degree to which existing programs require or encourage prevention of pollution. First, the sections of the act that dictate the rules under which EPA writes categorical effluent limitations (and related pretreatment standards for dischargers to public sewers) could be modified to reinforce the original pollution-prevention philosophy, emphasizing technology-based re-

quirements for the control of toxic pollutants.

Existing provisions require EPA to "take into account" such factors as "process changes" and "non-water-quality environmental effects." The former is designed to take EPA beyond treatment applied at the discharge point and the latter to prevent impacts on other parts of the environment besides surface water. Nothing, however, forces EPA to select such options over traditional treatment methods. The act should be modified to include a hierarchy of options, under which pollution-prevention activities such as chemical substitution and process changes that reduce pollution at the source must be exhausted before point-of-discharge treatment is considered. In addition, limitations on the concentration of a toxic pollutant in a discharge could be expressed in terms of the efficiency of particular industrial processes (as efficiency relates to chemical usage), as well as the amount of reduction of the chemical in the effluent that can be achieved by pollution prevention.

Closing loopholes in the water-quality-based approach also would stimulate pollution prevention. Dischargers should be induced to adopt prevention methods through discharge permits that require the application of WQC at the point of discharge rather than allowing dilution of the effluent in the receiving water. Elimination of the dilution allowance would require reductions in the concentration and mass of pollutants that could be discharged. Industries and waste-water treatment plants could achieve these reductions by employing more expensive treatment technologies or by potentially cheaper pollution-prevention techniques.

The act should also be modified to achieve consistency among state WQC for toxicants and in the procedures used to translate criteria into discharge limits. At present, states may set their own criteria and develop their own implementation procedures, albeit with EPA guidance and authority to approve criteria and procedures. This creates an opportunity for states to use lax standards to attract business. EPA's water-quality criteria should apply nationwide, unless a state's criteria are stricter. With this change, industries and waste-water treatment plants would be forced to find ways to meet national criteria through pollution prevention. They could no longer exert pressure for lower standards by threatening to move their factories and jobs to another state.

SPURRING INNOVATION

Although amendments to existing requirements may enhance the degree to which programs encourage pollution prevention, they will not necessarily encourage or require industries and waste-water treatment plants to alter their fundamental operations to prevent pollution. We suggest two principal strategies to encourage industrial innovation. One is based on traditional "technology-forcing" for the most dangerous pollutants, and the other is designed to promote more comprehensive pollution-prevention planning by all dischargers of toxic substances.

The first approach is to identify and then ban or phase out the use and release of the most toxic, persistent, and bioaccumulative pollutants. Specific substances would be identified by the criteria discussed earlier in this article. Several hurdles must be overcome to

achieve this result. The law must include a clear definition of the standards for identifying the specific toxicants subject to a ban or phaseout. A simple approach is to include a list of chemicals that warrant elimination. A specific set of criteria that EPA must use to expand the list should also be included.

Once a chemical is listed, it will be necessary to determine who decides the schedule and mechanism for phaseout. One possibility is simply to set a date and wait for technological innovation by industry, an approach that appears to have succeeded to phase out ozone-destroying chlorofluorocarbons. Another is to convene broadly representative panels that can evaluate replacements for each chemical and set reasonable deadlines for making substitutions. The least satisfactory option is to ask EPA to dictate the date and means by which processes and chemicals should change. Whatever approach is taken should be spelled out clearly in the act.

The second principal strategy is to require comprehensive pollution-prevention planning at the company, site, and production levels. At the company level, this might entail strategic decisions about how products are manufactured and sold. For example, a pesticide manufacturer might decide to phase out production of chlorinated pesticides in favor of new compounds that are less toxic to humans or that are less persistent in the environment. Or chemical pesticides might be eliminated entirely in favor of biological pest controls. At the site or plant level, pollution prevention could include covering storage areas to reduce runoff of spilled or open materials, or reuse of residues from one product or process as input into a related product or process.

At the production level, engineers are learning to substitute less-toxic input chemicals and to change the sequence, tuning, temperature, or other production conditions in ways that reduce residual toxic substances. One example of production-level pollution prevention is the replacement of elemental chlorine with chlorine dioxide or oxygen to bleach paper products. This substitution decreases chlorinated dioxins and furans as well as other highly toxic chlorinated organic compounds.

The major hook on which to hang this approach is the existing program that requires permits for all facilities that wish to discharge pollutants from point sources into surface waters. The original philosophy of this permit requirement is that no one has the right to discharge pollutants unless there is a need to do so—that is, unless it can be shown that eliminating the discharge is, for technological or economic reasons, not feasible. Over the years, this legal presumption has been implicitly reversed. Permittees can discharge until the government limits the amount and nature of the effluent. Pollution-prevention planning would help turn this presumption around.

The *Water Quality 2000* report, prepared by representatives from industry, environmental groups, academia, and government, recommended that pollution-prevention planning be conducted at all industrial facilities but that the facilities themselves decide on pollution-reduction goals and methods. Facilities would have to disclose the results of their planning to the public, stating their goals for reducing pollution and reporting on their success in achieving those goals. Such an approach could readily be included by requiring pollution-prevention plans as a condition for receiving a permit. This would take an important step back toward the direction of the original law because facilities would have to evaluate all alternatives to pollution creation and discharge as part of the permit process.

NONPOINT SOURCES

Preventing pollution may be particularly important for dealing with runoff and other nonpoint sources of toxicants, such as atmospheric deposition and contaminated sediments. The problem is extensive and in many ways more difficult to control than point sources. Furthermore, the time may be right to push for pollution prevention for nonpoint sources because this approach does not carry the political baggage of the established (and inadequate) regulatory process that governs point sources of toxic pollutants.

The 1987 amendments to the CWA require states to identify which waters are impaired by polluted runoff and other nonpoint sources and to describe measures to control these sources. Most states have met these requirements, and many have recommended voluntary implementation of "best management practices," which include approaches to pollution prevention. Therefore, there may be less resistance to mandatory implementation of newer prevention-based strategies, particularly when pollution prevention is cheaper—as it can be, for example, with the substitution of biological pest control for the use of expensive pesticides in farming.

Although we have yet to make significant progress in reducing nonpoint-source pollution from agriculture, numerous opportunities to do so exist.

These include changes in crop rotation patterns, which result in more efficient use of chemicals; substitution of less hazardous for more hazardous pesticides, along with phaseout of particularly hazardous chemicals; product changes, such as selection of disease- and pest-resistant crops that require smaller quantities of pesticides; and persuading consumers to change their behavior—by, for example, being more willing to buy cosmetically imperfect (but perfectly nutritious) produce. We do not have quantitative estimates of their pollution-prevention potential, but there is widespread agreement that concurrent implementation of a mix of them will reduce polluted runoff. And at least some of them—especially reduced use of pesticides—will probably also save money.

One promising approach that might encourage use of pollution-prevention techniques in agriculture and other land uses is site-specific planning, as incorporated in the 1990 amendments to the Coastal Zone Management Act (CZMA). This legislation requires EPA and the National Oceanic and Atmospheric Administration to publish detailed guidance on pollution-prevention measures for nonpoint sources. Each coastal state must, as a condition of its programs under both the CWA and the CZMA, develop enforceable mechanisms to ensure that such practices are employed on a site-specific basis by all major sources of polluted runoff affecting water quality in coastal areas. The *Water Quality 2000* report recommended a similar strategy for agriculture. Under this proposal, the CWA would be amended to require major landowners in impaired watersheds to develop, with EPA and state guidance, site-specific pollution-prevention plans designed to help restore the health of disturbed watersheds. This could provide the incentive for farmers to implement available pollution-prevention techniques.

CAN WE AFFORD IT?

No one has conducted a comprehensive analysis of the costs of implementing pollution prevention. Some preventive strategies may indeed entail high upfront costs. However, at least in some cases, pollution prevention can also be profitable. According to a recent GAO report, the installation of a $50,000 system to recover waste at a Clairol haircare products plant resulted in savings of about $240,000 a year. The report also describes how a campaign in Palo Alto, California, to encourage industrial users of silver to deliver their wastes to a silver reclaimer and to urge hobbyists to dispose of their silver solutions at hazardous waste-collection sites made it possible to avoid a $20 million per year expenditure for installing and operating new equipment to remove silver from the waste stream of its waste-water treatment plant.

Uncertainty about the economics of various pollution-prevention strategies is only one of the complexities with which the CWA must deal. The large number of toxic pollutants that are entering the nation's surface waters, the wide array of point and nonpoint sources of these pollutants, and the broad diversity of possible pollution-prevention activities are challenges for lawmakers considering reauthorization of the CWA. We believe that our proposals incorporate the flexibility and the scientific rigor necessary to continue the critical work of protecting our rivers, lakes, and streams.

NO

Robert W. Hahn

CLEAN WATER POLICY

The first major piece of environmental legislation to reach President Clinton's desk is likely to be the reauthorization of the Clean Water Act, last amended in 1987. Over the past two decades, water pollution regulation has been aimed at cleaning up municipal waste and reducing industrial water pollution. This effort has successfully reduced pollution and improved water quality in some circumstances. For example, between 1972 and 1988, there was a 69 percent increase in the population being served by technically sophisticated sewage treatment plants. The overall trends in water quality are less clear, however. Between 1978 and 1987 no significant progress was made in traditional measures of quality such as the levels of dissolved oxygen and bacteria in the water. Water in many parts of the country, moreover, is still priced well below its economic value, leading to excessive consumption and, in some cases, to lower levels of water quality. In addition, agricultural and other sources of water pollution such as runoff from urban areas (called nonpoint sources because of their diffuse nature) remain largely unregulated.

Three bills are presently circulating in Congress to strengthen clean water regulation, all of which focus primarily on water quality. Senators Max Baucus (D-Mont.) and John Chafee (R-R.I.) have recommended expanding the bureaucracy that enforces current laws, increasing the funding for sewage treatment, and adding toxic substances and nonpoint sources to existing regulations. Congressman Jim Oberstar's (D-Minn.) bill focuses on the regulation of nonpoint sources of pollution. Finally, a bill introduced by Congressman Gerry Studds (D-Mass.) calls for a system of user fees on toxic discharges and products known to contribute to water pollution, and for an excise tax on ingredients in pesticides and fertilizers. The revenue from these taxes would be invested in clean water infrastructure such as stormwater controls.

All of these bills would increase regulation with little regard for the economic consequences. Moreover, none of them promotes innovative approaches to regulation that could achieve better water quality at a cost lower than traditional methods of regulation.

From Robert W. Hahn, "Clean Water Policy," *The American Enterprise* (November/December 1993). Copyright © 1993 by The American Enterprise Institute. Reprinted by permission.

There is an alternative to traditional water quality regulation. We now can achieve improved levels of water quality at lower cost to the public, provided that Congress is willing to embark on a new approach.

DIRECTIONS FOR REFORM

The great British economist Joan Robinson once asked: "Why is there litter in the public park, but no litter in my back garden?" The answer, of course, involves incentives—we have clear incentives to keep our backyards clean. And while each of us would like to see the park kept clean, we would prefer that other people do it.

The same problem arises in managing water resources. Because we collectively own most of our major water bodies, none of us has an incentive to take care of these resources the way we would our own homes and yards. Congress should therefore change the incentive structure so that individual consumers, governments, and businesses have a direct stake in taking better care of our precious water resources.

There are basically two ways to change the incentive structure and achieve better management of water resources. The first is to sell off major public waterways, including rivers, lakes, and streams. Putting these assets into private hands would improve water quality and quantity, provided that property rights for water quality and quantity were well defined and enforceable. The new owners of these assets would have a very strong incentive to manage these water resources as well as they take care of their own backyards. Acting rationally, they would keep the water clean and allow people to use it only if they paid a price that reflected the water's value. But this approach, however meritorious, simply isn't realistic in many situations. Privatizing the nation's water resources would start a political firestorm, if not a revolution.

A less radical way to manage water resources is to apply basic economic analysis to the public management of them. This involves two steps: first, identifying appropriate goals for water quality and water use; and second, choosing appropriate methods for achieving these goals.

The level of water quality we aim for will be determined, among other things, by the economic benefits associated with consuming or using the water resource and the economic costs of providing that resource. High water quality can help preserve species habitat; allow both commercial and recreational uses of water bodies including fishing, swimming, and boating; and provide a safe drinking water supply and the satisfaction that comes from knowing waterways are clean.

INTRODUCING COST-BENEFIT ANALYSIS

According to conventional methods of cost-benefit analysis, standards should be set so that the incremental benefit of cleaning up the water just equals the incremental cost. The costs and benefits of water improvement, however, are difficult to quantify, particularly the benefits. Nonetheless, it is absolutely imperative to try to quantify them if clean water policy is to be developed in a way that leads to improvements in our standard of living.

The Environmental Protection Agency (EPA) has not devoted significant resources to developing analyses that pinpoint the areas where regulatory efforts should be best focused under the Clean Water Act. The most comprehensive analysis of the costs and benefits of current plans to achieve the objectives of the Clean Water Act was performed by economists Randy Lyon, then at Georgetown University, and Scott Farrow of Carnegie Mellon. They argue that in many current implementation plans the incremental costs of improving water quality exceed the incremental benefits. This means that many existing EPA standards and regulatory approaches are wasteful. At the same time, there are certainly heavily polluted and/or heavily used water bodies where significant improvements in water quality are well worth the cost.

Results from studies by these authors and from other studies suggest that more cost-benefit analyses should be done so that Congress and the states can concentrate on the right water problems in the right water bodies. Specifically, EPA should commission a state-of-the-art cost-benefit analysis of the current Clean Water Act so that the political debate on reauthorization can be better informed. This analysis should attempt to point out where standards should be tightened and where they should be relaxed.

The analysis should also identify key areas of uncertainty in the estimation of benefits so that more informed decisions about appropriate standards can be made. At present, relatively little is known about the relationship between the level of pollution and human health for many water contaminants, or the extent to which people value clean water that they themselves do not use.

EPA should also develop a database that permits a more accurate assessment of the benefits and costs of the Clean Water Act, and the agency should be re-quired to submit a report to Congress every two years that addresses the benefits and costs of controlling different pollutants in different waterways. (A provision in the Clean Air Act Amendments of 1990 mandates that a cost-benefit analysis be used for selected statutes in the act.) Without such information, Congress will not be in a position to make informed decisions about the economic consequences of proposed statutes.

ECONOMIC INCENTIVES

Once a standard has been chosen, the government must determine how that standard should be achieved. One way is to prescribe a technology that each company in an industry must use. This is sometimes referred to as "command-and-control" regulation. Command-and-control regulation has been criticized by economists because it does not give businesses and individuals much choice in how they achieve an environmental goal. For example, a law may require that a power plant use a scrubber to reduce air pollution, even though another technology or group of technologies might be more effective in achieving the same level of air quality. Because this approach does not take into account differing circumstances and costs, society ends up paying more.

There is a better way to meet the government's standard. The introduction of economic incentives can address many pollution problems effectively. The idea behind using economic incentives is to save resources while achieving a particular environmental goal. For example, in 1990, Congress adopted an economic incentive approach for reducing acid rain that could save as much as $1 billion annually when compared to a conventional command-and-control approach that required the largest polluters to install scrubbers.

There are, moreover, many different kinds of economic incentives. They include subsidies, taxes, deposit-refund schemes, pollution charges, marketable permits, and the removal of institutional barriers that lead to price distortions. In the interest of brevity, I will discuss only pollution charges and marketable permits.

Charge systems impose a fee or tax on pollution. For example, a chemical manufacturer would be charged for every unit of a pollutant that it discharged into a river. Several European nations, including France, the Netherlands, and Germany, currently use water pollution charge systems.

Pollution charges by themselves do not restrict the amount of pollutants that may be emitted; rather, they tax emissions. Such taxes ensure that a firm will internalize the previously external pollution costs. A firm can choose to pay the full tax or to reduce its emissions partially or completely—whichever option best fits its interests.

The advantage of the system is that all businesses face the same incentive to limit pollution at the margin. A firm will control pollution up to the point where the marginal cost of control just equals the tax it must pay. The result is that the total costs of pollution control are minimized, unlike other methods of allocating the pollution control burden across businesses. Pollution charges, like other market-based mechanisms, also provide ongoing incentives for businesses to develop and adopt better pollution control technologies.

MARKETABLE PERMIT SYSTEMS

Marketable or tradable permits can achieve the same cost-minimizing allocation of the pollution control burden as the pollution charges do, while achieving a particular environmental target. Under a tradable permit system, an overall allowable level of pollution is established for the affected area, portions of which are then allotted to businesses and government entities in the form of permits. A business that keeps its emission levels below its allotted level may sell or lease its surplus permits to others.

As with a charge system, the marginal cost of control is identical across businesses and thus the total cost of control is minimized for any given level of total pollution control. In the case of local water pollution control, for example, this approach could be substantially more efficient than current regulatory methods, both because its inherent flexibility takes advantage of differences in control costs and because it allows individual businesses to decide where and how to make desired reductions in pollution.

In the event that overall environmental targets are viewed as too strict, the government may choose to increase the supply of permits. Likewise, regulators could take the opposite stance and reduce the supply of permits in order to reduce allowable emissions.

Permit systems have been used primarily in the United States. Examples include the Environmental Protection Agency's Emissions Trading Program for reducing air pollution; the nationwide lead phase-down program for gasoline, which allowed fuel refiners to trade reductions in lead content; and the gradual phaseout of chlorofluorocarbons, where businesses are allowed to trade the right to produce or import limited quantities of these chemicals. In addition, several Western states have implemented water quantity trading in limited forms. Some states are also considering trading programs to control discharges from farms and municipal wastewater treatment plants in the least costly way.

BETTER WATER MANAGEMENT

Congress could encourage EPA to implement both pollution charge systems and marketable permit approaches. But because charges are likely to encounter political resistance, Congress should promote more widespread use of marketable permits by requiring EPA to use them as the tool of choice for improving water quality or to justify in writing why it has not chosen this alternative.

This would move the agency away from the command-and-control approach it has used for the last 20 years. A system of marketable permits could promote trading of environmental credits among a variety of sources.

Municipal treatment plants and private companies, such as chemical plants and pulp and paper plants, that can measure the amount of pollution they produce at specific points within their plants (so-called point sources) can trade permits among themselves. This approach will be effective in areas where current requirements have not succeeded in achieving water quality goals as well as in areas where load-based requirements are used, which specify a target level of pollution for a waterway. Those entities that treat their own waste and can easily reduce pollution will do so, and they will be able to make money by selling surplus permits to those who cannot cheaply reduce their own effluent. Polluters whose efflu-

ent is treated at a sewage plant can also trade permits among themselves.

Nonpoint sources—farms with fertilizer or pesticide runoff, for example—can trade both among themselves and with point sources. Many current problems with water quality have arisen because nonpoint sources, such as agricultural runoff, are typically unregulated or minimally regulated. Over 18,000 water bodies will not attain water quality standards even if all point sources meet their technical requirements due to pollution from nonpoint sources. While EPA has acknowledged that nonpoint sources are a major problem, little has been done to cope with the problem.

Potentially, great cost savings can be achieved if nonpoint sources can be brought into the system. One way to do this is for EPA to develop guidelines for trading with nonpoint sources. Even if nonpoint sources remain largely unregulated, heavily regulated point sources should have the ability to trade antipollution permits with nonpoint sources provided they can show that water quality will improve as a result.

Technical uncertainties make it hard to judge how pollution levels from nonpoint sources affect water quality; there is no smokestack, for example, that can be easily fitted with a measuring device. These difficulties may initially lead to problems in determining acceptable emissions levels. Where monitoring can only be done at great cost, experts may need to rely on their practical judgment to ensure that water quality will improve. One promising application for controlling nonpoint source pollution involves the farms just north of Florida's Everglades. I have proposed a marketable permit system to limit phosphorous entering the Everglades by restricting the amount of phosphorous leaving the Everglades Agricultural Area. If a marketable permit system is not practical, it may be possible to tax a pollutant, such as phosphates in detergent, to limit its use.

Markets and permit trading can play an important role in reducing nonlocalized contaminants such as phosphorus in a cost-effective way. For example, I am working with the government in Sydney, Australia, to establish trading rules for farmers along the Hawkesbury-Nepean river system; the new rules will encourage the cost-effective phosphorus reductions needed to limit the growth of the blue-green algae that sometimes clogs parts of the river system.

The technical challenges of regulating nonpoint sources are not unique to a market-based approach, but apply to all regulatory systems including command-and-control ones. A key advantage of trading with nonpoint sources is that it will provide environmental benefits while lowering the overall cost of regulation. If regulation remains largely voluntary, a market-based approach will provide a positive incentive to limit water pollution.

Congress should also direct EPA to develop and implement rules for trading among different kinds of wetlands. Wetlands trading would provide property owners with appropriate incentives for preserving wetlands, while giving owners greater flexibility in deciding how they can develop their property. For example, Disney World agreed to restore and maintain a wetland in exchange for the right to develop its site. Because artificial wetlands can be constructed and wetlands can be restored, there is latitude for trading among wetlands. Establishing the rules for trading will be a challenge, but EPA should provide guidance on this issue.

Congress should also encourage EPA and the states to establish total maximum pollution levels for water bodies that do not meet water quality standards. The focus on environmental outcomes is likely to lead to better environmental quality at lower cost. Where there are unacceptable damages associated with pollution from specific sites, some command-and-control regulation may be necessary to set the maximum ceilings on pollution from these sites. Nonetheless, the goal of regulation should be to provide the maximum improvement in environmental quality per dollar spent. This is best achieved through making greater use of market-based approaches.

Most, if not all, of the preceding recommendations could be implemented under the existing Clean Water Act, but explicit congressional support for marketable permits will spur their use. Congress should make it clear that it is primarily concerned with making necessary improvements in water quality in a timely manner. The precise method of achieving these environmental improvements should be left to the business and government entities responsible for making the needed reductions.

WHITHER WATER REGULATION?

Integrating water quantity and water quality concerns will be a fundamental aim of the 1990s. The recommendations here have focused primarily on quality issues, but the two issues are inextricably linked. Just as water quality can be improved through the introduction of markets, so too can water quantity. Moreover, markets for water quantity can improve water quality by encouraging water conservation. While water quantity issues are generally subject to state law, the federal government could help by endorsing the use of water markets and allowing the transfer of water contracts for federal reclamation water supply projects.

We have the technical know-how to apply market-based economic methods that will improve water quality and allocation. The question is whether we have the political will. I am optimistic that more markets for improving water management will be introduced. The only question is whether Washington will lead the charge or follow. The reauthorization of the Clean Water Act provides Congress with a unique opportunity to demonstrate leadership in a way that benefits the health and welfare of the American people.

POSTSCRIPT

Should the New Clean Water Act Aim at "Zero Discharge"?

Although Hahn includes the preservation of species habitats among the goals of water quality protection, the cost-benefit approach that he advocates typically ignores such ecological benefits whose economic value is difficult to assess. Environmentalists who opposed the incorporation of pollution permit trading into the Clean Air Act amendments, on the grounds that treating the right to pollute as a commodity is unethical, will surely react the same way to Hahn's marketplace strategy. Requiring comprehensive pollution-prevention planning, as Foran and Adler propose, may prove difficult to write into law in a way that will ensure its effectiveness in achieving toxic pollutant control.

One of the water quality problems that most experts agree needs more attention is pollution caused by runoff. For a critique of the provisions to deal with this problem that were first introduced in the 1987 amendments to the Clean Water Act see "Runoff Runs Amok," by Julie St. Onge, *Sierra* (November/December, 1988). For a thorough critique of the entire federal program to regulate water pollution and a set of recommendations for a strategy that differs from both the proposals of Hahn and those of Foran and Adler, read "Turning the Tide on Water Quality," by William F. Pedersen, Jr., *Ecology Law Quarterly* (vol. 15, no. 1, 1988).

The complexities that prevent scientists from reliably answering many basic questions about water quality is the theme of a review and analysis of the 20-year history of the Clean Water Act written by Debra S. Knopman and Richard A. Smith in the January/February 1993 issue of *Environment*. A more detailed treatment of the same theme is Robert Adler's book *The Clean Water Act: 20 Years Later* (Island Press, 1993). Adler's book is excerpted in the Summer 1994 issue of *EPA Journal*, which is entirely devoted to analyzing approaches to water protection legislation.

Two recent articles that focus on the safety of drinking water are "Clean Drinking Water Becomes a National Problem," by Peter Nye, *Public Citizen* (July/August 1993) and "Something in the Water," by Jonathan King, *The Amicus Journal* (Fall 1993).

For an attack on existing policies and environmentalists' proposals for wetlands protection that depict programs such as raising public health risks and violating property rights, see William F. Jasper's article in the March 8, 1993, issue of *The New American*.

ISSUE 10

Does Feeding People and Preserving Wildlands Require Chemical-Based Agriculture?

YES: Ronald Bailey, from "Once and Future Farming," *Garbage: The Independent Environmental Quarterly* (Fall 1994)

NO: Paul Faeth, from "We've Been Down That Road Before," *Garbage: The Independent Environmental Quarterly* (Fall 1994)

ISSUE SUMMARY

YES: Environmental journalist Ronald Bailey claims that intensive farming, relying on pesticides and fertilizers, is needed to feed the world's people without requiring increased land use, which would destroy wildlife.

NO: A senior research associate in the economics and population program of the World Resources Institute, Paul Faeth counters that chemically intensive farming is more environmentally damaging and ultimately less economically effective at increasing agricultural yields than organic farming would be.

The use of naturally occurring chemicals in agriculture has a history that dates back many centuries. After World War II, however, the application of synthetic chemical toxins to croplands became sufficiently intensive to cause widespread environmental problems. DDT, used during the war to control malaria and other insect-borne diseases, was promoted by agribusiness as the choice solution for a wide variety of agricultural pest problems. As insects' resistance to DDT increased, other chlorinated organic toxins— such as heptachlor, aldrin, dieldrin, mirex, and chlordane—were introduced by the burgeoning chemical pesticide industry. Environmental scientists became concerned about the effects of these fat-soluble, persistent toxins whose concentrations became magnified in carnivorous species at the top of the ecological food chain. The first serious problem to be documented was reproductive failure resulting from DDT ingestion in such birds of prey as falcons, pelicans, osprey, and eagles. Chlorinated pesticides were also found to be poisoning marine life.

Marine scientist Rachel Carson's best-seller *Silent Spring* (Houghton Mifflin, 1962) raised public and scientific consciousness about the potential devastating effects of continued, uncontrolled use of chemical pesticides.

In 1966 a group of scientists and lawyers organized the Environmental Defense Fund in an effort to seek legal action against the use of DDT. After a prolonged struggle, they finally won a court ruling in 1972 ending nearly all uses of DDT in the United States. In that same year amendments to the Federal Insecticide, Fungicide, and Rodenticide Act gave the Environmental Protection Agency authority to develop a comprehensive program to regulate the use of pesticides. By 1978 many other chlorinated organic pesticides had been banned in the United States because of evidence linking them to health and environmental problems. Pesticide manufacturers switched to more biodegradable organophosphate and carbamate pesticides. However, the acute human toxicity of many of these chemicals has caused a rise in pesticide-related deaths and illnesses among agricultural field workers. Pesticide manufacture has also resulted in the poisoning of many workers and in serious environmental problems such as the contamination of Virginia's James River. The 1984 Bhopal disaster, which caused 3,500 deaths and 200,000 injuries, was due to the release of a chemical precursor being used by Union Carbide to manufacture a pesticide.

Since 1975 the sale and use of insecticides has leveled off due to environmental effects and economic considerations, but use of herbicides (weed killers) has continued to increase worldwide. These plant poisons also pose environmental and human health threats. Five million acres of Vietnamese countryside was decimated by Agent Orange (a mixture of two potent herbicides), 12 million gallons of which were sprayed on that country by the U.S. Air Force during the Vietnam War. The dioxin contaminant in Agent Orange is a proven, potent carcinogen and an immune system poison—and the resulting exposure to this toxin by Vietnamese people and U.S. soldiers has resulted in claims that they have suffered from its effects.

The role of pesticides in world agriculture is hotly contested. Many high-yield varieties of grains have been developed that are dependent on the intensive use of both pesticides and fertilizers. Increased crop yields in developed countries have been accompanied by significant environmental degradation. The greatly increased cost of this type of farming has limited the value of this high-technology agriculture in solving local food problems in Third World countries, where the principal effect has often been to increase the fraction of acreage used to grow export crops.

Ronald Bailey, a journalist who writes about environmental issues, contends that only by using chemically intensive agriculture will we be able to feed the world's growing population without decimating most of the remaining wilderness that nurtures the flora and fauna needed to maintain biodiversity. Paul Faeth, a senior research associate in the economics and population program at the World Resources Institute, agrees with the need to increase crop yields, but he argues that research shows that the most efficient, sustainable way to achieve this is by using resource-conserving farming practices with limited, rather than intensive, use of chemicals.

YES

Ronald Bailey

ONCE AND FUTURE FARMING

For those of us who wish to preserve the planet's diversity of species, high-tech, chemically-assisted agriculture is an environmentalist's best friend.

That's right. Soaring growth in human population threatens to destroy most of the world's remaining rainforests, wetlands, and montane ecosystems, drastically reducing species diversity. Despite advances in organic farming techniques, such as integrated pest management and fertilizing with "green" manures, overly relying on these practices will result in the plow down of forests to feed a population that is estimated to nearly double by 2050.

Environmentalists must face up to the fact that unless high-yield crop varieties, pesticides, and fertilizer are widely adopted in developing nations, the world's food supply will be outstripped by spiraling demand. Inadequate crop yields translate directly into more forests falling under the plow.

Many of the environmental community resist this conclusion. They tend to be very skeptical of high-tech, chemically-assisted farming.[1] Some pine for a smaller scale, more communitarian type of agricultural system. They dismiss modern agriculture as a form of "industrialization," or demonize it for its "chemicalization." Some activists badly assert that the "drive to industrialize agriculture and increase output has also led to major ecological disasters because of the artificial nature of all agricultural systems."[2]

Much of the environmental community's disenchantment with modern, high-intensity agriculture can be traced to Rachel Carson's 1962 book, *Silent Spring*. She was certainly right to warn of the dangers of excessive pesticide use. But ironically, the real threat to birds, mammals, and even insects comes not from modern farming methods and agricultural chemicals, but from what would happen if they were eliminated.

AS DEATH RATE SLOWS, POPULATION SOARS

The central ecological fact of our time is that the world's human population is going to increase substantially for at least another generation. No matter what urgent steps we take now, another 2 billion people—at minimum—will join us during the first part of the next century. The more likely scenario, according to United Nations' projections, is that the world's population will probably double in the next 50 years.

It is a popular misconception that skyrocketing birth rates are causing the increase in human population. That is simply not true. Such rapid growth is a result of a dramatic reduction in the death rate during the 20th century. Human life spans have increased dramatically, from a global average of 30 years in 1900 to more than 65 years by 1990.[3]

"Rapid population growth commenced not because human beings suddenly started breeding like rabbits, but rather because they finally stopped dying like flies," says Nick Eberstadt, a demographer at Harvard University.[4]

Despite all the hype that you heard from September's United Nations' Population Conference in Cairo about reducing population growth, the plain fact is that billions more people need to be fed. "Just to keep pace with population growth and rising incomes, the world will need to produce an extra 32 million tons of grain (principally rice, what, and corn) every year," predicts agronomist and Nobel Peace Laureate Norman Borlaug.[5]

The methods we employ for feeding such a vast population will make all the difference to the kind of world we will live in. Will humanity inhabit a planet still rich with millions of wild species, or will we need to farm countless acres of wildlife habitat to feed our vast numbers?

BOOSTING CROP YIELDS PRESERVES LAND

Biologists such as Harvard University's E. O. Wilson fear that thousands of irreplaceable plant and animal species may soon go extinct, as farmers redouble their efforts to sustain the world's expanding population. In his book *The Third Revolution: Environment, Population and a Sustainable World* (Penguin, 1992), Paul Harrison estimates that "loss of habitat to humans menaces two-thirds of threatened vertebrate species." But modern, high-yield farming, if not derailed by bad environmental and economic policies, will guarantee that this won't happen, say a growing number of agricultural researchers.[6]

By dramatically increasing the amount of food grown on land already under cultivation, humankind has already managed to save millions of square miles of natural landscapes from being plowed under. Higher yields were achieved by substituting more productive crop varieties, pesticides, and fertilizers for extra acreage.

Before the 20th century, the world increased its food supply chiefly by expanding the amount of land cleared and planted in crops. Yields of wheat, rice, and other staples were not much higher than in the Middle Ages. Only with the advent of science-based agriculture did crop productivity take off.[7] While world population has doubled over the past 40 years, agricultural productivity has tripled.[8] Much of that increased productivity resulted from the "Green Revolution" of the late 1960s and early 1970s. International teams of agricultural scientists led by Norman Borlaug developed highly productive dwarf varieties of staple grains such as wheat and rice. These fertilizer-responsive hybrids were adopted throughout the world, dramatically boosting crop yields and forestalling the massive famines forecast by famous population doomsters like Paul Ehrlich, who in 1968 predicted that during the

1970s, "due to famines—hundreds of millions of people are going to starve."

In fact, food is cheaper and more abundant than at any other time in modern history. Since 1980, according to the World Resources Institute, the global average price of food has plummeted by an astonishing 57%. And yet, worldwide, crops are grown on just slightly more land than in the 1960s—nearly 6 million square miles—an area equal to that of South America.[9]

Norman Borlaug recently told Congress that "by sustaining adequate levels of output on land already being farmed in environments suitable for agriculture, we restrain and even reverse the drive to open more fragile lands to cultivation."

U.S. Department of the Interior analyst Indur Goklany calculates that without the dramatic productivity increases that high-tech farming achieved since 1950, globally "an additional [910 million] hectares would have been converted from forest, wood, pasture, and grasslands—an amount equivalent to the net global loss of forest and wood lands between 1850 and 1980."[10] In other words, adopting chemical-based agriculture saved more than 3.5 million square miles of rainforests, wetlands, and mountain terrain from the farmer's plow.

Dennis Avery, who worked for many years on international food issues at the U.S. Department of Agriculture and who now heads the Hudson Institute's Center for Global Food Issues, thinks that Mr. Goklany's numbers for the amount of land spared through modern farming are too low. He figures roughly that tripling yields translates directly into preserving as much as 10 million square miles of wilderness from the plow—more than the total area of North America.

High-yield farming has already enjoyed marked success in India, reports agricultural researcher Paul Waggoner of the Connecticut Agriculture Experiment Station. In a paper titled "How Much Land Can 10 Billion People Spare for Nature?", Dr. Waggoner calculates that if India's wheat yields had remained at 1960s levels, local farmers would have been forced to clear an additional 42 million hectares (162,000 square miles) to grow the food they supply today.

"Environmentalists are guilty of bad ecological accounting," says Mr. Avery. "Today's typical environmentalist worries about how many spiders and pigweeds survive in an acre of monoculture corn without giving credit [to] the millions of organisms thriving on the two acres that didn't have to be plowed because we tripled crop yields."

PESTICIDES KEY TO HIGH-YIELD FARMING

Even if modern agriculture is responsible for saving millions of square miles of natural ecosystems, can yields increase enough to prevent future losses?

Lester Brown, head of the Worldwatch Institute, doesn't think so. Earlier this year, he declared in a Worldwatch press release that there is a "diminishing backlog of agricultural technology"; he further warned, in *State of the World 1994* (Norton), that there are "no new technologies that could lead to quantum leaps in world food output."

Dr. Brown's views are increasingly in the minority. The growing consensus among researchers is that scientific agriculture is nowhere near the limits for improving crop yields. And the biggest gains in yields will continue to come from breeding more productive, pest- and drought-resistant crop varieties.

Donald Plucknett, the recently retired senior scientific advisor of the Consultative Group on International Agricultural Research (CGIAR is the international network of agricultural research institutes which nurtured the Green Revolution), attributes 50% of the increase in today's yields to genetic improvements in modern cultivars.[11] For example, hybridization has already boosted top yields in corn by more than six-fold. The growing season for rice has been shortened from 180 to 110 days, allowing for double and triple cropping. And Dr. Plucknett believes farmers can increase rice productivity by 60% in the early 21st century.

Some of the credit for boosting yields must also go to pesticides and fertilizers. In 1962, Rachel Carson wrote in her classic *Silent Spring* that using pesticides was a "smooth superhighway" to disaster. She urged farmers to take "another road," free of "poisonous chemicals." In apocalyptic tones, she warned that turning away from pesticides was "our only chance to reach a destination that assures the preservation of the Earth."[12]

Ms. Carson argued that instead of relying on synthetic pesticides to control pests, we should develop and employ "biological solutions" (e.g., using pest predators and sterile males of insect pests, and applying organic pesticides). More than 30 years later, we now know that her hopes for biological pest controls were too optimistic. Many of the "solutions" she recommended are still little more than glimmers in the eyes of laboratory scientists. Those that are available for field application are relevant just for a few niche crops. In a very real sense, survival of the world's wildlands is due directly to continued use of the "poisonous chemicals" that Ms. Carson opposed.

High-yield agriculture, now and for the foreseeable future, will be impossible to sustain without herbicides, insecticides, and fungicides. Of course, we should reduce chemical residue and their adverse health effects on consumers and workers where practicable. But if pesticide use were significantly curtailed, crop yields here and abroad would fall dramatically. Which is worse for wildlife and biodiversity—millions of square miles of habitat cleared and planted in low-yield corn and wheat, or the relatively transient harm caused by pesticide residues?

Consider what's really at stake. A 1992 task force on pesticides for the Council for Agricultural Science and Technology estimated that "all crop production in the [world] would decline 30% and food costs would increase by 50% or more without the use of agricultural pesticides." Millions of acres of wildlife habitat would be destroyed to make up for the shortfall in crop production that would result from the total elimination of pesticides. This is not only true for farmers in the U.S. In the Philippines, "long-term trials on rice show that without pesticides, losses amount to more than 30% of the crop."[13] If yields were reduced to anywhere near these levels, clearly much more land would be converted to crop production to make up for the losses.[14]

Some environmentalists, hungering for a chemical-free utopia, point to "Integrated Pest Management" [IPM] or "organic" agricultural techniques. IPM can reduce pesticide use, but it is certainly not the royal road to completely chemical-free farming. IPM is very knowledge intensive, relying on a suite of nonchemical techniques to control pests. Such methods include, according to the World Resources Institute, "crop rotation, planting more than one crop, early or delayed planting to protect a crop during the most vulnerable stages of growth, manipulation of water and fertilizer, field sanitation (such as plowing under harvest stubble to remove pest hideaways), and the use of 'trap crops' to lure pests away from the main crop." IPM seeks to establish a threshold of "acceptable damage" to a crop, after which farmers will often need to resort to pesticides to protect their crops. "[IPM] is not a panacea, it is unlikely to eliminate the need for chemical pesticide use entirely," conclude International Food Policy Research Institute analysts Peter Oram and Behjat Hojjati.

Researchers have made advances in developing more environmentally benign pesticides such as glyphosate and the sulfanylureas, which are replacing longlasting organochlorides. Leonard Gianessi, a senior research associate at the National Center for Food and Agricultural Policy, points out that "many new herbicides are used at rates as low as 0.02 pounds per acre in comparison to 2 pounds per acre for older herbicides."[15] He adds that for many modern pesticides, the "active ingredients are present in amounts so small that their presence in the environment cannot be measured."

Some environmentalists herald new biological pesticides as a way to avoid synthetics. The problem is that many are very specifically targeted. This sounds good, but farmers often need wide-spectrum herbicides to control the huge variety of weeds they find in their fields at any one time. Dr. Gianessi predicts that for the foreseeable future, wide-spectrum pesticides of all types will be necessary to keep crop yields high.

The choice that environmentalists face is between saving the world's biodiversity by forestalling the plow-down of wildlife habitat through the continued use of farm chemicals, or protecting themselves from the minuscule health risks posed by pesticides. And the health risks *are* minuscule.

University of California at Berkeley biochemist Bruce Ames calculates that "about 99.99% of all pesticides in the human diet are natural pesticides from plants. All plants produce toxins to protect themselves against fungi, insects, and animal predators such as humans."[16] Plants are packed with potent natural rodent carcinogens such as caffeic acid in lettuce and hydrazines in mushrooms. Dr. Ames estimates the average person ingests daily about 1,500 milligrams of natural pesticides and just 0.09 milligrams of synthetic pesticide residues. Of the pesticides we consume, just one-ten thousandth are synthetic.

Dr. Ames, who developed the chief method used by laboratories worldwide for detecting carcinogens, estimates that far less than 1% of all human cancers are due to exposure to synthetic chemicals (including pesticides) or pollution. Toxicologist Robert Scheuplein of the Food and Drug Administration's Center for Food Safety agrees. "Ordinary food contains an abundance of cancer initiators which in total dwarf all of the synthetic sources," writes Dr. Scheuplein in an essay for *Global Food Progress* 1991 (Hudson Institute). "The total risk from all pesticides and contaminants is a thousand times less than the estimates of cancer risk due to naturally occurring carcinogens."..

CAN FARMING WITH CHEMICALS SAVE WILDLIFE?

The greatest threat to biodiversity remains the burgeoning populations in developing nations, particularly in the tropics, where many farmers continue to practice low-input, low-yield agriculture. Dr. Borlaug noted the unsustainability of "low-input" farming in recent testimony before the Agriculture Committee of the House of Representatives. He told Congress that "slash and burn agriculture [is] a practice that presently causes the annual loss of more than 25 million acres of tropical rainforest. As an aside, it is worth mentioning that slash and burn techniques supported agriculture in traditional societies for millennia. It was not until population pressures accelerated the demands on this system that it became unsustainable."

Interior Department analyst Indur Goklany also criticizes low-input farming: "One consequence of low-input sustainable agriculture (LISA) is that more land would be devoted to crops than would be otherwise. This extra land used for agriculture will mean that much less is available to other species. What we need is not LISA, but HOSA—high-output sustainable agriculture."

Can the agricultural productivity of developing nations be raised in time to save the world's biodiversity? Yes, according to a recent report by Donald Plucknett, the former chief scientist of the authoritative Consultative Group on International Agricultural Research. He concludes that worldwide harvests could be boosted by 50%, just by making existing improved crop varieties and agricultural know-how more widely available. For instance, corn yields in West Africa currently are a meager eight-tenths of a ton per hectare. By switching to hybrid seeds and using fertilizer, African farmers could boost production nine-fold, to seven tons per hectare. The Hudson Institute's Dennis Avery estimates that for every hectare converted to high-yield farming, as many as eight hectares could be allowed to return to their natural state.

Dr. Plucknett argues that until farmers in developing countries adopt high-yield techniques, they "tend to move more and more onto marginal lands to meet food and production needs, destroying natural ecosystems in the process." Once yields per hectare begin to increase, expansion of the agricultural frontier onto marginal lands slows dramatically. Thus, high-yield farming is "land-saving agriculture" and is very "environmentally friendly," says Dr. Plucknett.

Ironically, many environmentalists refuse to believe the good news. In *State of the World 1994*, Lester Brown warns that world grain production per capita peaked in the 1980s, and that the "bottom line is the world's farmers can no longer be counted on to feed the projected additions to our numbers."

It is true that world grain production has slowed, but that's because the U.S. and Europe, which are drowning in surpluses, are paying their farmers to cut production. "More is not produced because it is not needed," writes Nikos Alexandratos of the Food and Agriculture Organization of the United Nations, in a paper titled "The Outlook for World Food and Agriculture to the Year 2010."

Throughout the 1980s, grain production in developing nations rose at the spectacular rate of 5% per year, easily outpacing the Third World's population growth of 1.9% annually, according to the Hudson Institute. In the 1980s, China's agricultural output soared by an unprecedented 50%, while Indonesia increased its rice productivity by more than one-third. Looking to the future, Dr. Alexandratos predicts that once "satisfactory" levels of per capita food consumption have been achieved, extraordinary gains in productivity will no longer be necessary. More cautious than many analysts, Dr. Alexandratos expects that world food production could slow to a 1.8% increase per year—but adds that "it will continue to outpace a 1.5% growth rate in world population."

To show clearly how chemical-based agriculture slows land clearing, Douglas Southgate, an associate professor of agricultural economics at Ohio State University, contrasts the experiences of Chile and Ecuador. Ecuadorian farmers have not increased their yields and are clearing land at a blindingly fast pace—crop and pasture land is increasing 2% annually, the second highest rate in Latin America. Meanwhile, Chile has invested in high-tech agriculture, including higher applications of pesticides and fertilizers and increased irrigation. Consequently, Chile's agricultural frontier has hardly expanded at all—land cleared for crops has increased by just 0.1% annually.

"My statistical analysis pretty clearly shows that countries that boosted their agricultural yields are the same countries where land clearing is very, very slow," says Dr. Southgate. "By contrast, countries where yields are flat are the same countries that are losing tropical forests and other natural ecosystems at a rapid rate."

Abundant evidence suggests that environmentalists who want to preserve the world's diminishing biodiversity must become advocates of modern, high-yield agriculture. Those who refuse should attempt to honestly answer Dennis Avery's pointed question: "How many millions of square miles of wildlife habitat are [you] willing to give up in order to have chemical-free farming?" He adds, "This is a strange way to save wildlife." Indeed it is.

NOTES

1. See Carson, Rachel, *Silent Spring*, (Houghton Mifflin, 1962); Goering, Peter et al., *From the Ground Up: Rethinking Industrial Agriculture*, (Zed Books, 1993); Bender, Jim, *Future Harvest: Pesticide Free Farming*, (University of Nebraska Press, 1994); and Conford, Philip, ed., *A Future for the Land: Organic Practice From a Global Perspective*, (Green Books, 1992).

2. Conford, 1992, p. x.

3. Eberstadt, Nicholas, "Population, Food and Income: Global Trends in the Twentieth Century," July, 1994, manuscript, p. 25.

4. Eberstadt, p. 26.

5. Borlaug, Norman. Testimony of the Former General Director of the International Maize and Wheat Improvement Center before the House Agriculture Committee. Subcommittee on Foreign Agriculture and Hunger. March 1, 1994. Federal Document Clearinghouse, Inc.

6. See Waggoner, Paul, "How Much Land Can Ten Billion People Spare for Nature?", Task Force Report No. 121, Council for Agricultural Science and Technology & The Rockefeller University (February, 1994); Plucknett, Donald, Senior Scientific Advisor, Consultative Group on International Agricultural Research, Paper: "Prospects of Meeting Future Food Needs Through New Technology," prepared for the Roundtable on Population and Food in the Early 21st Century (February 14–16, 1994, Washington, D.C.); Oram, Peter & Behjat Hojjati, Paper: "The Growth Potential of Existing Agricultural Technology," prepared for the Roundtable on Population and Food in the Early 21st Century (February 14–16, 1994, Washington, D.C.); Goklany, Indur & Merritt Sprague, "An Alternative Approach to Sustainable Development: Conserving Forests, Habitat, and Biological Diversity by Increasing the Efficiency and Productivity of Land Utilization," Office of Program Analysis, U.S. Department of the Interior (Washington, D.C., April 4, 1994); Avery, Dennis, Director of the Center for Global Food Issues at the Hudson Institute, *Biodiversity: Saving Species with Biotechnology* (Hudson Institute, 1993); Avery, Dennis, "Saving the Planet with Pesticides and Plastics," unpublished manuscript, 1994.

7. Waggoner, Paul, 1994, pp. 24–30; Plucknett, Donald, 1994, pp. 7–18.

8. U.N. Long-Range World Population Projections, p. 14; *World Resources 1994–1995*, (Oxford University Press, 1994), pp. 27–42, 107–28, 262. Lester Brown et al. *State of the World 1994*, (Norton, 1994), p. 182; Avery, Dennis, *Biodiversity: Saving Species with Biotechnology*, p. 36.

9. Goklany, Indur. Paper "Is It Premature to Take Measures to Adapt to the Impacts of Climate Change on Natural Resources?" Office of Policy Analysis, U.S. Department of Interior, 1994, Table 1, p. 3; Avery, interview, October 1993.

10. Goklany, 1994, p. 2.

11. Plucknett, Donald. "Science and Agricultural Tansformation," International Food Policy Research Institute Lecture No. 1, September, 1993.

12. Carson, 1962, p. 244.

13. Oram et al., 1994, p. 34.

14. Pickett, John. Chemistry and Industry, "Safer Insecticides: Development and Use." January 6, 1992, p. 25.

15. Gianessi, Leonard. "The Quixotic Quest for Chemical-Free Farming," *Issues In Science and Technology*, Fall 1993, p. 32.

16. Ames, Bruce and Lois Gold. "Environmental Pollution and Cancer: Some Misconceptions," In *Phantom Risk: Scientific Inference and the Law,* edited by Foster et al. (MIT Press, 1993), p. 153; see also Gold, Lois et al., *Science*, "Rodent Carcingens: Setting Priorities," (October 9, 1992), p. 261; see also, Ames, Bruce et al., Proceedings of the National Academy of Science. (Vol. 87, 1990), pp. 7772–7776.

NO

Paul Faeth

WE'VE BEEN DOWN THAT ROAD BEFORE

In quoting Dennis Avery's line that environmentalists worry more about the fate of spiders and pigweed in monoculture cornfields than they do about getting higher crop yields, Ronald Bailey sets up a straw man—which he then easily demolishes. But his straw man is more akin to the "back to the Neolithic" fringe than to anyone in the environmental mainstream.

I couldn't agree more with Mr. Bailey's assertion that it's crucial to step up agricultural productivity to feed a global population projected to double by mid-century. My only quarrel with him on this score is over *how* to intensify agriculture, not whether it should be intensified. The paramount concern must be to increase crop yields in environmentally sensitive ways that protect human health and the soil and water that are agriculture's very foundation. Heavy use of agrochemicals can bring high yields in the short run, but the cumulative damages can be considerable. Those of us whose research demonstrates that resource-conserving farming practices can be just as productive as the chemical-intensive kind contend that the goal should be efficient use of chemicals, not wide use.

Compelling physical evidence from around the world suggests that current farming practices in many areas cannot be sustained much longer. Soil degradation from erosion, salinization, compaction, and depletion of organic matter have made an estimated 2 billion hectares of once-arable land irreversibly unproductive.[1] Without conservative measures, more than 500 million hectares of rain-fed cropland may become unproductive over the long term in Asia, Africa, and Latin America.[2]

Fortunately, readily available practices can improve crop yields while reducing environmental damage. Water harvesting techniques developed in Africa can reduce soil erosion and improve infiltration to make more water available to plants. Irrigation management practices can reduce soil salinization, keeping valuable land in production. Soil tests can reduce the amount of fertilizer applied, avoiding unnecessary damage to ground and surface water, while maintaining yields and saving farmers' money. Judicious use of insecticides and pest scouting in rice fields can help to maintain populations of natural predators, avoiding outbreaks of pests and unnecessary expenses.

Crop rotation can help farmers to avoid chemical dependencies that occur when pest populations build up under monocultural cropping practices.

Where agrochemicals are heavily used, the off-farm environmental costs of farming may be even greater than the soil-productivity losses. A tiny percentage of the pesticides applied to a given field—less than 0.1% for many insecticides—actually reaches the target pest; the rest, by definition, becomes an environmental contaminant.[3] The farm workers who apply these chemicals and the ecosystems downstream suffer by far the worst impacts. Fertilizers don't stay put, either. Crops take up only about half the nitrogen fertilizers applied to them, and much of the rest—about 4.7 million tons a year in the U.S.—seeps into groundwater or drains into rivers, lakes, and estuaries. In rural Nebraska, for instance, the water supplies of nearly one in five communities contain nitrate levels near or above the Environmental Protection Agency's limit for drinking water.[4] What's more, farm run-off has become the single largest source of surface-water pollution in the U.S.[5]

How can developing countries—with little or no capacity to regulate or monitor these problems—avoid replicating this pattern and still increase production? Pouring vast amounts of high-priced agrochemicals on every field cannot be the answer. The supply is not unlimited, after all, since these countries are hard-pressed for the hard currency needed to buy agrochemicals. Farmers who use integrated pest management (IPM) need much smaller amounts of pesticides; the more efficient a country's farmers are in using these chemicals, the greater the economic gain.

Mr. Bailey considers IPM too knowledge-intensive for developing-nation farmers, but he ignores the fact that pesticides are even more so—and that dire consequences result when illiterate farmers apply powerful chemicals (some of them banned in the U.S., but still exported) that they aren't trained to use. In one region of the Philippines, for instance, 4,031 cases of acute pesticide poisoning were reported in just seven years, 603 of them fatal. In the group of farmers studied, nearly one-third had four different pesticide-related impairments. When the health costs for pesticide-related illnesses are factored in, farmers income rises as their pesticide use declines.[6] The problem is not unique to the Philippines. Occupational pesticide poisoning may affect as many as 25 million farm workers a year—or 3% of the developing world's agricultural workforce.[7]

Mr. Bailey also ignores the inconvenient fact that pesticides have by no means ended the problems they were meant to solve. After 50 years of widespread pesticide use, insects, weeds, and plant diseases still claim 30 to 35% of total crop production, about the same as in the prechemical era. Some pests develop resistance, making efforts to control them with the same chemicals increasingly futile, a process that has accelerated since it was first seen in the 1940s with DDT. Today, some 500 insect and mite species—as well as 113 weed species and 150 plant pathogens—are immune to one or more pesticides. Compounding this problem is that insecticides are often more deadly to insect predators than to the pests themselves. Once these natural predators are wiped out, pests multiply, and farmers often respond by increasing dosages or spraying more often—which may bring temporary relief but only hastens the trend toward resistance. Farmers become trapped on the pesticide treadmill, a cycle of diminishing returns and increasing cash outlays.[10]

IPM can help developing countries get off this treadmill. Indonesia's experience shows how much can be gained on several fronts: when the nation banned 57 of 66 pesticides and adopted an IPM program, pesticide use declined by 60%, the rice harvest increased by 15%, and the government saved $120 million a year in pesticide subsidies. The UN Food and Agriculture Organization is sponsoring IPM programs in eight Asian countries besides Indonesia, which together have trained hundreds of thousands of farmers and saved millions of dollars in pesticides, not to mention the associated health and environmental benefits.[11]

One reason that resource conserving farm practices haven't made more headway is that conventional farm accounting systems measure agricultural productivity, meaning crop yields, but they ignore agriculture's impacts on the productivity of the natural resource base—the maintenance of which is the *sine qua non* of sustainability. Mr. Bailey was very selective in quoting the congressional testimony Norman Borlaug gave earlier this year, for Dr. Borlaug clearly embraced the need for natural-resource accounting in the same testimony:

"At the very least, research must make explicit some of the costs associated with resource degradation and pollution when comparing alternative technologies and options for farmers and for society. When offsite effects are included, when inputs and products are properly valued, and when costs associated with degradation of the natural resource base are included, regenerative technologies may be more profitable than conventional technologies."[12]

Mr. Bailey's simplistic picture of farmers swarming onto fragile lands and "plowing down" forests completely ignores inequitable land tenure patterns. In Chile, for instance, the 4% of all farms that are bigger than 40 hectares make up 44% of all the land in production, and peasant farmers have been pushed onto steep slopes where the soils are most apt to erode. Nonetheless, our research demonstrates that peasant farmers who switch from traditional farming practices to organic ones, which entail less soil erosion, can maintain higher crop yields—and thus earn more income.[13]

Mr. Bailey is concerned that chemical-intensive farming might be "derailed by bad environmental and economic policies," but my concern is about the pernicious effects of existing policies on resource-conserving agriculture. Subsidies for such agricultural inputs as fertilizers, pesticides, and irrigation water are the chief culprit. Artificially cheapening these inputs encourages farmers to over-use them—while creating fiscal problems for governments—so it's bad policy on both environmental and economic grounds.

Mr. Bailey ends with a question that I consider specious, since it implies that to be an environmentalist is to oppose any use of agricultural chemicals. I've already made the point that this isn't the case, but I'd like to leave readers with a question of my own. First, a few relevant facts. A recent study by the Rodale Research Institute in Pennsylvania[15] shows that organic systems in many cases yield just as much as chemical-intensive ones—this despite the fact that U.S. policy has favored heavy agrochemical use for the past 50 years.

Billions of tax dollars have gone into agrochemical R&D since 1945, but only 2% of government agriculture research funds have been spent on alternative, low-input, or organic farming systems.[16] What yields might these environmentally benign systems be producing today—at how little cost to soil and water—if they had been supported as handsomely as chemical-intensive ones?

NOTES

1. Lal, R. and F. J. Pierce, "Soil Management for Sustainability" (Ankeny, IA: Soil and Water Conservation Society, 1991).

2. World Commission on Environmental and Development, *Our Common Future* (New York: Oxford University Press, 1989).

3. *World Resources, 1994–95.* (Washington, D.C.: World Resources Institute, 1994), p. 114.

4. Faeth, Paul, "Paying the Farm Bill: U.S. Agricultural Policy and the Transition to Sustainable Agriculture" (Washington, D.C.: World Resources Institute, 1991).

5. Faeth, Paul, "Agricultural Policy and Sustainability: Case Studies from India, Chile, the Philippines, and the United States" (Washington, D.C.: World Resources Institute, 1993).

6. Faeth, 1993, p. 8.

7. *World Resources, 1994–95,* p. 114.

8. *World Resources, 1994–95,* p. 115.

9. *World Resources, 1994–95,* p. 115.

10. *World Resources, 1994–95,* p. 113.

11. *World Resources, 1994–95,* p. 116.

12. Bourlag, Norman. Testimony of the former General Director of the International Maize and Wheat Improvement Center before the House Agriculture Committee, Subcommittee on Foreign Agriculture and Hunger. March 1, 1994. Federal Document Clearinghouse, Inc.

13. Faeth, 1993, p. 44.

14. Faeth, 1993, p. 6–7.

15. Faeth, 1991, p. 39.

16. Faeth, 1991, p. 24.

POSTSCRIPT

Does Feeding People and Preserving Wildlands Require Chemical-Based Agriculture?

Bailey repeatedly asserts that his perspective on how to feed the world's people while preserving biodiversity is supported by a growing consensus of agricultural experts. In fact, it is primarily those researchers and analysts affiliated with the agricultural establishment in the United States and other developed nations who continue to advocate chemically intensive agriculture. Many independent agronomists and entomologists would agree with Faeth's argument that the practices Bailey advocates will result, at best, in only short-term productivity gains, because the practices are not sustainable. In *Food First* (Houghton Mifflin, 1977), Frances Moore Lappe and Joseph Collins popularized the results of their research on the effects of the use of pesticide- and fertilizer-intensive agriculture in the developing world. They conclude, in support of Faeth's arguments, that the result was an exacerbation of local food shortages due to the shift to producing export crops, often accompanied by the pesticide poisoning of poor agricultural laborers.

A report frequently quoted by pesticide advocates is "Benefits and Costs of Pesticide Use in U.S. Food Production," by David Pimentel et al., *Bioscience* (December 1978). The conclusion reached by noted agricultural scientists Pimentel and his coworkers is that ending all U.S. pesticide use—a more extreme restriction than that advocated by integrated pest management (IPM) proponents—would cause an immediate increased annual crop loss worth $8.7 billion, whereas the cost of chemical controls is $2.2 billion. Those who cite these conclusions usually fail to mention that the authors admit they have not included the ecological and social costs of pesticide use and that much of the crop loss may be eliminated once pest predators reestablish a natural balance.

Another problem concerning pesticides that have been banned in wealthier counties, which tend to have stricter environmental and health regulations, results when these chemicals contaminate food imported into these wealthier nations from developing countries where there are few restrictions on agricultural toxins. For details about this widespread practice see *Circle of Poisons* by D. Weir and M. Shapiro (Institute for Food and Development Policy, 1981). An effective means of banning the small fraction of such pesticide-contaminated crops that are actually discovered by inspections has been a U.S. law known as the Delaney Amendment. In the January/February 1994 issue of *Sierra*,

Paul Rauber argues against the Clinton administration's plan to eliminate this law.

Faeth refers to "the pesticide treadmill." For a detailed explanation of this problem associated with intensive reliance on chemical toxins, see Michael Dover's article in the November/December 1985 issue of *Technology Review*. Omar Sattaur's article in the July 14, 1988, issue of *New Scientist* describes the successful use of IPM strategies in Third World countries. A much less optimistic assessment of the potential of IPM programs, and an argument that supports Bailey's advocacy of chemical controls, is contained in Leonard Gianessi's article in the Fall 1993 issue of *Issues in Science and Technology*.

Bailey implies that the new generation of insecticides and herbicides are relatively safe. This view is refuted by Ted Williams in his article in the March/April 1993 issue of *Audubon*. In the September/October 1993 issue of the same magazine, John Grossman discusses another growing concern about pesticides and herbicides due to the pollution caused by their highly intensive use on golf courses throughout the world.

Several biotechnology companies are using genetic engineering techniques to produce herbicide-resistant crops. Depending on how this development is implemented, the result could either increase or decrease the environmental impact of pesticides. This issue is discussed by Roger Wrubel in the May/June 1994 issue of *Technology Review*.

ISSUE 11

Is Protecting the Spotted Owl a Clever Strategy for Preserving Old-Growth Forests?

YES: Jon Jefferson, from "Timmmberr! How Two Lawyers and a Spotted Owl Took a Cut Out of the Logging Industry," *ABA Journal* (October 1993)

NO: Gene W. Wood, from "Owl Conservation Strategy Flawed," *The Journal of Forestry* (February 1991)

ISSUE SUMMARY

YES: Freelance writer Jon Jefferson lauds the successful legal strategy of environmental activists who organized their campaign to protect old-growth forests around a plan to save the northern spotted owl from extinction.

NO: Forest wildlife ecology professor Gene W. Wood critiques the government strategy for protecting the spotted owl and concludes that choosing the owl as a surrogate for the forest is not the best plan for achieving the worthy goal of preserving both of them.

Concern about the environmental impact of the destruction of forests by the wholesale harvesting of trees for timber is not a new issue. By the end of the 1800s the massive clear-cutting of forests in the eastern and midwestern regions of the United States had produced devastating results. Severe floods resulted from the loss of trees that had previously reduced surface water runoff. Branches and other debris left in clear-cut areas fed uncontrollable forest fires that swept through populated areas, causing significant loss of life and property. This crisis helped to spawn the conservation movement championed by President Theodore Roosevelt, who empowered a newly created U.S. Forestry Service to implement laws aimed at regulating the most destructive practices of the timber industry.

The construction boom that followed the end of World War II resulted in a dramatic increase in lumbering activity. The continuing dispute in the United States between the timber industry and the environmental community heated up again. In recent years one focus of this struggle has been the destruction of old-growth forests in the Pacific Northwest because of the practice of clear-cutting rather than selective, sustainable tree harvesting.

The major forestry industry companies claim that they are responding to legitimate material and economic needs. They maintain that severe curtailment of their activities will result in economic distress, due both to the loss of high-paying jobs in the timber industry as well as to the escalating price of wood and wood products. Many of them also point out that they have already modified their practices to make the forests sustainable by planting new trees at a rate greater than the harvesting rate.

Opponents assert that the industry's economic arguments are self-serving distortions and exaggerations of the truth. They raise objections to the fact that the industry, which operates largely on publicly owned forest lands, is subsidized by taxpayers, since the roadbuilding and maintenance provided by the Forestry Service is worth far in excess of what the companies are charged. Furthermore, the claim of sustainable timber harvesting ignores the fact that the newly planted tree farms do not in fact replace the old-growth forest ecosystems that are rapidly being depleted. These ancient forest ecosystems provide vital habitats for numerous threatened and endangered species.

This latter concern has provided the successful strategy that has been used by a coalition of environmental organizations, including the Sierra Club, the Audubon Society, and the National Wildlife Federation, to significantly curtail the destructive timber harvesting in old-growth forests in the states of Oregon and Washington. Beginning in the late 1980s, a series of precedent-setting lawsuits were won against the lumber industry. The basis for this strategy, which had the effect of forcing the Clinton administration to devise a plan to significantly slow down forest destruction, was the requirement under the Endangered Species Act that the northern spotted owl, which had been listed as a threatened species, had to be protected.

The authors of the pro and con articles for this issue agree that there is a need to protect old-growth forests. What they disagree about is whether the strategy devised to achieve this goal is appropriate. Jon Jefferson, a freelance journalist who frequently writes about legal issues, describes the evolution of the strategy by which lawyers for the Sierra Club Legal Defence Fund used the spotted owl's plight to win a series of court injunctions against the timber industry. He quotes a counsel for the Fish and Wildlife Service who judges the result to be "probably the most stunning series of victories ever put together by an environmental litigation team." Gene W. Wood, professor of forest wildlife ecology at Clemson University, examines the methodology employed by the Interagency Scientific Committee (ISC) in developing its spotted owl conservation strategy. While complementing the committee's response to its charge, Wood attacks the underlying premise that the ancient forests and an endangered species can best be protected by making the latter a surrogate for the former.

YES

Jon Jefferson

TIMMMBERR! HOW TWO LAWYERS AND A SPOTTED OWL TOOK A CUT OUT OF THE LOGGING INDUSTRY

When President Clinton convened his April "timber summit" in Portland to seek peace in the war between the Pacific Northwest's loggers and environmental activists, Seattle lawyer Vic Sher seemed just one among the dozens of speakers. Then Interior Secretary Bruce Babbitt sat down next to him and said, "So you're the one responsible for all this."

It was only a slight exaggeration. Sher, managing attorney for the Seattle office of the Sierra Club Legal Defense Fund, had indeed played a pivotal role in bringing everyone there, including the president, the vice-president, three Cabinet secretaries, and impassioned advocates for both environmental interests and timber companies.

During the past six years, Sher and his partner, Todd True, have litigated every major case that has halted logging sales from federal lands in the Northwest. Along with defense fund forester Andy Stahl and Oregon law professor Michael Axline, they forced a logjam, so to speak, that brought the White House to the Northwest in search of a way to save a resource without killing an industry.

The final verdict is not in yet: The only results so far are a proposed plan, unveiled July 1, and a draft report on its environmental impact, now undergoing public review and comment. That plan's adoption is far from certain: Timber-industry advocates say its sharp reduction in federal timber sales is economic disaster for lumber towns; environmental watchdogs fret publicly that it may be too little, too late. Even before its release, the plan sparked a fierce argument between Babbitt and House Speaker Tom Foley, D-Wash., whose opposition to it could cause political trouble.

Still, say scientific and legal analysts, by focusing on entire ecosystems—the complex web of forests, streams and wildlife, rather than merely owls or logging—the Clinton plan represents one of the most dramatic shifts ever in federal land-use policy.

Here's the story of how a few environmental lawyers set the legal stage for that dramatic shift, by forcing an end to business as usual in the federal forests of the Pacific Northwest.

* * *

In hindsight, the fight over the Pacific Northwest's forests had been taking root for years; in fact, the first seeds were sown a half-century ago, according to land-use expert Charles Wilkinson, a University of Colorado law professor and the author of "Crossing the Next Meridian: Land, Water, & the Future of the West" (Island Press, 1992).

"The problem really traces to the big construction boom right after World War II in the West," says Wilkinson. "The national forests had traditionally had an annual timber harvest—a 'cut'—of about 1 billion board-feet a year," half of it from the Northwest, Wilkinson says. (A board-foot equals a 12-inch square of wood an inch thick.) During the war, the yearly harvest increased to about 3 billion board feet.

It never went back down. By 1965, the annual cut had soared tenfold, to 11 billion board-feet—roughly 15 million trees a year. The cut would stay at that level for the next quarter century, and the federal forests were suffering for it. "I'm not one for shutting down timber harvesting in the national forests," says Wilkinson, "but that's too high—it's too high for forest health, too high for the animal species that live there, and too high for public acceptability. The policy had just spun out of control."

As the cut rose, so did concerns of local and national environmental groups, including the National Audubon Society. "I moved to the Northwest in 1963," says Brock Evans, now a vice-president of the society in Washington, D.C. "When I got there, I joined the Seattle Mountaineers, a climbing club. But as soon as I started climbing mountains, I started seeing all this logging. Eight-foot-thick trees—they were like cathedrals—being cut."

During the 1960s, Evans said, "our method was just to take land away from the Forest Service—we won [wilderness designation for] 7,000 acres in the North Cascades, for example." But then, in 1984, after Congress had set aside about 2 million more acres of wilderness in California, Oregon and Washington, says Evans, "The political leaders of the Northwest said, 'That's it—we're not [allow]ing this anymore.' And so the assault with the chainsaws began."

It was shortly afterward that the Sierra Club Legal Defense Fund [SCLDF] came to the Northwest. Nationally, SCLDF had been around since 1971. The nonprofit law firm was spawned by the Sierra Club's court fight against a proposed Disney ski resort next to Sequoia National Park. (*Sierra Club v. Morton*, 405 U.S. 727, 92 S.Ct. 1361, 31 L.Ed.2d 636. The Sierra Club lost the legal battle—and the personal goodwill of nature-flick king Walt Disney, whom it had earlier named an honorary life member—but it won the public-opinion war and quashed the resort.)

Today, the fund has offices in nine cities, 33 lawyers, a staff of more than 100, and an annual budget of $10 million, two-thirds of it raised by private contributions.

The Seattle office was opened by Sher and True in January 1987. "Even before we got the office open," True says, "people from regional and national environmental organizations came to us and explained the problems they were facing in getting federal agencies to protect this old-growth ecosystem." A key staff member from the outset was forester Stahl, hired from the National Wildlife Federation, who had spent the past three years pinpointing weaknesses in U.S. Forest Service and Bureau of Land Management plans to protect the spotted owl and the old-growth forest it inhabits.

Sher and True weren't the first attorneys to recognize the potential importance of the linkage between the spotted owl and old growth. They were, however, the first to plunge in for the long haul. "What had been missing in the region before was the availability of attorneys practicing full-time in the public-interest area who could take on cases that might span years and require thousands of hours to pursue," says True.

"One of the things we realized early on was that the kind of change needed in policy and environmental awareness was not something that could be accomplished with one lawsuit," he says. "It would take a coordinated effort, a coordinated series of lawsuits to bring the issues into focus in a way that would change agency behavior. That was our goal in selecting the cases we selected and pursuing them the way we did."

What emerged was a three-pronged strategy: 1) Get the Northern spotted owl protected as an endangered or threatened species; 2) halt or slow timber sales by the Forest Service, which manages 70 percent of the remaining spotted-owl habitat, until stricter habitat protections were implemented; and 3) force the Bureau of Land Management [BLM] to consider the impact on owl habitats of logging in its Oregon lands.

Down in Oregon, the groundwork for a case against the BLM had already been laid by Stahl and law professor Michael Axline, who teaches the environmental

ABOUT THE NORTHERN SPOTTED OWL AND LOGGING

Subspecies: California spotted owl, Mexican spotted owl and Northern spotted owl. Mexican and Northern owl are threatened. Total population: 6,000 to 10,000 (est.).

Height: 16–17 inches. Weight: 1.25–1.5 pounds.

Wingspan: About 40 inches.

Life span: 9–12 years, some up to 17 years.

Range: From southern British Columbia to northern California and from the eastern base of the Cascade Mountains of Washington and Oregon to the Pacific coast.

Home range: A pair of owls needs 1,000 to 10,000 acres to live, mate and reproduce. Owls without a home range join the "floating" population and are less likely to reproduce.

Pacific Northwest logging areas: Washington state, Oregon and parts of northern California.

Old-growth forest during 19th century in spotted owls' principal range of western Washington and western Oregon: 19.5 million acres (est.).

Old-growth forest now in principal range: 3.4 million acres (est.).

Annual timber harvest in principal range: 4.5 billion board feet annually from 1980–89, 2.4 billion from 1990–92 and an estimated 1.08 billion in 1993 and also under Clinton plan.

Forest product industries employment (lumber, wood and paper) in principal states of Washington and Oregon: 118,000 jobs in 1992.

Sources: U.S. Fish and Wildlife Service, U.S. Forest Service, Journal of Forestry

law clinic at the University of Oregon (and who stirred up some controversy of his own: a teacher at a tax-supported Oregon law school fighting tax-paying Oregon timber interests). Sher and True joined Axline as co-counsel in the Oregon BLM case, then filed other cases of their own against other government agencies with jurisdiction over old-growth forests and the spotted owl.

* * *

What followed, over the next five years, was a series of victories in federal district courts in Seattle and Portland that rapidly chipped away at federal timber sales in the Northwest. Under a court order to reconsider the owl's status, the U.S. Fish and Wildlife Service agreed in 1989 to list the bird as threatened. More damaging to the timber industry, though, was a string of injunctions, beginning in 1989, barring new timber sales by the BLM and Forest Service.

The injunction strategy suffered a temporary—but major—setback in 1989 and '90. After the first injunctions, Northwest members of Congress pushed through an appropriations-bill rider "determin[ing] and direct[ing]" that the Forest Service and BLM plans challenged by the lawsuits were, in fact, adequate—in effect, insulating the agencies' actions from judicial review.

The rider was a vastly expanded version of a similar measure first passed in 1985 to allow sales in a contested Oregon tract. The new version—"The Rider from Hell," environmental groups called it—was struck down by the Ninth Circuit, but not before 600 new timber sales had occurred.

According to True, the congressional rider was a "key turning point" in his firm's battle. "That's when we realized this was a major regional and national issue," he says, "and that to achieve policy changes, we'd have to protect our access to the courts. Suspending the laws is a giant policy mistake," he adds. "It's like taking the batteries out of a smoke alarm, because the ability to go to court and call the government to account is the smoke alarm you use when the government starts trampling on the law."

For the fight on the congressional front, True and Sher enlisted attorney Kevin Kirchner of SCLDF's Washington, D.C., office. Beginning in 1990, Kirchner built a coalition of public-interest organizations —including hundreds of law-school faculty and deans and 24 state attorneys general—to lobby Congress against further riders. The lobbying has warded off subsequent re-enactments of the rider and may continue to prove strategically important, since the Supreme Court in 1992 upheld the rider's constitutionality.

In the end, SCLDF's strategy was so successful that by the time Bill Clinton was elected president, timber sales from millions of acres of Northwest forest had been blocked until completion of court-ordered forest management plans and environmental impact statements.

Three months after taking office, Clinton and company came to Portland, seeking an airing of the issues and, ultimately, a breakup of the logjam. Two months after that, a dramatic new direction in forest policy was announced. The plan proposed sharply curtailing logging on federal lands in the Northwest—average harvests of 1.2 billion board-feet a year, compared with harvests of up to 5 billion board-feet per year in the 1980s. To ease the economic pain, though, it also proposed $1.2 billion in economic aid for retraining workers and retooling timber-dependent local economies.

In perhaps the most far-reaching change of all, the Clinton plan broadened the focus beyond owls and trees, aiming instead to preserve or restore entire ecosystems, including streams where Pacific salmon have been steadily losing ground to logging's effects.

According to Forest Service biologist Eric Forsman, "For the first time, this is an attempt to truly do an ecosystem plan, which is something we sorely needed all along." Forsman, one of the nation's leading spotted-owl researchers, figures that in the past three years he's spent 16 full-time months on scientific panels wrestling with issues raised by the spotted-owl cases.

He's philosophical both about the time required and about the pounding the Forest Service has taken in court. "The fact that they're now taking a pounding from both sides indicates that perhaps they're closer to doing the right thing," he says. "If both sides are upset, hopefully we're reaching a reasonable compromise position."

As Clinton himself had predicted, the plan didn't make anyone happy, least of all the timber industry. According to timber industry lawyer Mark Rutzick, "This plan is a disaster for the forest-products industry, for the workers, for the communities, for the school districts, for the children."

Rutzick, a partner in the Portland office of Seattle's Preston Thorgrimson Shidler Gates & Ellis, has been on the opposite side of the courtroom from True and Sher in most of the key timber cases—a matter, he says, of "being in the right place at the right time... or the wrong place at the right time."

* * *

What next? Some things are already known, others remain uncertain, at best. Until October 28, the timber industry, environmentalists and anyone else who wants to can comment on the Clinton administration's draft environmental impact statement—and, by extension, on the ecosystem-management plan that underlies it.

By December 31, according to an order from Seattle district judge William Dwyer, the administration must issue a final environmental impact statement, which could incorporate a variety of changes: scientific fine-tuning, economic considerations, political horse-trading.

What happens beyond that is uncertain, although here are some educated guesses from observers and participants in the legal process that has brought matters to this stage.

- According to Rutzick, "Businesses in the forest-products industry are likely to reach the conclusion that the president's proposal is neither legal nor balanced."
- "The final result, I think, will be pretty close to the Clinton plan," says public land law professor Wilkinson. "This whole process has been a great political debate in the Northwest, and one of the most important collective decisions any society in the world has ever made on natural resources."
- Owl biologist Forsman predicts, "The Forest Service, the BLM and the Fish and Wildlife Service are going to be under a lot of intense scrutiny. There's a real legacy of distrust, and it's going to be a real challenge to change that— a long, slow, painful process."
- Patrick Parenteau, law professor and director of the Environmental Cen-

ter at Vermont Law School, observes: "Theoretically, the Clinton plan could be implemented administratively. But its long-term success—certainly the pieces that relate to community development and even the harvest levels—will depend on legislative support. If it goes into the courts, my strong sense is that this time around the courts are going to be much more inclined to approve it [than prior plans]."

- "All of us hope that this administration will take a very simple and straightforward approach of telling the truth and obeying the law," says SCLDF attorney True. "If it does that, I'm sure it will achieve a credible resolution of the issue; if it departs from that concept, it will have trouble."

- "I have no idea where it goes from here," admits Forest Service biologist Jack Ward Thomas. "I've quit trying to guess at that. It's kind of a test case for how science and technology combine with political decision-making. It's an interesting thing to watch unfold—maybe not a lot of fun, but certainly interesting."

* * *

Regardless of the final result—regardless even of continuing debate over the proper balance between economics and environment—the cases Sher, True and Axline have litigated represent a watershed in environmental law, says law professor Parenteau.

Two years ago, Parenteau was hired by the Fish and Wildlife Service as special counsel to oppose a Bureau of Land Management effort to exempt 44 timber sales from provisions of the Endangered Species Act. He calls the string of cases filed by SCLDF and Axline "probably the most stunning series of victories ever put together by an environmental litigation team."

There's room for argument, Parenteau concedes, "about whether [forcing policy changes] is a legitimate use of the courts." (Actually, Rutzick is quick to acknowledge that "everything that spotted owl litigants have done is a legitimate use of the courts. People are free to file lawsuits," he says, "and if they win, more power to 'em." But he adds, "There's no doubt in my mind that this litigation strategy is an example of the environmental community's effort to shift decision-making power away from Congress and into the courts.")

But philosophical differences notwithstanding, says Parenteau, "Their conception of the strategy and its execution were absolutely brilliant. They forced the political system to its knees, in effect: forced it to deal with the issue and to dramatically change the direction of forest policy in the United States.

"I've been in this business for 20 years," he adds, "and I've never seen anything so successful as this litigation strategy Vic Sher and Todd True have pursued. They literally shut the forest down."

NO

Gene W. Wood

OWL CONSERVATION
STRATEGY FLAWED

The preparation of *A Conservation Strategy for the Northern Spotted Owl* may well have been the most concerted and intensive effort in the history of American wildlife management. Federal agencies, spurred by their increasing embroilment in the issues of loss of old-growth forest, declining northern spotted owl populations, the eminent listing of the owl as a threatened species, and the spotted owl as a surrogate for old-growth, initiated a blitzkrieg strategy aimed at defusing the crisis before another episode of "courtroom land management" could begin. To that end, they appear to have been highly successful.

An agreement between the Bureau of Land Management, Fish and Wildlife Service, Forest Service, and National Park Service established the Interagency Scientific Committee (ISC) on October 5, 1989, with Jack Ward Thomas as chair. The final report of this committee, 427 pages and 3 maps long, was published in May 1990.

EARLY HABITAT MANAGEMENT

The ISC offered compelling evidence that the fate of the northern spotted owl was highly dependent upon future changes in the Pacific Northwest forest landscape, especially with respect to the amount and distribution of forests having attributes of old-growth. The ISC found that while the geographic range of the owl covered a variety of coniferous forest zones in northern California, Oregon, and Washington, "suitable to superior" habitat over most of the range could be defined as "a dominant overstory >200 years old, with a multilayered, multispecies canopy, relatively high canopy closure, and large number of snags and logs." They noted that these attributes could be found in redwood forests 50 to 100 years old in northern California and that these habitats supported substantial numbers of owls. However, it was important to note that the northern California redwoods accounted for only 7 percent of the habitat in the owl's geographic range. The ISC acknowledged that while there were currently 7.1 million acres of "suitable to superior" (old-growth) habitat left, that habitat was being lost, primarily through forest cutting, at the rate of 1 to 2 percent per year.

Spotted owl habitat management began in Oregon in 1977 and later evolved into the spotted owl habitat area (SOHA) strategy. By 1989, SOHAs accounted for about 2 million acres of forestland. Most biologists and many managers agreed that the SOHA strategy could not succeed in perpetuating the owl because of biological insufficiency (resulting primarily from demographic problems). Furthermore, the strategy had become an administrative nightmare due to a lack of coordination among responsible agencies and other landowners. The ISC proposed a conservation strategy to meet the ecological requirements necessary to maintain a viable population of northern spotted owls throughout their geographic range and with a predicted population persistence exceeding 100 years.

CONSERVATION AREAS

The plan calls for a network of habitat conservation areas (HCAs) that will be managed to protect and enhance "suitable to superior" owl habitat, overlain on a forest matrix where management for a broad array of resources, including spotted owls, will continue. The ideal HCA (Category 1) would support twenty or more pairs of owls. The strategy allowed a 25 percent overlap of owl home ranges. Under this guideline, an HCA for twenty pairs and an appropriate home range median of 4,000 acres would encompass 60,000 acres. The next Category 1 HCA boundary would have to be within 12 miles, a spacing estimated to be the dispersal distance of 67 percent of dispersing juvenile birds. The ISC report established

four categories of HCAs based on estimated carrying capacity.

The conservation strategy begins by providing a habitat niche that provides for the owls' need to nest, roost, and find adequate amounts of prey. The habitat niche acquires a landscape perspective as population demographics come into consideration. The following postulates were set forth:

- Likelihood of persistence diminishes as number of pairs in an HCA declines from twenty.
- Likelihood of isolation and insufficient immigration and exchange between clusters becomes greater as spacing between HCAs becomes large (greater than twelve miles).
- Likelihood of mate replacement decreases as HCAs become smaller and more widely spaced.
- Likelihood of successful dispersal becomes less as connective habitats become poorer and more scarce.
- Stochastic events (storm, fire, disease, insect epidemic, etc.) are less likely to have a catastrophic effect on the species if its subpopulations are adequately dispersed over a large area.

According to the ISC, there may be as many as 6,000 northern spotted owls spread across the geographic range of the subspecies. There are 925 known pairs on currently proposed HCAs on Forest Service, Bureau of Land Management, and National Park Service land. The goal is to increase this number to 1,750 pairs by the year 2100. Mapped HCAs total about 7.7 million acres and cover all land types (lakes, streams, highways, etc.) and ownership classes. Except for owl habitat protection or enhancement or for silvicultural research on owl habitat management, timber harvests will be prohibited within HCAs and road construction will be discouraged.

The ISC would likely admit that it has not formulated a perfect scheme. On the other hand, these workers labored strenuously to produce the best approximation in response to their charge; the effort was no less than Herculean. Nevertheless, in my opinion there are some points that deserve debate.

TUNNEL VISION

My first two concerns are outside the committee's assigned responsibility. The ISC was to develop the best practicable strategy that would ensure a viable population of spotted owls for at least 100 years. It was not to consider ecological and economic tradeoffs or benefits resulting from that strategy. The current strategy is the best approximation for the owl —but is it the best for 7.7 million acres of landscape? The ISC maintains that yet another committee should assess the impact on other resources and goals. However, a major conflict is created by this line of thinking. How could a new committee begin such a task without some negativism toward ISC conclusions?

Furthermore, there are those who charge the ISC overlooked the potentially far-reaching effect of gearing a large amount of land to a single goal. It also seems notable that the Forest Service, mandated to pursue multiple-use management, should have provided the leadership for this single-use approach to land management while the National Park Service found single-species management inconsistent with its policies.

NO MIDDLE GROUND

My second point concerns the old-growth/owl/logging issue. While the ISC recognized that "to some degree" the spotted owl is a surrogate for old-growth, it denied complicity with the surrogate process. However readers cannot help but note the contradiction involved. When the ISC proposes a strategy that prohibits all commercial forestry on all HCAs, it has taken the position that there is no middle ground between logging without concern for the owl and protecting the owl by eliminating logging. In today's world this is not only poor multiple-use management, it is also a poor land ethic. It represents an unblinking subscription to the theory that goals for the spotted owl and commodity resources are mutually exclusive and that we possess neither the desire nor intellect to integrate them. The ISC notation that future research might cause a reevaluation of this aspect was only weakly reassuring.

A number of technical points raise my concern about the scientific foundation for the conservation strategy. First, when do habitats really become fragmented? Fragmentation, a term that has permeated applied ecology literature, is usually the first and most frequent missile fired in preservationist vs. logger battles, regardless of forest type or the issue at hand. Preventing fragmentation appears to be the highest priority guiding the owl conservation strategy. The ISC assumed that any type of even-aged management causes fragmentation. That point is hard to accept. Is there such a thing as a continuous habitat, i.e., one in which absolutely no discontinuities exist? How great does a discontinuity have to become before the habitat becomes fragmented?

Inappropriate logging has caused fragmentation, which has subsequently led to instances of subpopulation isolation. On the other hand, proposing that all logging necessarily results in fragmentation may be a convenient assumption but it is not an established fact, and it is not acceptable in a society that seeks to preserve sensitive species while remaining dependent on forest products.

DEBATABLE ASSUMPTIONS

There are some other ISC propositions [that] are of debatable scientific merit: cutting may result in an edge effect manifested by greater predation on spotted owls by barred and great horned owls; cutting negatively affects the prey base of spotted owls; old-growth forest conditions are a requirement for the northern flying squirrel (a primary prey species); logging one stand critically predisposes an adjacent stand to blowdown; owl-pair cluster size will respond sluggishly to increases in HCA size; owl populations must stabilize at densities lower than predicted carrying capacity of the HCA; and the spotted owl is a keystone species in old-growth forests. It was also disconcerting to note that while the collective studies on spotted owls yielded mixed results on such basic points as habitat (forest condition) requirements, home range size, and dispersal distance, variability in the data seemed to be of less concern to the ISC than the need to produce a number for a model.

Finally, while I am convinced that the experienced field biologists understood what constituted owl habitat, I am not convinced that knowledge was shared by the modelers. This is very troubling because the conservation strategy was greatly influenced by models, using critical parameter values that were largely best-educated guesses. In reality, such models are prone to subjective influence. Given the mixed results of the empirical data, my concerns were not alleviated by the claim that the role of computer simulation models was secondary to that of the empirical studies.

The creation of *A Conservation Strategy for the Northern Spotted Owl* was a historic effort in wildlife preservation. The ISC deserves high praise for completing its charge. While the strategy and science upon which it was based can be debated, I cannot imagine any finer product given the current state of knowledge, the time frame, and the administratively defined objective. It is unfortunate however that this accomplishment carries with it the ominous specter of a continuing surrogacy process and offers only single-species management response. It bodes ill as a guide to future management of the forests upon which society depends for a broad array of resources.

POSTSCRIPT

Is Protecting the Spotted Owl a Clever Strategy for Preserving Old-Growth Forests?

Jefferson's praise for the legal campaign waged by the Sierra Club Legal Defense Fund lawyers ignores the possibility that choosing the spotted owl as a surrogate for the ancient forests that they were committed to protect was not an ecologically wise decision. Most ecologists would probably agree with Wood's contention that it is better to devise a plan for conserving the old-growth forest based on the specific needs of that diverse ecosystem. But the political reality is that it is far easier to get the public and the politicians to respond to the plight of an attractive, feathered creature than to the less tangible, more complex issue of ecosystem protection. Some of the concerns raised by Wood could be realized by changing the management principle of the Forest Service from timber production to preserving biological diversity. This is proposed in H. Michael Anderson's article in the Winter 1993 issue of *Issues in Science and Technology*.

In his campaign for reelection, then-president Bush stated his support for the timber industry in terms of "jobs versus owls." He cited the industry's claim that proposed restrictions on its activities would result in the loss of 100,000 jobs in the industry. As documented in a front-page news story in the October 11, 1994, issue of the *New York Times*, this prediction has failed to materialize, as has often been the case with regard to dire industrial warnings prior to environmental regulations. In fact, as stated in the newspaper story, Oregon has gained nearly 100,000 jobs since the court injunctions began constraining the timber industry in 1991. Nine out of ten woodworkers who have participated in job retraining have found new jobs at salaries that average about 90 percent of their former wages. Instead of using 300-year-old trees, the mills are making two-by-fours out of wood from tree farms and are, according to the news story, "getting more out of the timber, using parts that used to be discarded."

The leaders of the Western Ancient Forest Campaign have recently been confronted with another obstacle. The Forestry Service has proposed a plan to curb forest fires that includes building roads and cutting trees in some forested areas that are now protected from such activity by wilderness designation. Gregg Easterbrook raises an even more fundamental objection to the owl-protection strategy for preserving old-growth forests by questioning whether the northern spotted owl qualifies for endangered species protection in his March 28, 1994, article in *The New Republic*. Kathie Duben analyzes the owl-based forest protection strategy from a more ecological, less legalistic perspective than Jefferson in her feature article in the March/April 1992 issue of *E Magazine*. Carrie Casey focuses on the extent to which the plight of the spotted owl is an indicator of the condition of old-growth forests in his article in the September/October 1991 issue of *American Forests*.

Critics of the Endangered Species Act frequently demand that it should require a cost-benefit analysis before prescribing actions that may have serious economic consequences. For such an analysis of the northern spotted owl issue that concludes that the benefits of protection outweigh the costs, see the article by Jonathan Rubin, Gloria Helfand, and John Loomis in the December 1991 issue of the *Journal of Forestry*.

PART 3

Disposing of Wastes

Modern industrial societies generate many types of waste. Manufacturing and construction activities yield hazardous liquid and solid residues; treatment of raw sewage produces sludge; mining operations generate mountains of tailings; radioactive waste results from the use of nuclear isotopes in medicine and in the nuclear power and nuclear weapons industries. Each of these forms of waste, in addition to ordinary household garbage, contains toxins and pathogens that are potentially serious sources of air and water pollution if they are not disposed of properly. We must now deal with the legacy of waste contamination problems that have resulted from years of neglect and inappropriate waste disposal methods. This section exposes some of the major controversies concerning proposed solutions to three important waste categories.

■ Hazardous Waste: Should the "Polluter Pays" Provision of Superfund Be Weakened?

■ Municipal Waste: Can Management Plans Based on Mandated Recycling Succeed?

■ Nuclear Waste: Should Plans for Underground Storage Be Put on Hold?

ISSUE 12

Hazardous Waste: Should the "Polluter Pays" Provision of Superfund Be Weakened?

YES: Bernard J. Reilly, from "Stop Superfund Waste," *Issues in Science and Technology* (Spring 1993)

NO: Ted Williams, from "The Sabotage of Superfund," *Audubon* (July/August 1993)

ISSUE SUMMARY

YES: DuPont corporate counsel Bernard J. Reilly argues that in both defining standards and assigning costs related to waste cleanup, "Congress should focus the program on reducing real risk, not on seeking unattainable purity."

NO: *Audubon* contributing editor Ted Williams claims that insurers and polluters are lobbying to change the financial liability provisions of Superfund, and he warns against turning it into a public welfare program.

The potentially disastrous consequences of improper hazardous waste disposal burst upon the consciousness of the American public in the late 1970s. The problem was dramatized by the evacuation of dozens of residents of Niagara Falls, New York, whose health was being threatened by chemicals leaking from the abandoned Love Canal, which was used for many years as an industrial waste dump. Awakened to the dangers posed by chemical dumping, numerous communities bordering on industrial manufacturing areas across the country began to discover and report local sites where chemicals had been disposed of in open lagoons or were leaking from disintegrating steel drums. Such esoteric chemical names as dioxins and PCBs have become part of the common lexicon, and numerous local citizens' groups have been mobilized to prevent human exposure to these and other toxins.

The expansion of the industrial use of synthetic chemicals following World War II resulted in the need to dispose of vast quantities of wastes laden with organic and inorganic chemical toxins. For the most part, industry adopted a casual attitude toward this problem and, in the absence of regulatory restraint, chose the least expensive means available. Little attention was paid to the ultimate fate of chemicals that could seep into surface water or groundwater. Scientists have estimated that less than 10 percent of the waste was disposed of in an environmentally sound manner.

The magnitude of the problem is truly mind-boggling: Over 275 million tons of hazardous waste is produced in the United States each year; as many as 10,000 dump sites may pose a serious threat to public health, according to the federal Office of Technology Assessment; and other government estimates indicate that more than 350,000 waste sites may ultimately require corrective action at a cost that could easily exceed $500 billion.

Congressional response to the hazardous waste threat is embodied in two complex legislative initiatives. The Resource Conservation and Recovery Act (RCRA) of 1976 mandated action by the Environmental Protection Agency (EPA) to create "cradle to grave" oversight of newly generated waste, and the Comprehensive Environmental Response, Compensation, and Liability Act, commonly called "Superfund," gave the EPA broad authority to clean up existing hazardous waste sites. The implementation of this legislation has been severely criticized by environmental organizations, citizens' groups, and members of Congress who have accused the EPA of foot-dragging and a variety of politically motivated improprieties. Less than 20 percent of the original $1.6 billion Superfund allocation was actually spent on waste cleanup.

Amendments designed to close RCRA loopholes were enacted in 1984, and the Superfund Amendments and Reauthorization Act (SARA) added $8.6 billion to a strengthened cleanup effort in 1986 and an additional $5.1 billion in 1990. While acknowledging some improvement, both environmental and industrial policy analysts remain very critical about the way that both RCRA and Superfund/SARA are being implemented. Once again both of these hazrdous waste laws are up for reauthorization and proposals for major changes are stimulating heated debate.

Bernard J. Reilly, who manages the legal aspects of DuPont's Superfund program, thinks the legislation has turned into an "unjustifiable waste of the nation's resources at the expense of other critical society needs." He calls for major changes, which would "focus the program on practical risk reduction." One specific change he advocates is in the "polluter-pays" provision of the law, which he argues holds companies liable for more than their fair share of the costs. The scheme he advocates would assess more of the costs to the EPA. Ted Williams, a contributing editor to *Audubon*, acknowledeges that the Supefund program has been very costly and has cleaned up little waste. But he blaims this on sabotage of the law by the Bush and Reagan administrations. He specifically warns against recommendations to abandon the policy of holding polluters strictly liable for the damage they have caused, which he fears would "turn it into a public works program" whereby "citizens will pay twice, once with their environment and once with their tax money."

YES

Bernard J. Reilly

STOP SUPERFUND WASTE

President Clinton's economic plan is a clear attempt to reorder federal spending priorities by putting more money into "investments" that will spur economic growth and increase national wealth, while cutting unproductive activities. One important way he could further his agenda would be to push for reform of one of today's most misguided efforts: the Superfund hazardous waste cleanup program. The President has already paid lip service to this goal, telling business leaders in a February 11 speech at the White House that, "We all know it doesn't work—the Superfund has been a disaster."

Superfund, created by the Comprehensive Environmental Response, Compensation, and Liability Act of 1980 (CERCLA) in the wake of the emergency at the Love Canal landfill in Niagara Falls, New York, was designed as a $1.6-billion program to contain the damage from and eventually clean up a limited number of the nation's most dangerous abandoned toxic waste sites. But in short order it has evolved into an open-ended and costly crusade to return potentially thousands of sites to a near-pristine condition. The result is a large and unjustifiable waste of our nation's resources at the expense of other critical societal needs.

No one questions that the nation has a major responsibility to deal with hazardous waste sites that pose a serious risk to public health and the environment. It is the manner and means by which the federal government has pursued this task, however, that are wasteful. Superfund legislation has given the U.S. Environmental Protection Agency powerful incentives and great clout to seek the most comprehensive, "permanent" cleanup remedies possible—without regard to cost or even the degree to which public health is at risk. Although the EPA does not always choose the most expensive remedial solution, there is strong evidence that, in many cases, waste sites can be cleaned up or sufficiently contained or isolated for a fraction of the cost, while still protecting the public and the environment. Further, EPA's selection of "priority" cleanup sites has been haphazard at best. Indeed, it has no system in place for determining which of those sites—or the many potential sites it has not yet characterized—pose the greatest dangers.

From Bernard J. Reilly, "Stop Superfund Waste," *Issues in Science and Technology* (Spring 1993), pp. 57–60, 62–64. Copyright © 1993 by The University of Texas at Dallas, Richardson, TX. Reprinted by permission.

A 180-degree turn in policy is needed. When the Superfund program comes up for reauthorization next year, Congress should direct the EPA to abandon its pursuit of idealistic cleanup solutions and focus the program on practical risk reduction, targeting those sites that pose the greatest health risks and tying the level and cost of cleanup to the degree of actual risk. Only by making such a fundamental change can the nation maximize the benefits of its increasingly huge investment in the remediation of hazardous waste sites.

COSTS ARE ESCALATING

Estimates for cleaning up, under current practice, the more than 1,200 sites on the EPA's "national priority list" (NPL) range from $32 billion by EPA (based on a $27 million per-site cost) to $60 billion by researchers at the University of Tennessee (based on a $50 million per-site cleanup cost). These estimates are likely to be well below the ultimate cost, since EPA can add an unlimited number of sites to the list. The agency plans to add about 100 sites a year, bringing the total by the year 2000 to more than 2,100. But more than 30,000 inactive waste sites are being considered for cleanup and the universe of potential sites has been estimated at about 75,000. Most experts believe that far fewer—from 2,000 to 10,000—will eventually be cleaned up. The University of Tennessee researchers make a best guess of 3,000 sites, which would put the cost at $150 billion (in 1990 dollars) over 30 years, not including legal fees.

This $150 billion might be acceptable if the U.S. economy were buoyant and limitless funds existed for other needs. It most certainly would be justified if many sites posed unacceptable dangers to the public. But neither of these situations exists.

SKEWED PRIORITIES

A key flaw in Superfund is that most of its effort and money are directed to a relatively small number of "priority" sites, while thousands of others are ignored and, in most cases, not even sampled or studied. For this reason, it is doubtful that the NPL includes all the worst sites.

"Deadly" chemical landfills buried under residential neighborhoods have hardly been typical of the sites EPA has placed on the NPL. Indeed, EPA's efforts to create a system for ranking hazards have not been geared to actually finding the riskiest sites but to satisfying the letter of the CERCLA law. In the first ranking scheme, sites were evaluated for various threats and a score of 28.5 (on a scale of 100) was determined to be sufficient for an NPL listing. However, the listings were not necessarily based on an actual determination of the degree to which they posed threats to public health or the environment. Rather, the sites were included because Congress had determined that 400 sites must be on the NPL, and a score of 28.5 resulted in 413 listings.

Several years ago, the ranking scheme was made much more elaborate, with threats from contaminants in the air, water, and soil weighed differently. The same maximum score of 100 and listing score of 28.5 were used. Why? EPA said that it was "not because of any determination that the cutoff represented a threshold of unacceptable risk presented by the sites" but because the 28.5 score was "a convenient management tool." So much for the rigors of a system designed to cull the Love Canals from town dumps.

A 1991 report by a committee of the National Research Council (NRC) strongly faulted EPA's methods of selecting sites and setting priorities. The report said that EPA has no comprehensive inventory of waste sites, no program for discovering new sites, insufficient data for determining safe exposure levels, and an inadequate system for identifying sites that require immediate action to protect public health.

In a perfect world, every "dirty" site would be cleaned, regardless of the degree of risk it presented. In practice, this is impossible, so we should be spending more to prioritize in order to focus our limited resources on real risks.

EXTREME REMEDIES

However it is accomplished, once a site makes the NPL, money is no object in the remediation process. This was not necessarily the case under the original 1980 Superfund law. CERCLA left some ambiguity about how extensive the cleanups had to be—whether only reasonable risks needed to be eliminated or whether the site had [to] be returned to a preindustrial condition. When it enacted the Superfund Amendments and Reauthorization Act (SARA) in 1986, however, Congress, motivated by a deep distrust of the Reagan-era EPA, took a hard-line stance. SARA, which increased funding for the program to $8.5 billion and ordered action to begin at ever more sites, directed EPA to give preference to cleanup remedies that "to the maximum extent practicable" lead to "permanent solutions." The emphasis on permanence was further reinforced by a requirement that cleanups must comply with any

"applicable or relevant and appropriate requirement" (ARAR) in any other state or federal law relating to protection of public health and the environment.

SARA was deeply flawed. For one thing, it effectively forced EPA to continue remedial action even after all realistic risks at a site had been eliminated. One example is the Swope Superfund site, a former solvent reclamation facility in Pennsauken, New Jersey. Although all major sources of contamination had been removed from the site, EPA ordered the installation of a $5-million vapor extraction system to remove more contaminants. The purpose was to protect groundwater in case any private wells were sunk in the future. But EPA neglected to consider the fact that private wells had been banned in the area.

SARA's requirements also serve to exclude the use of other far less costly remedies that would give the public the same or at least acceptable protection from harm. For example, at the Bridgeport Rental and Oil Services Superfund site in Logan Township, New Jersey, EPA ordered the construction of an onsite, $100-million incinerator after PCBs were found in several sludge samples. In making its decision, EPA used the ARAR requirement to retroactively apply the federal Toxic Substances Control Act (TSCA), which requires incineration of currently generated wastes if samples indicate that PCBs in the soil exceed 500 parts per million.

The absurdity of the plan became apparent when EPA decided to create an on-site landfill to dispose of the heavy metal residues from the incineration. Given that a landfill was to be created anyway and that PCBs at the site were so scarce that EPA had to import them for trial burns of the incinerator, the agency could have opted to contain the sludge on site in the first place —using existing proven technologies— while more than adequately protecting the public at an estimated one-fifth of the cost of incineration.

A similar tale is unfolding at another Superfund site in Carlstadt, New Jersey, which is contaminated with solvents, PCBs, and heavy metals. A trench has been cut around the site to an underlying impervious soil layer and then filled with clay to prevent any migration of the contaminants. The site has also been pumped dry to protect groundwater and capped to keep out rain. Remediation work has cost about $7 million, and DuPont as well as other responsible parties have pledged to maintain these containment systems for as long as necessary. However, despite the absence of any current or reasonably foreseeable public exposures, EPA may decide to require incineration of the top 10 feet of soil at an estimated cost of several hundred million dollars. This would be a foolish waste of money.

EPA must also consider that extreme, costly remediation solutions often are not without costs of their own. Incineration, for instance, cannot destroy metals. Does the public really benefit when lead is released into the air as a byproduct? By the same token, when contaminated soil is ordered excavated and carted elsewhere, one neighborhood gets a "permanent" solution, whereas another gets a landfill with toxic residues.

RISKS EXAGGERATED

Superfund legislation is not the only force driving EPA to seek "permanent" solutions. EPA decides on a remedy only after assessing the risks at a site. However, EPA often uses unrealistic assumptions that exaggerate the risks and lead to excessive actions. For example, according to the Hazardous Waste Cleanup Project, an industry group in which DuPont has been involved, EPA may make estimates of exposure based on a scenario in which an individual is assumed to reside near a site for 70 years, to consume two liters of water every day during those 70 years, and to obtain all of that water from groundwater at the site. It has even made exposure estimates based on the length of time a child will play (and eat dirt) on a site in the middle of an industrial location surrounded by a security fence. Each of these scenarios is highly improbable.

Questions involving risk assessment are, of course, going to be contentious ones for some time to come. Clouding the Superfund debate is the fact that there is no scientific consensus as to the precise magnitude of the dangers posed by chemicals typically found at Superfund sites.

The existence of toxic wastes at a site does not necessarily mean that they pose a threat to nearby residents. Epidemiologic studies of waste sites have severe technical limitations, and it is difficult at best to determine whether exposure to hazardous wastes can be blamed for medical problems when a long gap exists between exposure and disease. Even at such a well-known site as Times Beach, Missouri, where the entire community was evacuated, research in recent years has shown that the potential health risks were relatively small or even nonexistent.

The most comprehensive assessment of the risks from Superfund sites came in the 1991 NRC report, which concluded that "current health burdens from hazardous-waste sites appear to be small," but added that "until better evidence is developed, prudent public policy demands that a margin of safety be provided regarding public health risks from exposures to hazardous-waste sites."

No one can argue with a margin of safety. However, that is not the focus of the current Superfund program, which, far more than any other environmental program, makes no rational attempt to link costs with benefits. EPA's own Science Advisory Board, in a 1990 report that attempted to rank the environmental problems for which the agency is responsible, concluded that old toxic waste sites appeared to be "low to medium risk." Other hazards, such as radon gas in homes and cigarette smoke, were considered to pose much larger risks.

THE LIABILITY MESS

The bulk of the Superfund tab will be picked up by industry, through taxes imposed under CERCLA, out-of-pocket cleanup costs, or settlements with insurance companies. Industry recognizes that it must assume its fair share of the financial and operating burden of the cleanup effort, and it acknowledges that Superfund has compelled it to become exceptionally vigilant not only in disposing of toxic wastes but also in minimizing their generation in the first place. But it objects to a system in which EPA seemingly has put a higher priority on pinning the blame and the bill on companies than on ensuring the protection of public health.

CERCLA dictated a "polluter-pays" philosophy to deal with what had largely been lawful disposal of wastes. CERLCA and court interpretations of it also have created an extremely broad liability scheme. Virtually any company remotely

involved in a site-waste generators, haulers, site owners or operators, and even, in some cases, the companies' bankers—could be held responsible. One or a few companies could be forced to pay the entire bill, even though they were only minor participants and other parties were involved—a provision called joint-and-several liability. No limits were imposed on the amount of money that could be extracted from "guilty" parties.

One problem with this liability system is that it completely lacks cost accountability. With industry paying for most of the cleanup, the funds are not in EPA's budget and thus do not have to compete in budget battles with other cash-starved federal programs. And given the strictness of the law, why should EPA regulators subject themselves to possible congressional criticism by selecting a less-than-perfect solution, especially if money is no object? But let us not kid ourselves. Although this money may seem "free" to Congress, EPA, and the public, companies must make up the difference by raising prices, cutting investment and jobs, or taking other undesirable actions.

An even more damning problem is that the liability provisions have spawned countless legal brouhahas that are consuming a large and increasing share of Superfund resources—even as the cleanup process itself has languished. (The average length of a site cleanup is 8 years, and fewer than 100 sites have been "permanently" remediated.) In the approximately 70 percent of Superfund sites that involve multiple parties, companies must fight with the EPA, among themselves, and with their insurance companies over who dumped what, when, and how much—questions extremely difficult to answer many years after the alleged "dumping" is thought to have occurred. Some experts believe that these "transaction costs" will eventually account for more than 20 percent of all Superfund expenditures. This is a boon for lawyers but a waste for the nation.

Legal costs—as well as burdensome technical and administrative expenses—could potentially be greatly reduced if Congress would allow EPA to take a more practical approach to risk reduction. Unlike other environmental laws, such as the Clean Air Act and Clean Water Act, which have sought to deal with problems in successive stages, Superfund's emphasis on finding a one-time, complete, and permanent solution magnifies the stakes to all parties, prolonging disputes and greatly increasing the costs. If companies could count on a more realistic remediation approach, they might be more willing to compromise, which could lead to faster cleanups.

The liability mess could get completely out of hand if Congress goes along with a patently unfair proposal to exempt municipalities from liability at closed municipal landfills, which account for about 20 percent of NPL sites. Municipal governments argue that most of these landfills largely contain household wastes not covered by Superfund and thus they should not be billed for the cleanup. But in many cases this is not true. For example, at the Kramer Superfund site in Mantua, New Jersey, municipal governments contributed the greatest share of hazardous substances. Despite this, EPA is no longer even naming municipalities in cost-recovery suits. (EPA's tendency to selectively enforce the law has been increasing. At Kramer, EPA sued 25 parties even though hundreds were potentially responsible.)

Industry recognizes that many municipal governments are severely strapped for revenues. Yet companies, which provide jobs and help create the tax base needed to support municipal services, should not be milked to pay for Superfund shares properly owed by others.

One last concern with the liability provisions is that they may be having a chilling effect on new investment at sites in older urban areas—areas that sorely need such investment. The reason is that any party that buys such a property would be caught in Superfund's liability web. For example, investors seeking to build a coal-fired power plant in an area with a projected need for such a use recently approached DuPont about buying a property that had been used for manufacturing for more than 100 years and clearly contains some contaminated soil. Virgin land is not needed for a site to burn coal, and risk assessments indicated that workers could be protected with commonsense steps such as paving. But efforts to get reasonable compromises from regulators on containing the site proved fruitless, and now the investment will not be made, at least in this area.

STEPS TO REFORM

It is time for a major redirection of the Superfund program. Congress should tell EPA to abandon its focus on idealistic cleanup remedies and emphasize practical risk reduction. Instead of continuing its haphazard site selection and unjustifiably costly cleanup remedies, EPA should first define the universe of sites that may present real health risks and then take steps to deal with the most immediate dangers, taking costs into consideration. Once a national inventory has been established, extensive site evaluations can be undertaken, with the purpose of setting priorities for cleanup. Only after these actions are taken will we be able to make non-hysterical decisions as to how much we should invest in cleaning these sites, balancing such factors as risks, costs, and other societal needs.

It is particularly crucial that remedy decisions be based on the expected future use of the land and the costs and practicality of the proposed solution. If residential development is planned near the site, the cleanup may need to be extensive. In many cases, however, especially when another industrial use is planned on or near an old waste site, use of containment technologies may be sufficient to protect against risk of exposure. In the most troublesome cases, where major remediation is necessary, costs are high, and existing technology has limitations, it makes much more sense to isolate the site until more cost-effective treatment techniques are developed or increased land values justify a large investment.

In making these decisions, it would be helpful if EPA had much better information on the benefits and costs of different levels of cleanup. Currently, less than 1 percent of EPA's Superfund budget goes for research on the scientific basis for evaluating Superfund sites. Much more should be spent. EPA also should increase its research on the environmental consequences of different types of remedial actions, such as whether incineration actually increases risk by transferring hazardous substances from the ground or water into the air.

The liability provisions of the Superfund program also need to be changed. DuPont and companies in the chemical, petroleum, and other industries favor replacing the very unfair joint-and-several liability provision (making one or a few companies liable for all the costs, even though many others, often defunct, were also responsible) with proportional liability. In other words, responsible parties would pay only in proportion to the share of the cleanup costs associated with the wastes that they contributed at a site. EPA would then be forced to either find and sue all responsible parties or pay for the remainder of the cleanup costs itself. EPA is already authorized to pay for cleanup costs in cases where parties cannot be found or cannot afford to pay—shares which are often sizable. But in practice it has sought to recoup all cleanup costs under the joint-and-several provision. Proportional liability would inject more fairness into the process, and since the polluter-pays principle would be retained, it would continue to encourage responsible parties to pressure EPA to pursue the most cost-effective cleanup remedy. Most important, proportional liability would impose much-needed financial discipline on EPA, since it would be forced to pay for more of the cleanups out of its own budget. For the first time, EPA would have to consider whether the benefits were worth the costs.

Proportional liability would not, of course, solve the problem of how to divide up responsibility in the first place. One possible way out of this morass is to formalize in the law an alternative dispute resolution process in which any or all potentially responsible parties could participate. It would be chaired by neutral parties satisfactory to all. Its findings on shares could be appealed to the courts, but any party that concurred with the decision would be authorized to pay its share and exit the process. This solution would help cut site contention, reward cooperative parties, and leave messy litigation to those unwilling to pay their fair shares. It would also diminish Superfund's luster as a federally mandated entitlements program for lawyers.

More extensive reform of the liability provisions has been proposed by the insurance industry, which wants to eliminate all liability at sites in which more than one party is involved and in which waste disposal occurred prior to enactment of either CERCLA in 1980 or SARA in 1986. Site cleanup would then be paid out of the Superfund budget, financed by increased taxes on industry, including insurers. Although this proposal would eliminate contentious fights over specific site responsibility, substantially cut transaction costs, and possibly speed up site cleanups, it would be unacceptable to DuPont and other parties at Superfund sites if the new taxes were unfairly levied on the same companies already paying disproportionately large shares of the current Superfund cleanups.

Finally, the liability scheme must be changed so that prospective owners of older urban sites are not deterred from making new investments in them. New owners should certainly not be held responsible for contamination that they did not cause. One approach would be for current owners to demonstrate, before sale, that their sites, while not pristine, are adequately contained and do not pose unacceptable risks to the public. The new owner would be expected to maintain or monitor whatever containment system was developed. If EPA later did a more extensive site evaluation and determined that greater threats existed, the new owner would not have to pay. In addition, current owners should be able to make new investments in their property if they demonstrate that the sites are adequately contained.

* * *

The limits of our national wealth have not been so obvious since the 1930s. More than ever, we must make choices among competing, compelling demands for scarce resources. We recognize that a dollar spent on defense cannot be spent on health care. We must also recognize that a dollar spent on hazardous waste cleanup is similarly unavailable. As with other federal programs, Superfund spending must be balanced and managed. This can be done if we refocus our Superfund investment on real risks, give EPA a stake in doing its job cost-effectively, and bring more fairness into the process.

NO

Ted Williams

THE SABOTAGE OF SUPERFUND

The setting was perfect: Cold rain and gull-filled mist blowing in from Buzzards Bay. Litter clinging to the bare ribs of dead brush like shards of rotten umbrella silk. Derelict, graffiti-streaked trailers stuffed to overflowing with bald truck tires. Ratty mattresses and broken easy chairs strewn about the cratered parking lot. Glass from the abandoned mill crunching under my boots and snatches of Eliot's *The Waste Land* resounding in my brain as I trudged along Wet Weather Sewage Discharge Outfall No. 022: "Sweet Thames run softly, till I end my song..."

Until this day, March 28, 1993, I had avoided Superfund sites. So this was my first visit to the waterfront of New Bedford—an impoverished, predominantly Hispanic seaport in southern Massachusetts, now as famous for the polychlorinated biphenyls (PCBs) on the bottom of its harbor as for its whaling history. PCBs, widely used in the manufacture of electrical components until banned in 1978, do hideous things to creatures that come in contact with them—such as causing their cells to proliferate wildly and warping their embryos. I wasn't about to touch anything without my rubber ice-fishing gloves.

Where the sewage dribbled into the dark Acushnet River I jumped down onto gray silt and, breathing through my teeth, scooped up five handfuls of muck. The Environmental Protection Agency's guideline for protecting marine life from chronic toxic effects of PCBs is 30 parts per trillion. I cannot accurately report the PCB content of my amateur sample (taken illegally, the EPA later informed me), but the greasy globules that floated up through the surface scum were likely very rich. Had I been able to get out into the river and upstream to the old Aerovox Inc. discharge pipe, I could have found concentrations of at least 200,000 parts per *million,* or 20 percent, among the highest ever recorded. That means that with a similar test dredging I'd have retrieved one handful of pure PCBs, along with a tangle of wriggling sludge worms, about the only creatures that can live in such habitat.

I was rinsing my gloves and boots in a rain-filled pothole when *The Waste Land's* Fisher King materialized through the gloom—a wispy, gray-haired figure in a red plaid jacket, toting a stout spinning rod. He had parked next to a sign that read in Spanish, Portuguese, and English: "Warning. Hazardous

Waste. No wading, fishing, shellfishing. Per order of U.S. EPA." His name, which he printed with his forefinger on the wet trunk of his car, was Robin Rivera; he knew only enough English to make me understand that he and his family eat the fish he catches here.

Not until 1978 did the nation get angry about the indiscriminate disposal of poisonous chemicals. In that year people who lived near Hooker Chemical Company's Love Canal dump in Niagara Falls, New York, were distressed to smell vile chemical odors in their basements and observe a malevolent secretion bubbling out of the ground at a local school yard. County health officials and Hooker reps tried vainly to contain the alarm, but their assurances that all was well sounded as wrong as the uncontained leachate looked and smelled.

Eventually the citizens took their case to the young commissioner of the state Department of Environmental Conservation—Peter A. A. Berle, now president of the National Audubon Society. Although Berle had no authority to act on public health issues, he sent his people out to test houses on the strength of his environmental mandate. The benzene levels they found were, in his words, "right off the chart." Eventually 600 homes were abandoned and 2,500 residents relocated.

In response to the Love Canal horror show Congress enacted the Comprehensive Environmental Response, Compensation, and Liability Act of 1980, better known as Superfund. Amended in 1986, the law uses taxes on crude oil and 42 commercial chemicals to maintain a fund with which the EPA may, as it likes to say, "remediate" hazardous-waste sites. If perpetrators can be found and are still in business, the EPA may require one or all to clean up the entire site. This essential principle of Superfund is called joint and several liability.

For an idea of the pace at which cleanup proceeds, consider that the EPA and its contractors have been studying and planning what to do about New Bedford's harbor ever since it was declared a "National Priority" Superfund site 11 years ago. Nationwide, the EPA has spent $7.5 billion on its Superfund program, with pitiful results. In some cases remediation has created more problems than it has solved by stirring up contaminants that had been dormant. In other cases vast sums have been squandered at sites that posed little threat to the public, while deadly brews seethed nearby. Superfund contractors have consistently ripped off the EPA, billing it for everything from office parties to work they were supposed to do and didn't.

At this writing only 163 of 1,204 sites have been remediated, and in many cases polluters have been granted what the EPA calls the "containment" option—a feline approach to toxic-waste management in which they just cover their messes and walk away. The average cleanup has cost about $25 million and taken 7 to 10 years to complete.

No one remotely connected with Superfund is happy about the way it has functioned. Polluters identified by the EPA have been madly rummaging through dumps, trying to identify other polluters by their trash and so spread liability. In the process small towns, businesses, and individuals that contributed legally and insignificantly to landfills have been intimidated and assessed for cleanup costs in a fashion utterly inconsistent with the intent of Congress. Environmentalists are at the throats of insurance companies who want to do away with the polluter-pay tenet. The insurance companies are warring in court with industries to whom they have rashly sold pollution-liability policies. People who live atop and beside toxic waste claim— often correctly—that they have been ignored and lied to by the EPA, and as a result, they sometimes oppose well-advised cleanup plans.

Hearings for Superfund's 1994 reauthorization are already under way. "We all know it doesn't work," says President Bill Clinton. "Superfund has been a disaster."

* * *

Even as I wished the Fisher King good luck, I found myself greeting the first of 94 demonstrators from the New Bedford–area citizen's group Hands Across the River. We stood in the rain, listening to fiery speeches amplified by bullhorn about the EPA's plan to dredge the five acres that contain roughly 45 percent of the PCBs extant in the 28-square-mile site, then cleanse the spoil by fire in portable incinerators set up on the downstream side of Sewage Outfall 022.

"You and I will be breathing their mistakes," bellowed rally leader Richard Wickenden. "They made their decision to incinerate behind closed doors with a total disregard for the local citizenry."

He spoke the truth. The New Bedford City Council had found out about the plan not from the EPA but from Hands Across the River, which had found out about it from federal documents at the library. "State-of-the-art incinerators" have a long history of malfunction, even when run by the most conscientious contractors. This one will be operated by Roy F. Weston, a large environmental-consulting firm based in West Chester, Pennsylvania, which in 1990 agreed to pay $750,000 to settle charges that it had defrauded the EPA by backdating data and submitting a bill for work it never did. Finally, people downwind— mostly people like Robin Rivera—are likely to be breathing mistakes, along with all manner of toxic PICs (products of incomplete combustion) that won't be monitored or even identified.

In attempting to clean up one point of pollution the EPA and its contractors will be creating others, asserted New Bedford City Councilman George Rogers. They'll be unleashing PCBs and heavy metals on moving seawater, hauling them onto the bank, then casting them to the four winds during dewatering and combustion. "They're doing this because New Bedford is a poor community; we don't have clout. They wouldn't do it in Miami Beach." He, too, spoke the truth. A study released last September by *The National Law Journal* reveals that the EPA is lenient in penalizing polluters of minority and low-income communities and that cleanups in such areas are slower and less thorough. Toxic racism, activists call it.

Equally veracious were the allegations of David Hammond, president and founder of Hands Across the River, that polluters love incineration because their liability goes up the stack along with the toxic PICs and that the EPA has undermined Superfund's effectiveness and its own credibility by ordering remediation studies from companies that make their money remediating. In particular, Hammond is upset that Weston was hired to do the New Bedford Remedial Action Master Plan, then wound up with the $19.4 million incineration contract.

Both the city council and Hands Across the River hasten to point out that they are not against remediation. But instead of incineration they favor the "Eco Logic" process—a relatively contained heat treatment developed in Rockwood, Ontario, which combines hydrogen with PCBs to form methane and hydrogen chloride and which has been getting rave reviews in the press. "Stunning New Method Zaps Toxic Chemicals Efficiently," shouted a headline in *The Toronto Star* on January 30, 1993.

After the New Bedford speechmaking the congregation marched back and forth over the Acushnet River bridge, waving placards, obstructing traffic (much of which honked in sympathy), and chanting, "No way, EPA," and "Hey, Carol [Browner], if you please, don't you burn those PCBs. Not New Bedford, not the nation. We don't want incineration."

The citizens could scarcely have done a better, more honest job of drawing public attention to the perils of dredging and incinerating PCBs. But this doesn't mean that the EPA ought not to press ahead with its plan for New Bedford. When PCB concentrations are this high, the perils of doing something else or nothing at all are probably greater. One day the Eco Logic process may indeed be a "stunning method" of remediation. Now, despite the effusions of *The Toronto Star*, it's largely an experimental technology and therefore fraught with risk. Meanwhile, the PCBs are spreading out into the Atlantic with every tide and every storm. Humans and marine ecosystems —including half the North American population of endangered roseate terns, which nests on a single island in Buzzards Bay—don't have another decade to wait while the EPA collects data and shuffles papers.

* * *

In other contract deals the EPA has paid the New England office of Roy F. Weston, which it has criticized for poor performance, $635,000 to administer fieldwork that cost $340,000. But Weston looks like a model contractor when compared with some of the others.

Take, for example, consulting-engineering colossus CH2M Hill, which has worked on 275 major sites, including Love Canal, and which holds $1.4 billion worth of Superfund contracts. An inquiry by the House Subcommittee on Oversight and Investigations revealed that as part of alleged Superfund work, CH2M Hill billed the EPA $4,100 for tickets to basketball, baseball, and football games; $167,900 for employee parties and picnics, including the cost of reindeer suits, magicians, and a rent-a-clown; $15,000 for an office bash at a place called His Lordship; "thousands of dollars' worth" of chocolates stamped with the company logo; $63,000 for general advertising; $10,000 for a catered lobbying cruise on the Potomac; and $100 for a Christmas-party dance instructor. "I am all for rocking around the Christmas tree," commented Congressman Thomas J. Bliley Jr. (D-VA) at the hearing, "but does it have to be at the taxpayers' expense?"

Apparently yes, according to the testimony of CH2M Hill's president, Lyle Hassebroek. "No matter what differences of opinion exist on the manner in which we allocate costs," he explained, "CH2M Hill's charges to the government are fair to the taxpayer."

By no means is CH2M Hill aberrant. Last summer EPA investigators found that 23 companies hired for hazardous-waste cleanup in 1988 and 1989 spent 28 percent of their $265 million budget on wasteful administrative costs. Such inefficiency is cited by polluters and their insurance companies as a reason to "overhaul" Superfund—i.e., turn it into a public-works program whereby Uncle Sam would bail them out by picking up toxic litter (provided the offense preceded some stipulated date —1987, according to one proposal) and citizens will pay twice, once with their environment and once with their tax money.

Major polluters further foment discontent with Superfund by attempting to squeeze alleged shares of cleanup costs from everyone who might ever have sent a can of shoe polish to a landfill. The EPA and the courts don't want a nickel a day for 1,000 years and so avoid going after mom-and-pop polluters. But Mom and Pop don't know this, and technically they are liable. The real motive, charge environmental leaders, is not so much to collect money as to contrive broad support for Superfund "reform."

When Ford, Chrysler, General Motors, BASF Corporation, and Sea Ray Boats were fingered by the EPA for fouling the Metamora, Michigan, landfill with arsenic, lead, vinyl chloride, and the like, they proclaimed that 382 towns, businesses, and individuals were copolluters and tried to assess them $50 million to settle alleged liability quickly, including any unforeseen costs. Even the local Girl Scout troop was assessed $100,000. "That's a lot of cookies," declared a troop spokesperson.

In another case Doreen Merlino, the 25-year-old proprietor of a two-table pizzeria in Chadwicks, New York, offered the court officer the following plea when he served her with a two-inch-thick lawsuit in October 1990: "Aren't you at least gonna buy a pizza?" He kindly complied, but she didn't feel much better. In fact, she felt terrified. Cosmetics giant Chesebrough-Pond's and Special Metals Corporation were trying to extract $3,000 from her for helping them poison the local landfill. They weren't sure just what the trashman might have collected from her during the seven months she'd been in business—maybe pesticide containers or empty cleanser cans, they opined. But Merlino tells me she's never used pesticides and that she has always rinsed out her cleanser containers. A cover letter advised her that if she settled fast, she'd only have to pay $1,500. As it turned out, she had to pay no one save her lawyer, and none of her anger is directed at Superfund. Not all the 603 defendants were so philosophical.

When the EPA hits up polluters for toxic-waste-cleanup costs, polluters, naturally enough, hit up the insurance companies from which they have purchased pollution-liability coverage. Now the insurance companies would like to hit up the public—that is, rewrite Superfund so bygones can be bygones and taxpayers can spring for cleaning up old sites.

"Superfund's mission should be protecting human health and the environment, not fund-raising," contends the American International Group, an insurance company marshaling support for what it calls a National Environmental Trust Fund, by which Superfund money could be raised "from all economic sectors without regard to site-specific liability" via a surcharge on commercial- and industrial-insurance premiums.

Generating pity for the insurance industry requires a greater heart than beats in the breast of environmental consultant Curtis Moore. As an aide to former Republican senator Robert Stafford of Vermont, Moore was instrumental in writing both the original Superfund law and the amended 1986 version. Insurance companies, he points out, tend not to cover purposeful acts by anyone, including God; so the policies were restricted to "sudden and accidental" pollution. "You dump crude oil on the ground for fifteen years," he says, "and over a twenty-five-year period it migrates to the water table. Would you consider that sudden? Accidental? No? Well, I got news for you: The courts do. There was a string of decisions that construed the terms *sudden* and *accidental* as covering groundwater contamination. This trend started a long time ago—in the 1970s or earlier. It was clearly discernible. Any insurance lawyer with manure for brains could see it happening. Notwithstanding, the insurance industry continued to use the terms *sudden* and *accidental* in its policies.

"So here comes Superfund, and the chemical companies start casting around, trying to figure out how they can get someone else to pick up the tab. They file suits against their insurance companies and win. Well, there's only one way to fix the insurance industry's problem. You can either shift liability or, failing that, repeal Superfund."

Presuming to speak for the insurance industry, the American International Group complains that Superfund is "bogged down in a morass of legal warfare that delays cleanup and wastes enormous financial and human resources." True enough, but what it doesn't mention is that the insurance industry has been responsible for a great deal of this legal warfare. A Rand Corporation study reveals that between 1986 and 1989 insurers spent $1.3 billion on Superfund. Of this, $1 billion went to defending themselves against their policyholders or defending their policyholders against the EPA. One

leading attorney for the policyholders—Eugene Anderson, of the New York City firm of Anderson, Kill, Olick & Oshinsky—has gone so far as to suggest publicly that refusing all large claims is now seen as smart business procedure by insurers: Half the policyholders get scared away, and most of the others will settle out of court for less than full coverage.

* * *

Superfund has bombed, as the President, environmentalists, inhabitants of toxic neighborhoods, brewers of toxic waste, and especially the insurance industry have observed. But it is essential to remember the difference between Superfund the law and Superfund the program.

"The law was a creation of people like Bob Stafford, Ed Muskie, Jennings Randolph, John Chafee, Jim Florio," remarks Moore. "The program was the creation of Ronald Reagan; the people who were put in charge of implementing the law six weeks after it was enacted were people who six weeks earlier had been lobbying against it. They set out with the intent of making it unworkable, and they succeeded."

There is nothing in the statute that directs the EPA's contractors to dress up like reindeer or distribute customized confections at government expense. They engage in such excess because the EPA lacks the personnel to keep them honest. Nor is there anything in the statute that mandates stonewalling and procrastination on the part of polluters. But they have learned that endless negotiation is profitable because the EPA lacks the personnel to haul more than a few of them into court. Mr. Clinton, who proposes to trim $76 million from Superfund the program, appears not to understand this.

Certainly, the statute could stand repair. It needs to define how clean is clean, provide a better, more flexible means of selecting remedies, ensure state and local participation, create incentives for companies to take voluntary action instead of suing everyone in sight. But the fact is that Superfund the law isn't broken.

Even Superfund the program, disastrous though it has been, has produced some splendid if accidental results. "Joint and several liability," says Peter Berle, "has put the fear of God into everybody, which means they are careful in ways they never were before in what they do with their waste. I also think the cost risk of inappropriate toxic-waste disposal has been the major impetus toward waste minimization. When it gets too expensive to deal with it, then you make less."

Rick Hind, toxics director for Greenpeace, agrees. "It doesn't cost you and me anything if a big company wants to spend ten million dollars on lawyers to avoid an eleven-million-dollar cleanup," he offers. "That costs the company. Good! So it costs them twice what it should. That will teach them a lesson. When a Colombian drug cartel is in court nobody cares what their legal expenses are. Nor should we care about polluters."

Insurers and polluters—not environmentalists—are the ones driving for major surgery on Superfund the law. If they are permitted to degrade it from a dedicated fund to a public-works program whereby big government passes around public-generated revenues, the hemorrhage of federal pork will make the EPA nostalgic for the days when it used taxes on crude oil and chemicals to rent clowns for CH2M Hill. If they are permitted to do away with Superfund's liability provisions and weaken its polluter-pay principle, the United States will be poisoned on a scale unimagined even in New Bedford, Massachusetts.

It may be that Superfund is mortally wounded from a dozen years of sabotage. But it also may be that it can be salvaged and made to work. We need to try. Vendors of insurance and chemicals will shriek and sob, but the law wasn't written for them. It was written for Love Canal couples forced to watch as bulldozers razed their homes, for Robin Rivera and his family, for roseate terns, for sick and deformed children, for children yet unborn.

POSTSCRIPT

Hazardous Waste: Should the "Polluter Pays" Provision of Superfund Be Weakened?

Note that although Reilly does not question the need to "deal with hazardous waste sites that pose a serious risk to public health and the environment," he later qualifies this responsibility by claiming that "the existence of toxic waste at a site does not necessarily mean that they pose a threat to nearby residents." As citizens' groups, such as the New Bedford activists, whose concerns are described by Williams, have made clear, "nearby residents" reject Reilly's qualification and invariably demand remediation of toxic waste that has been identified in their neighborhoods. The "joint-and-several liability" provision of Superfund that Reilly thinks is unfair is a common provision of tort law that is considered necessary by many legal experts to enable courts to aportion penalties when there are several disputing liable parties.

A slightly more positive assessment of the accomplishments of the Superfund is presented by Karen Schmidt in her article in the April/May 1994 issue of *National Wildlife*. One of the general changes being considered by drafters of the Superfund revisions is that more flexibility be given to local communities to decide how to respond to hazardous waste contamination. Two proposals along those lines are contained in articles by Charles Bartsch and Richard Munson in the Spring 1994 issue of *Issues in Science and Technology*, and by John D. Graham and March Sadowitz in the Summer 1994 issue of the same journal. The National Commission on the Superfund—established in 1992 as a joint project of the Environmental Law Center, Vermont Law School, and the Keystone Center—has recently issued its comprehensive *Final Consensus Report* (March 1, 1994). For a copy of this distinguished panel's report and recommendations, contact the Keystone Center, P.O Box 8606, Keystone, Colarado 80435.

One controversial response to hazardous waste problems is the practise of buying out neighboring communities by the companies responsible for the problem. The pros and cons of this practice are discussed in "A Town Called Morrisonville," by John Bowermaster, *Audubon* (July/August 1993).

Another serious dimension of the hazardous waste problem is the growing use of developing nations as the dumping grounds for waste from the United States and other wealthier nations. "The Basel Convention: A Global Approach for the Management of Hazardous Wastes," by Iwonna Rummel-Bulska, *Environmental Policy and Law* (vol. 24, no. 1, 1994), is an assessment of the international treaty designed to prevent such waste dumping.

ISSUE 13

Municipal Waste: Can Management Plans Based on Mandated Recycling Succeed?

YES: John S. Van Volkenburgh and Randall L. Hartmann, from "Recycling Incentives: An Example of the Public Process for Policy Development," *MSW Management* (May/June 1994)

NO: Virginia I. Postrel and Lynn Scarlett, from "Talking Trash," *Reason* (August/September 1991)

ISSUE SUMMARY

YES: Engineering analyst John S. Van Volkenburgh and county waste manager Randall L. Hartmann describe a successful, popular municipal waste management program in an Ohio county based on a residential recycling incentive strategy.

NO: *Reason* editor Virginia I. Postrel and solid waste researcher Lynn Scarlett argue that mandatory recycling programs and efforts to promote the use of recycled materials are failing because they are ill-conceived and not cost effective.

Since prehistoric times, the predominant method of dealing with refuse has been to simply dump it in some out-of-the-way spot. Worldwide, land disposal still accommodates the overwhelming majority of domestic waste. In the United States roughly 90 percent of residential and commercial waste is disposed of in some type of landfill, ranging from a simple open pit to so-called sanitary landfills where the waste is compacted and covered with a layer of clean soil. In a very small percentage of cases, landfills may have clay or plastic liners to reduce leaching of toxins into groundwater.

By the last quarter of the nineteenth century, odoriferous, vermin-infested garbage dumps in increasingly congested urban areas were identified as a public health threat. Large-scale incineration of municipal waste was introduced at that time in both Europe and the United States as an alternative disposal method. By 1970 more than 300 such central garbage incinerators existed in U.S. cities, in addition to the thousands of waste incinerators that had been built into large apartment buildings.

Virtually all of these early garbage furnaces were built without devices to control air pollution. During the period of heightened consciousness about urban air quality following World War II, restrictions began to be imposed on garbage burning. By 1980 the new national and local air pollution regulations had reduced the number of large U.S. municipal waste incinerators to fewer than 80. Better designed and more efficiently operated landfills took up the slack.

During the past decade, an increasing number of U.S. cities have been unable to locate suitable accessible locations to build new landfills. This has coincided with growing concern about the threat to both groundwater and surface water from toxic chemicals in leachate and runoff from dump sites. Legislative restrictions in many parts of the country now mandate costly design and testing criteria for landfills. In many cases, communities have been forced to shut down their local landfill (some of which had grown into small mountains) and to ship their wastes tens or even hundreds of miles to disposal sites.

The lack of long-range planning coupled with skyrocketing disposal costs created a crisis situation in municipal waste management in the 1980s. Energetic entrepreneurs seized upon this situation to promote European-developed incineration technology with improved air pollution controls as the panacea for the garbage problem. Ironically, the proliferation of these new waste incinerators in the United States coincided with increasing concern in Europe about their efficiency in containing the toxic air pollutants produced by burning modern waste. Citizen groups became aware of this concern and organized opposition to incinerator construction. The industry countered with more sophisticated air pollution controls, but these had the effect of trapping the toxins in the incinerator ash, which presents a troublesome and expensive disposal problem. The result has been a rapid decrease in the number of municipalities that are choosing to rely on modern incineration to solve their waste diposal problems.

Recycling, which has until recently been dismissed as a minor waste disposal alternative, has recently been encouraged as a major option. The Environmental Protection Agency (EPA) and several states have established hierarchies of waste disposal technologies with the goal of using waste reduction and recycling for as much as 50 percent of the material in the waste stream. Several environmental groups are urging even greater reliance on recycling, citing studies that show that more than 90 percent of municipal waste can theoretically be put to productive use if large-scale composting is included as a component of recycling.

John S. Van Volkenburgh, an engineer who was project manager for the development of the Hamilton County, Ohio, Solid Waste Management Plan, and Randall L. Hartmann, who is manager of the plan, describe how they gained public acceptance for an effective waste program designed to meet state recycling mandates. Virginia I. Postrel, editor of *Reason* magazine, and Lynn Scarlett, vice president for reasearch of the Research Foundation, object to economic and legislative means of promoting recycling, claiming they are restrictive, ineffective, and costly.

YES

John S. Van Volkenburgh
and Randall L. Hartmann

RECYCLING INCENTIVES: AN EXAMPLE OF THE PUBLIC PROCESS FOR POLICY DEVELOPMENT

When state law went into effect requiring the development of MSW management plans, this was the challenge faced by the Hamilton County Solid Waste Management District in Cincinnati, OH. By using a participatory, consensus-building process, the district developed a comprehensive solid waste management plan that achieved one of the highest approval rates of any plan developed in the state of Ohio. The plan was supported by political jurisdictions in the county representing more than 97% of the population.

A key aspect of the plan supported by the political jurisdictions was the residential recycling incentive program which assists local governments by funding recycling programs without limitation to the kind of program involved. Other elements of the plan included district-wide educational efforts; technical assistance for small businesses; a waste reduction code for business; a grants program; an HHW education and collection program; enforcement; reviews of new and emerging technologies; and awards and recognition for successful waste reduction and recycling efforts. But the real story of this solid waste management plan is the consensus-building effort used to develop every aspect of the plan. The residential recycling incentive program is a cornerstone of the plan and an example of the successful process.

THE LAW AND THE DISTRICT

Ohio House Bill 592 (HB 592), which became law in 1988, required the formation of solid waste management districts based on geographical limits ranging in size from a single to, in some cases, several counties. Significantly, individual municipalities or townships could not form their own districts.

Hamilton County formed a single-county solid waste management district with a legally mandated five-member policy committee representing the Board of County Commissioners; the largest municipality (Cincinnati); the townships (unincorporated areas); the health department serving the largest geographical area; and the public at large. The committee was charged with developing the comprehensive solid waste management plan.

The district has a population of approximately 870,000 with about 363,000 housing units comprised of 48 independent political jurisdictions, each having its own priorities, concerns, constituencies, and elected officials. The political jurisdictions are municipalities, villages, and townships with populations ranging from Cincinnati's 363,040 to North Bend's 541 residents. The population is projected to decline by 10,000 from 1990 to 2010, while employment is expected to increase by 100,000 during the same period to a total employment of 464,000.

Waste collection services in the district vary. Collection services traditionally have been determined by the local governments. Some governments, like Cincinnati and St. Bernard, use city vehicles and staff to collect waste from single-family dwellings. Services for multi-family dwellings and businesses are the responsibility of the property owners. Other governments, such as Anderson and Delhi townships, play no role in waste collection. Instead, individual residents contract with private collection companies operating without franchises or territory.

Recycling services are as diverse as waste collection services. Cincinnati contracts for curbside collection of recyclables from 100,000 single-family dwellings. Township residents use independent waste haulers to provide recycling services for an additional fee. Some local governments provide drop-off facilities, while others have no recycling services at all. Private buy-back operations exist in the district, and some private companies, such as two grocery store chains, provide free drop-off facilities at their stores. Nonprofit organizations also provide an array of recycling and reuse services.

Faced with the challenge of developing a legally compliant plan for such a diverse constituency, the district hired a consultant to navigate the complex issues. For instance, Ohio law required that the plan be approved not only by the Hamilton County Commissioners and the city of Cincinnati—principal jurisdictions involved—but by all the other political jurisdictions as well, representing more than 60% of the district's population (including Cincinnati's 42% of the population). The development of the plan was made even more challenging because of prior environmental concerns about incineration and toxic releases, contention among interest groups, and a history of independent intergovernmental activities within the county.

THE CONSENSUS BUILDING PROCESS BEGINS

The most immediate efforts were to clearly define the existing waste management conditions and to establish a public advisory council. The first effort was necessary because information had never before been compiled and available in one place. A task group set about defining the amounts and types of waste generated, recycled, and reused within the district, as well as pertinent aspects of its disposal. As part of the effort the group detailed the existing system along with the various companies and governments involved in the business of waste management. Starting from the definition of existing waste management conditions, the district provided the data to the public in order to solicit its recommendations and to forge ahead in the development of its plan.

* * *

From the outset it was recognized that the council was vital to the successful development of the plan, serving as the mechanism to receive the concerns and recommendations of the public as well as to advise interested citizens of the incorporation of the concerns and recommendations in the plan. Council activities were open to all interested individuals or groups in the district. In fact, the formation of the council was widely publicized through newspapers, local governments, business, environmental interest groups, and newsletters. Meetings with media editorial boards and environmental groups were held. Invitations were extended to individuals identified as having an interest in solid waste management. Many individuals were encouraged to participate through personal contacts.

In its recognition of the plan's tremendous impact throughout the district, the council encouraged the greatest possible community participation in the development of the plan. From the beginning of the process, community participation instilled a sense of partnership in a broad range of individuals and organizations. Community participation allowed for the consideration of as many concerns and recommendations as possible during the planning process, and ensured final support upon completion of the plan.

The process also encouraged governments to work together, defusing some of the distrust and tension among former adversaries by putting them together in the same room and getting them to work on a shared problem. Finally, the process left no opportunity for perennial nay-sayers to claim, with any credibility, that they were unable to participate in the plan's development. The process worked.

A meeting of the entire council was called for a Saturday. Approximately 75 individuals, who proved to be the backbone of the organization through the remainder of the process, attended the first meeting. Because of past confrontations and anticipation of the disparate views of many of the attendees, the council employed professional mediators to develop consensus on basic issues of MSW management. Views and concerns were put on the table without prejudice. Areas in which consensus existed were set aside for consideration in the planning process. Problem areas were identified for further work.

As an outgrowth of the meeting, the council formed committees to address areas of interest, including local government issues; generator, recycling, and disposers' issues; health department concerns; siting and regulatory matters; public awareness and education initiatives; and reduction, reuse, and minimization programs.

The recycling and local government committees were pivotal in developing the residential recycling incentive program. The recycling committee contained representatives of local governments, the general public, haulers, recyclers, and end users/markets. The local government committee was composed of elected officials and administrators for local governments throughout the district, and included a mix of township, village, and municipal representatives. It also included representatives from municipal leagues, chambers of commerce, and the public-at-large.

It was important that committee meetings were open to all interested parties and that meeting times and locations were well publicized. Several individuals served on more than one committee. The district or consultants provided staff support for each committee.

RECOMMENDATIONS ALLOW FLEXIBILITY

Each committee prepared and presented recommendations to the policy committee. The consultant provided staff support, data regarding the existing solid waste management system, and technical assistance. The district coordinated the committee efforts and eventually formed an executive roundtable of committee co-chairs to better coordinate these efforts. Recommendations were based on the needs and interests of the committee members, with guidance provided by the district and consultants regarding the law, technical issues, and the responsibilities of the district for waste management.

The recycling and local government committees recommended an approach allowing maximum flexibility for local governments to establish recycling programs for their constituencies. Both committees encouraged the development of a model recycling program which could be used as a guide. They identified education as an essential part of successful recycling programs, and, finally, they placed responsibility for residential recycling in the hands of local governments.

* * *

The recycling committee encouraged the development of incentives tied to performance and stressed the need for fairness, discouraging mandatory programs. For instance, front-end separation was identified as the preferred but not mandatory method of recycling. The committee recommended a $2 million revolving loan fund for local program development and called for assistance from the district to advance market development. It also recommended that the district take proactive educational and collection roles for HHW. In a particularly innovative move, the committee called upon the district to develop programs for those local jurisdictions that failed to develop their own, passing on the expense to nonparticipants through assessments on their improved property. Finally, the recycling committee suggested that other committees consider an information hotline, and that a grant program be considered as an alternative to the revolving loan fund.

Among recommendations made by the local government committee were establishment of host community fees for areas with MSW facilities; development of a grant program to assist local governments with one-time waste management costs; district-wide handling of yard-waste and HHW collection; development of a mixed-waste composting facility; technical assistance to local governments by district staff; and funding of health departments and local health authorities to mount strong enforcement efforts in cleaning up open dumps and eliminating litter. While volume-based collection fees were encouraged, the committee recommended that they be mandatory only where subscription service existed. The committee also recommended that the model recycling program be mandatory for non-participating local governments. These recommendations were the foundation of the residential recycling incentive program and other district programs.

In response to these recommendations, the district adopted an HHW education and collection program managed by the district; established goals and incentives to encourage voluntary waste reduction by the commercial and industrial community; and determined that technical assistance would be provided to local governments and the business community by district staff. When legal counsel indicated that the district had no authority to operate a revolving loan program, it created a grant program.

Although residential recycling is the responsibility of the local governments with incentives provided by the district, mandatory provisions are in place if recycling and reduction goals are not met. Aspects of a model program are incorporated into the incentive program.

RESIDENTIAL RECYCLING INCENTIVE PROGRAM

Incentives will be provided to local governments by the district through quarterly payments based on tons of material recycled. Flexibility is ensured by allowing each local government to select the means of recycling for its community. The district requires that participating local governments sponsor one or more recycling programs and report on recycling in the jurisdiction. Funding to the local governments is provided to assist them in developing recycling programs; it is not intended to pay for the entire cost of a community's program. Funding must be used by the participating local governments for solid waste management efforts that are conducted at the expense of the local governments. Among the purposes allowed for fund utilization are:

- Solid waste education, awareness, and promotion;

- Contracts for residential solid waste reduction and recycling efforts;
- Government-operated recycling efforts;
- Yardwaste management programs; and
- Labor, equipment, and materials for these efforts.

For local governments that choose not to participate in the program, the district may implement a basic drop-off program for their residents if residents do not already have the opportunity to recycle. Fairness is ensured by a provision in the plan that states that a non-participating community will not receive a district-provided program at a per capita expense greater than the lowest per capita incentive payment made to a participating community.

Funds are available in the district budget for the incentive program and for the district to develop drop-off programs. The amount of funding is defined by estimating the cost for a district-wide drop-off program that would provide the opportunity for all residents to recycle within five miles of their homes. SCS Engineers, the firm hired by the district to provide solid waste management consulting, estimated the costs of the hypothetical program by estimating equipment, facility, personnel, processing, and transportation costs.

*   *   *

In order to determine the success of the recycling effort, the district will review residential waste generation and recycling/reduction each year. It will conduct a waste composition study of the residential waste stream after four years of implementation. If the district's goals for residential waste reduction

(15% in 1994 and 30% in 2004) are not being achieved, the district may implement mandatory waste reduction efforts by bans on the disposal of certain materials, requiring volume-based fees, or mandatory recycling.

A reporting form has been provided to local governments in the district along with an explanation of the incentive program. Estimates of the available funds have been provided to the local governments and included in the plan. Incentive funding reimbursements will be provided by the district for the quarter beginning October 1, 1993. More than 90% of the communities in the district are expected to participate in the incentive program.

There already has been an increase in the number of recycling programs throughout the district as local governments prepare for implementation of the program, and a corresponding increase in residential recycling has been documented. The private sector has responded by developing two material recovery facilities and by providing subscription curbside recycling virtually throughout the district. At least five new local government environmental committees have formed to consider new waste collection and recycling contracts or services. One local government privatized waste collection in order to expand services, and another discontinued its drop-off program in favor of a contracted curbside recycling program. Four or five contracts for waste collection have been negotiated to include recycling services.

Baseline data were identified in 1990 and annual reports were prepared for 1991 and 1992.... Combined residential and commercial recycling is estimated to have increased from 170,000 tons in 1990 to 228,000 tons in 1992. This is an increase in recycling of 34%.

The annual reports for 1991, 1992, and 1993 will provide the basis for determining success in 1994. When the district's plan is revised, as required by law in 1997, significant data will be available to help identify success, failure, and areas in which the program can improve.

The recycling incentive program addresses the basic goals of the district and the recycling and local government committees. It is flexible and fair. It gives responsibility for residential recycling to the local governments that wish to accept the responsibility, while allowing the district to meet its requirement to provide recycling opportunities to all residents. The program is incentive-driven, not mandatory. It includes the appropriate expenditure of district funds.

The program is not without its concerns, however. Lack of accurate data may become a problem, since the district's ability to verify information provided is limited. Also the value of assistance provided to local governments is governed by the district's budget and other demands for district funds. The grant program in conjunction with the incentive program, initially may help smaller local governments develop recycling programs. Finally, actual participation levels by local government and the resulting need for district drop-off programs are unknown.

Preliminary discussion with the private sector, which will provide the bulk of the data, and with the local governments is encouraging. The lead time between program development and implementation has been sufficiently long to allow development of the systems necessary to support the program. The district is hopeful and looks forward to success.

The Hamilton County Solid Waste Management District and SCS Engineers crafted a comprehensive solid waste management plan that is responsive to the existing systems in the county and the tri-state region. The programs to reduce the waste stream and to comply with state law were developed in a public process and represent compromise and hard work. Awareness of the waste reduction requirements is high. Interest in the district's efforts is growing. Local governments are developing the recycling programs that are best for their constituents. The private sector has responded to help meet the area's needs. The district has recorded increased recycling.

NO

Virginia I. Postrel
and Lynn Scarlett

TALKING TRASH

The United States does have some real solid-waste problems, but they are amenable to fairly simple solutions that require less, not more, government planning.

Perhaps it all started with *Mobro*, the Islip, Long Island, garbage barge. Back in 1987, the barge wandered from port to port, searching for some place that would accept the garbage it carried. After six states and three countries rejected its load, *Mobro* returned to New York. A Brooklyn incinerator burned the trash, and the waste ash went home to a landfill in Islip.

The Northeastern landfill shortage became a national story. Newspapers and TV shows told tales of the nation's impending garbage crisis. Landfills were closing. Waste was mounting. Soon every city in the land would have a garbage-filled barge roaming the seas.

The reports scared people. Politicians who had been content to leave garbage management to specialists decided something had to be done. So they passed laws. In the early '80s, only 140 American cities had curbside recycling programs. Today, however, more than 2,700 communities nationwide pick up residents' cans, bottles, and newspapers for recycling. In most of these places, recycling is mandatory for at least some residents.

More important, 28 states enacted recycling or waste-reduction quotas—Florida, for instance, will require 30-percent recycling by 1994, a demand that has solid-waste managers there in a near panic. Another five states have set nonmandatory goals. (The Environmental Protection Agency recommends a 25-percent diversion of the solid-waste stream by 1992, 50 percent by 1997.) Once enacted, these increasingly common laws drive all solid-waste management decisions in their states. They shift the policy emphasis from safe and efficient waste disposal to reducing consumption.

Although its targets are only recommendations, the EPA has played a major role in that shift. In 1989 the agency issued a report, *The Solid Waste Dilemma: An Agenda for Action,* in which it identified four means of managing solid waste: 1) source reduction; 2) recycling; 3) incineration; and 4) landfilling. These are, in one form or another, the options people have had since the Stone

Age. But the EPA didn't just list the options. It ranked them. It created a waste-management hierarchy, with source reduction at the pinnacle, flanked by reuse and recycling. Incinerators and landfills were left groveling in the dust, grateful that they were allowed to exist at all. Although it acknowledged that sound solid-waste management would involve all four options, the EPA made it clear that in all situations source reduction and recycling are preferable to burning or burying trash. "Reduce-Reuse-Recycle" became the national standard.

The EPA hierarchy diverts government policy from "integrated waste management," the technocratic way of mixing the four options in whichever combination best fits local needs. Instead, it has prompted—and given political support to—a mania for aggressive recycling and source-reduction efforts, regardless of cost, overall resource use, or local conditions. The EPA has lent respectability, even urgency, to calls [that] "demand an immediate halt to policies that promote materials destruction. That would include not only stopping incinerators, but ending the promotion of degradable plastics whose destination is not the recycler but the landfill."

In the wake of the EPA's report, members of Congress have proposed amendments to the Resource Conservation and Recovery Act (RCRA) and Solid Waste Disposal Act (SWDA) that would, among other things:

- Require that nonrecyclable materials be biodegradable and prohibit, after five years, any material that is neither biodegradable nor recyclable.
- Create a National Packaging Institute to establish national packaging standards.

- Mandate a return deposit on plastic and glass containers.
- Ban in interstate commerce any plastic container that isn't marked with a code indicating its composition to recyclers.

RCRA, better known for its hazardous waste provisions, is up for reauthorization this year, so Congress will soon be seriously considering amendments.... So far, however, most of the action to move the country toward a national materials policy has occurred on a piecemeal basis, at the state level....

* * *

Solid-waste policy used to be left to calm problem solvers.... But the chance to pick and choose which products people should use—and dispose of—brings out emotional paternalists like California state Sen. Daniel Boatwright.

It's a Wednesday afternoon in early May. The state Senate committee on which Boatwright sits has been hearing testimony on a proposal to levy an excise tax on disposable diapers. The hearing has been perfunctory, with only two witnesses allowed to speak on each side. Another 10 or so have gone on record against the bill, many submitting written materials. To show how the tax would hurt poor mothers, for instance, Gloria Torres has given the Senate committee a breakdown of a couple of family budgets. Each family spends $84 a month on disposable diapers.

It's Sen. Boatwright's turn to speak. The quiet committee room explodes with his anger. "These are AFDC mothers, they have other clothes to wash, and if they're spending that much money, I would certainly urge those people to go to *cloth diapers* to save $84 a month." Boatwright gets madder, his voice more contemptuous. He points to committee members. "He, he, he, she, we raised our kids with cloth diapers. And you know, it didn't kill 'em at all. It didn't kill 'em. Got your hands a little dirty, maybe, but it didn't kill 'em. It's a hell of a lot more convenient to use disposable diapers, but you know what—*you save a lot of money* when you use cloth diapers."

Boatwright is a liberal Democrat, not especially prone to frugality. He doesn't begrudge the mothers the money they get from the state. He just doesn't approve of the diapers. Like Grumpy Old Man on "Saturday Night Live," he remembers the old days, when life was lousy "and we *liked* it that way." Despite Boatwright's outburst, the bill dies, failing to get a motion in its favor.

The diaper bill, and the outburst, are minor but indicative. Disposable diapers account for less than 2 percent of the nation's solid-waste stream. But they make great symbols. Mankind—or, more accurately, womankind—managed to do without them until about 1970. They're highly artificial, engineered of plastic and synthetics and paper. You use a diaper once, then discard it. Disposable diapers seem self-indulgent, the kind of silly convenience that puts the *waste* in solid waste. On similar grounds, Greenpeace has attacked facial tissues, and Hannah Holmes, an assistant editor of *Garbage* magazine, has denounced tampons.

In the water-short West, of course, it's easy to counter that cloth diapers consume a resource far more precious than landfill space. And much public debate has focused on whether, in fact, disposable diapers really are "worse" for the environment than their predecessors. Several life-cycle assessments—studies that try to look at all of a product's environmental impact from manufacture to disposal—have examined disposable diapers, each with somewhat different results. One assessment gave disposables a better environmental report card than cloth diapers; others showed the opposite. And so the debate goes on.

But arguments over cradle-to-grave studies miss the point. The studies show the costs of various options, the trade-offs between water use and energy needs and air pollution and solid waste. They don't show the benefits. They don't consider why consumers buy disposable diapers or why juice makers use aseptic packaging. Pampers or Huggies or, for that matter, Kleenex tissues may fill up landfills faster than cloth diapers or handkerchiefs. But the people who buy them care about other values, too—convenience, or health, or comfort....

* * *

Product regulations also treat similar products as though they serve identical needs, differing only in their environmental impacts. This may be true of some products—it's hard to see any substantive difference between bleached and unbleached coffee filters—but it isn't true of most. Both kinds of diapers cover Baby's bottom, but each offers a distinct bundle of other qualities. Cloth diapers are less expensive and, if changed promptly, may be more comfortable.

Disposables, on the other hand, appear to prevent diaper rash, leak less, and are much more sanitary and convenient for use in day-care centers. Indeed, the American Academy of Pediatrics and the American Public Health Association's day-care program performance standards state "that to protect the public's health, cloth diapers should not be used in day-care centers." Most state day-care regulations forbid caregivers to rinse cloth diapers, so that not using disposables means sticking dirty diapers in plastic bags or diaper pails and sending the whole package home with Junior. Needless to say, day-care providers have been vocal opponents of bans or taxes on disposables....

Products don't exist in isolation. The economy is a complicated web of interactions. Disposable diapers are substitutes for laundry facilities. They are complements to day care, as are drink boxes that let even tiny kids brown-bag it. On the manufacturer's level, packaging can substitute for warehouse space or factories. The exotic layering of metals and plastics that keeps Keebler cookies fresh for as long as nine months after they leave the oven lets the company distribute them throughout the United States without having a plant in every city. Combined with new recipes, the packaging lets you buy cookies that are still soft months after they're made.

And packaging often reduces waste. When William Rathje, of the University of Arizona, took his garbage-archaeology team to Mexico City, they found that the average household in Mexico City "discards 40 percent *more* refuse each day than the average USA household." Rathje writes, "This difference—1.6 pounds per household per day—is food debris, the skins, rinds, peels, tops, and other inedible parts discarded in food preparation."

For instance, in Mexico City, most consumers squeeze fresh oranges to make orange juice. The peels are then thrown away. Americans, by contrast, tend to buy packaged frozen concentrate. As a result, the typical Mexican household tosses out 10.5 ounces of orange peel each week; the typical American household throws out 2 ounces of cardboard or aluminum. Meanwhile, back at the orange juice factory, the peels are collected and sold to make animal feed and other products. If all the orange juice drinkers in New York City individually tossed away their orange peels, one day's haul would weigh as much as two ocean liners....

The economy's complex interactions can produce surprising results. Consider a study by the research group GVM that examined what would happen if all plastic packaging were eliminated in the Federal Republic of Germany. The report found that materials usage by weight would increase fourfold, as substitutes replaced plastic. Packaging costs would more than double. Energy consumption would almost double. And garbage would increase by 256 percent. The report comments, "all of the cost-intensive endeavors, over many years, to reduce the use of material through more suitable packaging and 'slimming down' individual packaging materials would be [reversed] with one stroke."

* * *

Richard Pence isn't at all happy with Ohio's new requirement that 25 percent of all garbage be recycled by 1994. His family business, Pence Refuse Service, has been hauling trash since 1958. Now the state says they have to get into the recycling business: "They want you to get started right away. There's not much chance to gear up for it." What's more, the company is required to weigh the trash it collects at each stop—not in order to charge customers by the pound but to see whether they're meeting the 25-percent target. "The bookkeeping is unreal," says Pence.

The nine-employee company is struggling to adapt. It is separating and baling cardboard, milk jugs, and such, despite the lousy economics. Baling 900 pounds of corrugated cardboard costs $25, not including collection and sorting, but buyers will only pay $20 to $30 a ton for it. Recycling, says Pence, "takes a lot of money to operate, and there's no money in it. It's rough on a little company."...

So far, Pence Refuse has managed with its regular trucks and small building. But Dick Pence expects he'll need to invest in more-specialized trucks and add a $200,000 building to use as a processing center. The costs, he figures, will be passed on to the businesses whose trash the company hauls away. Contrary to *The Recycler's Handbook* (from the folks who brought you *50 Simple Things You Can Do to Save the Earth*), it is not true that "recycling saves towns and consumers money."

In fact, the move to recycle rather than dump or burn trash can cost plenty. A survey of Rhode Island communities found that the total cost of recycling—including pickup and processing, minus revenue from the sale of recycled materials—often runs more than $180 a ton, compared to the $120 to $160 a ton for ordinary waste collection and disposal. The outlay is especially high in cities with many multifamily dwellings. In Chicago, for instance, curbside recycling costs from $625 a ton to more than $1,100 a ton, depending on the area of the city; from that fee, the city can deduct about $110 a ton in sales and the $38 a ton it would have paid the landfill.

Generally speaking, landfill "tipping fees," the price of depositing debris, have to be more than $50 a ton—compared to a national average of $30 and a median of around $15—to make recycling economically competitive for most materials. There are, however, notable exceptions. More steel is recycled in the United States than any other material. Scrap metal dealers and steel minimills, not government mandates, drive this profitable recycling.

Aluminum cans fetch $900 a ton on the open market, and more than half of empty cans are recycled; the first major aluminum recycling plants opened in 1904. The reason is simple: It takes only 5 percent as much electricity to produce aluminum from old beverage cans as it does from bauxite ore. And electricity is the major cost in making aluminum. "Aluminum recycling exists today as a viable industry not because the aluminum industry is interested in saving landfill space, but because it has had a variety of economic motivations to recycle aluminum," write Jennifer Gitlitz and Paul Relis in a report summarizing a 1988 California recycling conference.

* * *

Once states make people recycle materials for which the cost of recycling is greater than the recovered value, officials have to figure out who will pay for the difference. Certainly, Dick Pence doesn't plan to absorb the total cost of complying with Ohio's mandate. If he had to, he'd go out of business. Improving the economics of recycling, to would-be materials planners, requires more new laws and more regulations.

In some cases, the laws seek to create bigger markets for all the near-worthless stuff collected. Old newspapers—which make up about 7 percent of a typical city's solid-waste stream—are a particular problem. They would be cheaper to dump. But to build a resale market, California, Connecticut, Maryland, Missouri, and Wisconsin have passed laws requiring publishers to increase their use of recycled newsprint. Similar laws have been proposed in Illinois, New Jersey, and New York.

Beginning January 1, 1994, the District of Columbia will require anyone who distributes within the district a publication with a circulation of more than 30,000 or who sells more than 500 tons or $100,000 of paper a year to use only recycled paper. Only if the company can prove that using recycled paper would increase its paper costs more than 10 percent over virgin stock can it apply for an exemption. In deeming a 10-percent higher price "competitive" with virgin paper, "They don't understand that huge newspaper deals are made on the basis of a fraction of a percent," says Jack Schafer, editor of the weekly *City Paper*, which has a circulation of 89,000. The penalty for law breaking: a 15-percent "recycling surcharge" over the price of the illegal paper.

The law also specifies just how much recycled material different kinds of paper must contain: 50 percent for high-grade printing and writing paper; 40 percent for newsprint; 5 percent for facial tissues; 20 percent for toilet paper; 30 percent for paper napkins; 40 percent for paper towels; even 40 percent for doilies. In many cases, the recycled material must be "post-consumer," meaning that reusing factory scrap doesn't count.

The ordinance's content requirements "will stifle rather than encourage recycling," says Carol Melamed, director of government affairs and associate counsel for *The Washington Post*. The reason lies in the technical and economic limits of paper making. The mills that can produce recycled paper with 40-percent old newspaper stock are mills that were built originally to make recycled paper. But more and more virgin-paper mills want to get into the recycled-paper business. Rather than build an entirely new plant, at a cost of some $400 million, they add a deinking line, which costs $30 million to $50 million; this retrofitting lets them make paper with between 15 percent and 25 percent recycled content. That may not meet D.C.'s lofty goals, but its impact on the waste stream is significant.

Before the law passed, the Bear Island mill in Virginia—which produces paper for the *Post*, *The Washington Times*, and other local newspapers—had plans to add a deinking line that would have absorbed 60,000 tons of old newsprint a year. But the recycled paper produced at Bear Island would have contained only 20 percent recycled content. Since the D.C. ordinance would wipe out the market for its recycled paper, the mill has indefinitely postponed adding the new capacity.

Both content mandates and product bans can become vehicles for favoring some corporations or industries over others. Diaper services have lobbied heavily for bans on disposables. And paper interests have had some notable successes in their decades-long struggle to beat out plastic—McDonald's switch, for instance, and a Maine law requiring retailers to use paper bags unless the customer requests a plastic bag. "Within a week of passage of that law, virtually all the orders for retail-store plastic bags were canceled if they were active, and if they were under consideration, they were rejected," says George A. Makrauer, president and chief executive of Amko Plastics Inc., a bag manufacturer.

Oddly enough, one way for plastics makers to fight back is to support content requirements like D.C.'s. With their emphasis on "post-consumer" content, such requirements raise paper costs. They also strip the "recycled" label from paper that contains factory scrap. Like orange-juice makers selling peels, both paper and plastic makers reuse their wastes—usually by putting them back through the production process. Paper manufacturers have long touted such paper as "recycled," while plastic makers haven't capitalized on the label.

Even within a single industry, bans and mandates get tangled up with corporate opportunism. Conservatree Paper Co., a distributor of post-consumer recycled paper, is a prominent lobbyist for laws that would mandate recycled content and forbid using the term "recycled" to describe paper made with factory scrap. Laws like D.C.'s increase the market for the paper Conservatree distributes. Mandates that lead paper manufacturers to invest in more recycling capacity should increase Conservatree's supplies —and the competition for its business— and lower its costs....

* * *

The most grandiose plans to regulate materials involve something called "advance disposal fees." Although these fees would require central planning on a scale unknown in this country since World War II, their proponents speak the language of markets, and some of them probably believe their own rhetoric.

The idea behind ADFs is that garbage represents a market failure. Manufacturers don't consider the costs of disposal when they make products. In theory, then, the government could charge manufacturers ADFs that would take into account such factors as: the actual collection and disposal costs of each product type or material; the actual collection and disposal costs in each different jurisdiction where a product is thrown away; current recycling rates; the actual length of product use per household; the actual con-

sumption and disposal path of each product by household; recycling and other behavior in response to new charges, which would change the cost picture over time. One ADF scheme envisions using barcoded information on each product to create a national database that would be used to regulate charges.

So far, such an elaborate system has yet to become a bill, much less a law. But more-stylized ADFs have been enacted. In late 1992, Florida will begin imposing fees on packaging materials that aren't recycled at a 50-percent rate. Rhode Island has introduced ADFs on items, such as tires and motor oil, that are difficult to dispose of. And in New Jersey, the governor's Solid Waste Task Force has recommended a pre-disposal fee to be assessed on manufacturers when they use virgin materials.

California Assemblyman Byron Sher has introduced a bill to tax materials used for packaging and nondurable goods unless their scrap values cover recycling costs. The bill draws its raison d'être from the 1989 law—also sponsored by Sher—that created the mandatory waste-reduction targets: "The costs of implementing the Act to local government, waste haulers and others are significant and should be borne by generators and disposers of solid waste."...

The Sher bill, like many such schemes, represents not a "true cost" system but an elaborate way to subsidize recycling. It seeks to penalize materials not because they actually harm the environment (by, for instance, releasing toxic gases) but because they can't be affordably recycled. The bill's backers speak the language of economics, but they don't understand it.

* * *

The basic problem with such schemes is that they start from a false premise. There is no market failure in solid waste. The economist will find no externalities in your garbage can, unless government subsidies put them there. But that doesn't mean there are no problems.

Take landfills. They really are closing. In fact, more than half the 18,500 landfills that existed in 1979 have shut down in the past 10 years. This is nothing new. Landfills have always had limited lifespans, usually about 10 years. What *is* new is that the old landfills aren't being replaced. The number of new landfills built from 1985 to 1990 was almost 50 percent lower than during the previous five years, the lowest level in 20 years. New landfills are much larger than old ones, but not large enough to make up the difference. As a result, it's hard to find space for trash. In a mini-version of the garbage barge, Santa Monica's trash haulers drive around in their trucks, calling each other on cellular phones to find out who's open to take their loads.

The cause of the landfill shortage isn't that we're "running out of space." A. Clark Wiseman, in a Resources for the Future study, calculates that "*all* municipal solid waste for the next thousand years would require [a landfill 120 feet deep in] a square area having 44-mile length sides." In other words, a hypothetical landfill that could accommodate the next 1,000 years of U.S. waste would take up less than 0.1 percent of the continental United States.

What's missing isn't land—it's prices. Cities used to be able to shove landfills anywhere they wanted. When surrounding communities rebelled, using lawsuits and environmental regulations to drag out the siting process, solid-waste managers griped about the NIMBY (not-in-my-backyard) syndrome and environmentalists declared landfills (and incinerators) remnants of a passing age of waste.

But entrepreneurs have found a way around NIMBY. It's called YIMBY-FAP: Yes, in my backyard—for a price. This new approach has two components. First, the landfill developer picks up the full costs of protecting the surrounding community from environmental harm. This includes such technical components as double landfill liners and leachate collection systems (to protect groundwater from the gop produced by decaying garbage) and methane-removal systems (to keep gas from building up underground). It also includes inspections, record-keeping, a detailed closing plan, and various monitoring systems.

Robert T. Glebs, a former city waste manager who now runs a business siting landfills, estimates that such a state-of-the-art landfill would cost about $55 million to build in the Midwest—including such additional costs as running local recycling programs and offering financial guarantees of local property values. Adding in a 25-percent margin—profit for private landfills, replacement cost for public ones—the tipping fee to cover such a landfill comes to $25.62 a ton, way, way below the cost of recycling programs.

The second component of a YIMBY-FAP landfill is to share the wealth—to pay the surrounding community. Charles County, Virginia, for instance, collects $5.00 for each ton of garbage dumped in the landfill Chambers Development Co. runs in the rural county. Chambers also picks up local garbage for free. "We're good capitalists; we realized there was money in garbage," county Administrator Fred Darden told *Forbes.*

Thanks to the landfill, the county collects more than $1 million a year, enough to cut property taxes by 20 percent while spending more on local schools. Such "host community fees" make landfill siting a win-win proposition.

They also bring the full cost of landfills into the marketplace by making the landfill operator pay not only to install safety measures but to compensate the people most directly affected by the landfill. The next step to internalizing garbage costs is to bring landfill costs back to the person with the bag full of trash.

* * *

... Looking through a nation's garbage, you can tell much about its people—how much they read, whether they're too poor to own refrigerators or rich enough to buy microwave ovens, whether they prefer gardening or fixing their cars. You can figure out how much their time is worth and whether they have a lot of kids. But it's hard, very hard, to see how everything fits together—how a Uneeda cracker box, resealable and lined with wax paper, could lead to national brands and mass marketing, how disposable diapers could make small-scale day care more feasible, how floppy disks could produce more paper waste.

Facing a solid-waste crisis, we have a choice. We can manage our garbage, getting rid of the barriers that keep people from seeing what their habits cost. Or we can assume omniscience and, thinking we know everything about the intricate connections between people and materials, we can try to manipulate both. If we choose the latter course, we will run into the old planner's problem. We just won't know enough to do the job. Garbage in, garbage out.

POSTSCRIPT

Municipal Waste: Can Management Plans Based on Mandated Recycling Succeed?

Volkenburgh and Hartmann stress how important citizen involvement in the planning process was in gaining acceptance for the Ohio program among an initially hostile constituency. The result is a waste management plan that is based on exactly the type of mandatory recycling requirements that are disparaged by Postrel and Scarlett. Initial results show that the Ohio plan appears to be succeeding. The recent upturn in the market price for many recycled materials reported in the front-page story in the October 8, 1994, issue of the *New York Times* will surely provide a significant boost for such programs.

Even more effective than setting goals for the percentage of waste that should be recycled are regulations (such as those now in effect in New York) that require the recycling of all waste components for which the cost involved would be less than other means of disposal. *Garbage in the Cities: Refuse, Reform, and Environment*, by Martin Melosi (Texas A&M University Press, 1981), is a historical analysis of the social, political, economic, and technological factors that led to our present waste disposal problems.

Two informative reports on a variety of problems and controversies concerning the garbage disposal issue are "Trash Can Realities," by Jon Luoma, *Audubon* (March 1990), and "Wasting Away," by Howard Levenson, *Environment* (March 1990). For an optimistic assessment of plastics recycling, see "Recycling the Plastic Package," by Robert Stone, Ambuj Sagan, and Nicholas Ashford, *Technology Review* (July 1992). Jeff Solomon-Hess describes some new ideas and programs that should aid recycling programs in his article in the March/April 1993 issue of *MSW Management*.

For another analysis that concludes that demand-side recycling is counterproductive, see the article by Christopher Boerner and Kenneth Chilton in the January/February 1994 issue of *Environment*. In "A Rationale for Recycling," by David G. Evans, *Environmental Management* (vol. 18, no. 3, 1994), it is concluded that simple financial factors alone are inadequate for assessing the value of recycling and that governmental intervention is appropriate when trying to meet societal objectives.

William Rathje is an archaeologist who has been studying the waste disposal problem by digging in old landfills. His research leads him to dispute much of what he reads about the "garbage crisis." For an elaboration of his views, see the recent book he coauthored with Cullen Murphy, *Rubbish! The Archeology of Garbage* (HarperCollins, 1992).

ISSUE 14

Nuclear Waste: Should Plans for Underground Storage Be Put on Hold?

YES: Nicholas Lenssen, from "Facing Up to Nuclear Waste," *World Watch* (March/April 1992)

NO: Luther J. Carter, from "Ending the Gridlock on Nuclear Waste Storage," *Issues in Science and Technology* (Fall 1993)

ISSUE SUMMARY

YES: Nuclear waste researcher Nicholas Lenssen proposes that due to technical uncertainties and political realities, the search for a permanent nuclear waste repository should be delayed until the future of nuclear power is decided.

NO: Science writer Luther J. Carter argues that Nevadans can be persuaded to accept the proposed Yucca Mountain site as safe for surface and underground storage of both civilian and military nuclear waste.

The fission process by which the splitting of uranium and plutonium nuclei produces energy in commercial and military nuclear reactors also generates a large inventory of radioactive waste. This waste includes both the "high-level" radioactive by-products of the fission reaction, which are contained in the spent fuel rods removed from the reactors, and a larger volume of "low-level" material, which has been rendered radioactive through bombardment with neutrons—neutral subnuclear particles—emitted during the reaction. "Low-level" waste also includes the refuse produced during medical and research uses of radioactive chemicals.

The amount of highly radioactive material that builds up in the core of a commercial nuclear power plant during its operation far exceeds the radioactive release that results from the explosion of a high-yield nuclear weapon. Because radioactive emissions are lethal to all biological organisms—causing severe illness and death at high doses and inducing cancer at any dose level —it is necessary to make sure that the radioactive wastes are kept isolated from the biosphere. Since some of the nuclear products remain radioactive for hundreds of thousands of years, this is a formidable task.

The early proponents of nuclear reactor development recognized the need to solve this problem. Confident that scientists and engineers would find the solution, a decision was made to proceed with a program, sponsored and funded by the U.S. government, to promote nuclear power before the serious issue of permanent waste disposal had been resolved.

Forty years later, with 100 commercial nuclear power plants licensed in this country, more than 300 in other countries around the world, and hundreds of additional military nuclear reactors piling up lethal wastes in temporary storage facilities every day, that early confidence that the disposal problem could be solved has long since disappeared. Nowhere in the world is there a proven, operating plan for permanent nuclear waste disposal. In the United States, several abortive plans and schedules have been mandated by Congress, only to be abandoned for a variety of technical and political reasons. The most recent Nuclear Waste Policy Act, legislated in 1982, set a step-by-step schedule to complete a permanent, operating "high-level" waste repository by 1998. This schedule has proven impossible to meet. In December 1987, recognizing that serious problems were again developing in implementing the new plan, Congress short-circuited the process by designating Yucca Mountain, Nevada, as the only site to be considered for the first high-level repository.

A solution to the problem of "low-level" waste has been equally elusive. Amendments were passed in late 1985 in an attempt to make the 1980 Low-Level Radioactive Waste Policy Act workable. But political and technological disputes continue unabated, and the timetable established in the legislation has not been met.

The history of the nuclear waste issue illustrates the folly of focusing on technological fixes without recognizing that solutions to real world problems must meet political, socioeconomic, and ecological criteria that are not revealed by isolating the results of laboratory investigations from the other aspects of the issue. The simplistic response of some nuclear scientists is to claim that the technological problems have been resolved and nuclear waste disposal is only a "political" issue. A careful examination of the situation reveals the inappropriateness of adopting such a perspective. The evaluation of a proposed technological solution to a problem is related to social values, which in turn affect the political position of the participants in the process. Serious differences exist as to the degree of isolation and period of time necessary for "high-level" waste containment. How certain need experts be about future geological processes before they can claim that burying wastes in a particular location will result in the required degree of isolation?

Researcher Nicholas Lenssen, author of a Worldwatch Paper on nuclear waste, proposes that in view of the uncertainty about the future of nuclear power, and because of the scientific and political difficulties with geological burial, above-ground "temporary" storage is likely to remain the only viable option well into the twenty-first century. Writer Luther J. Carter, author of a book on nuclear waste, sees the urgent need to resolve the disposal problem. He recognizes that present plans for Yucca Mountain are doomed, but he thinks that Nevadans could be convinced to accept a proposal to bury both commercial and military nuclear waste at the site, beginning with underground retrievable storage.

YES

Nicholas Lenssen

FACING UP TO NUCLEAR WASTE

A series of rapid-fire events has recently swept the nuclear field: amidst an almost celebratory atmosphere, *The Bulletin of the Atomic Scientists* rolled back the minute hand of its famed Doomsday Clock; the Soviet Union peacefully closed shop; the U.S. Nuclear Regulatory Commission's new chief pronounced an emphasis on "safety, safety, safety"; and the nuclear power industry made plans for a happy-days-are-here-again ad campaign proclaiming the virtues of the "new" nuclear power. The cumulative effect suggests that the atomic-age fears of the past are now safely behind us.

In fact, nothing could be farther from the truth. While the fall of the Soviet Union may have ended the superpower nuclear arms race, it has left the management of thousands of bombs, bombmaking facilities, nuclear materials, and radioactive waste sites in a state of near-chaos. And while the prospect of nuclear confrontation between superpowers has faded, the likelihood of more Saddam Husseins getting their hands on nuclear bombmaking materials is a growing concern.

But the most underestimated dangers of all may be those of the civilian nuclear power industry, which—after 50 years of costly research—has yet to find a safe and permanent way to dispose of its radioactive waste. In the United States, and possibly in the world as a whole, 95 percent of all radioactivity emitted by nuclear waste comes from the civilian sector—primarily from nuclear electric power plants. The cumulative discharge of irradiated fuel from these plants is fast growing; it is now three times what it was in 1980 and twenty times what it was in 1970.

Despite this increase, not a single one of the more than 25 countries producing nuclear power has found a solution that stands up to close scrutiny. The central problem is that nuclear waste remains dangerous for hundreds of thousands of years—meaning that in producing it, today's governments assume responsibility for the fate of thousands of future generations. Yet, neither technically nor politically has any way been found to assure that those generations—not to mention the present one—will be protected. The most prudent policy under such circumstances—to store waste in long-term temporary storage while searching for more responsible and permanent solutions—is being proposed by environmentalists and independent scientists in numerous countries; but even as that happens, the governments of the major nuclear nations continue their pursuit of more grandiose strategies for deep geologic burial, which also may entail greater long-term risks.

The nuclear waste issue has been marked by a series of illusions and unfulfilled promises. Like mirages, safe and permanent methods of isolating radioactive materials seem to recede from reach as they are examined closely. No government has been able to come up with a course of action acceptable either to advocates or opponents of nuclear power. Proponents insist that adequate permanent burial options have been developed and proved—and that it's time to jump-start the industry. Anti-nuclear advocates have identified flaws in every burial option proposed so far. They feel that in lieu of a commitment to abandon nuclear power, any waste site will become an excuse to start up the nuclear engine again. A political stalemate of this nature has formed in nearly every country.

Ironically enough, out of concern for the threat of global warming has come a political juggernaut that is being used to try to revive the nuclear power industry. Government officials and nuclear industry executives around the world believe that to achieve this "jump-start" will require a fast resolution of the nuclear waste problem. But just as earlier nuclear power plants were built without a full understanding of the technological and societal requirements, a rushed job to bury wastes may turn out to be an irreversible mistake.

BURY THE PROBLEM?

Since the beginning of the nuclear age, there has been no shortage of ideas on how to isolate radioactive waste from the biosphere. Scientists have proposed burying it under Antarctic ice, injecting it into the seabed, or hurling it into outer space. But with each proposal has come an array of objections. As these have mounted, authorities have fallen back on the idea of burying radioactive waste hundreds of feet below the earth's crust. They argue, as does the U.S. National Research Council (of the National Academy of Sciences), that geologic burial is the "best, safest long-term option."

The concept of geologic burial is fairly straightforward. Engineers would begin by hollowing out a repository roughly a quarter of a mile or more below the earth's surface. The repository would consist of a broadly dispersed series of rooms from which thermally hot waste would be placed in holes drilled in the host rock. When the chamber is ready, waste would be transported to the burial site, where technicians would package it in specially constructed containers made of stainless steel or other metal.

Once placed in the rock, the containers would be surrounded by an impermeable material such as clay to retard groundwater penetration, then sealed with cement. When the repository is full, it would be sealed off from the surface. Finally, workers would erect some everlasting sign post to the future—in one U.S. Department of Energy (DOE) proposal, a colossal nuclear Stonehenge—warning generations millennia hence of the deadly radioactivity entombed below.

Geologic disposal, though, as with any human contrivance meant to last thousands of years, is little more than a calculated risk. Future changes in geology, land use, settlement patterns, and climate all affect the ability to isolate nuclear waste safely. As Stanford University geologist Konrad Krauskopf wrote in *Science* in 1990, "No scientist or engineer can give an absolute guarantee that radioactive waste will not someday leak in dangerous quantities from even the best of repositories."

According to a 1990 National Research Council report on radioactive waste disposal, predicting future conditions that could affect a burial site stretches the limits of human understanding in several areas of geology, groundwater movement, and chemistry. "Studies done over the past two decades have led to the realization that the phenomena are more complicated than had been thought," notes the report. "Rather than decreasing our uncertainty, this line of research has increased the number of ways in which we know that we are uncertain."

THEY CALL IT DISPOSAL

In Germany and the United States, where specific burial sites have been selected for assessment and preparation, the work to date has raised more questions than answers about the nature of geologic repositories. German planners have targeted the Gorleben salt dome, 85 miles from Hanover in northern Germany, to house the country's high-level waste from irradiated fuel. But groundwater from neighboring sand and gravel layers is eroding the salt that makes up the Gorleben dome, making it a potentially dangerous location.

Groundwater conditions at the U.S. site at Yucca Mountain, a barren, flat-topped ridge about 100 miles north of Las Vegas, Nevada, are also raising concerns. According to the current plan, the waste deposited in Yucca Mountain would stay dry because the storerooms would be located 1,000 feet above the present water table, and because percolation from the surface under current climatic conditions is minimal.

But critics, led by DOE geologist Jerry Szymanski, believe that an earthquake at Yucca Mountain, which is crisscrossed with more than 30 seismic faults, could dramatically raise the water table. Others disagree. But if water came in contact with hot waste containers, the resulting steam explosions could burst them open and rapidly spread their radioactive contents. "You flood that thing and you could blow the top off the mountain. At the very least, the radioactive material would go into the groundwater and spread to Death Valley, where there are hot springs all over the place," University of Colorado geophysicist Charles Archambeau told the *New York Times*.

Other geologic forces could threaten the inviolability of underground burial chambers. For instance, in 1990 scientists discovered that a volcano 12 miles from Yucca Mountain probably erupted within the last 20,000 years—not 270,000 years ago, as they had earlier surmised. Volcanic activity could easily resume in the area before Yucca Mountain's intended lethal stockpile is inert. It is worth remembering that less than 10,000 years ago, volcanoes were erupting in what is now central France, the English Channel did not exist 7,000 years ago, and much of the Sahara was fertile just 5,000 years ago.

POLITICAL HOT POTATO

Since the early days of nuclear power, scientists have issued warnings about the long-lived danger of radioactive waste. In 1957, a U.S. National Academy of Sciences (NAS) panel cautioned that "unlike the disposal of any other type of waste, the hazard related to radioactive wastes is so great that no element of doubt should be allowed to exist regarding safety." In 1960, another Academy committee urged that the waste issue be resolved *before* licensing new nuclear facilities.

Yet such recommendations fell on deaf ears, and one country after another plunged ahead with building nuclear power plants. As government bureaucrats and industry spokespeople went about promoting their new industry, they attempted to quiet any public uneasiness about waste storage with assurances that it could be dealt with. However, early failures of waste storage and burial practices engendered growing mistrust of the secretive government nuclear agencies that were responsible. For example, three of the six shallow burial sites for commercial low-level radioactive waste in the United States—in Kentucky, Illinois, and New York—have leaked waste and been closed.

Trust also faded around the world as the public came to view government agencies as more interested in encouraging the growth of nuclear power than in resolving the waste problem. Grassroots opposition has sprung up against nearly any attempt to develop a radioactive waste facility.

The United States has perhaps the most dismal history of mismanaging waste issues; from the 1950s onward, the U.S. Atomic Energy Commission (AEC) and its successors have swept nuclear waste problems under the rug. Only following a stinging 1966 NAS critique of the AEC's waste policy (suppressed by the AEC until Congress demanded its release in 1970), and a 1969 fire at the U.S. government's bomb-making facility at Rocky Flats, Colorado (which created vast amounts of long-lived waste in need of storage), did the AEC concoct a rushed attempt to solve the problem by planning to bury nuclear waste in a salt formation in Lyons, Kansas.

By 1973, the AEC was forced to cancel the Lyons project because serious technical problems had been overlooked. For example, the ground around the site was a "Swiss cheese" of old oil and gas wells through which groundwater might seep. The Lyons failure set off a decade of wandering from potential site to potential site, and of growing opposition from apprehensive states.

A number of states, led by California in 1976, responded by approving legislation that tied future nuclear power development to a solution of the waste problem. Suddenly, the future of nuclear power seemed threatened. The nuclear industry pushed the AEC's successor, the Department of Energy (DOE), to bury waste quickly. But DOE had no better success in finding a state amenable to housing the nation's waste.

The department's repeated failures prompted Congress to pass the Nuclear Waste Policy Act of 1982. A product of byzantine political bargaining, the law required DOE to develop two high-level repositories, one in the western part of the country and the other in the east.

From the outset, the department was hampered in its response by an unreasonable timetable and its own insistence on considering sites that were technically and politically unacceptable. As DOE failed to gain public confidence, the process became embroiled in political conflicts at the state level. Finally, when the uncooperative eastern states forced the cancellation of the unsited eastern repository in 1986, the legislation fell apart. With the whole waste program in jeopardy, and over the strong objections of the Nevada delegation, Congress ordered DOE in 1987 to study just one site—Yucca Mountain, adjacent to the federal government's nuclear weapons test area.

While the federal government is determined to saddle Nevada with the country's waste, the state is vigorously seeking to disqualify the site, claiming in part that DOE—given that Yucca Mountain is the only site being investigated—cannot conduct research objectively. So vehement are the objections of Nevadans that the state legislature in 1989 passed a law prohibiting anyone from storing high-level waste in the state. Former U.S. Nuclear Regulatory Commissioner Victor Gilinsky describes Yucca Mountain as a "political dead-end."

GOING IN REVERSE

Although most of the countries using nuclear power are now preparing for geologic burial of their waste, almost every disposal program is well behind its own schedule. In 1975, the United States planned on having a high-level waste burial site operating by 1985. The date was moved to 1989, then to 1998, 2003, and now 2010—a goal that still appears unrealistic. Likewise, Germany expected in the mid-1980s to open its deep burial facility by 1998, but the government waste agency now cites 2008 as the target year. Most other countries currently plan deep geologic burial no sooner than 2020, with a few aiming for even later [see Table 1].

So charged is the atmosphere surrounding the waste disposal issue that it's questionable whether any government has the political capacity to build and operate nuclear waste repositories. In most countries, even the study of a location as a potential nuclear waste burial site brings people to the streets in protest, as in South Korea and the former Soviet Union. So far, most governments have made short-term decisions on waste while leaving their long-term plans vague, hoping to muddle through.

Even in France, the acknowledged leader in European nuclear power generation, the waste issue defies ready solution. In 1987, the French waste agency, ANDRA, selected four potential sites for burying high-level radioactive wastes. Officials in those locales, disturbed that they had not been consulted, joined with farmers and environmentalists to paralyze the research program. Blockades obstructed government technicians at three of the four sites, and work proceeded only with police protection. In January 1990, in one of the country's largest anti-nuclear demonstrations since the late 1970s, 15,000 people marched in Angers against one site. By February, then-Prime Minister Michel Rocard had imposed a nationwide moratorium on further work, providing the government a cooling-off period to try again to win public support.

The French Parliament approved a new plan in June 1991. The number of sites to be investigated was reduced from four to two, and the government claims the selection process will be more open this time around. Also, ANDRA officials have a new approach for winning support. They will pay the two communities contending for the site up to $9 million a year for

Table 1

Selected Programs for High-Level Waste Burial

Country	Earliest Planned Year	Status of Program
Argentina	2040	Granite site at Gastre selected.
Canada	2020	Independent commission conducting four-year study of government plan to bury irradiated fuel in granite at yet-to-be-identified site.
China	none announced	Irradiated fuel to be reprocessed; Gobi desert sites under investigation.
Finland	2020	Field studies being conducted; final site selection due in 2000.
France	2010	Two sites to be selected and studied; final site not to be selected until 2006.
Germany	2008	Gorleben salt dome sole site to be studied.
India	2010	Irradiated fuel to be reprocessed, waste stored for twenty years, then buried in yet-to-be-identified granite site.
Italy	2040	Irradiated fuel to be reprocessed, and waste stored for 50–60 years before burial in clay or granite.
Japan	2020	Limited site studies. Cooperative program with China to build underground research facility.
Netherlands	2040	Interim storage of reprocessing waste for 50–100 years before eventual burial, possibly in another country.
Soviet Union	none announced	Eight sites being studied for deep geologic disposal.
Sweden	2020	Granite site to be selected in 1997; evaluation studies under way at Äspö site near Oskarshamn nuclear complex.
United States	2010	Yucca Mountain, Nevada, site to be studied, and if approved, receive 70,000 metric tons of waste.
United Kingdom	2030	Fifty-year storage approved in 1982; exploring options including sub-seabed burial.

Source: Worldwatch Institute, based on various sources.

"the psychological inconvenience" of being studied, according to then-Industry Minister Roger Fauroux. However, parliament has delayed any decision on a final burial site for 15 years. In that time, the country's high-level waste inventory will more than triple.

In Germany, the controversy over radioactive waste mirrors that surrounding nuclear reactor construction, which has come to a standstill. Local opposition to any nuclear project appears deeply entrenched, and there is a general inability of the major political parties to agree on nuclear policy.

The German waste controversy erupted in 1976, when the federal government's investigation of three sites in Lower Saxony created such an uproar among local farmers and students that the state government rejected every one. The following year, the federal government selected another site in Lower Saxony—the salt dome at Gorleben.

Large protests erupted even before the official announcement; 2,500 people took over the drilling site for three months before police hauled them off and set up a secure camp from which scientific work could be conducted. Although the federal government has put all its bets on Gorleben, continuing technical problems and strong opposition from the Lower Saxony government make plans to bury waste by 2008 highly improbable. Critics have warned that the site's geology is unstable. Public confidence in the project sank even lower when a worker was killed by collapsing rock during a 1987 drilling accident.

In Sweden, nuclear issues have been —erupting since the 1970s, when two governments were thrown out of office following attempts to promote nuclear energy. Only after a national referendum in 1980 to limit the number of reactors in the country to 12 and to phase even these out by 2010, was the country able to focus on the waste issue. One immediate dividend from the agreed phase-out was a clarification of exactly how much waste would eventually need to be dealt with: 7,750 tons of irradiated fuel, and 7.2 million cubic feet of other radioactive waste.

Sweden's high-level waste program has won international praise for relying not simply on deep burial but on a system of redundant engineering barriers, starting with corrosion-resistant copper waste canisters that have four-inch thick walls with an estimated lifetime of 100,000 years or longer if undisturbed by humans or geologic forces. Even with the announced phase-out and international scientific praise, Swedish public support has not been forthcoming for burial. Protests halted attempts to site a permanent high-level burial facility 12 years ago, and efforts to explore other sites have met determined local opposition.

The Japanese government also has run into public opposition to its burial plans. In 1984, planners selected an amenable village, Horonobe, near the northern tip of Hokkaido island. But opposition from the Hokkaido Prefecture governor and diet and from nearby villages and farmers has blocked the government from constructing a waste storage and underground research facility there.

There are signs that Japan is now looking beyond its borders for a high-level waste disposal site. Since 1984, China has shown interest in importing irradiated fuel or waste for either a fee or in return for assistance with its own fledgling nuclear program. In November 1990, China and Japan agreed to build an underground facility in China's Shanxi province, where research is to be undertaken on high-level waste burial.

WALK, DO NOT RUN

Because of the scientific and political difficulties with geologic burial, aboveground "temporary" storage is likely to remain the only viable option well into the 21st century. Fortunately, there need be no rush to bury nuclear waste, other than for public relations reasons. As a result, rather than continue focusing on developing controversial and potentially dangerous burial sites, governments can still choose a course of action that will buy time—and gain public support—to continue the search for a dependable long-term solution.

To choose this course requires, first, that nations employ safer methods of temporary storage for radioactive waste, particularly irradiated fuel. For instance, most spent radioactive material is stored in cooling ponds at nuclear power plants —an inherently risky proposition, since electric pumps are needed to circulate cooling water to prevent the fuel from overheating. Yet both governments and independent analysts believe that storage technologies such as dry casks, that rely on passive cooling and are capable of containing materials for at least a century are safer than water-based systems. Such storage would allow radiation levels to fall 90 percent or more.

Even with improved temporary storage systems, however, an institution for the careful monitoring and safeguarding of the waste will be needed to prevent catastrophic accidents or even terrorism. But no government can guarantee the durability of an institution whose responsibilities must continue many times longer than any human institution has ever lasted.

Temporary storage does not solve the problem of nuclear waste, but it could allow time for more careful consideration than is now witnessed in many countries of longer-term options, including geologic burial, seabed burial, and indefinite storage. It also could permit long-term, in-situ experiments with promising technologies such as the Swedish copper canisters.

But addressing the waste problem demands much more than a reduction of technical uncertainties. It also requires a fundamental change in current operating programs as well as new measures to regain public confidence. A lack of credibility plagues government nuclear agencies in most countries. Public distrust is rooted in the fact that the institutions in charge of nuclear waste cleanup also promote nuclear power and weapons production—and have acquired reputations for equivocation, misinformation, and secrecy.

In the United States, the U.S. Office of Technology Assessment, the National Research Council's Board of Radioactive Waste Management, and private research groups have called for an independent government body to take over the task of managing the country's nuclear wastes from DOE. So far, Congress has responded merely by requiring more oversight of DOE. Forming autonomous and publicly accountable organizations to manage nuclear waste would go a long way toward regaining public support, and getting waste programs on track.

BEYOND ILLUSION

In the end, some observers believe that the nuclear waste issue is a hostage of the overall debate on nuclear power, which increasingly tears at nations. "If industry insists on generating more waste, there will always be confrontation. People just won't accept it," believes David Lowry, a British environmental consultant and coauthor of *The International Politics of Nuclear Waste*. Because the political controversies are so intense, true progress on the waste issue may only come about when nations come to decisive resolutions, once and for all, of the nuclear power issue.

Sweden, which has perhaps the broadest (though not universal) public support for its nuclear waste program, made a national decision to phase out its twelve nuclear power reactors by 2010. Without such a decision, public skepticism toward nuclear technologies and institutions could grow only stronger.

While most countries do not have formal policies requiring phase-out of nuclear power, there is a de facto phase-out of new plants imposed by rising costs and concern over safety. Worldwide, roughly 50 nuclear power plants are under construction today—fewer than at any other time in the last 20 years.

Despite this trend, nuclear advocates continue to call for a rapid expansion of atomic power. They've seized upon the threat of global warming and public anxieties about dependence on Middle Eastern oil, aroused by the Gulf War, to push their point.

Yet a world with six times the current number of reactors, as called for by some nuclear supporters, would require opening a new burial site every two years or so to handle the long-lived wastes generated —a gargantuan financial, environmental, and public health problem that nuclear power proponents conveniently continue to ignore. President Bush's 1991 National Energy Strategy, for example, proposed a doubling in the number of U.S. nuclear power plants over the next 40 years, but did not discuss the need for future waste sites.

As experience with nuclear power plants has demonstrated, it will not necessarily become any easier to site and construct future geologic burial facilities once the first is opened. A single accident could set back government and industry efforts for decades. While waste is but one of the problems still facing nuclear power, it is clearly the longest-lasting one.

NO

Luther J. Carter

ENDING THE GRIDLOCK ON NUCLEAR WASTE STORAGE

In light of the nation's hard-won experience with the political and technical realities of nuclear waste storage and containment, it's time to take another hard look at the Nuclear Waste Policy Act (NWPA) of 1982. The U.S. Department of Energy's existing program to investigate Yucca Mountain at the Nevada Test Site (NTS) for use as a geological repository for nuclear waste is in trouble. The costs are huge, the progress is slow and uncertain, and the anticipated benefits are not up to emerging needs.

With exploratory excavation of the site about to begin, we need to reconsider the fundamental parameters of this federal program. Is it possible to evaluate the suitability of the site for *permanent* storage under the proposed schedule, or should we set our sights on a *retrievable* storage facility for now? Should facilities for surface as well as underground storage be located at the NTS? Should the site be considered for deposit only of irradiated (or "spent") fuel from commercial power reactors and glassified high-level waste from past production of plutonium for the military stockpile, as now planned, or should we also include surplus plutonium recovered from dismantled warheads?

Answering these questions is made the more difficult because at the heart of our nation's nuclear waste policies lies a profound ambivalence: the desire to achieve at least a rough consensus in siting a repository versus the recognition that the only way to serve the nation's best interest may be to act without consensus. The original NWPA reflected this ambivalence: It sought to establish a consensus of sorts by screening many sites, providing for public participation and environmental assessments, seeking regional equity, and assuring veto rights for prospective host states. Yet Congress granted the Department of Energy (DOE) the authority to make all the key siting decisions and explicitly kept for itself the right to override a state veto.

The NWPA produced not consensus but conflict. Loud and bitter protests arose across the country in response to DOE's widespread search for sites. In late 1987, Congress was forced to rescue the waste program from a state of

From Luther J. Carter, "Ending the Gridlock on Nuclear Waste Storage," *Issues in Science and Technology* (Fall 1993), pp. 73–79. Copyright © 1993 by The University of Texas at Dallas, Richardson, TX. Reprinted by permission.

political paralysis by drastically amending the NWPA, abruptly limiting the investigation for a geological repository to Yucca Mountain in Nevada.

The decision met with strong disapproval among Nevadans, not to mention a pervasive cynicism about the perceived sacrifice of principle in favor of political expediency. As a sop to an angry Nevada congressional delegation, Congress provided that a surface monitored retrievable storage (MRS) facility for interim placement of spent reactor fuel could not be located with the permanent repository project at the NTS—even though establishing an MRS facility there would have been the surest way for DOE to meet its obligation to begin accepting utilities' spent fuel in 1998. Instead, the siting of a surface MRS facility was put on a purely voluntary basis.

Today, nearly six years later, the Yucca Mountain plan is at a pivotal point. At long last, the deep exploratory testing of Yucca Mountain is near at hand. A 12-acre North Portal support facility is being built for a state-of-the-art tunnel boring machine, similar to one used for the English Channel Tunnel. Next summer, the machine will begin excavating a five-mile long "loop" tunnel through Yucca Mountain from north to south.

However, the program as now defined cannot possibly meet the schedule that's been set for it and, indeed, seems doomed to frustration. The goal set by the sponsors of the 1982 act—establishing a licensed operational repository by 1995 —was never a serious possibility. The date has twice been readjusted, first to the year 2003, then to 2010. Similarly, the costs of "characterizing" the site— that is, determining its suitability—have escalated astronomically. Cost estimates have gone from about $100 million in 1982 to $6.3 billion today, of which about $1.4 billion already has been spent.

To arrive at a realistic schedule and budget for characterizing the site actually is not possible today because the NWPA was drafted on an erroneous assumption. That is, the act reflects a mistaken belief that geologic isolation and containment of nuclear waste are within the known state of the art and, hence, are now licensable under standards established by the U.S. Nuclear Regulatory Commission (NRC) consistent with Environmental Protection Agency criteria. But in reality, developing a geologic repository and credible containment system for long-lived, heat-generating waste is exploratory and experimental. It calls for an iterative, design-as-you-go approach, as advocated by the National Research Council's Board on Radioactive Waste Management in its July 1990 report "Rethinking High-Level Radioactive Waste Disposal." Legislative goals and requirements need to be adjusted in light of this technological reality.

TAKING AN EXPERIMENTAL APPROACH

One major shortcoming of the existing program is that the current schedule allows only four to five years for collecting data crucial to the first licensing application, a constraint sharply criticized by the Nuclear Waste Technical Review Board (NWTRB). Created in 1987 by Congress to look over DOE's shoulder, the NWTRB recently warned that the project is "driven by unrealistic deadlines" and noted that certain key questions about the Yucca Mountain site could take decades to resolve.

An independent reevaluation of the Yucca Mountain plan now appears inevitable. Two senior program officials recently issued a report highly critical of the plan. Rep. Philip R. Sharp (D-Ind.), chairman of the House Energy and Power Subcommittee, the General Accounting Office, and the NWTRB have also called for a thorough program review.

At the urging of Nevada's Gov. Bob Miller, Secretary of Energy Hazel O'Leary has promised to at least review the project's costs and financing. But what Miller and the Nevada congressional delegation really want is for DOE to stop everything. In the view of the state and its allies among the antinuclear and environmental groups, Congress should change course just as drastically as it did in 1987 and abandon the repository and MRS siting programs in favor of continued, and indeed indefinite, storage of spent fuel at the reactor stations. This is the alternative also favored by some academic critics of the present program.

A sharp change of course is now in order, but not in the direction proposed by the state of Nevada. Indeed, Congress has more cause than ever to understand, and to make everyone else understand, that the nation's need for a solution to the nuclear waste problem must now be put ahead of the desire not to impose that solution on an unwilling host state. What is required is to make the NTS the national center for surface as well as deep underground nuclear storage. This would be an important new mission to replace the weapons-testing mission that is fading away.

WHY YUCCA MOUNTAIN?

When Congress decided to make Yucca Mountain, a barren desert ridge formation of volcanic tuff that straddles the southwest boundary of the NTS, the sole candidate site for the first repository, it was picking the location that DOE had rated the best, technically and economically, of the five sites that had been selected as most promising. In many ways, the NTS, where more than 709 nuclear weapons tests have been conducted since 1951, is uniquely suited to nuclear storage. The site is large; at 1,350 square miles, it is bigger than Rhode Island. Its geology, dry climate, and geographical location in a remote area of a sparsely populated desert region offer important advantages. And it has a ready-made infrastructure that includes hundreds of miles of roads and a tradition of tight security.

Scientists at the U.S. Geological Survey see a signal advantage for waste isolation in Yucca Mountain and similar sites in and around the NTS. It's that a repository can be built hundreds of feet above the water table, so that casks of radioactive materials can be kept relatively dry and that retrieval will be relatively easy. As these scientists see it, this advantage offsets what is probably the site's principal drawback—the fact that over geologic time the NTS and the larger Great Basin region have been racked by earthquakes and vulcanism.

Nuclear materials storage in Yucca Mountain should be made robustly defensible by adopting new policies for dealing with the uncertainty inherent in safely containing and isolating radioactive materials for thousands of years. To this end, the repository should be limited, at least initially, to underground retrievable storage (URS). The URS concept, which Lawrence Livermore Laboratory's L. D. Ramspott probably has done more than anyone else to define, is based on the use of massive, self-shielded storage casks containing corrosion-resistant inner canisters. The casks would rest on the floor of the emplacement tunnels, possibly on rail carriages to ease moving them in and out. As Eugene H. Roseboom, Jr., an adviser to the director of the U.S. Geological Survey on the Yucca Mountain project and a URS advocate, describes it, "The repository could be essentially an underground railroad switchyard with canisters on flatbed rail cars parked in the tunnels." Temperatures inside the tunnels would increase from the heat of radioactive decay but could be kept within tolerable limits by means of a ventilation system.

If necessary, the casks could be brought up out of the repository by the access ramps to form a storage array at the surface. For the longer term, however, storage deep underground offers a major advantage over surface storage because if the repository were ever abandoned, as in the case of a societal collapse, the radioactive materials sequestered there would be more likely to remain secure and safely contained.

Location of a surface MRS with a geologic repository makes sense because each adds credibility to the other. Just as storage at an MRS facility cannot be deemed temporary unless progress is being made toward an underground repository, deep geologic storage cannot truly be termed retrievable without a convenient place at the surface for storage of any spent fuel or high-level waste that may be retrieved.

Accordingly, Congress should direct DOE to make preparations for the necessary licensing applications. Most urgently, DOE should ask the NRC for permission to build an MRS facility at the NTS in time to begin receiving spent fuel in 1998. DOE should also begin revising its Yucca Mountain program plans to support a licensing application to cautiously begin introducing spent fuel into a Yucca Mountain URS and test facility, say by the year 2005.

Development of a URS system could give vital support to scientific investigation of the site's suitability for permanent isolation of nuclear materials. Consider, for instance, these two separate but closely related questions: Will the Ghost Dance Fault zone, which runs through the mountain, prove to be so extensive that a repository of the size now contemplated cannot benefit? Will a "hot repository" or a "cool repository"—as determined by the density of spent fuel emplacement—best keep waste casks free from the corrosive effects of moisture? If the fault zone turns out to be much larger than now expected, the adequacy of the site for a full-scale repository might turn on the hot versus cool repository question and the density of fuel storage. Extensive testing with retrievably emplaced spent fuel could be essential to providing an answer.

MEETING AN EMERGING NEED

The need for surface and deep underground nuclear materials storage at the NTS is now proving pressing indeed. Consider the three principal categories of nuclear materials that should go there.

Spent commercial fuel. Spent fuel is generated by 110 reactors at nearly 70 commercial nuclear stations in 33 states. The existing spent-fuel inventory comes to roughly 27,000 metric tons; by 2010, this figure is expected to rise to nearly 59,000 tons. Nearly all of the spent fuel is kept at the reactors in pools used for cooling and storage. Many of these pools are nearing their capacity, forcing the utilities to look to storage of their older, cooler fuel in dry vaults or casks at the nuclear station.

The NRC regards this as a safe means of temporary storage for up to a century. The state of Nevada and others thus can argue that continued "at-reactor" storage affords a ready alternative to deep geologic storage and indeed buys time for developing safer, more acceptable methods for waste disposal. This argument is open to several objections. First, the belief that a better solution will turn up is entirely speculative. Second, the nuclear waste program is funded by a fee on nuclear electricity. This funding may not last indefinitely—particularly if existing nuclear plants are decommissioned without being replaced. Finally, indefinitely continued at-reactor storage will almost certainly meet with strong public opposition. In the absence of a long-term geological repository or a DOE-operated MRS facility for temporary central storage, at-reactor storage is likely to be seen —and rejected—as a *de facto* permanent solution.

Two current disputes in the upper Midwest bear on this point. In Minnesota, an appellate judge ruled in June against a Northern States Power Company plan for dry-cask storage at its Prairie Island station on the grounds that such storage might in fact be permanent. In Michigan, Consumers Power, which recently went to dry-cask storage at its Palisades station on Lake Michigan, has met opposition from the state Attorney General and from environmental activists who chanted, "We don't want your cask(et)s."

High-level military waste. Use of a Yucca Mountain repository to receive high-level waste from the nuclear weapons production sites is of central importance to the effort to clean up these sites.

Given the huge sums devoted to it (about $6 billion this year alone), the defense site cleanup surely ranks as a national priority and should be lending urgency to the need for greater progress at Yucca Mountain.

The Savannah River Plant's inventory of 34 million gallons of high-level waste, now stored in tanks, is all to be processed into about 7,000 canisters of borosilicate glass, possibly beginning next year. These canisters can be kept in temporary surface storage at Savannah River but will not be securely isolated for the long term until committed to an underground repository. The Yucca Mountain repository could in the longer term receive an even larger consignment of high-level waste from DOE's Hanford reservation in Washington state, and even an impressive amount from the Idaho National Engineering Laboratory. The volume of high-level waste stored at Hanford is nearly twice that kept at Savannah River, and most of it would be many times more difficult to recover, process, and reduce to a vitrified form. DOE's preliminary cost estimates for recovering and glassifying all the Hanford high-level waste run to nearly $50 billion, and there would also be the risk of significant radiation exposures to workers. Clearly, taking on so formidable and expensive a task would make no sense at all unless the waste recovered is to be securely isolated and contained in a geologic repository.

Warhead plutonium. A growing amount of plutonium is being recovered from the decommissioning of warheads required by recent arms-reduction agreements. About 1,800 warheads are being disassembled at DOE's Pantex plant in the Texas Panhandle, near Amarillo, each year, and a total of some 15,000 must be disassembled over the coming decade if the United States is to honor its arms-reduction obligations. By the early part of the next century, surplus warhead plutonium could amount to as much as 50 metric tons, which would be about half the existing military stockpile but less than a tenth of the plutonium present in the spent fuel of a fully loaded Yucca Mountain repository....

But DOE would have the plutonium kept as warhead pits or finished weapons parts and retained essentially as part of the military stockpile to await future decisions as to its disposition, which might include a return to weapons use. This policy defies convincing explanation because the existing plutonium stockpile is several times what will be needed for the downsized U.S. nuclear arsenal expected after the turn of the century. It is also at odds with U.S. policy to have the Russians remove surplus nuclear explosives from *their* military stockpile, and it weakens the moral force of U.S. appeals for the Nuclear Nonproliferation Treaty to be made permanent when it comes up for renewal in 1995....

Chris Whipple, chairman of the National Research Council's Board on Radioactive Waste Management, observes that, "By bringing the plutonium and the spent fuel to the same repository, you would be taking a further step toward international management of the spent fuel as well. The technical challenges are slightly different but the overall requirements for secure isolation of spent fuel, high-level waste, and weapons plutonium seem to be similar. I can't see anything but merit in the idea."

Princeton University's Frank von Hippel, a leading arms control expert recently appointed assistant director for national security in the White House Office of Science and Technology Policy, personally would prefer to see plutonium blended with high-level waste (HLW) for glassification and permanent geologic disposal. But he believes that retrievable storage, with the containers of plutonium placed together with canisters of HLW in the same storage casks, would be a "good compromise" with those (including Russian nuclear specialists) who believe that some day the plutonium will be valuable as a fuel for reactors.

CHANGING THE POLITICAL DYNAMIC IN NEVADA

There is, to say the least, the possibility of a wholly negative and outraged response by the state of Nevada to a federal initiative designating the NTS as the national center for storage of spent fuel, high-level waste, and surplus warhead plutonium. Indeed, state leaders in Nevada have been able to profit politically by crying "Never!" They spurn all federal efforts to enlist state cooperation and point to opinion polls showing that a large majority of Nevadans are opposed to nuclear waste storage at Yucca Mountain, never mind their own considerable part in shaping that opinion.

Nevada's Sen. Richard Bryan and Governor Miller, in particular, have told their constituents that the so-called waste dump is not inevitable, that time is on the state's side in opposing the Yucca Mountain project, and that appeals to negotiate for federal benefits in return for state cooperation must be flatly rejected. The Republican majority leader of the Nevada Senate and several other legislators actually would welcome such negotiations, but on this issue Bryan and

Miller have kept them in the minority and on the defensive.

Yet Nevadans know that, despite all its problems, the Yucca Mountain project has persisted and, with exploratory drilling soon to begin, may gain a new momentum. They also realize that, in the end, Nevada could have the repository but no benefits and no real part in deciding the outcome of safety issues.

Congress could break up the political dynamic that has favored all-out state resistance by declaring unequivocally that the NTS is to become the nation's center for nuclear storage and by directing that a spent-fuel surface storage facility be built and ready to operate by 1998. Elected state officials might suddenly find their political survival in jeopardy unless they are resourceful in having the state gain a critical but seriously constructive and well-rewarded role with respect to such nuclear storage.

To make the project more palatable, Congress could give Nevada and the counties principally affected a significant new place in the nuclear storage program. They could, for example, be invited to appoint a number of appropriately qualified scientists and engineers to product design teams. They might also be allowed a leading role in setting up a Nevada-based, but rigorously independent, project oversight agency similar to New Mexico's highly respected Environmental Evaluation Group (EEG), which oversees, and has significantly influenced, DOE's Waste Isolation Pilot Plant project—a geologic repository near Carlsbad for low-level plutonium-contaminated waste from past production of nuclear weapons. For emergencies, a Nevada EEG might be given authority to stop further loading of nuclear materials or even order the retrieval of materials already emplaced. Nevada has long had a nuclear waste project oversight group but, being answerable to the governor, it is far too politicized to have scientific credibility.

Nuclear storage at the NTS could also be made more palatable by joint federal/state high-technology ventures bringing Nevada important economic benefits. The expected loss of thousands of jobs from the ending of nuclear weapons testing is already cause for deep apprehension among some labor groups in southern Nevada and would be felt by the larger regional economy. To counter this disturbing trend, a Nevada Technology Development Trust could be established with money from the Nuclear Waste Fund, which is now collecting well over a half-billion dollars a year from a fee imposed on nuclear electricity....

Nevada, it should be noted, not so very long ago viewed nuclear storage as an opportunity, not a scourge. In 1977, faced with the threat of job losses due to a proposed nuclear test ban, the Nevada Legislature actually petitioned to have nuclear waste stored at the NTS. This receptive attitude did not, in the main, survive the national uproar over repository siting in the 1980s. Even today, however, rural counties in and around the NTS do not, by and large, go along with the state's categorical rejection of the Yucca Mountain project. For these counties, the critical considerations are whether the project can be built safely and whether the state and federal governments will respect their interests. What Congress and the Clinton administration have an opportunity to do now is to act firmly to give the NTS a new nuclear storage mission while letting all Nevadans know that, in carrying out this mission, the government will indeed respect their legitimate interests.

POSTSCRIPT

Nuclear Waste: Should Plans for Underground Storage Be Put on Hold?

Carter claims that U.S. Geological Survey scientists are convinced that a repository built at Yucca Mountain can be kept dry. As Lenssen points out, other scientists disagree with this conclusion and fear that a future rise in the water table could disperse the stored waste. Carter acknowledges that local opposition is one of the key problems with the present plan, but he doesn't fully explain why expanding the proposal to include a much larger quantity of nuclear waste would make it politically more viable.

Nevada's former governor Richard Bryan's outspoken rejection of the congressional decision to designate Yucca Mountain as the permanent storage site set the stage for the state's continued opposition. For an elaboration of Bryan's arguments read his article "The Politics and Promises of Nuclear Waste Disposal: The View from Nevada," *Environment* (October 1987).

A very pessimistic assessment of the effort to resolve the low-level waste problem is contained in "The Deadliest Garbage of All," by Susan Q. Stranahan, *Science Digest* (April 1986).

On the optimistic side is a report by researchers George Wicks and Dennis Bickford entitled "Doing Something About High-Level Nuclear Waste," *Technology Review* (November/December 1989). They describe the process of "glassifying" nuclear waste, which they claim is the key to permanent safe disposal. (Glassifying means to form a glass that incorporates the radioactive metallic ions and thereby immobilizes them; this would prevent leaching.)

A scandal has erupted concerning nuclear waste issues related to the U.S. nuclear weapons program. For an account of this problem, which predates the publicity given to recent revelations, see William F. Lawless's article "Problems With Military Nuclear Waste," *Bulletin of the Atomic Scientists* (November 1985). In "Hanford Cleanup: Explosive Solution," published in the October 1990 issue of the same journal, environmental researchers Scott Saleska and Arjun Makhijani present a frightening assessment of ongoing nuclear waste storage and treatment practices at the large military nuclear reservation in Hanford, Washington. Equally distressing is the history of incompetence in building the Waste Isolation Pilot Plant in New Mexico for permanent storage of military nuclear waste, as told by Keith Schneider in "Wasting Away," *The New York Times Magazine* (August 30, 1992). For a chilling expose of the hazardous nuclear waste disposal practices of the former Soviet Union, see William Broad's article, which begins on the front page of the November 21, 1994, issue of the *New York Times*.

PART 4

The Environment and the Future

In addition to the many serious environmental problems of today, there are several potential future crises that might be averted or diminished if preventive measures are taken now: the destruction of tropical rain forests, which play a life-sustaining role in the biosphere; pollution of the atmosphere, which could raise the average global temperature or destroy much of the protective ozone layer; and the continued use of developmental strategies based on nonsustainable technologies, which could deplete resources, increase pollution, and exacerbate world hunger.

- Can Incentives Devised by Industrial Nations Combat Tropical Deforestation?

- Do the Projected Consequences of Ozone Depletion Justify Phasing Out Chlorofluorocarbons?

- Are Aggressive International Efforts Needed to Slow Global Warming?

- Are Major Changes Needed to Avert a Global Environmental Crisis?

ISSUE 15

Can Incentives Devised by Industrial Nations Combat Tropical Deforestation?

YES: Martin T. Katzman and William G. Cale, Jr., from "Tropical Forest Preservation Using Economic Incentives," *BioScience* (December 1990)

NO: Hannah Finan Roditi and James B. Goodno, from "Rainforest Crunch: Combating Tropical Deforestation," *Dollars and Sense* (November 1990)

ISSUE SUMMARY

YES: Economist Martin T. Katzman and science and mathematics dean William G. Cale, Jr., propose a scheme whereby a consortium of industrialized nations would develop, fund, and help administer an economic incentive program they claim could preserve tropical forests at a reasonable cost.

NO: *Dollars and Sense* editorial associate Hannah Finan Roditi and staff editor James B. Goodno emphasize the importance of grassroots tactics and the involvement of representatives of indigenous populations in creating equitable plans to combat tropical deforestation.

The area of the Earth that is covered by forests has decreased by approximately 33 percent as a result of human activity. The clearing of land for crop production or animal grazing, the harvesting of timber, and the gathering of wood for fuel have been the principal human activities that have shrunk the world's forests.

Rapid regional decimation of tree cover is not a new phenomenon. By the end of the eighteenth century, France had cleared almost 85 percent of its forested land over a period of less than two centuries. Other contemporary industrialized countries, including the United States, have engaged in wholesale deforestation. Until recently, however, these practices have had relatively minor deleterious effects on human welfare.

Today, hundreds of millions of poor people in South and Central America, Africa, and Asia find their principal source of fuel for cooking and home heating threatened by the accelerating clear-cutting of tropical forests. Natives of the forested areas are being uprooted and driven from their only available source of sustenance. The economic forces that promote this plague are large lumbering, cattle ranching, and land speculation entrepreneurs. The beneficiaries include foreign investors as well as local elites with strong ties to the entrenched minority who maintain political control in much of the developing world.

The problem is exacerbated by the displaced forest dwellers who contribute to Third World urbanization. In the cities charcoal, which is easier to transport, replaces wood as the predominant fuel. In the process of converting wood to charcoal, half of the fuel value of the wood is lost. Thus the movement of rural villagers to city slums results in a doubling of per capita fuel wood needs.

The recognition that as much as one-third of the annual contribution to the increase in atmospheric carbon dioxide, which contributes to global warming, comes from deforestation has greatly heightened worldwide concern about forest depletion. (The global warming connection is a result of the fact that the cutting and combustion of trees release carbon dioxide that would only be balanced by an equal number of new trees removing that same amount of carbon dioxide as they grow.) Since global warming is an issue of universal concern, there is hope among environmentalists that it will serve to mobilize the enormous number of people needed to save the forests.

Tropical forests supply many useful commercial products and are the source of a wide variety of chemicals, including natural products that are used in the pharmaceutical industry. Among the serious consequences of rain forest destruction would be the loss of a principal source of organic chemicals used in medical research.

Among the proposals for halting tropical deforestation are various plans whereby funds are provided by the governments, entrepreneurs, or financial institutions of industrial nations in exchange for some form of agreement by the governments and institutions of developing nations to take action to preserve their forests. One such proposal is offered by research economist Martin T. Katzman and university math and science dean William G. Cale, Jr., who claim that it could protect 10 percent of Brazil's rain forest at a cost of only a 2 percent increase in present foreign aid. Hannah Finan Roditi and James B. Goodno are on the editorial staff of *Dollars and Sense* magazine and have each written a book on the economic problems of a developing tropical country. They are concerned that economic plans developed in the industrialized world to save tropical forests are doomed to failure because they often ignore the real needs and conditions of the indigenous people of the forested areas.

YES

Martin T. Katzman and William G. Cale, Jr.

TROPICAL FOREST PRESERVATION USING ECONOMIC INCENTIVES

The destruction of tropical forests, long a source of alarm to professional ecologists and environmental activists, has been of increasing public concern in Western industrial nations. Citizens of industrial nations often respond to the phenomenon of tropical deforestation with pedagogical or moral exhortation: If only we could explain the long-term consequences to the people of the tropics.... If only tropical citizens could be more responsible (than we were).

In fact, deforestation is the result of innumerable individual decisions that are rational on a small scale (e.g., subsistence farming, ranching, or lumbering for profit), even though the consequences are irrational on the large scale (e.g., alteration of hydrological patterns, effects on global climate, or reduction of biodiversity). Any attempt to stanch tropical deforestation must recognize the economic basis of these decisions and change the incentive structure that generates them.

Whereas ecologists and environmentalists often view economics as an apology for environmental degradation, this article shows how economic analysis can provide useful insights into policies to protect specific rainforest habitats. We begin by framing the problem of deforestation in economic terms and presenting a discussion of some of the limitations of existing proposals to reduce deforestation. Next, we offer a proposal for a system of conservation easements that can overcome these limitations. Finally, we give an example to indicate the order-of-magnitude costs for a plan to preserve 10% of Amazonia.

FRAMING THE PROBLEM IN ECONOMIC TERMS

The basic problem of tropical deforestation can be stated simply. Habitat destruction in the tropical rain forests is proceeding at an average annual rate of 100,000–200,000 km², an area the size of England. The tropics contain a disproportionate share of the world's species, many endemic to tiny habitats. Above and beyond the species they comprise, tropical forest habitats offer several classes of local and global values: hydrological, in preventing soil erosion and downstream siltation, and climatological, in maintaining local precipitation and the atmospheric balance of gases.

Rather than exhorting the inhabitants of tropical nations to cease and desist in deforestation, it is necessary to understand the underlying pattern of their material interests in order to alter their destructive behavior. For analysis, we assume that tropical governments place no value on forest protection per se. Many tropical nations have, of course, formally established forest reserves in response to international concerns and alarms about ecological destruction sounded by native scholars. We cannot assume, however, that the degree to which these reserves are actually protected fully reflects interests of the global population.

The Winners

We begin by identifying winning and losing interests in the tropical nation where deforestation occurs and in the rest of the world. There are large gains from deforestation to narrowly circumscribed producer groups in tropical nations. These groups include ranchers in Latin America and loggers in Southeast Asia, who produce mainly for the market. The population growth of subsistence farmers provides the main pressure on forests in Africa, and this pressure is increasing in Latin America and Asia. In terms of output value per unit of land, ranching uses far more land than logging, mining, or agriculture.

For the winning interests in tropical nations, the activities resulting in defor-estation can result in extremely large increases in income, compared with using the land otherwise. A small number of individuals enjoying intense gains are often able to protect these interests by obtaining favors and concessions from the state, even if their activities impose aggregate losses to a diffuse, larger group within the same state. An example is the granting of tax concessions by the Brazilian government for ranching in Amazonia.

In addition, there are diffuse market-mediated gains from deforestation in nontropical nations, whose consumers obtain cheaper food, fiber, and building materials. By diffuse gains, we mean that a reduction in the export of these tropical products would not greatly lower the current material standard of living to each of these consumers.

We can illustrate the diffuseness of gains to the industrial world with the case of timber from Southeast Asia, the region where deforestation for logging is most pronounced. The world's three largest exporters—Malaysia, Indonesia, and the Philippines—exported approximately $3 billion worth of timber during the 1980s. These sources account for approximately 12% of the imports of all wood products into advanced, industrial nations.

These trade figures inflate the importance of these exporters to the world's supply. Total world production (and consumption) of industrial roundwood, sawn wood, and panels was approximately 2.1 billion cubic meters in the 1980s. Combined production of these materials in these three nations is only 85 million cubic meters, approximately 4% of the world supply. If Southeast Asian wood exports were to decline by, say, half, the impact on the world wood supply system would be relatively small. Industrialized countries in East Asia would have to obtain wood supplies from non-tropical sources, and the consumption of wood substitutes would rise.

A similar argument can be made about the diffuseness of the gains to advanced countries from meat exports from tropical Latin America. Imports of meat into advanced industrial countries from Brazil, only some of which comes from Amazonia, comprise only 3% of total meat imports into advanced industrial countries. The value of meat imports from Brazil, approximately $450 million, is similar to those from Argentina and Taiwan, nations without tropical rain forests. The reduction in meat exports from tropical Latin America would induce expansion in nontropical regions, in net, scarcely denting the world meat supply.

The Losers
Tropical deforestation produces losses among the citizens of the tropical nations. The displacement of powerless nationals, such as indigenous people or poor peasants, has been a common theme in Latin American development. Even if the losses to these citizens outweigh the gains to interests engaged in deforestation, the losers lack the power to induce the winners to desist.

Other losers, most relevant to our analysis, are inhabitants of advanced, industrial nations. Through tropical deforestation, they forgo aesthetic-moral, scientific, climatological, and economic option values. The relevance of these losers is their economic power to change the incentives of parties engaged in deforestation.

An Economic Approach
In economic terms, tropical deforestation imposes external diseconomies on the remaining inhabitants of the globe. (A diseconomy results from factors that increase cost, or decrease value, and are not compensated in the marketplace. An external diseconomy is a cost borne by those not directly involved in the activity creating the diseconomy. Exploitation of a common resource is a familiar example.)

To correct for external diseconomies, the economic approach relies little on education or moral suasion, no matter how desirable these efforts may be. Rather, the economic approach seeks ways to internalize external diseconomies by compensation, creating incentives for alternative behavior. If the polluter always paid, the parties responsible for deforestation would compensate the rest of the world for the lost aesthetic, scientific, climatological, and economic option values. Because no supranational government can enforce such compensation, we must rely on the opposite flow of funds: the losers in advanced industrial nations compensate the winners in the tropical nations to desist. We envision state-to-state agreements, although arrangements between private parties or nongovernmental organizations are not ruled out.

Any compensation must be subject to several constraints. First, tropical nations are sovereign. They will not willingly accept intervention into their internal matters, especially any roadblock to their definition of development. Any agreement must therefore be voluntary, and must also raise the tropical nation's welfare, defined in its own terms.

Second, many tropical nations are politically unstable. International agreements made by one regime may be conveniently repudiated by a successor. Workable agreements must give both parties a continuing incentive to maintain the contract.

The third constraint may pose the greatest difficulty. An agreement to refrain from cutting forests is a restriction on property rights. These rights in tropical forests may be poorly defined and costly to enforce. For one, overlapping claims to a given parcel are common in sparsely settled regions of Latin America. Furthermore, traditional hunter-gatherers and other native people may assume rights to harvest the forest on a sustainable basis without claiming the right to transform the forest. Finally, poachers may treat forests as common property to be exploited and transformed as they wish.

SUGGESTED SYSTEMS AND THEIR LIMITATIONS

The most noteworthy schemes for protecting specific habitats and for preserving a certain proportion of the tropical forest are debt-for-nature swaps, public-private partnerships, extraction reserves, and the Tropical Forest Action Plan. Each has its advantages and limitations.

Debt-for-Nature Swaps

The debt of developing countries with poor credit ratings sells for a few cents on the dollar. In several instances, conservation groups have bought a nation's debt and turned it back in exchange for the country agreeing to conservation measures. This approach has some serious disadvantages.

In one transaction, a conservation group bought $650,000 of Bolivia's debt on the secondary market for approximately $39,000. In exchange for turning the debt back to Bolivia, the country pledged to establish a reserve. But we are worried because, first, there was no provision for enforcement of property rights.

Second, if population or economic pressures heightened in the near future, leaders in such an unstable political system may have little reluctance to repudiate an agreement with a foreign-influenced conservation group, especially an agreement of so little continuing benefit.

On a large scale, debt-for-nature swaps are not attractive to debtor nations. One attempt to buy a total debt of $37 million resulted in bidding up the price 11 cents on the dollar. After the prices rose, the remaining debt was still valued at approximately $35 million, although the face value of the virtually unpayable debt was cut in half.

Public-Private Partnerships

There are interesting possibilities for nongovernmental organizations to employ market incentives to offset deforestation. For example, a Connecticut electric utility has dedicated $2 million to plant enough trees in Guatemala to offset the carbon dioxide releases from coal combustion. However, this is not strictly a scheme of habitat preservation, but rather reforestation.

Among the most praiseworthy public-private partnerships is University of Pennsylvania professor Daniel Janzen's effort to restore a dry tropical forest in Costa Rica. Working with Costa Rican officials and citizen groups, Janzen has obtained donations from private citizens to purchase grazing land for incorporation into Guanacaste National Park, which has been delineated by the government. Part of the success owes to the broad domestic constituency established for the park. The inherently beautiful area is accessible for recreational purposes. Costa Rica's large middle class is ecologically sensitive and supports instruction in the school curriculum on the nation's ecological heritage. Reforestation provides Costa Ricans with tangible benefits and an incentive to support the enforcement of the public's property rights in the park against poachers.

Remote areas in rain forests like Amazonia lack these bases of support; they offer less-tangible recreational or scenic advantages. Although admirable, the Guanacaste model does not solve the free-rider problem. A relatively few individuals or firms with intense interest in forest preservation or reforestation are providing global benefits. Such models can only operate on a small scale. The problem is to bring all of the beneficiaries into the circle of contributors.

Extractive Reserves

Zoning can limit certain areas of tropical forests to sustainable extractive use. For example, rubber tappers in Brazil have proposed restricting exploitation of the forests to traditional technologies. While providing protection for relatively powerless inhabitants such as rubber tappers, extractive reserves do not guarantee the interests of the global population.

The protection of the powerless depends on the beneficence of the state, and the state may have little material incentive to restrict conversion of the forest to other uses if the opportunities arise. Experience suggests that such beneficence is unreliable. At any time, a tropical state may protect its virgin forests for a wide variety of internal reasons, such as maintenance of natural systems or falling export prices. The losses and gains to the global population do not necessarily play a role in such internal decision making about forest policy.

Tropical Forest Action Plan

The World Resources Institute in Washington, DC, has stimulated the development of a Tropical Forest Action Plan (TFAP) that is being supported by several multilateral institutions, led by the Food and Agricultural Organization and the World Bank. On a country-by-country basis, TFAP initiates a process that brings together potential donor nations, multilateral institutions, and nongovernmental organizations on one side of the table with agencies from a developing country on the other. Projects ranging from industrial forestry to watershed reforestation, fuelwood production, and nature conservation are explored. Forest preservation projects may include transferring public property to a conservation agency and the support for enforcing conservation efforts.

It is too early to determine the success of TFAP as an instrument of habitat preservation. Achieving goals such as developing sustainable, industrialized forestry or fuelwood production is no guarantee. For the habitat-preservation objective to be achieved, there must be continuing financial inducements. The following proposal spells out the details of such an inducement.

A CONSERVATION EASEMENT PROPOSAL

We propose a set of institutions for overcoming the limitations of current approaches to preserving tropical habitats. One party to the proposal is a consortium of industrialized nations, perhaps an existing group such as the Organization for Economic Cooperation and Development. As in an earlier proposal of Rubinoff, the consortium would compensate individual tropical nations for protecting specific habitats. Unlike Rubinoff's, this proposal emphasizes five institutional keys to success:

- Tropical nations establish a legal distinction between conservation easements and other claims of ownership to forests.
- Industrialized nations evaluate, and establish priorities for, habitats globally.
- Each tropical nation establishes an offering price for conservation easements on various habitats.
- Industrialized nations agree to a budget for the acquisition of easements and for enforcement.
- A foundation is established in each tropical nation to administer the financial transfer.

Let us consider how this system would work with the voluntary cooperation of tropical nations.

Creating the Legal Concept of Conservation Easement

Zoning laws have traditionally recognized the right to develop urban land at different levels of intensity. In the past few decades, similar concepts were extended to rural areas in the form of the conservation easement. In exchange for a payment, a farmer forgoes the right to develop land at a higher intensity.

The public purpose of the easement is to protect open space. In the context of tropical forests, granting an easement allows the traditional use of the forest by indigenous people or others on a self-sustaining, extractive basis, but it forbids the clear-cutting of trees. Unlike an extraction reserve, where the easement is implicitly held by the tropical state, the conservation easement is granted to a foundation. A conservation easement can be granted in perpetuity or for a fixed term. We envision a minimal period of 50 years, which may allow the development of technological substitutes for rainforest products.

Setting Priorities for Habitats

The preservation value of all rainforest habitats is not necessarily equal. Because funds are unlikely to be available to preserve all habitats, priorities must be set. The consortium of industrialized nations may delegate the task of rank ordering to ecologists. Obviously, these rankings have to be performed under considerable time pressure in the absence of full information about all the potential habitats. Nevertheless, the task is not impossible. For example, Jacobs suggests assigning greater value to habitats that show large intraspecies variation in tree diameter, high species diversity, and mixture of topographic and soil types; that are proven Pleistocene refugia; and that serve as migration routes. Brazilian ecologists have implemented a similar scheme of prioritizing habitats.

Ultimately, these rankings must be converted into a willingness of industrial nations to pay for conservation easements. It has long been recognized that, however one sets priorities, the final decisions must be based primarily on human understanding. No formal ranking system can evaluate subjective values such as biodiversity, climax condition, or perceived worth 50 years hence. Ranking is important as an aid in making choices, but, in the end, establishing a willingness-to-pay does not require formal cost-benefit analysis.

Setting an Offering Price

Independent of the consortium's evaluation, the tropical state establishes an offering price for easements on various habitats. The offering price includes compensation for granting the easement and the cost of enforcement. The state may wish to exclude from the preservation program a wide swath of its rainforest that it wishes to develop for strategic or economic reasons. Each tropical nation then makes a bona fide offer of these easements to the consortium.

The offering price for a habitat is likely to be proportional to its perceived developmental value. The developmental value of a given habitat depends on natural resources (such as oil fertility or mineral riches), population pressure, and transportation access. Many colonization schemes in the tropics have gone bankrupt because of low yields and high transportation costs for imported inputs and exported outputs. With the improvement of rail and highway transportation, the developmental value of all habitats should rise. The implementation of sustainable agroecosystems should also raise these values.

Setting a Budget

To begin, the consortium establishes a budget for the purchase and protection of 50-year easements. The apportionment among the contributors may be based on such indicators as gross national product, population, or United Nations assessments.

Given the budget constraint and the habitat prioritization, the consortium compares the tropical state's offering price and its own willingness to pay for each habitat. The difference between the two is termed the *global ecological profit* of each habitat. In decreasing order of profitability, the consortium then accepts the offers until the budget is exhausted....

Administering the Funds

Each tropical nation establishes a tripartite foundation, with representatives of the nontropical donors, the tropical state, and multilateral organizations. The foundation is to receive funds for the easement and for enforcement.

On reaching a bargain, the capital for the easement and its enforcement is deposited in a multilateral bank. When the protection of the preserve by the tropical nation has been certified each year, an annuity (some capital plus annual interest) is released to the foundation. If the foundation were held strictly liable for damages to the preserve, the consortium could reduce its annuity by, say, double the amount of the damages.

The preservation agreement can permit continued extraction on a traditional basis, the construction of recreational trails, or the establishment of basic scientific research stations. In addition, the foundation can sell research rights to commercial chemical and pharmaceutical companies. The disposition of the annuity transferred through the foundation to the tropical government is an internal matter.

Enforcement is the most serious problem plaguing current proposals for tropical forest preservation. In a sparsely populated area, the management of a guard force is difficult, and collusion between poachers and guards is a cause of concern. Jacobs notes that in Southeast Asia the value of a tree can exceed the monthly salary of a guard. Conceivably, the cost of enforcement can exceed the cost of the easement itself. For example, economic pressures to develop coca production on the periphery of Amazonia render the enforcement of any easements prohibitively costly there.

There is an important purpose in transferring funds to the tropical state annually instead of as a lump sum. The annuity overcomes the problem of repudiation of agreements with unstable governments. Also, the annuity gives the tropical state a continuing interest in enforcing the easement.

EASEMENT: AN EXAMPLE

Brazilian Amazonia consists of 370 million hectares. In 1980, approximately 41 million hectares in the region were incorporated into agricultural, pastoral, or silvicultural enterprises. Only approximately 10 million hectares, approximately 3% of the area, were cleared of forest by these enterprises. In the 1980s, as much as 23 million hectares may have been cleared in Brazil, much of this in Amazonia. Approximately 90% of the region remains forested in 1990. Let us consider the cost of preserving 10% of Amazonia.

Easement Acquisition Costs

The developmental value of habitats depends on natural resources and transportation costs. The developmental value of Amazonia can be calculated by comparing the value of land in agriculture, broadly defined, with the value of land in virgin forest.

The market value of land in agriculture is the expected discounted value of the stream of annual profits from the raising of crops and animals and the planting of trees. These annual profits are the difference between the value of outputs and the value of inputs. The shorter the life expectancy of the agricultural

system, the lower will be the land value. The market value of land in forest is the extractive value of the forest (i.e., collection of tree products and associated subsistence cultivation). The difference between the two values is the maximal private gain that could be achieved if forest were transformed into agriculture.

The developmental value of Amazonia can be calculated from market values of land, which are meaningful only in areas of greatest developmental pressure. In 1984, the median price of pasture and arable land in Brazilian Amazonia was approximately $140/ha, whereas the median value of virgin forest was approximately $40/ha. These data suggest that if sufficient transportation investments were made to transform forest into arable land, land values would increase by $100/ha at most. This figure is an upper bound, because more remote forests have lower values in both agriculture and extraction.

A more direct measure of developmental value is provided by Fearnside, who notes that annual profits from ranching in Para, a fairly accessible Amazonian subregion, were approximately $10–$20/ha (in 1985 dollars) in the early 1970s. Because of the rapid degradation of land under contemporary ranching techniques and the necessity for compensating fertilizers, profits rapidly disappear after approximately 5 years. This calculation suggests that $100/ha is the right order of magnitude. These private gains overestimate the narrow economic benefits to Brazilian society, which bears the costs of building the access roads. Private developers may gain even more than $100/ha if they forcibly expel rather than compensate the population engaged in extraction, as has often happened to indigenous people, rubber tappers, and subsistence farmers. At $100/ha, preserving 10% of Brazilian Amazonia (37 million hectares) should cost at most $3.7 billion.

Under the proposal, these funds would not be transferred immediately to the tropical nation. Funds would be disbursed in annual payments, contingent on protection of the easement by the host nation. Financially, this plan resembles receiving an inheritance or a retirement income as an annuity. In this case, Brazil receives $203 million a year for 50 years.

Enforcement Costs

The cost of enforcement is probably proportional to developmental pressure. In areas of great accessibility, fertility, or alluvial gold, the foundation would have to fend off invasions of poachers, squatters, and rogue ranchers.

The Brazilian government estimated a need for approximately 120 guards and 120 other supervisory personnel for the 2,000,000-hectare Araguaia National Park, which faces heavy developmental pressure. This ratio of approximately one protector per 10,000 hectares may be too low. Amerindian tribes in the Amazon generally protect, with only modest success, habitats of approximately 250 thousand hectares, a ratio of one adult male per 1000 hectares. Nevertheless, these numbers provide an order-of-magnitude estimate of the personnel requirements.

The minimal wage in Amazonia is approximately $2500/year. Let us assume that a guard earning this wage can patrol 100 hectares. At $2.50/ha, annual enforcement costs are nearly $100 million for the target area. Over 50 years, the current discounted value of enforcement costs is approximately $1.7 bil-

lion. The annualized value would be $93 million.

Basic Research Costs

Basic research is not essential to the success of preservation, but it can clarify the value of continued preservation beyond the 50-year horizon of the easement. Wilson provides rough-and-ready figures for calculating research costs. Although no one knows how many of the world's species are unique to Amazonia, 3 million is not out of the question. If one biologist can catalog 20 species per year, then 3000 scientists working for 50 years can catalog 3 million Amazonian species.

At $100,000 support per scientist, the annual cost may be $300 million simply for cataloging species. Over 50 years, the discounted current cost of this research is approximately $5.5 billion. Costs might be cut dramatically by training researchers from the tropical nations and employing local people as ethnobiologists. Research on how these species interact in the ecosystem, however, would cost even more.

CONCLUSIONS

The proposed scheme assumes that it is necessary to transfer resources from developed industrial nations to developing tropical nations to provide incentives for rainforest preservation. It confronts the difficult problem of providing continuing incentives to enforce conservation easements.

An analysis of the costs of preservation can put them into perspective. The cost of easement acquisition and protection for 10% of Brazilian Amazonia might incur an annual cost as high as $300 million. Undertaking related research might cost another $300 million. The annual grants of industrial nations to the developing nations is approximately $25 billion. Therefore, the proposed scheme would increase foreign aid expenditures by a mere 2%. This is quite a bargain for the world.

ACKNOWLEDGMENTS

The authors thank Thomas Eisner, Robert Goodland, Daniel H. Janzen, Donald Jones, Waud Kracke, Emilio Moran, Marianne Schmink, and Charles Wood for comments on an earlier draft.

NO

Hannah Finan Roditi
and James B. Goodno

RAINFOREST CRUNCH: COMBATING TROPICAL DEFORESTATION

Fire, chainsaws, and bulldozers consume tens of thousands of square miles of tropical forests each year, wiping out more than a hundred species of animals and plants daily. From Brazil to the Philippines, from Sub-Saharan Africa to the South Pacific, more than 40% of the earth's rainforests have been cleared since 1960.

Activists and some government officials in the South and North now realize that this rapid destruction threatens to wipe out precious natural resources and eventually to undermine whole Third World economies, and they are doing something about it. Grassroots tactics confronting deforestation include consumer boycotts, lobbying development agencies, marketing alternative forest products, and struggling for new forms of land tenure.

Pressure has built to the point where even the World Bank, the U.S. Agency for International Development (AID), and the United Nations are finally paying considerable attention to the plight of the forests. But the official agencies are still doing more harm than good, and further change will depend on continued grassroots action.

A PLAN THAT ISN'T

More than any single organization, the World Bank has solicited and received praise for placing environmental concerns on the front burner. Yet scores of grassroots groups from various countries North and South have sharply criticized the World Bank's efforts. They say the Bank has encouraged widespread logging, clearing of forests for plantations and cattle ranches, construction of roads into previously pristine forests, and damming of rivers running through the jungles. *Outside,* an outdoor recreation magazine, has labelled the Bank "perhaps the greatest global rainforest villain."

The centerpiece of the World Bank's effort has been the Tropical Forestry Action Plan (TFAP), a program developed in 1985 by the U.N. Food and Agriculture Organization (FAO), the Bank, and the World Resources Institute,

From Hannah Finan Roditi and James B. Goodno, "Rainforest Crunch: Combating Tropical Deforestation," *Dollars and Sense* (November 1990). Copyright © 1990 by *Dollars and Sense.* Reprinted by permission. *Dollars and Sense* is a progressive economics magazine published six times a year. First-year subscriptions cost $18.95 and may be ordered by writing to *Dollars and Sense*, 1 Summer St., Somerville, MA 02143.

a Washington, D.C., environmental think tank. Administered by the FAO, TFAP is supposed to provide participating states with funding, technical assistance, and a rough model for forest management.

The basic assumption behind TFAP is that timber industries can sustain forests adequately by practicing selective logging, revegetating cleared lands, and introducing industrial forestry, which replaces naturally diverse forests with single-species tree farms.

Financial support for the $8 billion TFAP program comes from the World Bank, related regional development banks, U.S. AID, and its counterparts in other industrialized nations. Since 1985, 73 tropical countries have expressed interest in participating in TFAP, while eight have formally adopted national forestry plans guided by the TFAP model.

But looking at national plans developed under the auspices of TFAP, critics question whether many of the schemes are sincere attempts at conservation. To start with, they encourage practices that contribute to heavy deforestation. In addition, architects of the plans emphasize commercial solutions that would satisfy the biggest corporations, largely ignoring options to take the land off the market or to address the needs of indigenous forest dwellers who harvest nuts, fruits, and medicinal plants to make a living. Lacking confidence in TFAP, many environmentalists are both pushing to reform the model and working toward solutions of their own.

The level of deforestation allowed by some TFAP-guided plans appalls environmentalists. A plan for the Ivory Coast, for example, provided funding for logging half the country's remaining forest, says Alex Hittle of the environmental organization Friends of the Earth (United States). A study by the Malaysia-based World Rainforest Movement, an international coalition of anti-deforestation groups, says Peru's plan calls for increasing logging five to seven fold in that country's Amazon region, while a Nepalese proposal would increase industrial forestry in the Himalayas by 250%.

In a 1988 survey, the Sierra Club found that banks funneled close to 70% of their loans for national TFAPs to the timber industry, while fewer than 20% were devoted to conservation, watershed protection, or clearly sustainable activities like agro-forestry.

TFAP has also come under criticism for its refusal to challenge existing patterns of land-ownership or involve grassroots organizations in planning. Its "only way of valuing the forest is to benefit the big companies," says Larry Lohmann, an author of the study by the World Rainforest Movement (WRM).

Notably excluded from the planning have been indigenous or long-time forest dwellers who make their living harvesting non-timber forest products, running small farms, or tapping rubber. Instead, the plans result from collaboration between Third World aristocracies and First World financial wizards.

"Many of the national plans ignore politically delicate issues such as the causes of landlessness—the main factor causing the rural poor to colonize the rainforests," write Larry Lohmann and Marcus Colchester. "Instead of challenging the present economic and political forces responsible for deforestation, the TFAP offered a 'business as usual' approach, which would divert efforts away from making radical changes in national land use policies." ...

The immediate aim of environmentalists seeking to reform TFAP is to challenge the leadership of the U.N. Food and Agriculture Organization. "We do not feel comfortable with the FAO in a leadership position," says Robert Winterbottom of the World Resources Institute. According to Winterbottom, pressure from Third World states seeking quick profit from selling timber has unduly influenced the FAO.

World Rainforest Movement's Colchester agrees TFAP cannot be reformed while it remains under the control of the FAO. He proposes a three-part international steering committee of funders, tropical country governments, and representatives of rural peoples in the Third World. The WRM has, in fact, called for a moratorium on all funds for TFAP activities pending its restructuring to address the main causes of deforestation and the lack of grassroots participation in planning.

Participants in the TFAP have not been completely deaf to criticism. The FAO has placed its role in TFAP on its agenda. And even the World Bank is holding up loans to the forestry sector while it reviews its policies.

But environmentalists, many of whom met in September to hammer out strategies and lobby the World Bank, are less than sanguine about the possibility of radically reforming Bank or FAO practices, believing, as Meg Ruby of Greenpeace says, "the record [of the World Bank] is abysmal." So while they push the authorities to change, they are also pursuing their own strategies.

ALTERNATIVES TO TFAP

Some First World activists opposed to large-scale logging and agro-forestry have promoted creative, though less far-reaching, commercial alternatives. One is to enlarge the market for non-timber forest products that are harvested by longtime forest dwellers and are gaining popularity in the North. These include resins and saps used in industrial glues and perfumes, fruits, nuts, medicinal plants, honey, mushrooms, rattan, and spices.

Already, there have been some success stories: Socially conscious traders and consumers have made a multimillionaire of Anita Roddick, owner of the Body Shop, a firm that markets perfumes derived from tropical oils and other nature-based cosmetics. Roddick says she has paid her suppliers "First World prices" for their commodities.

Cultural Survival, a Massachusetts-based advocate for indigenous people, plans to buy a thousand tons of Brazil nuts over the next year from Indians and rubber tappers in Brazil, Bolivia, and Peru. Many of the nuts will go to Community Products, a Vermont company that will use them to make Rainforest Crunch candy. The firm has promised to return 40% of its profits to rainforest protection efforts, says Jason Clay of Cultural Survival. Last year's profits were enough to finance the first local factory to shell nuts owned by the people who collect them, he says.

Advocates of trade in non-timber products argue this strategy can protect the forest while providing jobs and income to forest dwellers and tax revenue and foreign exchange to Third World governments. A recent study by researchers at the New York Botanical Garden points to the dramatic potential of harvesting the Amazon's renewable resources. It suggests long-term harvesting of non-timber products would yield two to three times as much income as commercial logging or ranching would.

Despite these attributes, this market-oriented approach has its dangers and limitations. Unfamiliar products can be hard to introduce, and once they start selling, large firms might take over. "Corporations will simply come and set up plantations of whatever product is successful," predicts Yoke Ling Chee, secretary of Malaysia's Friends of the Earth Organization. "More land will be cleared to create [plantations]; so the creation of demand in Western countries is not only doomed to failure, it is dangerous."

CONSUMER BOYCOTTS

Other activists have developed a different strategy to control the market—the consumer boycott of products sold by deforesters. The San Francisco-based Rainforest Action Network (RAN), a scrappy four-year old organization, often takes the lead in such campaigns in the United States. By deluging corporate headquarters with letters and leading boycotts, RAN and like-minded organizations have forced Burger King to halt beef imports from tropical ranches in Central America and stopped Scott Paper's attempt to establish a tree farm and pulp plant in Indonesia.

Despite this enviable record, the boycott strategy is also controversial. "It's likely to have a perverse market effect," warns Alex Hittle of Friends of the Earth. "A reduction in demand for tropical woods could cause prices to fall. If prices fall, standing forests become a less valuable resource, giving governments an incentive to convert land to agricultural uses." Instead, he argues, "we should aim to increase the value of standing timber to [encourage] more careful forest management."

To avoid conflict with Third World groups and to gain some control over the market, some environmental organizations, like Greenpeace, recommend integrating consumer action—such as boycotts and alternative product development—in the North with political activities in the South.

QUESTIONS OF CONTROL

In the Third World, questions of who will control the forest are central to conservation strategies. Activists in various countries advocate control by local people rather than outside interests or market dictates. Through concerted struggle, Amazonian Indians and rubber tapper unions compelled the Brazilian government to start deeding parts of the forest to indigenous groups and other forest dwellers in the late 1980s. Some Brazilians hail the so-called "extractive reserve" as a way to arrest deforestation while advancing the economic well-being of forest dwellers. Regulations generally limit harvests and ban logging and other destructive practices.

As the 1989 murder of labor leader Chico Mendes shows, advocates of the extractive reserve still must contend with violent opposition from local elites. Nevertheless, the rubber tappers and Indians have mustered enough strength to force the government to act. In one case, the state deeded 1.5 million acres of land in the Amazonian southwest to local inhabitants, creating the Mapia-Inui Extractive Reserve. While few expect the reserve to produce the sort of short-term income timber corporations expect to make, its managers hope it will ultimately benefit 600 families. Once completed, the reserve should make $3–4 million a year, without cutting one tree, says Paulo Robert Silva e Sousa, the reserve's general manager.

For the rubber tappers and Indians of the Amazon, the extractive reserve is but one part of a more comprehensive program for regional development and environmental protection. Other aspects of the program include: recognition of Indian and rubber tapper land rights, an end to debt peonage on large rubber estates, local authority over health and education, and the promotion of cooperatives and public investment in the processing of forest products.

The World Rainforest Movement deems several elements in this program essential to protecting tropical forests. "The most effective agents of change in what is happening to the tropical forests are the popular organizations in the Third World, whose increasing mobilization offers the best, some would say only, hope of checking the forces presently destroying the forests," points out Marcus Colchester.

Colchester believes Northern and international organizations still have a role to play, as long as they cooperate with people in the South. Outsiders can't save the rainforests without recognizing the needs of forest dwellers and their compatriots, he and others maintain.

"Tropical forests will never be protected if their continued existence is seen as a tradeoff for economic development of the people who live in tropical countries," agrees Robert Buschbacher, director of the World Wildlife Fund's Tropical Forestry Program.

In the short run, environmentalists and other activists have an array of tactics to choose from and, when appropriate, to mix and match. Marketing strategies in the North linked to land reform in the South and consumer boycotts coordinated by First World and Third World organizations are examples of cooperation that can help slow the pace of deforestation today. But to have a serious impact on the pace of deforestation, these efforts will have to be integrated into a new development strategy: One that recognizes the needs of Third World people.

POSTSCRIPT

Can Incentives Devised by Industrial Nations Combat Tropical Deforestation?

The struggle between Brazil's rubber tappers and ranchers trying to clear the forested area they occupy illustrates the need to consider the plight of indigenous people, which is the focus of Roditi and Goodno's skepticism about proposals such as the one offered by Katzman and Cale. The worldwide publicity that followed the murder of Chico Mendes in 1988 did much to popularize the plight of the Amazonian natives. Mendes, the leader of the rubber tappers, had established an international reputation as an effective nonviolent labor organizer and environmentalist before he was killed by ranchers opposed to his forest preservation efforts. "Whose Hands Will Shape the Future of the Amazon's Green Mansions?" is a very vivid and moving description of the struggle of the Brazilian rubber tappers by Michael Parfit, *Smithsonian* (November 1990). Unfortunately, Parfit is pessimistic about the chances that the Brazilian government's policy of "extractive reserves" will succeed. A more optimistic view of the chances for success in dealing with these issues in Brazil and countries facing similar problems, which builds on the discussions and actions at the recent Earth Summit in Rio de Janeiro, is presented by Sandra Hackman in "After Rio—Our Forests, Ourselves," *Technology Review* (October 1992).

"Sustaining the Amazon," by Marguerite Holloway, *Scientific American* (July 1993) examines the conflict between the inevitability of economic development and the need to preserve biodiversity. Increasing the economic value of forest products other than wood is a strategy explored by Holloway, as well as by Fred Pearce in "Brazil, Where the Ice Cream Comes From," *New Scientist* (July 7, 1990). Other proposals are included in "The Peruvian Experiment," by Scott Landis, *Wilderness* (Spring 1990); "Pardo's Law for Saving Tropical Forests" by Richard Pardo, *American Forests* (September/October 1990); and "Ecotourism: New Hope for Rainforests?" by Edward Warner, *American Forests* (March/April 1991).

Debt-for-nature swaps are a form of incentive program that Katzman and Cale reject as being unattractive to debtor nations. In their article in the June 1994 issue of the *Journal of Forestry*, Dana R. Visser and Guillermo A. Mendoza contend that the latest version of these programs have been much more successful and are designed to meet the objections raised by Roditi and Goodno, as well.

The importance of rain forests as a source of new medicinal substances derived from plants is the subject of "Rainforest Rx," by Joseph Wallace, *Sierra* (July/August 1991).

ISSUE 16

Do the Projected Consequences of Ozone Depletion Justify Phasing Out Chlorofluorocarbons?

YES: Mary H. Cooper, from "Ozone Depletion," *CQ Researcher* (April 3, 1992)

NO: Patricia Poore and Bill O'Donnell, from "Ozone," *Garbage: The Independent Environmental Quarterly* (September/October 1993)

ISSUE SUMMARY

YES: *CQ Researcher* staff writer Mary H. Cooper details the development, the theory, and the evidence that chlorofluorocarbons (CFCs) are depleting the ozone layer—an issue that has resulted in an extraordinary international effort to ward off the predicted health and environmental consequences.

NO: *Garbage* magazine's editor and publisher Patricia Poore and associate publisher Bill O'Donnell claim that their analysis of conflicting evidence leads to the conclusion that ozone depletion is not a crisis requiring an outright ban on CFCs.

In 1974 a short paper by M. J. Molina and F. S. Rowland was published in *Nature* magazine. Based on laboratory experiments, the paper warned of a potential threat to the stratospheric ozone layer resulting from the rapidly expanding use and release of a family of synthetic chemicals. This speculative prediction gave rise to an immediate controversy among the scientific, environmental, and industrial communities because of the essential role played by atmospheric ozone in shielding human beings, as well as other terrestrial flora and fauna, from the harmful effects of the high-energy ultraviolet radiation emitted by the sun.

The molecules in question, chlorofluorocarbons (CFCs), were developed by the chemical industry as inert, volatile nontoxic fluids. They have been used as the working fluids in refrigeration and air conditioning systems, as the propellants in pressurized spray cans for a variety of industrial and consumer products, as foaming agents for plastic foams, and as cleansing solvents in the electronics industry. Ultimately, CFCs find their way into the atmosphere where, because of their chemical inertness and insolubility in water, they neither decompose nor get washed out in rainfall. Molina and Rowland proposed that CFCs would, over a period of about a decade, rise to levels in the stratosphere where they would be exposed to the UV radiation that fails to reach the lower atmosphere because of ozone absorption. They would then photodecompose, producing atomic chlorine, which laboratory studies have shown would act as an effective catalytic agent in destroying ozone.

The predictions of Molina and Rowland met with much skepticism and stimulated intense activity on the part of scientists, particularly those associated with companies and industries that had a vested interest in selling or using CFCs, who tried to disprove the dire prediction of serious ozone depletion. Rowland has devoted much of his professional and private life to defending and substantiating his prediction as well as seeking an international response to the need to phase out the use of CFCs. Gradually, through both laboratory work and environmental sampling, data accumulated that supported the ozone depletion prediction and refuted proposed alternative mechanisms for the removal of CFCs from the atmosphere.

Predictions of the extent of ultimate ozone loss from the continued use of CFCs rose and fell as new data accumulated. Then in 1985 came definitive reports of large-scale seasonal losses of ozone over the Antarctic. Follow-up studies have resulted in a growing consensus that this effect is indeed a result of the increasing atmospheric concentrations of CFCs and related compounds. Furthermore, estimates of the health and environmental consequences (including increased incidence of human skin cancers and phytoplankton destruction) if CFC use is not drastically curtailed are again on the rise.

The ozone depletion problem is of global dimensions and requires a response based on international agreements that are difficult to achieve. The first action to reduce ozone destruction was the unilateral banning of CFCs in aerosol spray cans by the United States, Canada, and Scandinavia in 1976–1978. Stimulated by the Antarctic findings, international conferences on the problem have been held since 1985. In 1987, in Montreal, a landmark agreement was reached to phase out the use of ozone-depleting chemicals. Subsequent meetings have broadened the scope and hastened the timing of these actions.

Mary H. Cooper, a staff writer for *CQ Researcher* (published by Congressional Quarterly, Inc.), presents a detailed history of how the problems with chlorofluorocarbons were identified, and she explains the subsequent scientific findings that have resulted in the unprecedented international effort to ban CFCs. Patricia Poore and Bill O'Donnell, respectively the publisher and editor and associate publisher of *Garbage* magazine, assert that their "rational analysis of the facts" leads to the conclusion that ozone depletion is not an urgent crisis that justifies the economic disruption that will result from the planned rapid phaseout of ozone-depleting chemicals.

YES

Mary H. Cooper

OZONE DEPLETION

Scientists at the National Aeronautics and Space Administration (NASA) hadn't planned to hold a news conference on February 3 [1992]. But, they decided at the last minute, their preliminary findings about Earth's upper atmosphere were too important to sit on. Earth's protective ozone layer,[1] they announced, was losing ozone much faster than anyone had predicted, exposing humans to higher amounts of harmful radiation.

Even more ominous, they said, it seemed likely that a highly depleted section of the ozone layer, known as a "hole," would develop over the Arctic, exposing populated areas of the Northern Hemisphere. A similar hole had first been observed over Antarctica in 1985.

The scientists based their startling announcement on new data collected over northern New England, eastern Canada and much of Europe and Asia. What their airborne instruments—carried aloft by a satellite and two high-flying planes—detected was the highest concentration of ozone-destroying chlorine monoxide ever measured in the atmosphere.

Chlorine monoxide is a derivative of an important family of synthetic chemicals that are known as chlorofluorocarbons (CFCs). They have enjoyed wide use for decades as coolants in refrigerators and air conditioners, propellants in aerosol spray cans, blowing agents in the manufacture of plastic and rubber foam products and as solvents in the production of electronic equipment.

Once released into the atmosphere, CFCs drift upward until they reach the ozone layer, which begins in the stratosphere. As long as they remain in their original molecular form, CFCs are harmless. But intense ultraviolet radiation can break the CFC molecule apart, producing chlorine monoxide and setting off a series of reactions that destroy ozone.

High levels of chlorine monoxide are alarming enough by themselves. But NASA's scientists found evidence of even more worrisome atmospheric problems: high levels of bromine monoxide. A byproduct of halons, man-made chemicals used in fire extinguishers, bromine monoxide is even more destructive than chlorine monoxide.

Michael Kurylo, NASA's program manager for the study, estimated that the two chemicals could destroy 1 to 2 percent of the ozone layer daily during brief periods of late winter. At that rate, as much as 40 percent of the ozone over populous areas of the Northern Hemisphere could be depleted by early spring, when ozone destruction ends each year. The resulting hole, scientists said, could be almost as serious as the one over Antarctica, where ozone depletion has been known to reach 50 percent.

In addition to high levels of ozone-destroying chlorine monoxide and bromine monoxide, the NASA team found reduced levels of nitrogen oxides, which protect ozone from the other two gases by converting them into harmless compounds before they have time to destroy ozone. The loss of nitrogen oxides, which scientists attribute to high levels of volcanic ash ejected into the stratosphere last summer during the eruption of Mount Pinatubo in the Philippines, diminishes the atmosphere's natural ability to recover from ozone depletion.

"The latest scientific findings indicate pretty clearly that the atmosphere all over the place, and not just in the polar regions, is nearly devoid of some of the constituents that protect ozone against depletion," says Michael Oppenheimer, senior scientist at the Environmental Defense Fund in New York City.

... [R]ecent findings are serious enough that several countries, including the United States, have taken new steps to slow ozone depletion. In 1987, for example, the main producers and consumers of CFCs and halons signed the Montreal Protocol, which mandated phasing out these destructive chemicals by the year 2000, or sooner. The phaseout was subsequently accelerated in 1990, and several signatories to the protocol have since committed themselves to beating the deadline. ...

How Dangerous Is Ozone Depletion?

Ozone-destroying chemicals are extremely stable, so they last in the atmosphere for many decades. That means that even if production of all CFCs and halons stopped today, the chemicals already in the atmosphere would go on destroying ozone well into the 21st century. And because large quantities of these chemicals are contained in existing air conditioners and refrigerators, from which they continue to escape through malfunction or intentional venting, it may be a century before the ozone layer has built itself back up.

Just how devastating widespread ozone depletion would be is not known. But a 1975 government study on the environmental effects of an all-out nuclear war—which scientists say would destroy much of the ozone layer—provided a chilling glimpse of the aftermath. Ozone depletion of 50 percent, the study postulated, "would cause [skin] blistering after one hour of exposure. This leads to the conclusion that outside daytime work in the Northern Hemisphere would require complete covering by protective clothing. ... It would be very difficult to grow many (if any) food crops, and livestock would have to graze at dusk if there were any grass to eat."

The study speculated that a 25 to 30 percent depletion of stratospheric ozone —which NASA's findings indicate already may have occurred over parts of the Northern Hemisphere—would make it "difficult to imagine how survivors could carry out postwar recovery operations.

HOW OZONE-DEPLETING AGENTS ATTACK THE OZONE LAYER

Beginning in the stratosphere at an altitude of about 15 miles and extending up into the mesosphere, the 25-mile-wide ozone layer protects Earth by blocking out most of the sun's harmful ultraviolet light. Breakdown of ozone by chlorofluorocarbons and other chemicals allows harmful radiation to reach Earth.

1. Oxygen molecules in the stratosphere are transformed into ozone by solar ultraviolet (UV) radiation, which splits the oxygen molecule and releases highly reactive oxygen atoms. The free oxygen atoms then bind to oxygen molecules to form ozone molecules, which also are broken up by UV radiation. This continuous creation and destruction of oxygen and ozone occurs normally in the stratosphere.
2. Once certain chemicals, chiefly chlorofluorocarbons (CFCs), reach the ozone layer, UV radiation bombards the CFC molecule, breaking off an atom of chlorine.
3. The free chlorine atom attacks an ozone molecule, breaking off one of ozone's three oxygen atoms to form one chlorine monoxide molecule and leaving one oxygen molecule.
4. When the chlorine monoxide molecule encounters a free oxygen atom, produced during the natural mixing of oxygen and ozone, the oxygen atom breaks up the chlorine monoxide molecule and binds to its oxygen atom, forming a new oxygen molecule and leaving behind a free chlorine atom.
5. The newly freed chlorine atom can continue to destroy ozone molecules for many years. Oxygen molecules continue to break apart and form ozone, but this natural replenishing process is slowed in the presence of chlorine monoxide.
6. Because oxygen, unlike ozone, does not reflect UV radiation, the sun's potentially harmful UV rays penetrate the depleted areas of the ozone layer and reach Earth's surface.

Since the ozone hole opened over Antarctica in 1985, scientists have been assessing the impact of increased ultraviolet (UV) radiation on phytoplankton, the micro-organisms that make up the essential first link in the food chain that maintains all animal life in warm southern waters, including whales. Preliminary findings show that phytoplankton populations have dropped by up to 12 percent in areas where surface UV radiation has increased under the Antarctic ozone hole.

This is the first evidence outside the laboratory that links ozone depletion to damage of living organisms on Earth.

Excessive UV radiation is also thought to disrupt photosynthesis, the process by which green plants use the sun's radiant energy to produce carbohydrates. Ozone depletion could thus cause reduced yields in crops such as soybeans and rice, crops that are essential to feeding large parts of the Third World.

Ultraviolet radiation has long been known to cause health problems in animals, including cataracts in humans— the leading cause of blindness. The United Nations Environment Programme (UNEP), which was set up in 1972 to foster international cooperation in protecting the environment, predicts that ozone depletion will cause an additional 1.6 million cases per year.

There are also preliminary reports of widespread blindness among rabbits, sheep, horses and cattle in southern Chile, where high UV radiation exposure resulted from the ozone hole over Antarctica.

UNEP also foresees an annual increase of 300,000 cases of skin cancer, by the year 2000, particularly in Argentina and Australia, which have come under increased UV radiation. UNEP also estimates that a 10 percent depletion of the ozone layer would cause up to 26 percent more basal and squamous-cell skin cancers. The agency cites new evidence that UV radiation may also contribute to cancers of the lip and salivary glands.

Other studies project that a 10 percent increase in UV penetration would cause up to a 9 percent increase in the incidence of the more deadly malignant melanoma among light-skinned people, the group that is most vulnerable to this virulent form of cancer.

Ultraviolet radiation may also undermine the immune system's ability to ward off infectious diseases. This, says Margaret L. Kripke, an immunologist at the University of Texas' M. D. Anderson Cancer Center in Houston, is the biggest unknown health effect of UV radiation.

Animal experiments have indicated that UV radiation may reduce lymphocytes' ability to destroy certain microorganisms that enter the body through the skin, such as Leishmania, malaria, schistosoma and the leprosy bacillus.

Although it is not known whether UV radiation actually reduces human resistance to these agents, Kripke testified last fall, "infectious diseases constitute an enormous public health problem worldwide, and any factor that reduces immune defenses... is likely to have a devastating impact on human health."

Kripke's research was particularly ominous for sun worshipers. She found that commercial sunscreen preparations, which protect against sunburn and other damage to the skin from UV radiation, don't block the immunosuppressive effects of UV radiation. Similarly, skin pigmentation, which protects darker-skinned people from skin cancers that are prevalent among Caucasians, doesn't seem to protect the immune system from UV damage....

FIRST SIGNS OF TROUBLE

Even as industry was finding new uses for CFCs in the early 1970s, scientists were beginning to link them to ozone destruction. In 1974, Ralph Cicerone, then at the University of Michigan, and his colleague, Richard S. Stolarski, investigated the possible effects on stratospheric ozone of chlorine released by NASA rockets. They concluded that a single atom of chlorine would destroy many thousands of ozone molecules.

However, because the number of rockets passing through the ozone layer was small, and no other sources of chlorine at that altitude had been identified, their findings did not cause widespread alarm.

Findings reported later that year, however, showed that rocket engines were not the only source of chlorine in the stratosphere. Sherwood Rowland and Mario Molina at the University of California at Irvine decided to study CFCs after they are released into the atmosphere. They found that CFCs are so durable that they do not break down under the forces of solar radiation and precipitation in the lower atmosphere, but continue to float around in their original state for many years, eventually drifting upward into the stratosphere.

"What we did was to ask a question that hadn't been asked before: What is going to happen to the CFCs?" Rowland recalls. "The conclusion we came to was that nothing would happen quickly, but on the time scale of many decades CFCs would go away into the stratosphere and release chlorine atoms and then that the chlorine atoms would attack the ozone.... We concluded that there was danger to the ozone layer and... that we should quit putting CFCs into the atmosphere."

Not surprisingly, Rowland and Molina faced hostile reactions from the producers of CFCs when they published their results in 1974. "The public was probably more likely to believe it than the chemistry community," Rowland says. "Within the chemistry community then and still now there is a feeling that most environmental problems are really just public relations problems, that they are not real problems."

Rowland says the chemicals manufacturers set up the Committee on Atmospheric Science to discredit the two researchers' findings. Indeed, he adds that many critics dismissed their conclusions as "kooky. One of my favorites was an aerosol-propellant company that claimed [our results were] disinformation put out by the KGB."

But their data held up. In 1976, after a nationwide research effort involving NASA and the National Oceanic and Atmospheric Administration (NOAA), the National Academy of Sciences confirmed that CFC gases released into the atmosphere from spray cans were in fact damaging the ozone layer.

Two years later, after consumer boycotts had reduced the market for spray cans by almost two-thirds, the United States banned the use of CFCs as aerosol propellants in spray cans for most uses.

OZONE HOLE DISCOVERED

Although other industrial nations continued to produce and use CFCs for aerosol sprays and other purposes, the international scientific community continued the search for data on ozone depletion launched by Rowland and Molina. During the early 1980s, most research was confined to computer models of the atmosphere. Then, in 1985, British scientists discovered that ozone depletion had become so severe over a vast area of Antarctica that it amounted to a virtual "hole" in the ozone layer.

Still, resistance to the ozone-depletion theory remained so strong that the British team was refused additional government funding to continue their research. Ironically, they obtained backing instead from the U.S. Chemical Manufacturers Association, whose members had the most to lose from confirmation of Rowland and Molina's theory. Because of mounting pressure at home to find substitutes for CFCs, however, the American chemical industry wanted to resolve the issue once and for all before abandoning CFCs.

Meanwhile, Rowland and other scientists were learning more about ozone depletion and why the phenomenon was so strong over the Antarctic.

They discovered that CFCs are concentrated over the South Pole because of strong circular winds known as the "polar vortex," which sweep unimpeded over the flat, barren continent of Antarctica. The vortex gathers the destructive gases from the surrounding atmosphere into a wide funnel over Antarctica, where they remain isolated during the dark, frigid winter months.

Equally important, they found that as CFCs break down, the resulting chlorine monoxide clings to the ice crystals that form clouds in the stratosphere. These ice crystals provide the surfaces needed for the catalytic reaction in which chlorine breaks down ozone.

With the return of sunlight to Antarctica during September and October, the beginning of spring in the Southern Hemisphere, solar radiation acts as a catalyst enabling the chlorine monoxide produced by CFCs to destroy the surrounding ozone layer.

As the days lengthen, the air over Antarctica warms up, breaking up both the stratospheric ice clouds and the polar vortex. The destruction of ozone slows as the chlorine atoms are once again bound into harmless chlorine nitrate and hydrogen chloride molecules, and the hole disappears as the vortex dissipates, allowing ozone from the surrounding regions to fill the void.

The final confirmation of Rowland and Molina's theory linking CFCs to ozone depletion came in 1987, when NASA undertook a series of aerial tests over Antarctica. From inside the ozone hole, the NASA instruments detected high concentrations of chlorine monoxide.

Montreal Protocol Signed

International reaction to the proof that CFCs were destroying the ozone layer was swift. On Sept. 16, 1987, just nine months after formal negotiations began, 24 nations signed the Montreal Protocol on Substances That Deplete the Ozone Layer. The agreement garnered an unprecedented degree of international support for such a sweeping program to protect the environment: The ratifying nations accounted for 99 percent of the world's production of CFCs and 90 percent of their consumption.

The Montreal Protocol called for freezing halon emissions at 1986 levels by 1992; for halving CFC emissions by 1998; and halving CFC production and importation by 1999. To compensate for their low levels of production of ozone-depleting chemicals, developing nations were given an additional 10 years to meet these deadlines. By Jan. 1, 1989, the protocol had been ratified by enough countries to go into effect. ...

The drafters of the Montreal Protocol also assured its success by making the agreement flexible. As such, it could be rapidly amended to reflect subsequent changes in environmental conditions or new findings. And new findings were soon to test the agreement's flexibility.

The ozone hole over Antarctica continued to appear each September and October after its initial discovery in 1985. In 1988, scientists were encouraged to find that the hole was not as big as before. But the following year, the ozone hole reappeared, covering more than 15 million square miles.

Arctic Expedition Launched

The same year, NASA and NOAA launched an airborne expedition to the Arctic to investigate whether conditions were ripe near the North Pole for another ozone hole. Because the Arctic terrain is not as flat as that of Antarctica—and because temperatures at the North Pole do not fall as low as they do at the South Pole—the polar vortex was found to be weaker in the north. But the scientists did find higher than expected concentrations of chlorine compounds and concluded that an ozone hole could easily develop.

Because more people live at far northern latitudes than in southern Chile, Argentina, Australia and New Zealand, which border the area exposed to UV radiation in the Southern Hemisphere, an ozone hole over the Arctic would pose far greater risks to human health.

Other research revealed a new potential source of ozone depletion in areas far from the polar regions. American chemists Susan Solomon and Dave Hoffman found that sulfate particles spewed into the stratosphere by strong volcanic eruptions could act in much the same way as ice crystals in polar stratospheric clouds by providing surfaces on which chlorine and bromine compounds can destroy ozone more efficiently than when they are floating free.

Studying the impact of volcanic ash in the aftermath of the 1982 eruption of El Chichon in Mexico, Solomon and Hoffman found that ozone concentrations over the middle latitudes were significantly depleted. They concluded that ozone depletion was likely following other major volcanic eruptions.

Although their research was limited to El Chichon, Solomon, a NOAA chemist in Boulder, Colo., says, "We found that similar processes could also take place on the liquid sulfuric acid and water particles that form following major volcanic eruptions."

The implications of Solomon and Hoffman's research are clear. While ice clouds form only over the polar regions, volcanic ash can travel anywhere. If volcanic ash does facilitate ozone depletion even in the absence of ice crystals, an ozone hole could open over any region on Earth.

In the summer of 1990, NASA reported that, globally, the ozone layer had been depleted by 2 to 3 percent over the previous two decades. It was also reported that the ozone layer had already begun to thin over the United States and other populated areas in the middle latitudes.

At the same time, the chemicals industry was quickly bringing into production substitutes for CFCs that are less damaging to the ozone layer. While not completely benign, these hydrochlorofluorocarbons, or HCFCs, were hailed as temporary substitutes for CFCs in many applications, particularly as coolants. Most important, the HCFCs and other substitute chemicals facilitated the rapid phaseout of CFCs.

Montreal Protocol nations were quick to respond to the news that ozone depletion was intensifying. In June 1990, in London, they amended the agreement to accelerate the phaseout of ozone-depleting chemicals. Under the new guidelines, all production and importation of CFCs and halons must stop by the year 2000. Other ozone-depleting agents, such as carbon tetrachloride and methyl chloroform, were added to the list of chemicals to be phased out of production. Developing countries still have an additional 10 years to meet the deadline. As a result of the new deadlines, chlorine pollution was expected by 2075 to fall below levels recorded prior to the first appearance of the ozone hole.

The amendments also addressed the special problems faced by developing nations. Although they produce few ozone-depleting chemicals, India, China and other countries have counted on introducing cheap refrigeration and air conditioning as part of their plans for modernization. They succeeded in convincing the industrial world to set up a fund to help them pay for the more expensive substitutes they will be forced to purchase, as well as information and equipment to help them produce environmentally sound refrigerators and air conditioners themselves.

Also in 1990, Congress passed the far-reaching Clean Air Act Amendments, which call for the complete phaseout of CFCs, halons and carbon tetrachloride by 2000, of methyl chloroform by 2002 and HCFCs by 2030. The law made the United States the first nation to legislate a ban on these chemicals. To reduce emissions of existing stores of ozone-depleting agents, the law called for regulations to require recycling of refrigerants and air-conditioning coolants. Finally, the new law mandated faster elimination of ozone-depleting substances if warranted by new scientific findings of damage to the ozone layer.

VAST AREA AT RISK

No sooner had the ink dried on the revisions to the Montreal Protocol than new information pointed to an even more dire situation. In October 1990, scientists found the lowest ozone levels ever recorded over Antarctica and discovered that the hole had stretched into southern Chile including Purna Arenas, a city of 100,000. There was also further evidence that parts of Australia had been exposed to high levels of UV radiation when bits of the ozone hole broke away as the polar vortex weakened and drifted northward from Antarctica.

On Oct. 22, the UNEP and the World Meteorological Organization announced that ozone depletion had begun to occur at the middle and high latitudes of both the Northern and the Southern Hemispheres in spring, summer and winter.

"Ozone depletion in the middle and high latitudes means that it covers almost all of North America, Europe, the Soviet Union, Australia, New Zealand and a sizable part of Latin America," said UNEP Director Mostafa K. Tolba. "The only area with no indication of change, that is, no visible reduction of ozone, is the tropical belt around the Earth."

European researchers, building on Solomon and Hoffman's volcano-ash findings, are now predicting that last year's eruption of Mount Pinatubo threatens to erode the ozone layer to dangerous levels over much of Europe this spring. Researchers participating in the 17-nation European Arctic Stratospheric Ozone Experiment based in northern Sweden have yet to complete their experiments. But they issued a recommendation in early February that governments in Northern Europe should take more urgent steps to protect the ozone layer.

The most recent signs of severe ozone loss were detected by NASA's Upper Atmosphere Research Satellite (UARS), launched last September [1991] to monitor the ozone layer and measure substances that destroy ozone. On Feb. 3, two months before the current study was scheduled for completion, NASA announced that the satellite had detected high levels of chlorine monoxide over Scandinavia and northern Eurasia, an area that includes London, Moscow and Amsterdam. The levels were comparable to concentrations found in the ozone hole over Antarctica.

NASA predicted that an ozone hole could open over the Northern Hemisphere this spring if chlorine monoxide levels remain high enough. Final results of the study are due in mid-April.

The bad news was not limited to the far north. NASA's satellite observations also showed ozone depletion over the tropics, which the agency suggested was due to plumes of ash from Mount Pinatubo. In addition, the satellite detected areas of low ozone across the western United States. These findings were confirmed by separate measurements taken in Boulder, Colo.

Confirming the satellite data were new findings from the NASA-led Airborne Arctic Stratospheric Expedition, which monitors ozone depletion from two specially equipped aircraft: the ER-2, a converted U-2 spy plane that gathers data at 70,000 feet, and the DC-8-72, a "flying lab" that operates at 41,000 feet. The expedition reported Feb. 3 that it had found even higher levels of chlorine monoxide than the satellite had over eastern Canada and northern New England. The readings—at 1.5 parts per billion by volume—surpass anything ever measured in either polar region.

"These findings have increased our concern that significant ozone loss will occur during any given winter over the Arctic in the next 10 years," scientists announced. "This is based on significant new data with improved instrumentation obtained with broader geographic and seasonal coverage and the knowledge that past release of CFCs will increase chlorine substantially in the stratosphere in the decade to come."

NOTES

1. The ozone layer is a 25-mile-wide band above the Earth with a high but uneven concentration of ozone gas. Starting at an altitude of about 15 miles, it shields humans and other organisms from the most harmful effects of the sun's ultraviolet (UV) radiation.

NO

Patricia Poore and
Bill O'Donnell

OZONE

No journalistic "lead" for this story. No weary scientists peering through the frozen antarctic mist after a restless night spent dreaming of blind rabbits. No international chemical-industry conspiracies. We won't try to hook you. We won't promise an easy read, either. But we will try to remain neutral, even as we suggest that conventional wisdom may be deeply flawed.

We have spent the better part of two months deeply engrossed in the literature of ozone depletion. Our editorial interest had been aroused by the recent popular books[1] which present vastly different interpretations of science. We moved in further with the original scientific papers of Dobson, Rowland and Molina, Teramura, et al. We then read expert reviews of the literature by Elsaesser, Singer, et al.

We found compelling arguments on both sides, only to find credible contradictory information in the next day's reading. Let us warn you up front, anything resembling a final conclusion eludes us.

Although the science around ozone depletion is a continuum—an as-yet incomplete mosaic of postulates and findings—politics and media hype have transformed the argument into a battle between philosophical adversaries: Camp Apocalypse and Camp Hogwash. We may be accused of adding to the confusion by developing our arguments around this artificial divide, but there is really no choice. The escalating volley of counterpoints and rebuttals has given rise to overstatement, simplification, and a growing tendency to lie by omission, suppressing information that doesn't fit. It is to that situation that this article must be written.

Representing Camp Apocalypse are Sharon Roan, author of *Ozone Crisis*, and Vice President Al Gore, author of *Earth in the Balance*. They were preceded by, and continue to find support from, the environmental group Greenpeace and other environmentalist public-interest groups.

Representing Camp Hogwash, we found Rogelio (Roger) Maduro, primary author of *The Holes in the Ozone Scare*, and, less hysterically but just as dismissively, Dixy Lee Ray, primary author of *Trashing the Planet and Environmental Overkill*.

From our reading, we find that the truth may lie in the middle—in this arena, a radical place to be. Our views echo those of Ronald Bailey in his book *Eco-Scam*,[2] and Dr. S. Fred Singer (*Global Climate Change*), a physicist and climatologist oft-quoted by both camps.

We are comfortable making these statements for the record: (1) Both camps are engaging in hyperbole and lies of omission. (2) The chemical industry is not "dragging its feet" in coming up with substitutes for CFCs [chlorofluorocarbons] indeed they are responding deftly to market demand and will make huge profits from the phase-out. (3) There is currently no "crisis," nor any documented threat to human health, inasmuch as (a) the so-called ozone hole is an ephemeral disturbance over a mostly unpopulated area; (b) ozone thinning over populated latitudes, if it exists, is within the range of natural fluctuation and is seasonal; (c) no documentation exists for actual sustained increase in UV-B radiation at ground level.

We believe, however, that there may be cause for concern. We are skeptical of the debunkers' claims. No, it is not chlorine from oceans and volcanoes which is responsible for creating the effect seen in the polar region; yes, chlorine from CFCs does apparently make it to the stratosphere and does destroy ozone.

We consider the lack of disclosure and debate regarding the real costs of a precipitous halocarbon phase-out to be near-criminal. The costs that will be involved (monetary, opportunity, and human) receive scant coverage, in spite of the fact that the "threat" of ozone depletion is demonstrably lesser than any number of real threats both worse in scope and more immediate.

WHAT WAS THE QUESTION?

Let's review briefly the points of debate, both to define the scope of our discussion and to inform those who have not been reading carefully the science sections of newspapers in the past four years.

A theory advanced in 1973 by F. Sherwood Rowland and Mario Molina (Univ. of California-Irvine) holds that chlorofluorocarbons (CFCs) and related molecules, owing to their tremendous stability, eventually reach the stratosphere and, photolyzed by intense ultraviolet radiation, split to release energized chlorine atoms that then destroy ozone (O_3) molecules. Obviously, O_3 is always being created and destroyed, but it is thought that the increased destruction from man-made chemicals has tipped the balance and caused a temporary net depletion in the O_3 concentration. This is potentially harmful because O_3 is one mechanism that controls the amount of UV-B radiation reaching the biosphere (UV-B is an ultraviolet wavelength that affects the body, in ways that are both life-sustaining and, in excess, damaging.)

The "ozone hole" is the graphic name given to a phenomenon that so far exists only seasonally over the Antarctic region; namely, a thinning of the concentration of O_3 molecules that represents a depletion of up to two-thirds for a limited amount of time. Scientists on all sides of the debate agree that preexisting conditions unique to the Antarctic zone create the possibility of the "ozone hole."

Those scientists and politicians calling for an immediate CFC ban believe that very recent minor, unsustained, localized depletion of ozone in the stratosphere in some areas outside the polar regions is caused by CFCs, and is a harbinger of increasing future depletion. The issue was presented strongly enough that a phase-out was planned in 1987 in an international treaty called the Montreal Protocol; the dissemination of certain findings since that time resulted in a decision for a near-total ban by 1996.

In the meantime, a strong counterpoint to the ozone theory and the proposed ban has been presented, which many people refer to as a "backlash." Regardless of the personal political motivations of the skeptics, good reasons for this "backlash" include the discovery of information suppressed in the politicking for a ban, as well as a growing realization of the extraordinary costs inherent in phasing out the relatively safe, useful and ubiquitous chemicals.

POINTS OF CONTENTION

Each camp purports to interpret the original data. Only since the publication of the popularized books, or since about 1989, has the debate escalated into a war, with each side battling the other point by point. Let's look at Camp Apocalypse first, as it gained favor earlier and still holds sway. Here are their major points:

1. CFCs, HCFCs, and halons are proven to be responsible for a sudden (in a 40-year period) depletion of stratospheric ozone, which created the "ozone hole" over Antarctica. The effect of CFCs on the stratosphere will lead to a similar hole over the Arctic, and will change the ozone layer over populated areas for at least 100 years, even with a phase-out and ban.
2. The "ozone hole" gets worse every year, starting sooner or growing in area or breaking up later.
3. Ozone loss causes increased UV-B at ground level, which has resulted

in severe sunburns and will cause increases in skin cancer, cataracts, and immune deficiency.
4. Increased UV-B at ground level will affect the food chain, from phytoplankton to soybeans, and may have apocalyptic results.

As you can see, their points are a mix of the known and the projected. Context is often missing from the arguments of both camps, as well. For example, saying "the ozone hole gets worse every year" sounds definitive (and terrifying), but the period referred to is only 14 years —an insufficient baseline from which to chart real deviation. Now, the salient points from Camp Hogwash, themselves a mixture of red herrings and truth:

1. CFCs are heavier than air and therefore can't get up into the stratosphere.
2. In any case, chlorine from CFCs pales in comparison to the chlorine released by the oceans and volcanic eruptions.
3. There has always been an ozone hole, we just didn't know how to look for it.
4. There is no long-term "thinning" of the ozone layer.
5. The relationship between stratospheric ozone concentration and UV-B at ground level is unknown, and no sustained increase in UV-B at ground level has been demonstrated.

* * *

Both camps bring up the same topics; only their conclusions differ. Let's look at those topics, one by one, with a more neutral perspective, based on a reading of both and reference to some of the original documents.

THE OZONE HOLE

The argument regarding whether or not the "ozone hole" existed before CFCs remains murky. The question, apparently, is what did ground-breaking researcher Gordon Dobson really find when he examined ozone concentration in the 1950s (i.e., before the proliferation of CFCs). Did he discover the ozone hole or not? Some in the hogwash camp have publicly asserted that Dobson found ozone levels as low as 150 Dobson Units [D.U.] over Halley Bay [on the Antarctic continent at approx. 75° S].

We looked it up ourselves. Here is Gordon Dobson reviewing his findings of the late 1950s in a paper written for *Applied Optics* in March 1968—long before the controversy erupted.

"One of the more interesting results on atmospheric ozone which came out of the IGY [International Geophysical Year] was the discovery of the peculiar annual variation of ozone at Halley Bay. The annual variation of ozone at Spitzbergen [a Norwegian Island at approx. 80° N.] was fairly well known at that time, so, assuming a six months difference, we knew what to expect. However, when the monthly telegrams from Halley Bay began to arrive and were plotted alongside the Spitzbergen curve, the values for September and October 1956 were about *150 units lower than we expected.* [our emphasis] We naturally thought that Evans had made some large mistake or that, in spite of checking just before leaving England, the instrument had developed some fault. In November the ozone values suddenly jumped up to those expected from the Spitzbergen results. It was not until a year later, when the same type of annual variations was repeated, that we realized that the early results were indeed correct and

that Halley Bay showed most interesting difference from other parts of the world. It was clear that the winter vortex over the South Pole was maintained late into the spring and that this kept the ozone values low. When it suddenly broke up in November both the ozone values and the stratosphere temperatures suddenly rose."

So, while Dobson's group didn't find levels as low as those measured in the mid 'eighties, it's clear from his language that he was shocked at how low ozone concentrations were over Halley Bay, and at a loss to explain how such a phenomenon could exist. Whether or not the "hole" (that is, levels as low as 150 D.U.) is a recent occurrence, it is clear that the physical environment particular to Antarctic had depleted ozone in the austral spring before CFCs could be credibly implicated.

Dobson's group didn't have converted spy planes, high-tech satellite imagery, and countless researchers available to them. They had one instrument in one place. Today, we see the exact position of maximum ozone depletion shifting location from year to year. Could it be that Halley Bay was outside of the "hole" in '56 and '57? We can never know.

CAN CFCs MIGRATE TO THE STRATOSPHERE?

"CFCs are much heavier than air, and so could never reach the stratosphere." It is clear to us that this is a bogus argument. While it's true that CFCs weigh anywhere between four and eight times as much as air, and will sink to the floor if spilled in a laboratory, in the real world, they won't stay on the ground. Our atmosphere is a very turbulent place. Says Rowland: "The atmosphere is not a quiescent laboratory and its mixing processes are dominated to altitudes far above the stratosphere by the motions of large air masses which mix heavy and light gaseous molecules at equal rates. Throughout most of the atmosphere, all gaseous molecules go together in very large groups, independent of molecular weight.

"By 1975, stratospheric air samples... had been shown regularly to have CFC-11 present in them. During the past 17 years, CFC-11 and more than a dozen other halocarbons have been measured in literally thousands of stratospheric air samples by dozens of research groups all over the world."

WHAT ABOUT NATURAL SOURCES OF CHLORINE?

Say the skeptics: "The amount of chlorine hypothetically released by CFCs pales in comparison to that available from natural sources." They are talking about seawater evaporation and volcanoes. Dixy Lee Ray tells us in *Trashing the Planet:* "The eruption of Mount St. Augustine (Alaska) in 1976 injected 289 billion kilograms of hydrochloric acid directly into the stratosphere. That amount is 570 times the total world production of chlorine and fluorocarbon compounds in the year 1975."

The hogwash camp has said that one billion tons of chlorine are released into the atmosphere from natural sources, as compared to a theoretical 750,000 tons from man-made sources. Taken at face value, these seemingly scientifically arrived-at proportions would lead one to believe that man-made sources are insignificant.

Most unfortunately for the hogwash camp, Ray had made a terrific blunder.

Her calculation came not from Alaska in 1976, but from a theoretical extrapolation of the total HCL released (not necessarily reaching the stratosphere) by a mammoth eruption 700,000 years ago. She may have made the same argument (which rested on a 1989 paper by Maduro) even with accurate numbers, but noise over the mistake has eclipsed the question.

Indeed, what about volcanoes, spewing chlorine compounds at high velocities? Again, the amount released by volcanoes is not the same as the amount reaching the stratosphere. Yet Maduro insists: "No matter what figure is used, the basic point remains that the amount of chlorine emitted by Mother Nature through volcanoes dwarfs the amount contained in man-made CFCs."

Ozone-depletion researchers counter that whatever the amount of chlorine compounds released through natural sources, all of it is washed out in the lower atmosphere through precipitation —before it has reached the stratosphere.

In summary, the hogwash camp is vastly overstating the importance of natural sources of chlorine. The apocalyptic camp entirely dismisses the importance of natural sources of chlorine because it is removed by rainfall, with negligible amounts reaching the stratosphere.

Whom to believe? Is it really true that only organic, water-insoluble compounds (e.g., CFCs) can deliver chlorine to the stratosphere? Are we really to believe that there's enough precipitation in the antarctic night to wash out all the chlorine being emitted by Mount Erebus (a volcano, continuously active since 1972, six miles from the monitor station at McMurdo Sound)—before any of it can move up to the stratosphere in the great, turbulent polar vortex?

GLOBAL OZONE DEPLETION? FROM WHAT BASELINE?

For the record, no solid evidence exists to suggest ozone depletion over the northern latitudes poses any health hazard. Are you shocked? It's no wonder. Environmental groups and the popular press tell us the threat is now.

Case in point: On February 3, 1992, NASA "interrupted their research" to announce their prediction of a full-scale ozone hole over much of the U.S. and Europe: the infamous "hole over Kennebunkport" referred to by then-Senator Al Gore. It didn't happen. The October 1992 Greenpeace report entitled *Climbing Out of the Ozone Hole* claimed: "The formation of an ozone hole over the Northern Hemisphere in the near future, and possibly as early as 1993, now appears inevitable." Greenpeace's "inevitable hole" over the Northern Hemisphere didn't materialize, either.

That the alarms were false didn't stop them from becoming common knowledge. The July 1993 issue of the women's fashion magazine *Vogue* tells us that "thorough sun protection is the cornerstone of any summertime beauty strategy. As government scientists report ozone over the Northern Hemisphere is at its lowest level in fourteen years." The ominous warning appears in a feature article called "Beauty and the Beach," which shows page after page of bathing beauties soaking up the summer sun in the latest bikinis.

What the article fails to mention is that the 10 to 15% reduction government scientists reported occurred in March and April, when the amount of UV-B reaching the northern latitudes was but a small fraction of what the summertime sun delivers. We have to be careful when we interpret these diminished percentage-point results. A ten percent depletion over Kennebunkport in April (and its corresponding as-yet theoretical increase in UV-B) is still but a small fraction of that received in New York or Boston in June— when people really are out on the beach. We also must be careful to understand what baseline is being used to report these "depletions."

Of those who either discredit the degree of ozone thinning or differ on its range of effects, few carry greater weight or generate more controversy than S. Fred Singer, who holds a doctorate in physics from Princeton University and is now president of an Arlington, VA-based think tank called Science and Environmental Policy Project.

Dr. Singer is skeptical about claims by other scientists that, on average, global ozone levels are falling: "One cannot estimate whether there has been any long-term change from short-range observations because the natural fluctuations are so large." According to Singer, long-term analyses are compounded by daily ozone fluctuations that double naturally from one day to the next [without any cataclysmic outcome, by the way]. "Seasonal fluctuation, from winter to summer, are as much as 40% and the eleven-year solar cycle is three to five percent, on a global average. Extracting long-term variations from a few percentage points of change in a decade is like observing temperatures for one season and judging whether climate has changed over the long term. It can't be done.

"It is not possible to eliminate the chance that what we are seeing is a natural variation.

"The Antarctic hole is a genuine phenomenon," Singer concedes. "But it is nothing much to worry about because it lasts such a short while and has already stabilized. Besides, it is controlled more by climate than by CFCs."

THE UV-B QUESTION

The scary part of ozone depletion is, of course, the correlation to increased UV-B penetration. The most often-cited theoretical relationship is that for every 1% decrease in stratospheric ozone, we can expect a 2% increase in ground-level UV-B. It would seem a good check of diminishing ozone claims would be to quantify the penetration of UV-B. Problem is, the few who are looking can't find any increase at the Earth's surface.

Despite the analysis of TOMS (Total Ozone Mapping System) satellite data released by former EPA-administrator William Reilly indicating *springtime* average ozone levels over the United States have dropped 8% in the last decade, there are no data to suggest increased penetration of UV-B on the ground. In fact, a report published in the September 28, 1989, issue of *Nature* cites a study that found a 0.5% average *decrease* in UV-B between 1968 and 1982, despite an overall decrease in ozone column density of 1.5% over the same period.

Ozone doomsayers counter by arguing: 1) The monitors used are not capable of making distinctions between UV-A and UV-B radiation, and 2) UV-B is not reaching the surface because it's being absorbed in the troposphere by man-made pollutants. They reason that we shouldn't count on our fouling of the lower atmosphere to protect us from damage we're inflicting above.

If the monitors are antiquated, you'd think we'd be funding new ones, given our fear of the sky. The second argument is a red herring. The reported 8% depletion in stratospheric ozone (which should theoretically create a hard-to-miss 16% increase in UV-B) occurred during a decade when tropospheric pollution was decreasing over the U.S.—courtesy of the Clean Air Act.

The Connection to Human Health

All claims regarding human health risks associated are related not to ozone thinning *per se*, but to increased UV-B exposure. So far, researchers have not in fact tied increases in skin cancer and cataracts to increased UV-B exposure due to thinning ozone. There is no epidemiological evidence of suppressed immune function due to UV-B exposure caused by thinning ozone.

(No one questions that people get more UV exposure than in the past. Only a few generations ago, a tan was considered unhealthy. Only since the 1950s have so many people had the leisure and desire to be out in the sun, wearing scant clothing. And only with technological advances have so many white people been living in previously inhospitable "sunbelts.")

But is there more UV-B, overall, sustained, at ground level? What would it mean if we can find ozone depletion without a corresponding rise in UV-B penetration to ground level?

WHERE WE ARE—AS OF AUGUST '93

Public policy is driven by the public, not by scientists. A recent survey gave these results: 67% of Americans consider themselves "extremely concerned about the environment." But only one in five is aware that CFCs are used in refrigeration, and only one in 30 is aware that CFCs are used in air conditioning. Are a well-meaning public and the politicians who serve them not well enough informed to make global decisions that will cost hundreds of billions of dollars? Will future generations look back at the "ozone crisis" as the greatest waste of resources in human history? Or will they thank us for taking lifesaving action without delay? (The apocalyptics talk about political foot-dragging "for 14 years," but the Montreal Protocol is perhaps the fastest, largest non-military global response to a perceived threat in human history.)

The following observations are based not on our own scientific experiments, of course, but rather on a rational analysis of the facts following a great deal of reading. We have no vested interest in either camp.

1. Attributing the Antarctic "ozone hole" to CFCs is overstatement to the point of fallacy. Natural conditions have always existed which deplete the concentration of ozone in that region during a specific time of year. However, scientific data do support the theory that stable, man-made chlorinated molecules are implicated in a localized net ozone loss during the natural cycle.

2. Ozone depletion is not an epic crisis. Remember, even if ozone maintains 100% of its "normal level," skin cancers will still occur. On a day when ozone levels over Punta Arenas, Chile, are reduced by 50% because of the "hole," the theoretical maximum increase of UV-B levels would be equal to only 7% of what reaches the ground at the equator on the same day.

3. We must monitor UV-B at ground level to see if in fact there is any correlation with stratospheric ozone fluctuations.

4. A outright ban on CFCs and other useful halocarbons (before adequate substitutes are available) would cause more human suffering and economic mayhem than the theoretical increase in ozone depletion under a more managed phase-out. In the U.S. we have the financial means and perhaps the political will to accept the challenge —albeit at tremendous cost and lost opportunities. In other parts of the world, an already insufficient supply of affordable refrigeration would be exacerbated. The result will be more disease from food-borne bacteria, and greater hunger.

What do you think?

NOTES

1. *The Holes in the Ozone Scare/The Scientific Evidence That the Sky Isn't Falling* by Rogelio A. Maduro and Ralf Schauerhammer. 21st Century Science Associates, Washington, D.C., 1992. *Ozone Crisis/The 15-Year Evolution of a Sudden Global Emergency* by Sharon Roan. John Wiley & Sons, New York, 1989. *Trashing the Planet/How Science Can Help Us Deal with Acid Rain, Depletion of the Ozone, and Nuclear Waste (Among Other Things)* by Dixy Lee Ray with Lou Guzzo. Regnery Gateway, Washington, D.C., 1990. *Earth in the Balance/Ecology and the Human Spirit* by Al Gore. Houghton Mifflin Co., Boston, 1992.

2. *EcoScam/The False Prophets of Ecological Apocalypse* by Ronald Bailey. St. Martin's Press, New York, 1993.

POSTSCRIPT

Do the Projected Consequences of Ozone Depletion Justify Phasing Out Chlorofluorocarbons?

In November 1992 the parties to the Montreal Protocol (the international agreement to phase out CFCs) gathered in Copenhagen, Denmark, and once again agreed to earlier deadlines for eliminating the use of CFCs and other ozone-depleting chemicals. A detailed report on this meeting by Ian H. Rowlands was published in the July/August 1993 issue of *Environment*. Poore and O'Donnell claim that public policy is driven by the public, not by scientists. Surely, Dr. Rowlands would agree that scientists have a difficult time getting a response from political leaders to their pleas for action on environmental threats. But for many years, it was not the public who opposed his warnings about ozone layer depletion. It was CFC producers and other powerful economic interests who attempted to refute the accumulating evidence that he doggedly presented to world leaders. The ultimate collapse of the opposition is a clear indication that the remaining skeptics constitute a very small minority of the scientists who have studied this issue. Poore and O'Donnell profess to have no vested interest that influenced their analysis of this issue. But this claim is suspect considering that the magazine they publish has featured many articles that refute or downplay the seriousness of many prominent environmental problems. Environmentalists are still not satisfied with the Copenhagen agreement, and they fault the failure to restrict the use of methyl bromide, a pesticide shown to be one of the major ozone depleters.

Simply negotiating a treaty does not ensure compliance. Greenpeace and other environmental organizations are continuing to mobilize public pressure to guarantee enforcement of the provisions of the agreement. In "The World Can't Wait for DuPont," *Greenpeace* (July/August 1990), Judy Christrup accuses the principal U.S. producer of CFCs of hedging on its commitment to cooperate in efforts to end ozone depletion. Jack Doyle's article "Hold the Applause: A Case Study of Corporate Environmentalism," *The Ecologist* (May/June 1992), supports this accusation.

For an in-depth analysis of the provisions of the original Montreal Protocol, see "The Montreal Protocol: A Dynamic Agreement for Protecting the Ozone Layer," by Jamison Koehler and Scott Hajost, *Ambio* (April 1990). The ozone "hole" that was discovered over the Antarctic poses a specific threat to the Antarctic food chain. For a discussion of this local, but significant, aspect of the problem, see "Fragile Life Under the Ozone Hole," by S. Z. El-Sayed, *Natural History* (October 1986).

ISSUE 17

Are Aggressive International Efforts Needed to Slow Global Warming?

YES: Richard Elliot Benedick, from "Equity and Ethics in a Global Climate Convention," *America* (May 23, 1992)

NO: S. Fred Singer, from "Warming Theories Need Warning Label," *The Bulletin of the Atomic Scientists* (June 1992)

ISSUE SUMMARY

YES: U.S. environmental diplomat Richard Elliot Benedick presents the case for a global climate convention modeled on the ozone protection treaties and warns that waiting for scientific certainty about global warming could be disastrous.

NO: Environmental science professor S. Fred Singer claims that most experts do not think that greenhouse gases will lead to catastrophic warming and that the world should not invest huge sums of money in response to a "phantom threat."

The likelihood of a major worldwide meteorological disturbance that would drastically affect climate and thus profoundly alter the balanced web of ecological cycles has provoked speculation by scientists as well as authors of science fiction. A currently prominent theory proposes that the age of dinosaurs was brought to a sudden and spectacular end as a result of just such an event. Supporters of this theory have pointed to evidence that an asteroid or comet may have struck the Earth, causing an enormous dust cloud to blanket the planet for many years, blocking much of the incident solar radiation. The lush tropical forests of the time would have been decimated by the reduction of sunlight. The resulting loss in the dinosaurs' primary food source, coupled with the climate change, could have produced sufficient stress to cause short-term massive extinctions.

Only recently, however, has there been serious scientific concern that significant changes in the average surface temperature or other worldwide meteorological effects could result from intentional or inadvertent human intervention. Although it is generally accepted that the per capita production of energy would have to increase by a factor of 100 or more before a direct, observable atmospheric heating could occur, there are other aspects of present industrial activity that are widely believed to be potential causes of calamitous atmospheric effects.

Many atmospheric scientists now predict that our environment may be altered in a dramatic way as the result of the increase in carbon dioxide and other trace gas concentration in the air due to the burning of fossil fuels, destruction of forests, and other agricultural and industrial practices. Trace gases transmit visible sunlight but absorb the infrared radiation emitted by the Earth's surface, much as the glass covering of a greenhouse does. A continued increase in these gases could cause sufficient heat to be trapped in the lower atmosphere to raise the world's average temperature by several degrees over the next 50 to 100 years. This would result in major alterations in weather patterns and perhaps melt part of the polar ice cap. The rising ocean would then submerge vast low-lying coastal areas in all continents.

There is now little doubt that atmospheric carbon dioxide and other trace gas levels are rising. Most meteorologists now agree that there will be some resultant warming; but due to the complexity of the many interacting phenomena that affect climatological patterns, there is much uncertainty on how large the temperature increases will be and whether or not they will actually be sufficient to cause the apocalyptic effects that some predict.

During the summers of 1988 and 1989 many regions of the United States experienced unusually hot weather. This led to public speculation, and some by climatologists and meteorologists, that we were experiencing the beginning of the effects of the predicted greenhouse warming. These conjectures and the scientific data offered to support them are disputed by other scientists. One positive effect of this much-publicized debate is that more attention is now being paid to the causes and potential consequences of global warming, as demonstrated by the intense discussion of this issue at the 1992 Earth Summit in Rio de Janeiro.

Richard Elliot Benedick was the chief U.S. negotiator for the 1987 Montreal Protocol on protecting the ozone layer and a special advisor to the UN secretary-general for the 1992 Earth Summit proceedings. He argues that despite remaining uncertainties, the existing evidence supports the urgent need for international actions to forestall global warming. S. Fred Singer is an environmental science professor and director of the Science and Environmental Policy Project. He claims that most of the atmospheric scientists he has surveyed doubt that human-induced global warming will be sufficiently catastrophic to warrant the huge investment of funds that would be required to prevent it.

YES

Richard Elliot Benedick

EQUITY AND ETHICS IN A GLOBAL CLIMATE CONVENTION

INTRODUCTION: OZONE AND CLIMATE

It is not yet five years since representatives of a handful of governments signed a treaty that ushered in a new era of international environmental law. The "Montreal Protocol on Substances That Deplete the Ozone Layer" was hailed as the most significant international environmental agreement in history.

The Montreal Protocol was not inevitable. Most knowledgeable observers had long believed that a treaty would be impossible because the scientific data were so uncertain, the economic issues so complex and the initial positions of the negotiating parties so widely divergent. Like the governments currently attempting to deal with global warming, the ozone negotiators confronted theoretical, slow-developing dangers that could affect every nation and all life on earth over periods far beyond the customary time horizons of politicians.

Perhaps the most extraordinary aspect of the Montreal Protocol was that, unlike environmental treaties of the past, it was not a response to harmful events but rather a conscious preventive action on a global scale. Knowing what we have since learned about stratospheric ozone, it is sometimes forgotten today that during the nearly six years of negotiation, there was no measurable evidence that the ozone layer was being damaged by the actions of an extremely useful family of chemicals (chlorofluorocarbons and halons)—substances whose applications made them virtually synonymous with modern standards of living. The internationally agreed measures to control these important chemicals were wholly based on theoretical scientific models.

Under these circumstances, multi-billion-dollar global industrial interests claimed at the time that international regulations would impose immense economic hardship. Technological solutions were either nonexistent or were considered unacceptable by most major governments. It was argued that there was ample time to postpone actions pending resolution of the many scientific uncertainties. Some political leaders were well prepared to accept hypothetical future environmental risks rather than impose the indisputable near-term costs entailed in controlling substances used in thousands of products and processes.

All of this must sound familiar to observers of the debates over climate change.

NEGOTIATING A CLIMATE TREATY

Based primarily on complex but imperfect computer models of earth systems, the generally accepted scientific consensus is that an unprecedented planetary warming lies ahead because of increasing atmospheric concentrations of greenhouse gases derived from human activities. Coming at a time when human society is already struggling with the consequences of poverty, unprecedented population growth, wasteful consumption of energy and natural resources, and environmental degradation, climate change could imperil economic and social progress worldwide.

In December 1990, following over two years of coordinated international research on the scientific models and possible policy response strategies, the United Nations General Assembly established the "Intergovernmental Negotiating Committee for a Framework Convention on Climate Change," aiming at an international treaty to be signed at the June 1992 U.N. Conference on Environment and Development—the "Earth Summit"—in Rio de Janeiro.

These are very large multilateral negotiations, involving over 120 national delegations (at least 90 from developing countries) plus numerous U.N. programs and agencies and dozens of environmental, industry and other citizens' groups. Five negotiating sessions were scheduled over 18 months, a fast timetable by any standard of diplomacy, especially considering the complexity of the issues. Because of persisting unresolved issues, a sixth session was added for April 30–May 8, 1992 —practically on the eve of the Rio conference.

Greenhouse gas emissions are linked with modern energy, agricultural and industrial policies, and with forests, oceans and biological diversity. Because of the many interconnected aspects of the problem, there are no quick and easy solutions. It is necessary to take action on different fronts.

It appears essential for modern societies to reduce their dependence on fossil fuels, which account for more than half of all greenhouse gas emissions from human activities. This involves, in the first instance, measures to conserve use of energy and improve energy efficiency: changes in the transportation sector, more efficient manufacturing processes, improved construction techniques, low-energy lighting. As coal produces the most carbon dioxide per unit of energy produced, followed by oil and then natural gas, fuel switching— especially to natural gas—offers opportunities to reduce total emissions. Such renewable energy sources as solar energy, wind power and geothermal energy must be more aggressively promoted and developed.

The destruction of forests not only releases carbon dioxide into the atmosphere but also diminishes an important sink for absorbing carbon dioxide from other sources. Therefore, programs to reduce deforestation and encourage sustainable forest management, improved agricultural practices and reforestation are crucial. Because most forest destruction is related to the needs of populations in the poorer countries, solutions to this aspect of the climate problem are intimately connected to measures attacking poverty.

Some of the needed policies appear relatively straight-forward, but others will involve substantial changes in the way people live, work and consume. The need to stimulate research and development of new technologies in energy, industry and agriculture is critical. The implications of continued rapid population growth in the South also cannot be ignored.

Apart from the mitigation strategies just described, the international community must also cooperate in measures to adapt to some degree of climate change. Such policies would include contingency plans for dealing with climate-related emergencies, schemes for protection of coastal areas and development of agricultural practices and crops better able to resist drought and disease.

DIFFERING NATIONAL INTERESTS

Even though the threats are global and require an unprecedented degree of international cooperation and harmonization, nation-states remain preoccupied with traditional attributes of sovereignty —and with accountability to their own public opinion and electorates.

Regions and nations differ considerably in their vulnerability to climate change and in their ability to adapt. Prospects are generally less favorable in already ecologically fragile areas, primarily in the poorer parts of the world: arid areas of Africa, parts of South America and Southeast Asia, low-lying island states.

The industrialized North (including the new "economies in transition" of Eastern Europe and the former U.S.S.R.) are the major emitters of greenhouse gases, past and present—particularly carbon dioxide from fossil fuels. The wealthier among them now accept a responsibility to undertake stronger abatement measures than in the rest of the world. But there are also differences among them in their industrial structure that can influence their stance on specific proposals. For example, Australia, the United States, Eastern Europe and Russia are heavily dependent on coal; for Russia, Norway and Australia, fossil fuels constitute a significant share of export earnings.

Among the developing countries, those that are particularly vulnerable, such as the small island states and arid African countries, advocate strong mitigation measures. At the other extreme are the OPEC oil exporters, led by Saudi Arabia, who see their national patrimony threatened if a climate treaty imposes serious limits on fossil fuels. China's more than one billion citizens depend on energy to improve their living standards. Possessing roughly a third of the world's coal reserves, China is reluctant to forgo this energy source in the absence of economical options. Other newly industrializing nations of the South, such as India, Brazil and Mexico, share similar perspectives on energy. Countries with large forests, including Brazil, Indonesia, Zaire and Malaysia, are wary of the North trying to impose restrictions on how they can use their own national resources.

These widely varying national situations and interests will need to be reconciled in a climate convention. In many respects the negotiators are navigating uncharted waters.

ELEMENTS OF A
CLIMATE CONVENTION

A "framework convention" on climate change could be similar to the 1985 Vienna Convention for the Protection of the Ozone Layer, which preceded the 1987 Montreal Protocol. The Vienna Convention created a general obligation for nations to protect the ozone layer, established a mechanism for cooperation in research and exchange of information and provided the framework for future specific actions under an internationally agreed protocol. Many observers, however, stressing the long lead times needed to develop response policies and new technologies, urge that a climate convention should go beyond the Vienna model and also incorporate specific control measures analogous to the Montreal Protocol.

In any event, a climate convention would establish international agreement on a long-term general objective—for example, stabilizing greenhouse gas concentrations in the atmosphere at a level that minimizes the risks to the biosphere and to human societies.

In addition, the convention could move toward the Montreal Protocol model by including specific short-term goals of stabilization of net greenhouse gas emissions by a certain date (stronger) or "as soon as feasible" (weaker).

An important new element of the convention might be provisions for development of national action plans for responding to climate change, in particular for carrying out internationally agreed obligations in specific sectors, such as energy, transportation, forestry, agriculture. These plans would comprise measures designed to limit greenhouse gas emissions, to enhance sinks for carbon dioxide and to develop adaptation policies. While these strategies would probably require further elaboration and negotiation in future protocols, a start could be made in the framework convention.

Another significant innovation, going beyond the Vienna model, could be an agreement on specific instruments and modalities for providing financial assistance and technology to countries in need.

As in the Vienna Convention, the climate treaty would establish mechanisms for intensified international cooperation in research and monitoring—a major effort to resolve the scientific, economic and technical uncertainties.

Finally, the convention would doubtlessly include provisions to promote public education and awareness of climate change issues.

COMMITMENTS TO CHANGE

Amid the hundreds of pages of proposals and draft texts submitted by dozens of governments over the past 18 months, two overarching issues have emerged as the key elements of any eventual agreement on an international climate change convention: the nature of obligations by state-parties to the convention and the provision of assistance to developing nations.

The first of these issues relates to the principle of "common but differentiated responsibilities"—that is, the concept that all parties to an international accord undertake some obligations, but that these are varied according to the particular situation of the country concerned. Underlying the debate are fundamental questions of equity and fairness, not only between the wealthy North and the poorer but developing South, but also among the industrialized countries.

At their starkest, negotiators for some developing countries, notably India, maintain that the South should not be required to accept any obligations at all under a climate convention, beyond possibly some purely voluntary undertakings. According to this argument, since the North has grown wealthy while inadvertently polluting the atmosphere, the entire burden of reducing greenhouse gas emissions should rest with the industrialized nations. Citing the widening gap between rich and poor countries, proponents of this thesis argue that the highest priority of the South is alleviating poverty.

Negotiators for the industrialized countries recognize that the North has a primary responsibility because of its financial and technological resources. Timely actions in the energy and transport sectors by the North, which currently accounts for about 60 percent of the world's total carbon emissions from fossil fuels, could slow the warming trend and thereby buy time for development of new technologies and renewable energy sources. Such actions would make the expressed concerns of the North about climate change more credible: They would demonstrate to the South that the industrialized countries take the problem seriously and are willing to accept some sacrifice in the global interest.

But deciding on specific initial measures has revealed fissures among the industrialized nations. The European Community, joined by most other industrialized nations, has endorsed a concept of "targets and timetables," or specifically a commitment to stabilize carbon dioxide emissions at 1990 levels by the year 2000. They maintain that these targets are feasible through improvements in efficiency and fuel switching (mainly to natural gas), and that only firm timetables would provide a suitably strong incentive to the private sector to develop new technologies to curtail future use of fossil fuel.

This proposal has led the United States, which accounts for about 25 percent of the world's energy-related carbon dioxide emissions, to raise an equity issue. American negotiators have pointed out that the relative ease of meeting specific reduction targets may vary considerably among different countries, in part because of industrial structure and dependence on fossil fuel. They have argued that not enough is known about the costs of achieving a given target versus the benefits of any resulting slowdown in global warming. As an alternative to global targets, the Americans have advanced what they term a "bottoms up" approach, under which parties would identify and commit themselves to specific actions to limit greenhouse gas emissions.

Assuming that the North reaches some agreement on the form of a meaningful initial contribution to mitigate climate change, the next step is to delineate the responsibilities of the developing countries. The industrialized nations acknowledge that less-advantaged countries should not have to stifle development by reducing energy use. But it seems clear that if there is no change in the trend of greenhouse gas emissions from the South, any beneficial effects from efforts of the industrialized countries will be overwhelmed in the coming decades.

The South already accounts for roughly 30 percent of carbon dioxide emissions from energy use, and when effects of deforestation are counted, this proportion rises, in some estimates, to 40 percent or more of total carbon emissions. Even more troubling is the fact that emissions from the developing nations are rising steeply, pushed by industrialization, surging population growth and destruction of forests.

Some feasible changes in developing-country policies could be included in a climate convention. New programs promoting, for example, greater energy efficiency, improved forest and land management, more efficient industrialization and promotion of family planning represent reasonable convention commitments that would not only moderate the upward curve of greenhouse gas emissions but simultaneously improve economic and social progress.

ENLISTING AND ASSISTING THE SOUTH

The North-South debate at the climate negotiations has revealed deep mistrust in many developing nations of the underlying motivations of the richer countries. Fears have been openly expressed about a new form of "environmental colonialism." Developing countries see themselves relegated to an indefinite second-class status through measures to restrict energy use and new trade restrictions imposed by the North on the pretext of environmental protection. These anxieties are also reflected in the jealous guarding of recently acquired sovereign rights over their own natural resources (e.g., tropical forests).

Negotiators from developing countries repeatedly emphasize the inequities that mark economic relations between North and South and that consequently contribute to the perpetuation of poverty. They cite debt burden, vulnerability of commodity exports, trade barriers to their industrial products, deteriorating terms of trade and dependence on obsolete or inefficient technologies.

As the negotiations have unfolded, there is general agreement that the wealthier countries must assume the lion's share of responsibility and that the South's concerns about equity and fairness are justified. It is the negotiators' task to translate these principles into reasonable commitments on both sides.

Negotiators for developing countries have made very plain that a financial mechanism must be part of any climate convention, as it was in the Montreal Protocol. They contend that without external funding, they will not be able to transform their industrial, agricultural and energy sectors through new technologies to minimize greenhouse gas emissions. Furthermore, they argue that renewed efforts are necessary to reduce poverty, which is an underlying cause of poor land and forest management. It is likely that substantial aid will be required to enable countries with large tropical forests to develop alternatives to destroying those forests for purposes of agriculture, timber exports or basic fuel and shelter needs of growing populations. In addition, investment will be needed for measures to prepare for the anticipated impact of climate change, such as protecting coastal areas against sea-level rise.

The debate over financial assistance reflects long-standing frustrations on both sides of the North-South frontier. In the developing countries, there is disappointment that poverty remains pervasive, foreign indebtedness has become virtually unmanageable and access to markets in the North is restricted. There is a sense of being exploited by global financial and industrial forces that are not answerable to any forum.

In the donor countries, on the other hand, aid malaise riddles public opinion. It reflects disenchantment with corruption on the part of governments and leaders and misguided central planning policies in the South that have distorted markets, promoted waste and capital flight, and discouraged foreign investment. Open-ended commitments for new transfers of financial aid and technology over which donor governments would have no control are deeply resisted.

There is, however, no argument over the real investment needs of the South for reducing poverty, creating jobs, providing education and health care—and for managing and protecting the natural resource base. Many influential voices in the North acknowledge the necessity for additional aid flows, debt relief and opening up markets to developing countries. However, the ultimate responsibility for investment lies within the developing nations themselves. Resource transfers from abroad can provide only marginal help.

In the South itself there is increasing recognition that much external financing has been misused in the past. Officials and observers throughout the developing world are openly raising the issue of corruption, following revelations in recent years of gargantuan excesses by leaders of, among others, the Philippines, Haiti, the Central African Republic, Uganda and Zaire.

Perhaps the largest source of "new and additional" funds for the South could come from cutting their own expenditures for armaments. Despite the widening North/South gap, the military spending of developing countries has grown in recent years twice as rapidly as per capita income. Many countries spend two to three times more on weapons than on education and health combined. To be sure, reform in this area requires substantial cooperation from the governments of industrialized countries, whose weapons producers vigorously compete for expanding markets.

Closely related to the financial issue is the question of technology transfer. In order to limit significantly their greenhouse gas emissions, developing countries would need to utilize the most effective existing and new technologies, especially in the energy area. But these countries do not merely want to purchase licenses at possibly monopolistic prices. Rather, they demand guaranteed access to modern technologies on terms they can afford, or, in the words of the proposed convention language: "on preferential and non-commercial terms."

While accepting the need for technology transfer, the industrialized countries face a conflict over intellectual property rights. It is difficult to see how governments could mandate transfer on non-commercial terms of technology owned by private companies without diminishing their incentive to invest in research and development. In contrast, market theory holds that technology will gravitate, via joint ventures and licensing, toward developing countries with favorable investment climate and policies, and that international competitive forces will militate against unfair bargains.

PROSPECTS FOR SUCCESS

Given the differing national interests and the scientific and economic uncertainties, what are the prospects? Is the negotiation "doomed to success," with everything falling into place by June 1992 in Rio de Janeiro? Not necessarily. The negotiations on Law of the Sea are a sobering reminder that key parties to a negotiation can pull back.

What, then, would constitute a successful climate convention under the existing constraints? Perhaps the most important element in terms of near-term impact will be the extent of commitments by the industrialized countries to limit their greenhouse gas emissions by whatever formula is adopted. The convention should provide a genuine signal to the industrial, energy and agricultural sectors, and to consumers. It should begin to stimulate technology development and lifestyle changes in the direction of energy conservation and efficiency and decreased reliance on fossil fuels, particularly coal and oil.

A further crucial measure of the convention's success will lie in its provisions for financial and technological assistance, with corresponding commitments by developing countries on policies to moderate their own growth in greenhouse gas emissions.

The negotiators should aim for a flexible, even if imperfect, accord that can be reassessed and readily modified as the science evolves. The unusual strength of the Montreal Protocol was that it was deliberately designed not as a static solution, but rather as a dynamic instrument capable of evolving in accordance with increasing scientific knowledge, technical possibilities and political judgment.

A climate treaty could also include provisions for regular assessments of national policies for reducing greenhouse gas emissions—in effect a peer review process by other parties to the convention (similar to reviews under the International Monetary Fund of a member state's progress toward currency convertibility). Such a process would serve to exchange information and data; but more important, if the reviews were designed to be transparent to outside observers and the general public, they would help promote a convergence of national policies toward those strategies that most effectively address climate change.

Even without detailed provisions for strong controls over greenhouse gases, a climate convention could establish political momentum toward this objective by providing for early resumption of negotiations on protocols, perhaps focusing on such specific sectors as energy, transportation and forest management. In this spirit, it is essential to regard the climate convention not as an end in itself, but rather as a major landmark along a road —part of an incremental, ongoing process of addressing global climate change.

TO ERR ON THE SIDE OF CAUTION

It has been nearly 35 years since Roger Revelle and Hans Suess at the Scripps Institution of Oceanography voiced concern over the growing accumulation of carbon dioxide in the atmosphere: "Human beings are now carrying out a large-scale geophysical experiment of a kind that could not have happened in the past." We still do not know the consequences of this experiment.

With unnatural quantities of greenhouse gases in the billions of tons being emitted into the atmosphere and concentrations reaching every year into uncharted territory, policy-makers must ask themselves whether hidden thresholds in the climate system are being approached, unsuspected even by the scientists. Political leaders must consequently resist any tendency to assign excessive credibility to self-serving economic interests that demand scientific certainty and insist that dangers are remote. By the time the effects of ozone-layer depletion and climate change are beyond dispute, it may be too late to avoid serious damage and draconian costs.

During the ozone treaty negotiations, when some major countries were unwilling to agree to strong measures, I argued, as head of the U.S. delegation, that the risks of delaying action were simply too great: "If we are to err," I stated in a plenary address, "then let us, conscious of our responsibility to future generations, err on the side of caution." A strong convention on climate change signed at Rio in June 1992, containing meaningful goals and providing a framework for still more aggressive future limits on greenhouse gases, would be a prudent insurance policy for the world.

In the realm of international relations, there will always be resistance to change and there will always be uncertainties —political, economic, scientific, psychological. The ozone negotiations demonstrated that sovereign nations with varying circumstances can, even in the real world of ambiguity and imperfect knowledge, join hands in partnership for the benefit of future generations. The Montreal Protocol may thus be the forerunner of an evolving global diplomacy through which nations accept common responsibility for the stewardship of planet earth.

NO

S. Fred Singer

WARMING THEORIES NEED
WARNING LABEL

The conventional wisdom these days seems to be as follows: increasing carbon dioxide from burning fossil fuel is enhancing the natural atmospheric greenhouse effect. By the next century, the resulting global warming will present a clear and present danger to humankind. We need to find radical solutions as quickly as possible to avert catastrophes—including violent weather, parched farmlands, rising sea levels, flooded continents, complete ecological collapse, and millions of environmental refugees. I suppose that many readers of the *Bulletin* would agree.

Furthermore, some of the more ardent proponents of global warming theories seem to believe that it is somehow inappropriate, if not downright immoral, for any scientist to emphasize the theories' uncertainties. Their argument seems to be that it is better for national governments to do something, however costly(even if it turns out that warming theories are wrong), rather than risk waiting for more certain and persuasive data.

It is not surprising that such views are widely held. After all, the public has been exposed to a steady diet of hyped news stories and TV specials and propagandized by environmental pressure groups. However, these views are not shared by all specialists in atmospheric physics or climatology—scientists who actually study these problems. There is no scientific consensus in support of a greenhouse warming threat.

A growing number of experts have become concerned that opinion-making and "publication by press release" are being used to influence environmental policy. With momentum building toward the "Earth Summit"—the U.N. Conference on Environment and Development (UNCED) in Rio de Janeiro this month—the issue of climate warming has taken center stage. Many scientists have spoken out. Philip Abelson, in a lead editorial in the March 30, 1990, *Science*, observed that "if [global warming] is analyzed applying the customary standards of scientific inquiry, one must conclude that there has been more hype than solid fact."

Robert M. White, president of the National Academy of Engineering and a distinguished meteorologist, wrote in the July 1990 *Scientific American*, "Given this 'cry wolf' history, it is not surprising that many meteorologists harbor deep reservations about taking costly actions on the basis of predictions of a climate warming." And in late December, John Houghton, chief editor of the U.N.-sponsored Intergovernmental Panel on Climate Change (IPCC) Report, which forms the basis for the global warming portion of the UNCED Earth Summit, announced a much reduced prediction of future climate warming based on new studies. As reported in the December 29, 1991 *Sunday Times* of London, Houghton, who also directs the British Meteorological Office, castigated environmental activists for scaremongering.

ABOUT GLOBAL WARMING

During the summer of 1991, researchers at the Science & Environmental Policy Project (SEPP), an independent, foundation-funded research group, sent survey forms to more than 120 U.S. atmospheric scientists. Most of these scientists had contributed to or reviewed the IPCC report, which has been widely described by UNCED supporters as presenting a "scientific consensus" about the reality and danger of enhanced greenhouse warming. Colleagues who worked on the report had complained that its "Policymakers Summary" did not accurately represent the conclusions in the report itself. And journalists and bureaucrats presumably read only the summary, not the rather technical 400-page report.

The survey results were remarkable. Of over 50 scientists who responded, 23 agreed that the summary did not represent the report fairly and could be misleading to non-scientists. An overwhelming majority of respondents agreed that there was no clear evidence in the cli-

mate record of the last 100 years for enhanced greenhouse warming due to human activities. Nearly all respondents expressed skepticism about the adequacy of the global climate models (GCMs) used to predict future climate warming.

Other independent surveys support these findings. For example, a November 1991 Gallup poll of 400 members of the American Meteorological Society and the American Geophysical Union (actively involved in global climate research) responded to the question: Do you think that global average temperatures have increased during the past 100 years and, if so, is the warming within the range of natural, non-human-induced fluctuation? The poll found that only 19 percent believed that human-induced global warming has occurred.

Greenpeace International also surveyed scientists who worked on the IPCC report. Asked whether business-as-usual-policies might instigate a runaway greenhouse effect at some (unspecified) future time, only 13 percent of the 113 respondents thought it "probable" and 32 percent "possible." But 47 percent said "probably not"—far from a consensus. Jeremy Leggett, Director of Sciences in Greenpeace International's Atmosphere and Energy Campaign, described this same survey as revealing "an as-yet poorly expressed fear among a growing number of climate scientists that global warming could lead not just to severe problems but complete ecological collapse."

These surveys all guaranteed respondents' anonymity, although some did sign their names. But this February, SEPP went a step further and contacted some 300 atmospheric physicists and meteorologists (most of them serving on technical committees of the American Meteorological Society) and asked them to publicly endorse a strongly-worded statement (see box) expressing concern that policy initiatives being developed for the Earth Summit were being driven by "highly uncertain scientific theories." One of those who replied objected, four wanted changes, but more than 50 put their names to the statement.

These surveys all confirm that most climate scientists believe that some global warming may be occurring, but that catastrophic predictions are unsupported by the scientific evidence, and that predictions of disaster are based on yet-to-be validated climate models.

But what do the surveys mean in terms of greenhouse warming? Science is not democratic; truth is not arrived at by vote. The surveys tell us that there are still unanswered questions that need to be settled by additional research before drastic and far-reaching policies are undertaken. And there is time for this research.

MODEL SHORTCOMINGS

How can we tell if human activities are having a significant effect on the global environment, either good or bad? There are really only two methods available: one is theory—calculating the expected effects, based on some model of the earth's atmosphere and associated environments (oceans, biosphere, cryosphere or even lithosphere). The other is empirical—it requires an examination of data based on actual observations of the atmosphere or some other environmental parameter, like sea level or ice cover.

If theory and observations agree, then we can be confident that the theory is valid and that its predictions are likely to be correct. If the two methods do not

agree, then the observations could be faulty, or the theory incomplete, or both. This is the conclusion that logic demands when we are told that an event is "worse than expected." After all, expectations about the future can only be based on theory. When observations and theory disagree, the theory cannot be used to forecast future events.

Any theory that attempts to explain the effects of human interventions and predict future changes must inevitably be based on a model—a much simplified mathematical description—of the atmosphere or other relevant environment. There is no alternative. "Models are better than hand-waving," says Stephen Schneider of the National Center for Atmospheric Research, and an ardent proponent of global-warming theories. But how much better? A good model will incorporate those features of the atmosphere that are important, but leave out those that are not. The model builder has to decide what is important and what is unimportant—and thereby hangs the tale.

Ideally, one would like to calculate the characteristics of the atmosphere at every point in space with the finest possible resolution. But computational limits prohibit this. Current computers provide fairly coarse resolution. Sampling points on the globe are typically 300 to 500 kilometers apart, still not close enough to discern cloud systems, or even such surface features as the Florida peninsula. Vertical sampling of the atmosphere occurs only at a few levels, typically a dozen, ranging from the earth's surface to the stratosphere.

As computing power increases, finer topographic detail will be incorporated and climate models will move closer to reality. A similar argument applies to time steps: sampling at hourly intervals

DISSENT ON WARMING

In late 1991, the Science & Environmental Policy Project (SEPP) circulated this statement to some 300 atmospheric scientists in the United States. Thus far, more than 50 scientists at a wide range of institutions (including MIT, Yale, Woods Hole, and the University of Virginia) have signed it.

As independent scientists researching atmospheric and climate problems, we are concerned by the agenda for UNCED, the U.N. Conference on Environment and Development, being developed by environmental activist groups and certain political leaders. This so-called Earth Summit is scheduled to convene in Brazil in June 1992 and aims to impose a system of global environmental regulations, including onerous taxes on energy fuels, on the population of the United States and other industrialized nations.

Such policy initiatives derive from highly uncertain scientific theories. They are based on the unsupported assumption that catastrophic global warming follows from the burning of fossil fuels and requires immediate action. We do not agree.

A survey of U.S. atmospheric scientists, conducted in the summer of 1991, confirms that there is no consensus about the cause of the slight warming observed during the past century. A recently published research paper even suggests that sunspot variability, rather than a rise in greenhouse gases, is responsible for the global temperature increases and decreases recorded since about 1880.

Furthermore, the majority of scientific participants in the survey agreed that the theoretical climate models used to predict a future warming cannot be relied upon and are not validated by the existing climate record. Yet all predictions are based on such theoretical models.

Finally, agriculturalists generally agree that any increase in carbon dioxide levels from fossil fuel burning has beneficial effects on most crops and on world food supply.

We are disturbed that activists, anxious to stop energy and economic growth, are pushing ahead with drastic policies without taking notice of recent changes in the underlying science. We fear that the rush to impose global regulations will have catastrophic impacts on the world economy, on jobs, standards of living, and health care, with the most severe consequences falling upon developing countries and the poor.

will give greater precision than daily intervals.

Another difficult problem involves how much atmospheric physics to put into the model—how to incorporate clouds, small-scale convection in the atmosphere, transport of water vapor, effects of aerosols from air pollution, and how to incorporate and couple ocean circulation with that of the atmosphere.

Specialists argue endlessly about these important questions. It is clear that current models do not jibe with the climate history of the past 100 years. The challenge is to improve the models so that they represent the atmosphere/ocean circulation system more closely. Most models must be "tuned" to give the right mean temperature and seasonal temperature variations, but they often fall short of accurately reproducing many other atmospheric parameters.

A major component of the debate focuses on the question of water vapor and "feedback." It is generally agreed that most of the naturally occurring greenhouse effect is due to water vapor, rather than to carbon dioxide, methane, and other greenhouse gases. Some estimates ascribe 98 percent of the greenhouse effect to atmospheric water in its various forms.

Exactly what happens to water vapor —which is not under human control— as carbon dioxide increases? Current climate models demonstrate positive feedback—that is, water vapor reinforces and amplifies the effect of increasing carbon dioxide. (Air with higher temperature "holds" water vapor better than cool air.) But leading atmospheric scientists, such as Hugh Ellsaesser of Lawrence Livermore National Laboratory and MIT researcher Richard Lindzen, have argued to the contrary, that the feedback is smaller and could even be negative—it could oppose and diminish the greenhouse effects of increased carbon dioxide.

An example of such negative feedback might occur if increased ocean temperatures lead to increased evaporation and increased cloud cover. Although clouds induce cooling by reflecting sunlight back into space, they can also increase warming by keeping heat in. On balance, however, and as shown by actual observation, low clouds promote cooling. In contrast, a clear example of a positive feedback is ice cover. As it shrinks from warming, less sunlight is reflected back out to space and more is absorbed to warm the earth further.

GLOBAL OBSERVATIONS

In the presence of both positive and negative feedbacks of immense complexity, how can a non-specialist judge the adequacy of global climate models? One method is to examine their gross characteristics—consistency and validation. Consistency refers to the extent to which different modelers agree, and differences are rather large in greenhouse warming models. Warming predictions range from negligible or small (compared to naturally occurring year-to-year variations), all the way to catastrophic—from 1.5 to 5.0 degrees centigrade in response to a doubling of carbon dioxide in the atmosphere. Even more pronounced are the differences between predictions of regional temperature changes and precipitation patterns.

Consistency also refers to consistency over time. An analogy from the related field of ozone-depletion research is illustrative. In 1972, theories predicted decreases in stratospheric ozone of up to 70 percent as a result of the planned use of high-flying supersonic aircraft, which would produce nitrogen oxides. As theorists incorporated more data, these predictions gradually diminished. By around 1977, theorists suggested an increase in ozone. But after 1978, theorists predicted a modest ozone decrease. Current theory, however, holds that nitrogen oxides would protect ozone by counter-acting the ozone-destroying properties of chlorofluorocarbons.

The concept of enhanced greenhouse warming has been undergoing similar changes. Although modelers' predictions have never changed from positive to negative, the magnitude of the predicted change began to drop as greenhouse warming models incorporated ocean circulation, the effects of sulfate pollution, and a better understanding of cloud formation. Most startling has been the downgrading of the greenhouse effect on sea level rise. Only a few years ago, some modelers forecast a 30-foot rise in sea levels; current IPCC estimates range from a three- to 11-inch rise, far short of catastrophe.

Levels of carbon dioxide have increased by 25 percent over the past 100 years; and all greenhouse gases taken together have increased carbon-dioxide-equivalent levels by about 50 percent. In other words, we have already gone halfway towards the greenhouse gas doubling which is often taken as the benchmark for model predictions. One would have expected a warming of at least 0.75 degrees centigrade by now, and more likely a rise of 1.5 degrees centigrade, according to the predictions of many models.

The reality is quite different. Since 1880, temperature has increased only 0.5 degrees centigrade, and that primarily before 1940—that is, before appreciable greenhouse gases were added to the atmosphere. The global climate record during the last 50 years shows no appreciable temperature increase at all. In the United States, the warmest years were in the 1930s, not in the 1980s, based on the analyses of the U.S. Climate Center in Asheville, North Carolina, which uses the U.S. observational network and also corrects for the "urban heat island" effect.

Many climatologists identify the pre-1940 warming with a recovery from an anomalous cooling of the preceding centuries, known as the "Little Ice Age." Certainly, the observed global cooling that inspired a fear of a coming ice age in the 1970s is not in accord with greenhouse models. Adding to the problem, a November 1, 1991 *Science* article by Danish meteorologists, E. Friis-Christensen and K. Lassen, shows that average temperature and solar activity are closely correlated, as measured by the length of the sunspot cycle. If this is correct, then little or no warming can be ascribed to the greenhouse effect.

The most appropriate data for validating current climate models is the global temperature record from satellite microwave observations, which began in 1979. This is the only truly global and continuous set of data available with heat islands and other surface distortions of temperatures eliminated. Contrary to an expected 0.3 degree centigrade rise per decade, based on current theory, the satellite record shows no significant temperature trend.

TREND OR FLUCTUATION?

Temperature observations generally show large fluctuations from unknown causes. Some of the fluctuations may be due to natural influences such as volcanic activity. Other fluctuations are a consequence of the chaotic behavior of the system itself, involving feedbacks, both positive and negative, on many different time scales. These fluctuations make it difficult (if not impossible) to identify small long-term trends caused by human activities. Interannual and longer-term fluctuations of global temperature exceed those predicted by many greenhouse model calculations.

Disentangling natural changes from a greenhouse effect enhanced by human activities will require detailed examination and more refined indicators than simply average global temperature. The climatological record may contain specific "fingerprints" that are unique to specific mechanisms of change. But, as pointed out by Hugh Ellsaesser, neither the observed latitude, altitude, or hemispheric variations of global warming in the past century are in agreement with greenhouse theory.

(Even the 1990 IPCC report on climate change waffles on that issue. The report says that the data are too ambiguous to fully support greenhouse theory. Nevertheless, the data are not inconsistent with the greenhouse effect.)

One result of detailed climate studies was the discovery that U.S. temperature records reflect a warming trend mainly for night-time temperatures; that is, there is a decrease in the day-to-night temperature range. Data on the same effects in the former Soviet Union and China have now been published. If greenhouse gas increases were the cause of this increase in night temperatures—and we don't know that—then the obvious benefits to agriculture would make this climate change a plus rather than a minus. This argument is strengthened by the expectation that the present interglacial (warm) period, which started around 11,000 years ago, must soon come to an end. With a renewed ice age "on the horizon," the possibility of greenhouse warming takes on a relatively beneficial interpretation.

WHAT TO DO

We can sum up present understanding of the enhanced greenhouse effect as follows: experts generally agree that the expected doubling of greenhouse gases in the next century will not cause a severe or catastrophic warming. Many scientists and most agricultural experts would argue that a longer growing season and enhanced carbon dioxide levels are, on the whole, beneficial to crops, which require both warmth and carbon dioxide to flourish. It is also agreed that it will take years, maybe a decade or more, before satellite data can establish a definite climate trend and before theoretical understanding of the atmosphere is comprehensive enough to allow accurate predictions.

This uncertainty raises an important but controversial question. How long should governments wait before taking drastic policy actions—if we cannot now identify a long-term climate trend? And if a trend is eventually identified, how can we be sure of its cause—or whether the cause is man-made? Answers to these questions are crucial if the proposed policy actions have a negative impact on other human values—economic welfare, health, and life expectancy. Environmental pressure groups often say that "we cannot afford to play Russian roulette with the planet's future." But this is an appeal to emotion, instead of the careful analysis that is called for.

Delaying action is not an invitation to disaster, as often claimed. Calculations by atmospheric scientist Michael Schlesinger of the University of Illinois, a climate modeler, clearly demonstrate that postponing controls on carbon dioxide for even a decade would have no noticeable impact on the next century's temperature trends. Moreover, even the most drastic limits on carbon dioxide emissions by industrialized countries would delay the doubling of greenhouse gases in the next century by only a few years.

A contributing factor to global warming is thought to be population growth and economic development in Third World nations, which will soon determine the growth rate of greenhouse gases. Carbon dioxide will increase because of fuel burning and forest clearing, and methane emitted from rice paddies and cattle raising will increase. It is well recognized, but seldom said, that controlling these activities and thus condemning billions to continued poverty, starvation and misery—or to draconian restrictions on population growth—would rightly be regarded as immoral and as a form of "eco-imperialism."

If greenhouse warming should become a problem, two reports from the U.S. National Academy of Sciences during the past year have suggested that mitigation of the effects of climate change, or adjustment to the change, is quite possible, and not prohibitively costly. A wide range of technological options can be pursued. These include planting trees on a large scale to replace logged or burned forests, and fertilizing the ocean with trace nutrients for plankton growth to sequester and thus reduce atmospheric carbon dioxide. Using satellites to screen out some incoming solar radiation also has been suggested. Such schemes may sound farfetched, but at one time so did many other futuristic projects that have since been realized.

Drastic, precipitous, and especially unilateral steps to roll back carbon dioxide emissions simply to delay an unlikely greenhouse warming will imperil living standards—and even political freedoms—in the industrial world. Yale economist William Nordhaus, who has been trying to deal quantitatively with the economics of this issue, has pointed out that "those who argue for strong measures to slow greenhouse warming have reached their conclusion without any discernible analysis of the costs and benefits."

At this stage, there are major uncertainties about greenhouse theory, about the effects of a possible warming, and about the economic and political impacts of hasty, ill-considered policies. Does it make sense to waste $100 billion a year on what is still a phantom threat when there are so many pressing—and real—problems in need of resources?

POSTSCRIPT

Are Aggressive International Efforts Needed to Slow Global Warming?

Singer implies that the only alternative to the type of Third World development that would increase the release of greenhouse gases is a policy of "draconian restrictions" on population growth and other controls that would condemn billions to "continued poverty, starvation and misery." Surely neither Benedick nor the many other political and scientific leaders who favor action to reduce the global warming threat favor such a policy. They argue for a cooperative policy that takes into account the energy and resource needs of developing nations, as well as their economic limitations.

Singer claims that the longer growing season and increased carbon dioxide levels that would accompany global warming would be beneficial to crops. For an analysis of recent research that questions this assertion, see "Plant Life in a CO_2-Rich World," by F. A. Bazzaz and E. D. Fajer, *Scientific American* (January 1992).

One of the major proposed agreements to emerge from the 1992 United Nations' environmental summit in Rio was the Framework Convention on Climate Change, which has since been ratified by 93 nations. For a discussion of plans for the forthcoming meeting to begin negotiations on implementing this agreement see "Climate Change," by David G. Victor and Julian E. Salt, *Environment* (December 1994).

Policymakers have pointed out that many programs that are designed to curb greenhouse gas emissions, such as increased energy efficiency, would make good sense even if there were no threat of climate change. For an elaboration of this argument, see "Preventing Climate Change," by Claudine Schneider, *Issues in Science and Technology* (Summer 1989).

Other recent articles that contain useful information related to global warming are "The Great Climate Debate," by Robert White, *Scientific American* (July 1990); "Practical Responses to Climate Change," by Jill Jager, *Environment* (July/August 1990); "Global Warming on Trial," by Wallace Broecker, *Natural History* (April 1992); "Gazing Into Our Greenhouse Future," by Jon Luoma, *Audubon* (March 1991); "The Road to Reduced Carbon Emissions," by Rosina Bierbaum and Robert Friedman, *Issues in Science and Technology* (Winter 1991–92); "The New Team: Electricity Sources Without Carbon Dioxide," by David White, Clinton Andrews, and Nancy Stauffer, *Technology Review* (January 1992); and "Global Warming: The Worst Case," by Jeremy Leggett, *The Bulletin of the Atomic Scientists* (June 1992).

ISSUE 18

Are Major Changes Needed to Avert a Global Environmental Crisis?

YES: Russell E. Train, from "A Call for Sustainability," *EPA Journal* (September/October 1992)

NO: Julian L. Simon, from "More People, Greater Wealth, More Resources, Healthier Environment," *Economic Affairs* (April 1994)

ISSUE SUMMARY

YES: Former EPA administrator and current World Wildlife Fund chairman Russell E. Train calls for U.S. leadership to change the course of the world's economic and industrial policies toward the goal of sustainable development in order to prevent serious global environmental deterioration.

NO: Professor of economics and business administration Julian L. Simon predicts that over the long term the brain power of more people coupled with the market forces of a free economy will lead to improved standards of living and a healthier environment.

In 1972 the results of a study by a Massachusetts Institute of Technology computer modeling team triggered an avalanche of controversy about the future course of worldwide economic growth. The results appeared in a book entitled *The Limits to Growth* (Universe Books, 1972). The book's authors—Donella Meadows, Dennis Meadows, Jorgen Randers, and William Behrens —predicted that exponential growth in population and capital, accompanied by increasing pollution, would culminate in sudden resource depletion and economic collapse before the middle of the next century. The sponsors of the study, a group of rich European and American industrialists called the Club of Rome, popularized its conclusions by distributing 12,000 copies of the book to prominent government, business, and labor leaders.

Critiques of the study emerged from all sectors of the political spectrum. Conservatives rejected the implication that international controls on industrial development were necessary to prevent disaster. Liberals asserted that no-growth policies would hurt the poor more than the affluent. Radicals contended that the results were only applicable to the type of profit-motivated growth that occurs under capitalism. Among the universal criticisms of the study were the simplicity of the computer models used and the questionable practice of making long-term extrapolations based on present increasing growth rates. The book's authors admitted that no attempt was made to incorporate the complex sociopolitical interactions that can profoundly affect the type and level of international industrial activities.

Although the debate about the specific catastrophic predictions of Meadows et al. has died down, the questions raised during that controversy continue to receive attention. In 1980 a three-volume publication entitled *The Global 2000 Report to the President* was released by the U.S. government. This report, which has sold over 500,000 copies, is the result of a joint study by the Department of State and the Council on Environmental Quality under President Carter of trends in population growth, natural resource development, and environmental quality through the end of the century. The dire projections of this study include increased environmental degradation, continued abuse of natural resources, and a widening of the gap between the rich and the poor.

This study, like its predecessors, has had its share of methodological criticism. For example, anticipated changes in energy use during the period of the study are not taken into account. Despite these flaws, the *Global 2000 Report* has contributed to the growing consensus that present patterns and rates of worldwide industrial growth are likely to cause intolerable environmental stress. This issue, the potential for conflict between the need for development and the need for environmental protection, was the central focus of the 1992 UN Earth Summit in Rio de Janeiro. The concept of sustainable development, which requires a fundamental change in the technologies used by the world's economies in order to meet their energy, transportation, agriculture, and industrial production needs, has received increasing attention in the aftermath of the Rio meeting.

Russell E. Train, who is a former EPA administrator and is currently the chairman of the World Wildlife Fund, presents the view of most economists, developmental planners, and environmentalists that dramatic changes, promoted by governmental incentives and regulations, are needed to avert future ecological crises and massive starvation. This analysis has consistently been rejected by a small, vocal group of scholars. Prominent among the ecological and environmental optimistis is Julian L. Simon, professor of economics and business administration at the University of Maryland. Simon claims that there is no evidence that environmental degradation, health problems, or world hunger are increasing, and he predicts that unless governments restrict the free market trends, the world can look forward to an improved standard of living and a cleaner environment.

YES

Russell E. Train

A CALL FOR SUSTAINABILITY

The coming together of more than 170 nations under the auspices of the Earth Summit was, if nothing else, the first *global* acknowledgement that environmental quality and economic health are inextricably linked—that the economic well-being of the Earth's peoples depends directly on the continued health of its natural resources.

This synthesis of environment and economics—and put forward in *Agenda 21*, the lengthy charter for the future adopted by the conference plenery—known as sustainable development, was only advanced, not discovered, by the diplomats in Rio. I suspect that if one were to search the literature, one would find references to the basic relationship hundreds, if not thousands, of years ago. I do know that 85 years ago, in the annual message to Congress which has since become known as the State of the Union address, President Theodore Roosevelt said, "To waste our natural resources, to skin and exhaust the land instead of using it as to increase its usefulness, will result in undermining in the days of our children the very prosperity which we ought by right to hand down to them amplified and developed."

The choice between crisis and sustainable development is one our nation shares with the rest of the world, and the only way to address it is through international cooperation and through U.S. commitment to leadership at home and abroad.

As the world's single largest economy, the largest user of natural resources, the largest producer and consumer of energy, and the largest producer of carbon dioxide pollution, the United States has not just a special responsibility to exercise world leadership but a particularly high stake in meeting the environmental challenges of the future.

I am convinced that the natural processes that support life on Earth are in serious jeopardy and that by acting now—or not acting—our country is choosing between two radically different futures. If the United States continues down its current path, merely reacting to and trying to repair environmental injuries, then the nation's natural resources, economy, and way of life will deteriorate. However, if our country pioneers new technologies, realigns government policies, makes bold economic changes, and embraces a

From Russell E. Train, "A Call for Sustainability," *EPA Journal* (September/October 1992).

new ethic of environmentally responsible behavior, we can expect the coming years to bring a higher quality of life, a healthier environment, and a vibrant economy.

The time is now for new strategies to address the environmental challenges of the future. The National Commission on the Environment spent more than 18 months deliberating and debating ways to address the overwhelming environmental problems we face. Let me share some thoughts of mine that arose from the commission's work.

THE PICTURE TODAY

Over the past 20 years, an impressive array of federal, state, and local pollution control and resource management programs, both public and private, have been instituted in the United States. Total U.S. expenditures on environmental protection now average more than 2 percent of gross national product per year.

The United States had the foresight to begin adopting stringent environmental laws and regulations more than two decades ago and to make sizable economic investments in pollution control and energy efficiency. As a result, this country does not have to contend with landscapes as blighted, air and water as polluted, soils as poisoned, or public health as ravaged as those of Central and Eastern Europe. The measurable environmental progress made by the United States should be a source of national pride.

Still, our country's environmental achievements allow no room for complacency. Despite numerous victories, the United States is losing the battle:

- Global environmental problems to which we make no small contribution

---

> ### AGENDA 21
>
> "Humanity stands at a defining moment in history. We are confronted with a perpetuation of disparities between and within nations, a worsening of poverty, hunger, ill health, and illiteracy, and the continuing deterioration of the ecosystems on which we depend for our well-being. However, integration of environment and development concerns and greater attention to them will lead to the fulfillment of basic needs, improved living standards for all, better protected and managed ecosystems and a safer, more prosperous future...."
>
> Chapter 1 (Preamble)

—climate change, loss of biodiversity, stratospheric ozone depletion, for instance—are placing both human and natural systems at grave risk.

- The air in U.S. cities threatens to deteriorate further as improvements in auto emissions controls are overwhelmed by the sheer numbers of cars and miles driven and by congestion. Meanwhile, indoor air pollution is largely ignored.

- Disposal and cleanup of the vast amounts of waste generated each year pose ever greater difficulties and consume an increasing proportion of the limited funds available for environmental protection. Indirect sources of pollution, such as urban and agricultural runoff, continue nearly unabated.

- Encroaching land development is displacing and undermining critical ecosystems, such as wetlands, and threatens rural landscapes, natural areas, and biological diversity.

- Large areas of national forest and other public lands and resources are not managed sustainably.
- Farmlands are suffering from the loss of soil and excessive use of chemicals.
- Aquifers, a major source of water supply, are being consumed and contaminated at an alarming rate in many areas of the nation.
- Overfishing is seriously depleting our most important commercial fisheries.
- In many U.S. inner cities, the physical environment has the look of a wasteland.

While this litany of environmental ills, familiar-sounding and by no means complete, is a product of *today's* level of economic activity and human population, consider tomorrow. Over the next 50 years—within the lifetimes of many of us and of all of our children—economic activity in the United States is projected to *quadruple* and global population to at least *double*. If growth of this magnitude occurs with today's industrial processes, agricultural methods, and consumer practices, the result could be both environmentally and economically disastrous.

Forecasts based on linear projections are often wrong. In the case of environmental conditions, such projections may be too optimistic. Ample evidence suggests that, unless we act decisively, the price will be serious—in some cases, irreversible—environmental damage. Clearly, it would be the height of folly for the nation to sit back and simply hope that the future will be greened by an invisible hand. Excuses for inaction, such as budget deficits and opposition to taxes, abound. Yet the continuing pursuit of politics as usual will almost certainly guarantee failure.

There must be an end to ambivalence about both the importance of environmental policy and our environmental policy priorities. The United States must have a long-term strategy for pursuing the goal of sustainable development. Such a balanced strategy may anticipate or avoid severe local and regional economic dislocations or stimulate adjustment assistance and job retraining.

ECONOMIC GROWTH

Economic and environmental well-being are mutually reinforcing goals that must be pursued simultaneously if either one is to be reached. Economic growth will create its own ruin if it continues to undermine the healthy functioning of Earth's natural systems or to exhaust natural resources. By the same token, healthy economies are most likely to provide the necessary wherewithal for investments in environmental protection. For this reason, one of the principal objectives of environmental policy must be to ensure a decent standard of living for all.

Sustainable development innovations will themselves bring major economic benefits. The economic advantage of efficiently using materials and energy is obvious, and the domestic production and use of environmentally sound technologies will reap profits both for the U.S. firms that sell them and for those who use them.

The most efficient way to achieve environmental progress is to harness market forces. Here, the role of public policy is to send the right signals to the economy—"getting the prices right" and making the marketplace work *for*, instead of *against*, environmental protection. Available tools include social-cost pricing, taxes, and removing or instituting subsidies.

The National Commission on the Environment harbored no illusions that market economics alone will put the United States or the world on the path to sustainable development. Government, private, and personal initiatives are also required. Regrettably, the U.S. statutory and regulatory system is woefully inadequate, cumbersome, and sometimes even perverse. A regime that now emphasizes "end of the pipe" cleanup must be radically reformed into one that encourages pollution prevention. Changing product design or manufacturing processes to minimize or prevent pollution is obviously superior to mandating expensive cleanup after the fact. An environmentally literate public will encourage such efforts by demanding environmentally acceptable products.

If environmental prevention is to prevail over environmental cure, and if the United States is to remain an industrial leader, our country must rapidly develop and deploy a wide array of more efficient and environmentally safe technologies. This need for new technology is particularly acute in transportation and energy generation.

ENERGY

There must be a fundamental change in how our country produces and uses energy. No single area of activity is so closely interwoven with the environment. Were it not for the world's predominant reliance on fossil fuels for both energy production and transportation, the problems of global warming, acid rain, and urban smog would be relatively minor. A progressive shift away from fossil fuels as quickly as possible in both the energy and transportation sectors is therefore crucial. Because the United States uses in excess of one-fourth of the world's energy—most of it generated by fossil fuels—it must accord this matter the highest priority.

We need dramatically different economic incentives in the energy sector. Coal, oil, and gas prices, for instance, must reflect the environmental costs associated with their combustion. Over the long term, the United States must develop alternative nonpolluting sources of energy, principally from renewable sources. Meanwhile, the country must develop technologies that use energy more efficiently, thereby consuming less fuel.

In transportation, the long-range need is a shift in auto technology to a nonpolluting source of energy. Electricity —and in the long run, hydrogen—holds promise as a nonpolluting energy carrier. More research on nonpolluting sources is needed. The immediate need is for incentives for more fuel-efficient autos and for fewer miles driven.

In agriculture, in manufacturing processes, in consumer products, and in almost every other sector of the economy, new technologies will give the United States a competitive edge as well as a healthier environment. The worldwide market for such technologies can only continue to grow as the connections between environmental and economic well-being become more apparent. The economic potential of trade in such technologies is no secret: Japan and Germany, among others, have already moved aggressively into this field. If the United States moves up in this technology race, it will be because we have at last understood that we need a technological revolution, not just another technical fix.

LAND USE PLANNING

A key failure in the U.S. effort to address environmental needs has been widespread resistance to land use planning. I am not suggesting that the federal government should impinge on state and local governments in this area, though certainly it should manage its own property and facilities better. State and local governments and other regional groups should undertake land use planning for a variety of reasons: to protect environmentally sensitive areas, including watersheds, aquifers, and wetlands; to maintain biological diversity; to continue productivity of agricultural land; and to protect sites of natural beauty and of historic and cultural value.

THE GLOBAL ENVIRONMENT

While the United States must put its own environmental house in order, there is no denying it has a huge stake in addressing global environmental problems. As environmentalists Barbara Ward and René Dubos have said, all of us have two countries—"our own and Planet Earth." The threat of global climate change, for example, certainly requires national initiatives in the United States, but the problem really can be addressed only through a common worldwide effort.

Similarly, the destruction of forests will exacerbate global warming and accelerate the loss of species and ecosystems, foreclosing medical, recreational, and trade opportunities for the United States, as well as diminishing the world's shared biological heritage. Economically, the large and growing trade with developing countries will ultimately collapse unless these nations achieve sustainable development. Politically, U.S. national security interests depend increasingly upon achieving a level of international stability that can come only from sustainable development.

The most critical need facing the world is the control of human numbers. Continued global population growth of the current magnitude—1 billion more people every decade—will swamp economic and social progress, as well as efforts to protect the environment. Our country and every other country stands to gain by efforts to stabilize world population and improve living standards in developing countries, where 90 percent of projected population growth will occur. The burden placed on the environment is a product of population and consumption. The priorities for the developed countries must focus on switching to sustainable technologies to reduce wasteful consumption; the priorities for the developing countries are to develop sustainably and curb population growth.

The United States must make a major commitment to cooperate with the world community to stabilize global population, recognizing the linkages between birth rates, child survival, economic development, education, and the economic and social status of women. Universal access to effective family planning information, contraceptives, and health care is essential.

ENVIRONMENTAL LITERACY

An informed citizenry with an ethical commitment to care for the environment is essential to the future. Success with the necessary technological, economic, and governmental changes is predicated on the understanding and support of the American people—individuals and families, government at all levels, and business.

The U.S. society and its schools must pledge themselves to the goal of ecological literacy. U.S. citizens must have the knowledge, practical competence, and moral understanding to cooperate in building a sustainable civilization. The pursuit of environmental literacy will require curricular innovations from kindergarten through college, changes in teacher education programs, and expanded graduate programs.

All of us must develop a greater sense of ethical responsibility for the environment. Environmental ethics are founded on an awareness that humanity is part of nature and that nature's myriad parts are interdependent. In any natural community, the well-being of the individual and of each species is tied to the well-being of the whole. In a world increasingly without environmental borders, nations, like individuals, have a fundamental ethical responsibility to respect nature and to care for the Earth, protecting its life-support systems, biodiversity, and beauty, caring for the needs of other countries and future generations.

It is only within such a framework that sustainable development will be achieved. Religious institutions, schools, businesses, governments, the news media, and, perhaps, above all, families must share in the tasks of achieving it.

Humanity *can* live and prosper in harmonious and sustainable balance with the natural systems of the Earth. Americans have an opportunity to rise to the challenge of environmental leadership as they have to the causes of human liberty, of equality, and of free and open markets. The challenge starts at home.

NO   Julian L. Simon

MORE PEOPLE, GREATER WEALTH, MORE RESOURCES, HEALTHIER ENVIRONMENT

This is the economic history of humanity in a nutshell. From 2 million or 200,000 or 20,000 or 2,000 years ago until the 18th century there was slow growth in population, almost no increase in health or decrease in mortality, slow growth in the availability of natural resources (but not increased scarcity), increase in wealth for a few, and mixed effects on the environment. Since then there has been rapid growth in population due to spectacular decreases in the death rate, rapid growth in resources, widespread increases in wealth, and an unprecedently clean and beautiful living environment in many parts of the world along with a degraded environment in the poor and socialist parts of the world.

That is, more people and more wealth have correlated with more (rather than less) resources and a cleaner environment—just the opposite of what Malthusian theory leads one to believe. The task before us is to make sense of these mind-boggling happy trends.

The current gloom-and-doom about a 'crisis' of our environment is wrong on the scientific facts. Even the US Environmental Protection Agency acknowledges that US air and water have been getting cleaner rather than dirtier in the past few decades. Every agricultural economist knows that the world's population has been eating ever-better since the Second World War.

Every resource economist knows that all natural resources have been getting more available not more scarce, as shown by their falling prices over the decades and centuries. And every demographer knows that the death rate has been falling all over the world—life expectancy almost tripling in the rich countries in the past two centuries, and almost doubling in the poor countries in only the past four decades.

POPULATION GROWTH AND ECONOMIC DEVELOPMENT

The picture is now also clear that population growth does not hinder economic development. In the 1980s there was a complete reversal in the consensus of thinking of population economists about the effects of more people. In

1986, the National Research Council and the National Academy of Sciences completely overturned its 'official' view away from the earlier worried view expressed in 1971. It noted the absence of any statistical evidence of a negative connection between population increase and economic growth. And it said that 'The scarcity of exhaustible resources is at most a minor restraint on economic growth'. This U-turn by the scientific consensus of experts on the subject has gone unacknowledged by the press, the anti-natalist [anti-birth] environmental organisations, and the agencies that foster population control abroad.

LONG-RUN TRENDS POSITIVE

Here is my central assertion: Almost every economic and social change or trend points in a positive direction, as long as we view the matter over a reasonably long period of time.

For a proper understanding of the important aspects of an economy we should look at the long-run trends. But the short-run comparisons—between the sexes, age groups, races, political groups, which are usually purely relative—make more news. To repeat, just about every important long-run measure of human welfare shows improvement over the decades and centuries, in the United States as well as in the rest of the world. And there is no persuasive reason to believe that these trends will not continue indefinitely.

Would I bet on it? For sure. I'll bet a week's or month's pay—anything I win goes to pay for more research—that just about any trend pertaining to material human welfare will improve rather than

get worse. You pick the comparison and the year.

Let me quickly review a few data on how human life has been doing, beginning with the all-important issue, life itself.

THE CONQUEST OF TOO-EARLY DEATH

The most important and amazing demographic fact—the greatest human achievement in history, in my view—is the decrease in the world's death rate. Figure 1 portrays the history of human life expectancy at birth. It took thousands of years to increase life expectancy at birth from just over 20 years to the high twenties in about 1750. Then life expectancy in the richest countries suddenly took off and tripled in about two centuries. In just the past two centuries, the length of life you could expect for your baby or yourself in the advanced countries jumped from less than 30 years to perhaps 75 years. What greater event has humanity witnessed than this conquest of premature death in the rich countries? It is this decrease in the death rate that is the cause of there being a larger world population nowadays than in former times.

Then starting well after the Second World War, the length of life you could expect in the poor countries has leaped upwards by perhaps 15 or even 20 years since the 1950s, caused by advances in agriculture, sanitation, and medicine (Figure 2).

Let me put it differently. In the 19th century the planet Earth could sustain only 1 billion people. Ten thousand years ago, only 4 million could keep themselves alive. Now 5 billion people are on average living longer and more healthily than

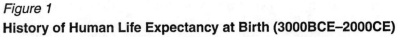

Figure 1

History of Human Life Expectancy at Birth (3000BCE–2000CE)

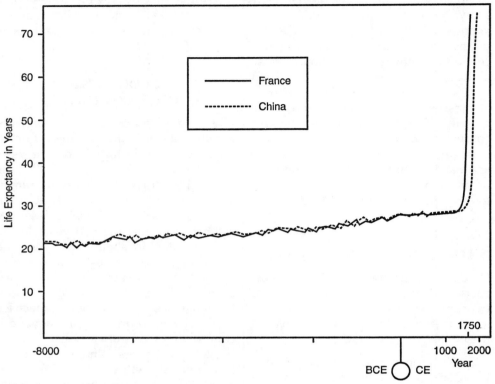

BCE: Before the Christian Era.

ever before. The increase in the world's population represents our victory over death.

Here arises a crucial issue of interpretation: One would expect lovers of humanity to jump with joy at this triumph of human mind and organisation over the raw killing forces of nature. Instead, many lament that there are so many people alive to enjoy the gift of life. And it is this worry that leads them to approve the Indonesian, Chinese and other inhumane programmes of coercion and denial of personal liberty in one of the most precious choices a family can make—the number of children that it wishes to bear and raise.

THE DECREASING SCARCITY OF NATURAL RESOURCES

Throughout history, the supply of natural resources has worried people. Yet the data clearly show that natural resource scarcity—as measured by the economically-meaningful indicator of cost or price—has been decreasing rather than increasing in the long run for all raw materials, with only temporary exceptions from time to time: that is, avail-

Figure 2
Female Expectation of Life at Birth

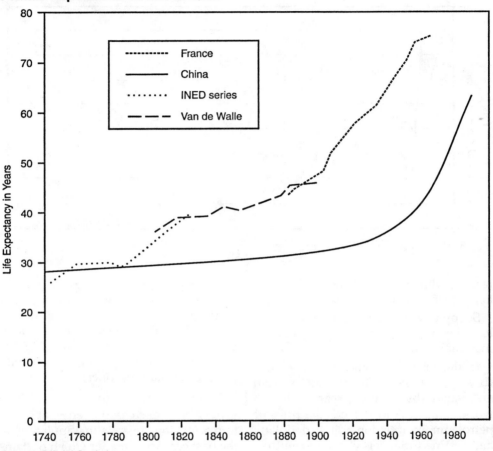

Source: Official Statistics

ability has been increasing. Consider copper, which is representative of all the metals. In Figure 3 we see the price relative to wages since 1801. The cost of a ton is only about a tenth now of what it was two hundred years ago.

This trend of falling prices of copper has been going on for a very long time. In the 18th century BCE in Babylonia under Hammurabi—almost 4,000 years ago—the price of copper was about a thousand times its price in the USA now relative to wages. At the time of the Roman Empire the price was about a hundred times the present price.

In Figure 4 we see the price of copper relative to the consumer price index. Everything we buy—pens, shirts, tyres—has been getting cheaper over the years because we have learned how to make them more cheaply, especially during the past 200 years. Even so, the extraordinary fact is that natural

Figure 3
Copper Prices Indexed by Wages

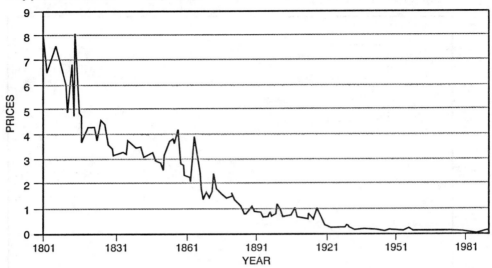

resources have been getting cheaper even faster than consumer goods.

So, by any measure, natural resources have been getting more available rather than more scarce.

In the case of oil, the shocking price rises during the 1970s and 1980s were not caused by growing scarcity in the world supply. And indeed, the price of petroleum in inflation-adjusted dollars has returned to levels about where they were before the politically-induced increases, and the price of gasoline is about at the historic low and still falling. Taking energy in general, there is no reason to believe that the supply of energy is finite, or that the price of energy will not continue its long-run decrease indefinitely....

FOOD—'A BENIGN TREND'

Food is an especially important resource. The evidence is particularly strong for food that we are on a benign trend despite rising population. The long-run price of food relative to wages is now perhaps only a tenth as much as it was in 1800 in the USA. Even relative to consumer products, the price of grain is down because of increased productivity, as with all other primary products.

Famine deaths due to insufficient food supply have decreased even in absolute terms, let alone relative to population, in the past century, a matter which pertains particularly to the poor countries. Per-person food consumption is up over the last 30 years. And there are no data showing that the bottom of the income scale is faring worse, or even has failed to share in the general improvement, as the average has improved.

Africa's food production per person is down, but by 1994 almost no-one any longer claims that Africa's suffering results from a shortage of land or water or sun. The cause of hunger in Africa is a combination of civil wars

Figure 4
Copper Prices Divided by CPI

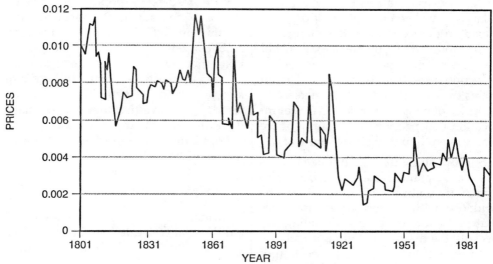

and collectivisation of agriculture, which periodic droughts have made more murderous.

Consider agricultural land as an example of all natural resources. Although many people consider land to be a special kind of resource, it is subject to the same processes of human creation as other natural resources. The most important fact about agricultural land is that less and less of it is needed as the decades pass. This idea is utterly counterintuitive. It seems entirely obvious that a growing world population would need larger amounts of farmland. But the title of a remarkably prescient article by Theodore Schultz in 1951 tells the story: 'The Declining Economic Importance of Land'.

The increase in actual and potential productivity per unit of land has grown much faster than population, and there is sound reason to expect this trend to continue. Therefore, there is less and less

reason to worry about the supply of land. Though the stock of usable land seems fixed at any moment, it is constantly being increased—at a rapid rate in many cases—by the clearing of new land or reclamation of wasteland. Land also is constantly being enhanced by increasing the number of crops grown per year on each unit of land and by increasing the yield per crop with better farming methods and with chemical fertiliser. Last but not least, land is created anew where there was no land.

THE ONE SCARCE FACTOR

There is only one important resource which has shown a trend of increasing scarcity rather than increasing abundance. That resource is the most important of all—human beings. Yes, there are more people on earth now than ever before. But if we measure the scarcity of people the same way that we measure the scarcity of other economic goods— by how much we must pay to obtain their services—we see that wages and salaries have been going up all over the world, in poor countries as well as rich. The amount that you must pay to obtain the services of a barber or cook— or economist—has risen in the United States over the decades. This increase in the price of people's services is a clear indication that people are becoming more scarce even though there are more of us.

Surveys show that the public believes that our air and water have been getting more polluted in recent years. The evidence with respect to air indicates that pollutants have been declining, especially the main pollutant, particulates. With respect to water, the proportion of monitoring sites in the USA with water of good drinkability has increased since the data began in 1961.

Every forecast of the doomsayers has turned out flat wrong. Metals, foods, and other natural resources have become more available rather than more scarce throughout the centuries. The famous Famine 1975 forecast by the Paddock brothers—that we would see millions of famine deaths in the US on television in the 1970s—was followed instead by gluts in agricultural markets. Paul Ehrlich's primal scream about 'What will we do when the [gasoline] pumps run dry?' was followed by gasoline cheaper than since the 1930s. The Great Lakes are not dead; instead they offer better sport fishing than ever. The main pollutants, especially the particulates which have killed people for years, have lessened in our cities. Socialist countries are a different and tragic environmental story, however!

... But nothing has reduced the doomsayers' credibility with the press or their command over the funding resources of the federal government....

With respect to population growth: A dozen competent statistical studies, starting in 1967 with an analysis by Nobel prizewinner Simon Kuznets, agree that there is no negative statistical relationship between economic growth and population growth. There is strong reason to believe that more people have a positive effect in the long run.

Population growth does not lower the standard of living—all the evidence agrees. And the evidence supports the view that population growth raises it in the long run.

Incidentally, it was those statistical studies that converted me in about 1968 from working in favour of population control to the point of view that I hold today. I certainly did not come to my current view for any political or religious or ideological reason.

The basic method is to gather data on each country's rate of population growth and its rate of economic growth, and then to examine whether—looking at all the data in the sample together— countries with high population growth rates have economic growth rates lower than average, and countries with low population growth rates have economic growth rates higher than average. All the studies agree in concluding that this is not so; there is no correlation between economic growth and population growth in the intermediate run.

Of course one can adduce cases of countries that seemingly are exceptions to the pattern. It is the genius of statistical inference, however, to enable us to draw valid generalisations from samples that contain such wide variations in behaviour. The exceptions can be useful in alerting us to possible avenues for further analysis, but as long as they are only exceptions, they do not prove that the generalisation is not meaningful or useful.

POPULATION DENSITY FAVOURS ECONOMIC GROWTH

The research-wise person may wonder whether population density is a more meaningful variable than population growth. And, indeed, such studies have been done. And again, the statistical evidence directly contradicts the common-sense conventional wisdom. If you make a chart with population density on the horizontal axis and either the income level or the rate of change of income on the vertical axis, you will see that higher density is associated with better rather than poorer economic results. . . .

The most important benefit of population size and growth is the increase it brings to the stock of useful knowledge. Minds matter economically as much as, or more than, hands or mouths. Progress is limited largely by the availability of trained workers. The more people who enter our population by birth or immigration, the faster will be the rate of progress of our material and cultural civilisation.

Here we require a qualification that tends to be overlooked: I do not say that all is well everywhere, and I do not predict that all will be rosy in the future. Children are hungry and sick; people live out lives of physical or intellectual poverty, and lack of opportunity; war or some new pollution may finish us off. What I am saying is that for most relevant economic matters I have checked, the aggregate trends are improving rather than deteriorating.

Also, I do not say that a better future happens automatically or without effort.

It will happen because women and men will struggle with problems with muscle and mind, and will probably overcome, as people have overcome in the past—*if the social and economic system gives them the opportunity to do so.*

THE EXPLANATION OF THESE AMAZING TRENDS

Now we need some theory to explain how it can be that economic welfare grows along with population, rather than humanity being reduced to misery and poverty as population grows.

The Malthusian theory of increasing scarcity, based on supposedly fixed resources (the theory that the doomsayers rely upon), runs exactly contrary to the data over the long sweep of history. It makes sense therefore to prefer another theory.

The theory that fits the facts very well is this: More people, and increased income, cause problems in the short run. Short-run scarcity raises prices. This presents opportunity, and prompts the search for solutions. In a free society, solutions are eventually found. And in the long run the new developments leave us better off than if the problems had not arisen.

To put it differently, in the short run more consumers mean less of the fixed available stock of goods to be divided among more people. And more workers labouring with the same fixed current stock of capital means that there will be less output per worker. The latter effect, known as 'the law of diminishing returns', is the essence of Malthus's theory as he first set it out.

But if the resources with which people work are not fixed over the period being analysed, the Malthusian logic of diminishing returns does not apply. And the plain fact is that, given some time to adjust to shortages, the resource base does not remain fixed. People create more resources of all kinds.

When we take a long-run view, the picture is different, and considerably more complex, than the simple short-run view of more people implying lower average income. In the very long run, more people almost surely imply more available resources and a higher income for everyone.

I suggest you test this idea against your own knowledge: Do you think that our standard of living would be as high as it is now if the population had never grown from about 4 million human beings perhaps 10,000 years ago? I do not think we would now have electric light or gas heat or cars or penicillin or travel to the moon or our present life expectancy of over 70 years at birth in rich countries, in comparison to the life expectancy of 20 to 25 years at birth in earlier eras, if population had not grown to its present numbers....

THE ROLE OF ECONOMIC FREEDOM

Here we must address another crucial element in the economics of resources and population—the extent to which the political-social-economic system provides personal freedom from government coercion. Skilled people require an appropriate social and economic framework that provides incentives for working hard and taking risks, enabling their talents to flower and come to fruition. The key elements of such a framework are economic liberty, respect for property, and fair and sensible rules of the market that are enforced equally for all.

The world's problem is not too many people, but lack of political and economic freedom. Powerful evidence comes from an extraordinary natural experiment that occurred starting in the 1940s with three pairs of countries that have the same culture and history, and had much the same standard of living when they split apart after the Second World War—East and West Germany, North and South Korea, Taiwan and China. In each case the centrally planned communist country began with less population 'pressure', as measured by density per square kilometre, than did the market-directed economy. And the communist and non-communist countries also started with much the same birth rates.

The market-directed economies have performed much better economically than the centrally-planned economies. The economic-political system clearly was the dominant force in the results of the three comparisons. This powerful explanation of economic development cuts the ground from under population growth as a likely explanation of the speed of nations' economic development.

THE ASTOUNDING SHIFT IN THE SCHOLARLY CONSENSUS

So far I have been discussing the factual evidence. But in 1994 there is an important new element not present 20 years ago. The scientific community of scholars who study population economics now agrees with almost all of what is written above. The statements made above do not represent a single lone voice, but rather the current scientific consensus.

The conclusions offered earlier about agriculture and resources and demographic trends have always represented the consensus of economists in those fields. And the consensus of population economists also is now not far from what is written here.

In 1986, the US National Research Council and the US National Academy of Sciences published a book on population growth and economic development prepared by a prestigious scholarly group. This 'official' report reversed almost completely the frightening conclusions of the 1971 NAS report. 'Population growth [is] at most a minor factor. . . .' As cited earlier in this paper, it found benefits of additional people as well as costs.

A host of review articles by distinguished economic demographers in the past decade has confirmed that this 'revisionist' view is indeed consistent with the scientific evidence, though not all the writers would go as far as I do in pointing out the positive long-run effects of population growth. The consensus is more towards a 'neutral' judgement. But this is a huge change from the earlier judgement that population growth is economically detrimental.

By 1994, anyone who confidently asserts that population growth damages the economy must turn a blind eye to the scientific evidence.

SUMMARY AND CONCLUSION

In the short run, all resources are limited. An example of such a finite resource is the amount of space allotted to me. The longer run, however, is a different story. The standard of living has risen along with the size of the world's population since the beginning of recorded time. There is no convincing economic reason why these trends towards a better life should not continue indefinitely.

The key theoretical idea is this: The growth of population and of income create actual and expected shortages, and hence lead to price rises. A price increase represents an opportunity that attracts profit-minded entrepreneurs to seek new ways to satisfy the shortages. Some fail, at cost to themselves. A few succeed, and the final result is that we end up better off than if the original shortage problems had never arisen. That is, we need our problems though this does not imply that we should purposely create additional problems for ourselves.

I hope that you will now agree that the long-run outlook is for a more abundant material life rather than for increased scarcity, in the United States and in the world as a whole. Of course, such progress does not come automatically. And my message certainly is not one of complacency. In this I agree with the doomsayers—that our world needs the best efforts of all humanity to improve our lot. I part company with them in that they expect us to come to a bad end despite the efforts we make, whereas I expect a continuation of humanity's history of successful efforts. And I believe that their message is self-fulfilling, because if you expect your efforts to fail because of inexorable natural limits, then you are likely to feel resigned; and therefore literally to resign. But if you recognise the possibility— in fact the probability—of success, you can tap large reservoirs of energy and enthusiasm.

Adding more people causes problems, but people are also the means to solve these problems. The main fuel to speed the world's progress is our stock of knowledge, and the brakes are (a) our lack of imagination, and (b) unsound social regulation of these activities.

The ultimate resource is people— especially skilled, spirited, and hopeful young people endowed with liberty— who will exert their wills and imaginations for their own benefit, and so inevitably benefit not only themselves but the rest of us as well.

POSTSCRIPT

Are Major Changes Needed to Avert a Global Environmental Crisis?

It is tempting to accept Simon's rosy predictions for the future and his faith in the ability of human beings to solve whatever problems they confront. Unfortunately Simon undermines his own argument early in his essay by suggesting that environmental degradation is a problem only in poor and socialist parts of the world because satellite photographs reveal a growing region of constant, hazy air pollution over much of the northeastern United States.

Simon's minority view that increasing world population is positive rather than problematic is fully explicated in his book *The Ultimate Resource* (Princeton University Press, 1981). For a recent look at Simon and his world view, his controversial standing among ecologists, and additional background to this debate on the earth's future, see John Tierney's "Betting the Planet," *The New York Times Magazine* (December 2, 1990).

It is important to distinguish Simon's views from those of environmentalists, such as Barry Commoner, who accept the premise that population explosion is a problem but argue against population control as the principal mode of controlling environmental degradation. Commoner, unlike Simon, sees the need for very active governmental involvement in technological planning and regulation in order to promote the economic conditions under which decreased population growth can be achieved.

The issue of resource depletion has recently been incorporated into the more general debate about the concept of "sustainable development." Very few experts share Simon's optimism that the 10 billion people that may inhabit the earth by the end of the next century, if present trends continue, will be able to thrive if current industrial practices and materialistic goals continue to prevail. The World Commission on Environment and Development published a much publicized report, entitled "Our Common Future," on many aspects of this issue in 1987. Commission chairperson Gro Harlem Brundtland, prime minister of Norway, has actively publicized its findings and recommendations, which include unprecedented efforts to obtain international cooperation in achieving a more equitable distribution of the world's wealth and new systems of sustainable developmental practices. Her keynote address at the 1989 Forum on Global Change, "Global Change and Our Common Future," was published in *Environment* (June 1989).

For a specific assessment of the future of world hunger that is generally less optimistic than the views of Simon, see "Can the Growing Human Population Feed Itself?" by John Bongaarts, *Scientific American* (March 1994).

CONTRIBUTORS
TO THIS VOLUME

EDITOR

THEODORE D. GOLDFARB is a professor of chemistry at the State University of New York at Stony Brook. He received a B.A. from Cornell University and a Ph.D. from the University of California, Berkeley. He is the author of 30 research papers, which have appeared in scientific journals, as well as the book *A Search for Order in the Physical Universe* (W. H. Freeman, 1974).

Professor Goldfarb is a member of several professional and community organizations, including the American Association for the Advancement of Science, the New York Academy of Sciences, and the American Chemical Society. His present research interests include public policy issues related to sustainable development, and the environmental effects of alternative energy, agriculture, and waste management technologies. He has served as an adviser to local citizen's groups and governments on environmental matters.

STAFF

Mimi Egan   Publisher
Brenda S. Filley   Production Manager
Libra Ann Cusack   Typesetting Supervisor
Juliana Arbo   Typesetter
Lara Johnson   Graphics
Diane Barker   Proofreader
David Brackley   Copy Editor
David Dean   Administrative Editor
Richard Tietjen   Systems Manager

AUTHORS

ROBERT W. ADLER is a senior attorney and the director of the Clean Water Project at the Natural Resources Defense Council in Washington, D.C., a national nonprofit organization staffed by attorneys, scientists, and resource specialists dedicated to the protection of public health and the environment. He is also an adjunct professor at the University of Virginia School of Law.

IVAN AMATO is an author who frequently writes about environmental issues. His work has more recently been published in *Science* and *Garbage: The Independent Environmental Quarterly.*

RONALD BAILEY, an environmental journalist, is the producer of *TechnoPolitics*, a weekly PBS television series. As a staff writer for *Forbes*, he has covered science and technology policy issues. His publications include *Eco-Scam: The False Prophets of Ecological Apocalypse* (St. Martin's Press, 1993).

RICHARD ELLIOT BENEDICK is a senior fellow of the Conservation Foundation and World Wildlife Fund in Washington, D.C. A former deputy assistant secretary of state for environment, health, and natural resources, he was the chief U.S. negotiator for the Vienna Convention on the Protection of the Ozone Layer and the Montreal Protocol on Substances that Deplete the Ozone Layer.

ROBERT D. BULLARD is a professor of sociology at the University of California, Riverside. His publications include *Unequal Protection: Environmental Justice and Communities of Color* (Sierra Club Books, 1994).

WILLIAM G. CALE, JR., is an ecologist and the dean of the College of Natural Sciences and Mathematics at Indiana University of Pennsylvania in Indiana, Pennsylvania. He served until 1989 as a professor and head of the Graduate Program in Environmental Sciences at the University of Texas at Dallas.

LUTHER J. CARTER is an independent, Washington, D.C.–based journalist. He is the author of *The Florida Experience: Land and Water Policy in a Growth State* (Johns Hopkins University Press, 1976) and *Nuclear Imperatives and the Public Trust: Dealing With Radioactive Waste* (Resources for the Future, 1987), which received the Special Forum Award from the U.S. Council on Energy Awareness in 1988.

MARY H. COOPER is a staff writer for the Congressional Quarterly's *CQ Researcher,* a weekly magazine that provides in-depth analyses of current issues. She is the author of *The Business of Drugs* (Congressional Quarterly, 1988).

JOHN DANIEL is the poetry editor for *Wilderness* magazine.

ENDANGERED SPECIES COALITION was formed to advocate the preservation and reauthorization of the Endangered Species Act. It includes more than 50 national wildlife and environmental organizations with a collective membership of more than 5 million citizens.

PAUL FAETH is a senior associate in the Economics of Population Program at the World Resources Institute.

JEFFERY A. FORAN is the executive director of the Risk Science Institute in Washington, D.C., and a former associate professor and director of the Environmental Health and Policy Program at George Washington University.

JAMES B. GOODNO, a former *Dollars and Sense* editor, is a freelance journalist based in Bangkok, Thailand.

MICHAEL GREENBERG is a professor of urban studies and community health at Rutgers University in New Brunswick, New Jersey. He is also the director of the environmental policy division at the Environmental and Occupational Health Sciences Institute.

ROBERT W. HAHN is a resident scholar at the American Enterprise Institute in Washington, D.C., a privately funded public policy research organization. He is also an adjunct research fellow of Harvard University in Cambridge, Massachusetts.

DOUG HARBRECHT is a Washington, D.C., *Business Week* correspondent.

PAUL HARRISON is the author of *The Third Revolution* (Penguin Books, 1993), which won a Population Institute Global Media Award.

BETSY HARTMANN is the director of the Hampshire College Population and Development Program in Amherst, Massachusetts, and the coordinator of the Committee on Women, Population, and the Environment.

RANDALL L. HARTMANN is the manager of the Hamilton County Solid Waste Management District.

RICK HENDERSON is the Washington, D.C., editor of *Reason*.

JON JEFFERSON is a freelance writer based in Knoxville, Tennessee.

MARTIN T. KATZMAN (1941–1989) was an economist working on the economics of research and development, innovation, and technological change in the Energy Division of the Oak Ridge National Laboratory in Oak Ridge, Tennessee. He has published 4 books, including *Cities and Frontiers in Brazil* (Harvard University Press, 1977), and 50 scholarly journal articles. He also created the software product "Solar Economics: Computer Programs."

LESTER P. LAMM is the president of the Highway Users Federation for Safety and Mobility in Washington, D.C., which was founded in 1970 to promote highway safety and to encourage sound highway transportation development on a national basis.

NICHOLAS LENSSEN is a senior researcher with the Worldwatch Institute, a nonprofit research organization devoted to the analysis of global environmental issues. His research and writing focus on energy policy, alternative energy sources, nuclear power, radioactive waste, and global climate change, and he has testified before the U.S. Congress and the European Parliament on energy issues. His publications include *Power Surge: Guide to the Coming Energy Revolution* (W. W. Norton, 1994).

WILL NIXON is an associate editor of *E* magazine.

BILL O'DONNELL is a former associate publisher of *Garbage: The Independent Environmental Quarterly*.

ROBERT A. PASTOR is a professor of political science at Emory University in Atlanta, Georgia, and the director of the Latin American and Caribbean program at Emory's Carter Center. He is the author of *Whirlpool: U.S. Foreign Policy Toward*

Latin America and the Caribbean (Princeton University Press, 1993).

PATRICIA POORE is a former publisher and editor of *Garbage: The Independent Environmental Quarterly.*

VIRGINIA I. POSTREL is the editor of *Reason,* a monthly current-affairs magazine published by the Reason Foundation in Santa Monica, California, a nonprofit, public-policy research organization. A former reporter for the *Wall Street Journal* and *Inc.* magazine, she writes regularly for the *Los Angeles Times* op-ed page and has contributed articles on a variety of political, economic, and cultural topics.

BERNARD J. REILLY is the corporate counsel at DuPont, where he has been managing the legal aspects of the company's Superfund program since 1986.

HANNAH FINAN RODITI, a former member of the Dollars and Sense Collective, is now a labor organizer in Florida.

STEVEN E. SANDERSON is a professor of political science and the director of the Tropical Conservation and Development Program at the University of Florida in Gainesville, Florida. His publications include *The Politics of Trade in Latin American Development* (Stanford University Press, 1992).

LYNN SCARLETT is the vice president of research for the Reason Foundation in Santa Monica, California, a nonprofit, public-policy research organization. She has written extensively on environmental and land-use regulations, solid waste, and recycling issues, and privatization, and she has testified on environmental and solid waste issues before the Federal Trade Commission, the U.S. House Subcommittee on Transportation and Haz-

ardous Waste, and the California Senate Committee on the Environment.

JULIAN L. SIMON is a professor of economics and business administration in the College of Business and Management at the University of Maryland at College Park. His research interests focus on population economics, and his publications include *The Economic Consequences of Immigration* (Basil Blackwell, 1989); *Population Matters: People, Resources, Environment, and Immigration* (Transaction Publishers, 1990); and *The Ultimate Resource,* 2d ed. (Princeton University Press, 1994).

S. FRED SINGER is the director of the Washington, D.C.–based Science and Environmental Policy Project (SEPP) and a professor of environmental sciences (on leave) at the University of Virginia in Charlottesville.

JOE THORNTON is the research coordinator for the Greenpeace Toxics Campaign in New York City.

RUSSELL E. TRAIN is the chair of the World Wildlife Fund in Washington, D.C., which emphasizes the preservation of endangered and threatened species of wildlife and plants as well as habitats and natural areas throughout the world. He is a former Environmental Protection Agency administrator.

WILLIAM TUCKER, a writer and social critic, is a staff writer for *Forbes.* His publications include *The Excluded Americans: Homelessness and Housing Policies* (Regnery Gateway, 1989), which was the winner of the 1991 Mencken Award for best nonfiction.

JOHN S. VAN VOLKENBURGH is a senior project analyst for SCS Engineers, and he was the project manager for the development of the Hamilton County Solid Waste Management District.

TED WILLIAMS has been a regular contributor to *Audubon* for 14 years, during which he has covered a variety of topics, including gold mining in Alaska and the Northern Forest of the Northeast.

SUZANNE WINCKLER is a freelance writer whose areas of interest include natural history and environmental issues.

Her interest in endangered species policies stems from long experience as a bird watcher and her concern for the declining numbers of many avian species. She currently works for the Nature Conservancy in Nebraska.

GENE W. WOOD is a professor of forest wildlife ecology in the Department of Aquaculture, Fisheries, and Wildlife at Clemson University in Clemson, South Carolina.

INDEX

Abelson, Phillip, 319
Adler, Robert W., on new Clean Water Act aiming at "zero discharge," 162–169
"advance disposal fees" (ADFs), 243
Agency for International Development (AID), 282
Agenda 21, 330, 331
agriculture, 333, 340–341; controversy over chemical-based, 180–191; NAFTA and, 15–17
agro-forestry, 284
air quality, controversy over need of law enforcement to improve, 146–157
Amato, Ivan, on phasing out industrial use of chlorine, 132–141
Atomic Energy Commission (AEC), 253
auto industry, clean air laws and, 150, 151–157
Avery, Dennis, 182, 185, 186
Axline, Michael, 196, 198–199, 201

Babbit, Irving, 40, 41
Bailey, Ronald, on controversy over chemical-based agriculture, 180–187, 188, 189, 190
bald eagle, as endangered species, 49, 51, 54–55, 58, 60, 62, 63
Bangladesh, 97
Bartram, William, 24
Benedick, Richard E., on global warming, 310–318
biodiversity, decline in, 272; Endangered Species Act and, 51–52, 63–64
birth control, 97–98
black-footed ferret, as endangered species, 49, 50, 51, 58, 63, 66
Boatwright, Daniel, 238–239
Boundary Water Canoe Area, 39
bromine monoxide, 290, 291
Brower, David, 36, 37
brown pelican, as endangered species, 49, 55
Browne, J. Ross, 39–40
Browner, Carol, 73, 74
Bullard, Robert D., on need for environmental justice, 70–75
Burley, F. William, 65

Buschbacher, Robert, 286

Cale, William G., on tropical deforestation, 272–281
California Desert Protection Act, 105
captive breeding programs, 50–51, 63
carbon dioxide emissions, air quality and, 314, 324, 325, 326
Carson, Hampton, 66
Carter, Luther J., on underground storage of nuclear waste, 259–265
Cascades, Oregon, 25
cattle ranching, in rain forest, 272, 273, 279
CFCs (chlorofluorocarbons), 126, 136, 137–138, 310, 323; controversy over ozone depletion and phasing out, 290–306
chemical-based agriculture, controversy over need for, 180–191
Chile, 186
chinook salmon, as endangered species, 54, 62, 63
chlorine, controversy over phasing out industrial use of, 120–141. See also CFCs
chlorine monoxide, 290, 291
chlorofluorocarbons. See CFCs
CH2M Hill, 223
Civil Rights Act of 1964, Title VI of, 73, 74
Clajon Corporation, 113–114
Clay, Jason, 284
Clean Air Act, 147, 148, 149, 150
Clean Air Act Amendments, 147, 152
Clean Water Act, controversy over "zero discharge" and, 162–176
Coastal Zone Management Act (CZMA), 169
Colchester, Marcus, 283, 286
Comprehensive Environmental Response, Compensation, and Liability Act (CERCLA). See Superfund
condor, California, as endangered species, 50, 51, 58, 63, 64, 65
conservation, controversy over intrinsic value of wilderness and, 24–43
conservation easement, in rain forest, 278–281
consumer boycotts, of rain forest products, 285
contraceptives, 97–98

Cooper, Mary H., on phasing out CFCs, 290–298
copper prices, decline in, 339–340, 341
Council on Environmental Quality, 53
Cultural Survival, 284

Daniel, John, on controversy over intrinsic value of wilderness, 24–31
DDT, 126, 136, 137–138
debt-for-nature swaps, 275
deforestation, 311–312; in Madagascar, 86–87; tropical, controversy over, 272–286
Department of Energy (DOE), 253–254, 259–260
desert tortoise, as endangered species, 58, 60, 62
diapers, waste disposal and, 238–240
Dobson, Gordon, 302
Dolan v. City of Tigard, 105, 106–107
Dubos, Rene, 43

eco-imperialism, 326
economic development, 332–333; population growth and, 336–346
Ehrlich, Paul, 87
Ellsaesser, Hugh, 322, 325
eminent domain, property rights and, 104–114
Endangered Species Act, controversy over, 48–66
Endangered Species Coalition, on Endangered Species Act, 48–59
energy efficiency, 314–315
environmental justice, controversy over, 70–81
Environmental Protection Agency (EPA): clean air laws and, 147; Clean Water Act and, 162, 171–172, 173–174; recycling and, 237–238; Superfund and, 212–215, 216–218, 219
Epstein, Richard, 105, 111–112
ethnobiology, 280
European Community, 314
Everglades, Florida, 174–175
extinction, controversy over Endangered Species Act and, 48–66
extraction reserves, in rain forests, 275, 276, 277, 285–286

Faeth, Paul, on controversy over chemical-based agriculture, 188–191
family planning, 91–92, 97–98
farming, subsistence, in rain forest, 272
Fay, John, 61

Fifth Amendment, property rights and, 105, 106, 111
First National People of Color Environmental Leadership Summit, 72
Food and Agricultural Organization (FAO), 276, 282–283, 284
Foran, Jeffery A., on new Clean Water Act aiming at "zero discharge," 162–169
forests: destruction of old-growth, 52, 53, 64; spotted owl and preservation of, 196–205. *See also* deforestation; wilderness
fossil fuels, 333; global warming and, 311, 312, 314, 317, 319; NAFTA and, 17–19
France, 254–255
Friends of the Earth, 283, 285
Friis-Christenson, E., 324

Gandhi, Mahatma, 52
gap analysis, 64–66
geothermal energy, 311
Germany, 252, 254, 255–256
GHASP (Galveston Houston Alliance to Stop Pollution), 149
global warming, controversy over, 310–316
Goldman, Benjamin, 78–79
Goodno, James B., on tropical deforestation, 282–286
Greenberg, Michael, against need for environmental justice, 76–81
grizzly bear, as endangered species, 48, 54, 55, 60, 62

habitat, loss of animal, 49, 51, 53, 56, 57–58, 272–273
Hage, Wayne, 113
Hahn, Robert W., against new Clean Water Act aiming at "zero discharge," 170–176
halons, 290, 291, 301
Harbrecht, Doug, on property rights, 110–114
Harris, Marvin, 41
Harrison, Paul, on population growth as key environmental factor, 86–92
Hartmann, Betsy, against population growth as key environmental factor, 93–99
Hartmann, Randall L., on success of management plans for recycling, 230–236
Hawaii, habitat loss in, 53, 65, 66
HCFCs (hydrochlorofluorocarbons), 296, 297, 301
Henderson, Rick, on property rights, 104–109
Hillman, James, 29
Hittle, Alex, 283, 285

Houghton, John, 320

Indonesia, 190
Information Superhighway, 28–29
integrated pest management (IPM), 183–184, 189, 190
Intergovernmental Panel on Climate Change (IPCC), 320, 325
Intermodal Surface Transportation Efficiency Act of 1991, 150, 152, 154
International Monetary Fund (IMF), 317

Janzen, Daniel, 275
Japan, 255, 256
Jefferson, Jon, on protecting spotted owls and preservation of forests, 196–201
Jenkins, Robert E., 52
justice, controversy over need for environmental, 70–81

Kaiser Permanente, 152
Kantor, Mickey, 10
Katzman, Martin T., on tropical deforestation, 272–281
Kauai, Hawaii, 36
Kirtland's warbler, as endangered species, 63, 66
Kripke, Margaret L., 293

Lamm, Lester P., against need to enforce laws to improve air quality, 151–157
Lassen, K., 324
Law of the Sea, 316
Lee, Charles, 74–75
Leggett, Jeremy, 320
Lenssen, Nicholas, on underground storage of nuclear waste, 250–258
Leopold, Aldo, 33, 61, 66
life expectancy, changes in, 337, 338, 339
Lindzen, Richard, 322
locally unwanted land uses (LULUs), environmental justice and, 70–81
Lohmann, Larry, 283
lumbering, in rain forest, 272, 273–274, 283, 285

M & J Coal Company, 113
Madagascar, 86–87
Malthus, Thomas, 87
maquiladoras, 5–6
marketable permit systems, Clean Water Act and, 173–714
Marshall, Robert, 33

Mexico, environmental effects of NAFTA and, 4–20
military, nuclear waste of, 263–264
mission blue butterfly, as endangered species, 51, 57–58
Molina, Mario, 294–295
Montreal Protocol, 310, 313, 315, 317, 318; controversy over phasing out CFCs and, 291, 295, 306
Muir, John, 25, 32, 37
Multiple Use and Sustained Yield Act of 1960, 34

NAFTA (North American Free Trade Agreement), controversy over benefit of, to environment, 4–20
NASA (National Aeronautics and Space Administration), on ozone depletion, 290–291, 293–294, 295–296, 297–298, 304
National Forest Service, 33, 34, 35
National Highway System, 153, 154–155, 156–157
National Wilderness Preservation System, 24, 25
natural gas, NAFTA and, 18
Natural Heritage Program, 53
natural resources, decreasing scarcity of, 338–340, 341
Nature Conservancy, The, 52, 65
NIMBY (not-in-my-backyard) syndrome, recycling and, 244
Nixon, Richard, 48
Nixon, Will, on need to enforce laws to improve air quality, 146–150
nonpoint sources, of water pollution, 168–169, 174–175
Nordhaus, William, 326
Norplant, 97–98
North American Free Trade Agreement. See NAFTA
nuclear waste, controversy of underground storage of, 250–265
Nuclear Waste Policy Act (NWPA), controversy over, 250–265

O'Donnell, Bill, on phasing out CFCs, 299–306
oil, NAFTA and, 17–19
orange juice, recycling and, 240
Oregon Cascades, 25
Organization of Economic Cooperation and Development (OECD), 276
ozone, climate and, 310–311, 317, 318, 323

ozone depletion, controversy over phasing out CFCs and, 290–306

panther, Florida, as endangered species, 54, 55, 60, 62
paper mills, controversy over phasing out chlorine and, 129–130
parrot, Puerto Rican, as endangered species, 60, 62, 66
Pastor, Robert A., on NAFTA's effect on the environment, 4–12
PCBs (polychlorinated biphenyls), 214–215, 220; phasing out chlorine use and, 124, 126, 133, 136, 137–138
PCDDs (polychlorinated dibenzodioxins), 136
PCDFs (polychlorinated dibenzofurans), 136
Pence, Richard, 240–241
Penn, William, 24
peregrine falcon, as endangered species, 49, 54–55, 62, 63
pesticides, 54–55; chlorine and, 124; controversy over need for chemical-based agriculture and, 180–191
Petróleos Mexicanos (PEMEX), 17–18
Pew Charitable Trusts Global Stewardship Initiative, 96
Pinchot, Gifford, 32, 34
plastics, controversy over phasing out chlorine use and, 129, 133, 135, 139
Poore, Patricia, on phasing out CFCs, 299–306
population, animal, definition of, 54
population growth, controversy over, as key environmental factor, 86–99; economic development and, 332–333, 336–346
Postrel, Virginia I., on success of management plans for recycling, 237–245
Powell, John Wesley, 24, 32
priorities, use of risk assessment in setting environmental, 278
Private Property Owners Bill of Rights, 108
Private Property Rights Restoration Act, 108
property rights, controversy over, 104–114
proportional liability, Superfund and, 218
public-private partnerships, rain forest preservation and, 275–276
PVC (polyvinylchloride), 129, 133, 135, 139

quinacrine sterilization pellet, 98

racism, controversy over need for environmental justice and, 70–81
rain forests, controversy over deforestation and, 272–286

recycling, controversy over success of management plans for, 230–245
Reilly, Bernard J., on "polluter pays" provision of Superfund, 212–219
renewable energy sources, 311
Resource Conservation and Recovery Act (RCRA), 238
Revelle, Roger, 317
Roadless Area Resources Evaluation (RARE), 35
Roddick, Anita, 284
Roditi, Hannah Finan, on tropical deforestation, 282–286
Rousseau, Jean-Jacques, 39
Rowland, Sherwood, 294–295, 302–303
Ruby, Meg, 284

Salinas de Gortari, Carlos, 4, 7
Sanderson, Steven E., on the effect of NAFTA on the environment, 13–20
Scarlett, Lynn, on success of management plans for recycling, 237–245
Schlesinger, Michael, 325
Schneider, Stephen, 321
Schumacher, E. F., 41
Science & Environmental Policy Project, 320–321, 323
Scott, J. Michael, 63–64
sea level, rise in, 315, 324
sea otter, as endangered species, 49, 50, 51, 52, 55, 62
Sher, Byron, 243
Sher, Vic, 196, 197–198, 199, 201
Sierra Club, 283
Simon, Julian, 87–88; against need for major changes to avert global environmental crisis, 336–346
Singer, S. Fred, on controversy over global warming, 319–326
soil erosion, population growth and, 89
solar energy, 311
Solid Waste Disposal Act (SWDA), 238
Southwest Network for Environmental and Economic Justice (SNEEJ), 72
species, definition of, 49
spotted owl, northern: as endangered species, 50, 57, 62, 64; preservation of forests and, 196–205
Standards and Sanitary and Phytosanitary Measures, 8
Suess, Hans, 317
Superfund Amendments and Reauthorization Act (SARA), 214

Superfund, controversy over "polluter pays" provision of, 212–226
Surface Transportation Efficiency Act of 1991, 150, 152, 154
Sweden, 255, 256, 257

Takings Clause of the Fifth Amendment, 105, 106, 111
tallgrass prairie, destruction of, 53
Tauzin amendment, 105, 108
taxon, definition of, 60
technology, wilderness conservation and, 27–29
Third World: controversy over global warming and, 310–326; controversy over tropical deforestation in, 272–286
Thomas, Lewis, 59
Thoreau, Henry David, 24–25, 30, 32, 66
Thornton, Joe, on phasing out industrial use of chlorine, 120–131, 132
threatened species, controversy over Endangered Species Act and, 48–66
Title VI of the Civil Rights Act of 1964, 73, 74
tradable permit systems, Clean Water Act and, 173–174
Train, Russell E., on need for major changes to avert global environmental crisis, 330–335
tropical deforestation, controversy over, 272–286
Tropical Forest Action Plan, 275, 276, 282, 283, 284
True, Todd, 196, 197–198, 199, 201
Tucker, William, on controversy over intrinsic value of wilderness, 32–43
Turner, Ted, 96

ultraviolet (UV) radiation, ozone depletion and harmful effects of, 292–293, 300, 301, 304, 305, 306

Van Volkenburgh, John S., on success of management plans for recycling, 230–236

Vienna Convention, 312–313

waste collection, recycling and, 230–245
Water Quality Criteria (WQC), 164, 167
whales, as endangered species, 51, 63
White, Lynn, 41–42
White, Robert M., 320
whooping crane, as endangered species, 50–51, 52, 60, 63, 66
Wilderness Act of 1964, 24, 25, 32–33
wilderness, controversy over intrinsic value of, 24–43
Williams, Ted, on "polluter pays" provision of Superfund, 220–226
Wilson, E. O., 181
Winckler, Suzanne, on controversy over Endangered Species Act, 60–66
wind power, 311
Winterbottom, Robert, 284
wolves, as endangered species, 54, 55, 58, 62
women, population growth and, 91–92, 96, 97–98
Wood, Gene W., on spotted owls and preservation of forests, 202–205
woodpeckers, red-cockaded, as endangered species, 62, 66
World Bank, 276, 281, 282
World Rainforest Movement, 283, 286
World Resources Institute, 283, 284
World Wildlife Fund, 286

YIMBY-FAP (Yes, in my backyard—for a price), 244
Yoke Ling Chee, 285
Yucca Mountain, underground disposal of nuclear waste at, 252, 259, 260, 261–262

"zero discharge," controversy over new Clean Water Act aiming at, 162–176